WILD ADAPTER

vol.5

by Kazuya Minekura

D0003222

TOKYOPOP®

HAMBURG // LONDON // LOS ANGELES // TOKYO

Wild Adapter Volume 5
Created by Kazuya Minekura

Translation - Alexis Kirsch
English Adaptation - Christine Boylan
Retouch and Lettering - Star Print Brokers
Production Artist - Vicente Rivera, Jr.
Graphic Designer - Louis Csontos

Editor - Lillian Diaz-Przybyl
Digital Imaging Manager - Chris Buford
Pre-Production Supervisor - Lucas Rivera
Production Manager - Elisabeth Brizzi
Managing Editor - Vy Nguyen
Creative Director - Anne Marie Horne
Editor-in-Chief - Rob Tokar
Publisher - Mike Kiley
President and C.O.O. - John Parker
C.E.O. and Chief Creative Officer - Stu Levy

A TOKYOPOP® Manga

TOKYOPOP and 🐾 are trademarks or registered trademarks of TOKYOPOP Inc.

TOKYOPOP Inc.
5900 Wilshire Blvd. Suite 2000
Los Angeles, CA 90036

E-mail: info@TOKYOPOP.com
Come visit us online at www.TOKYOPOP.com

© 2005 & 2006 Kazuya MINEKURA. All rights reserved. Original Japanese edition published by TOKUMA SHOTEN PUBLISHING CO., LTD. Tokyo. English translation rights arranged with TOKUMA SHOTEN PUBLISHING CO., LTD.

English text copyright © 2008 TOKYOPOP Inc.

All rights reserved. No portion of this book may be reproduced or transmitted in any form or by any means without written permission from the copyright holders. This manga is a work of fiction. Any resemblance to actual events or locales or persons, living or dead, is entirely coincidental.

ISBN: 978-1-4278-0219-4

First TOKYOPOP printing: May 2008
10 9 8 7 6 5 4 3 2 1
Printed in the USA

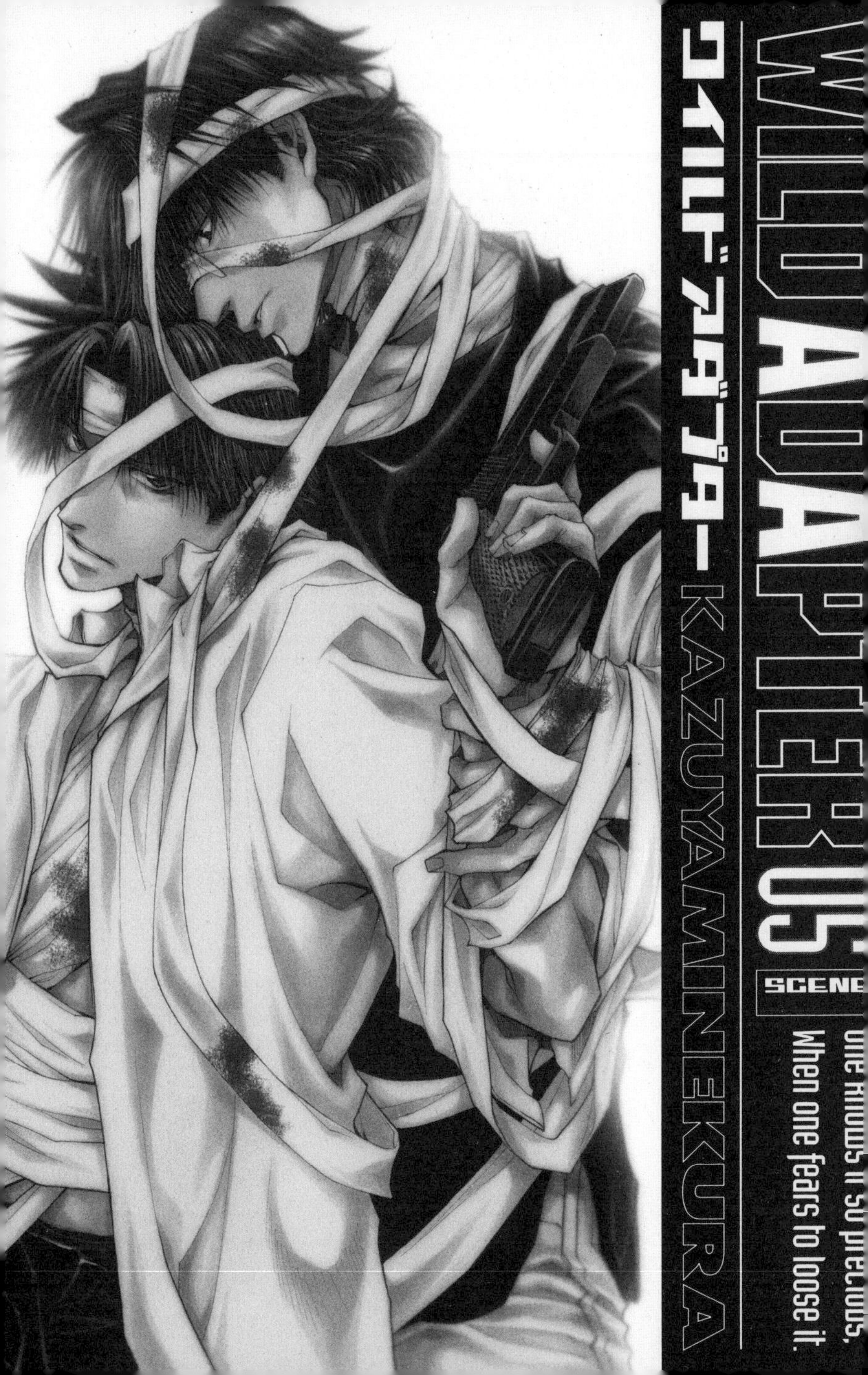
WILD ADAPTER 05
SCENE
one knows it so precious,
when one fears to loose it.
ワイルドアダプター
KAZUYA MINEKURA

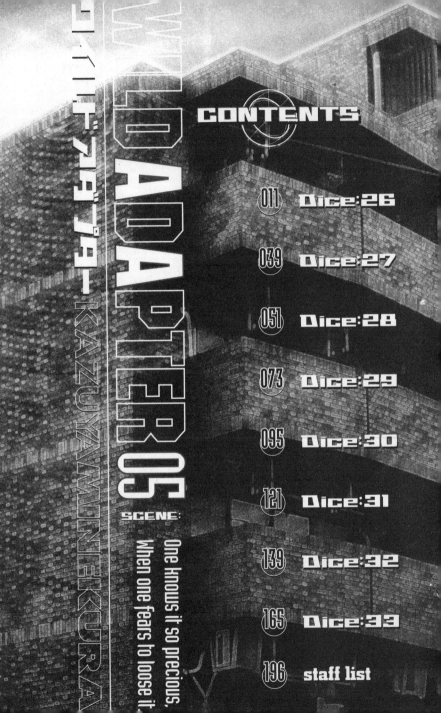

WILD ADAPTER 05

ワイルドアダプター -KAZUYA MINEKURA

SCENE: One knows it so precious, when one fears to loose it.

CONTENTS

CHARACTERS:

MAKOTO KUBOTA:
ILLEGITIMATE SON OF THE SHADOWY SEIJI
MUNAKATA, KUBOTA IS FASCINATED BY
EVERYTHING BUT ATTACHED TO NOTHING.
AFTER JOINING IZUMO MORE OR LESS ON A
WHIM, HIS CALM EXTERIOR LEADS ENEMIES AND
FRIENDS ALIKE TO UNDERESTIMATE HIM, UNTIL
KUBOTA DESTROYS TOJOU'S HEADQUARTERS
ON HIS WAY OUT OF THE YAKUZA WORLD.

MINORU TOKITO:
A YOUNG MAN WITH NO MEMORIES OF THE
PAST, AND A CREEPY ANIMAL-LIKE HAND
REMINISCENT OF THE DEAD BODIES LEFT
BEHIND IN THE WAKE OF THE NEW DRUG WILD
ADAPTER. KUBOTA LITERALLY PICKS HIM UP
OFF THE STREET, AND THE TWO NOW LIVE
TOGETHER. BRASH AND BOISTEROUS, IN
CONTRAST TO KUBOTA'S ETERNALLY PLACID
FAÇADE, TOKITO SEEMS TO BE THE ONE
PERSON WHO KUBOTA REALLY CARES ABOUT.

KASAI:
KUBOTA'S UNCLE AND A LOCAL POLICE
DETECTIVE. AN EXCELLENT MAHJONG PLAYER,
AND A BIT OF A CROOKED COP, KASAI IS
INVESTIGATING WILD ADAPTER WHILE TRYING
TO KEEP KUBOTA OUT OF TROUBLE.

SANADA AND SEKIYA:
HEADS OF RIVAL YAKUZA
ORGANIZATIONS, BOTH HAVE
THEIR OWN REASONS FOR
PURSUING WILD ADAPTER, AND
APPARENTLY KUBOTA, AS WELL.

KOU:
AN UNLICENSED PHYSICIAN AND PHARMACIST
WORKING OUT OF YOKOHAMA'S CHINATOWN,
KOU SELLS INFORMATION AND ILLEGAL
GOODS ALONG WITH HIS MEDICAL SERVICES.
HE OCCASIONALLY EMPLOYS KUBOTA ON A
PART-TIME BASIS FOR DELIVERIES AND KEEPS
A WARY EYE ON TOKITO'S RIGHT HAND.

STORY SO FAR:

MAKOTO KUBOTA'S TIME WITH THE IZUMO CRIME SYNDICATE IS SHORT-LIVED AND BLOODY. AFTER TAKING OVER AS THE HEAD OF THE ORGANIZATION'S YOUTH GANG, HE SPENDS SEVEN MONTHS PLAYING VIDEO GAMES WITH HIS YOUNG COHORTS, BEFRIENDING SMALL ANIMALS AND WRECKING RIVAL YOUTH GANGS UNTIL HIS ONE FRIEND IN IZUMO IS KILLED OVER A MYSTERIOUS DRUG CALLED "WILD ADAPTER." KUBOTA QUITS THE YAKUZA, TAKING OUT THE HEAD OF THE RIVAL TOJOU ORGANIZATION AS A PARTING GIFT. BUT SANADA, THE CURRENT BOSS OF IZUMO, ISN'T QUITE SATISFIED WITH THIS TURN OF EVENTS.

AND THEN...

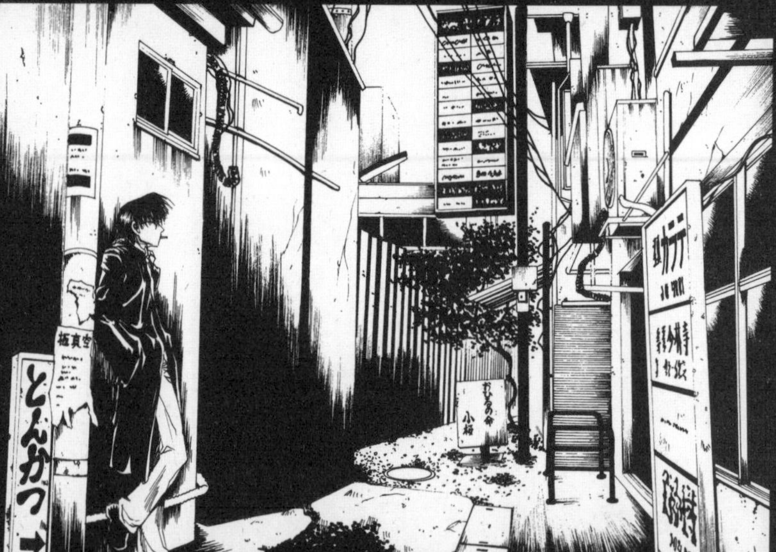
とんかつ

I PICKED UP A STRAY CAT.

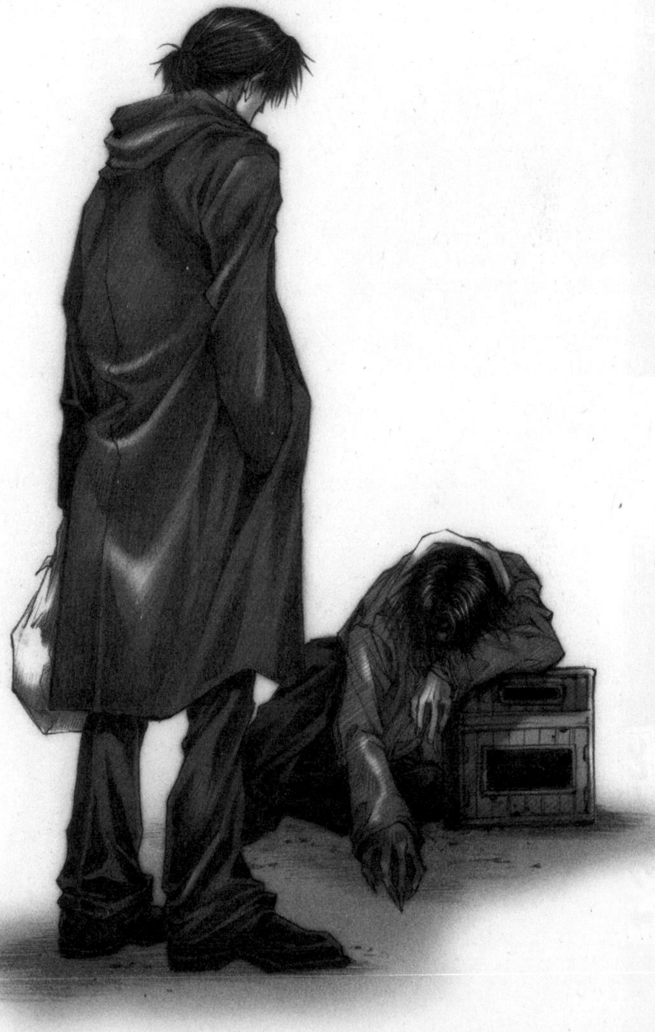

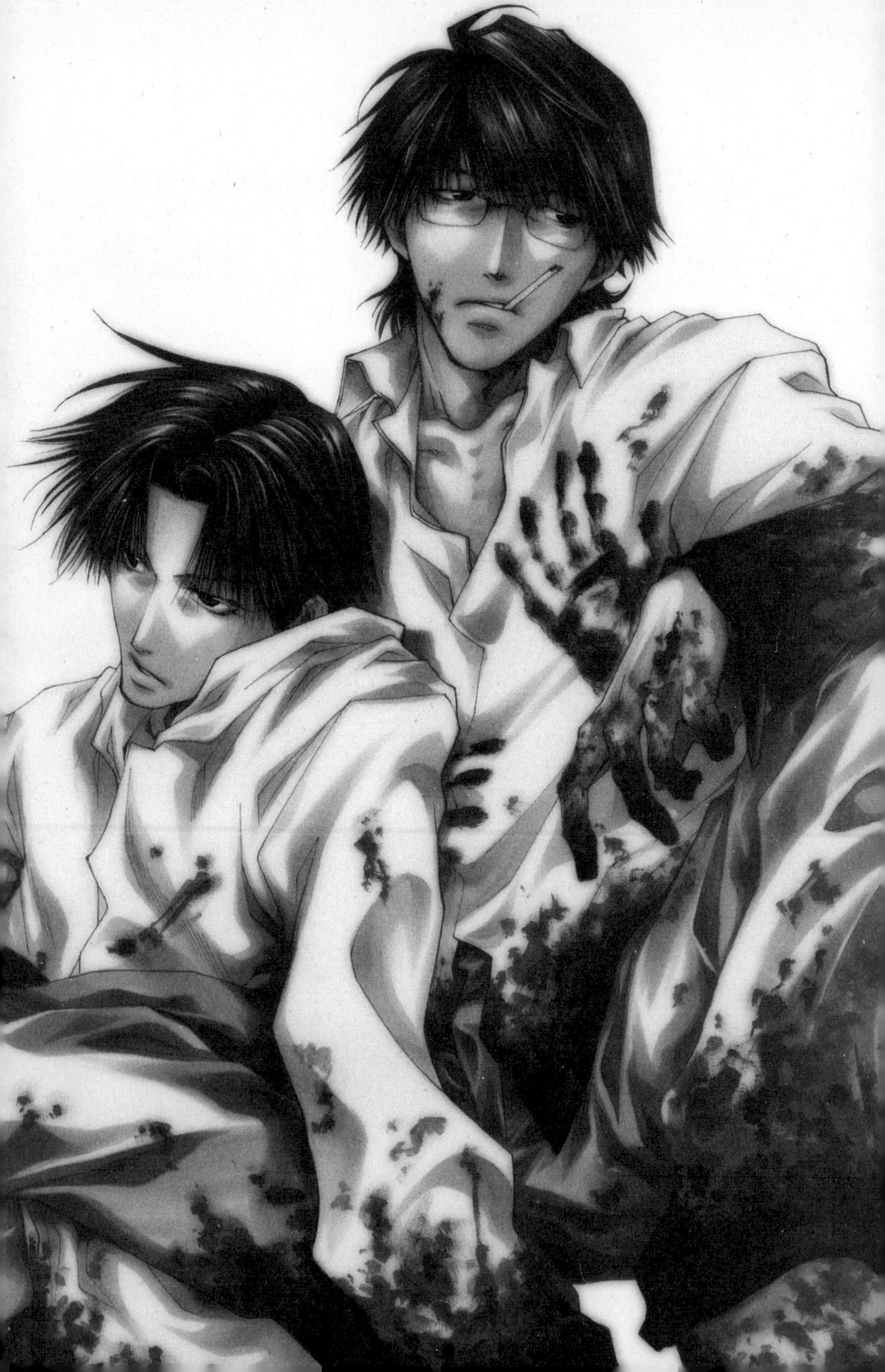

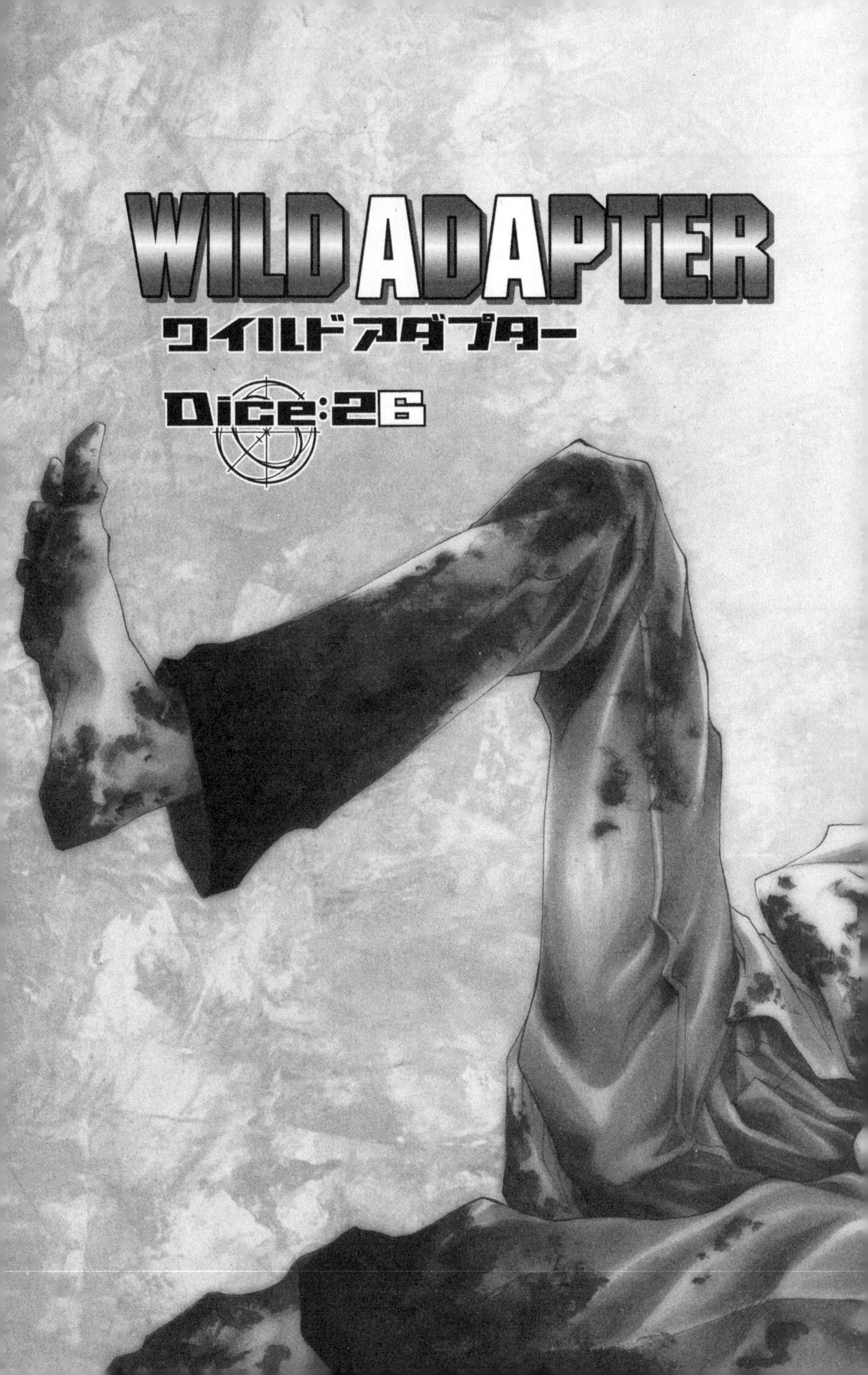
WILD ADAPTER
ワイルドアダプター
Dice:26

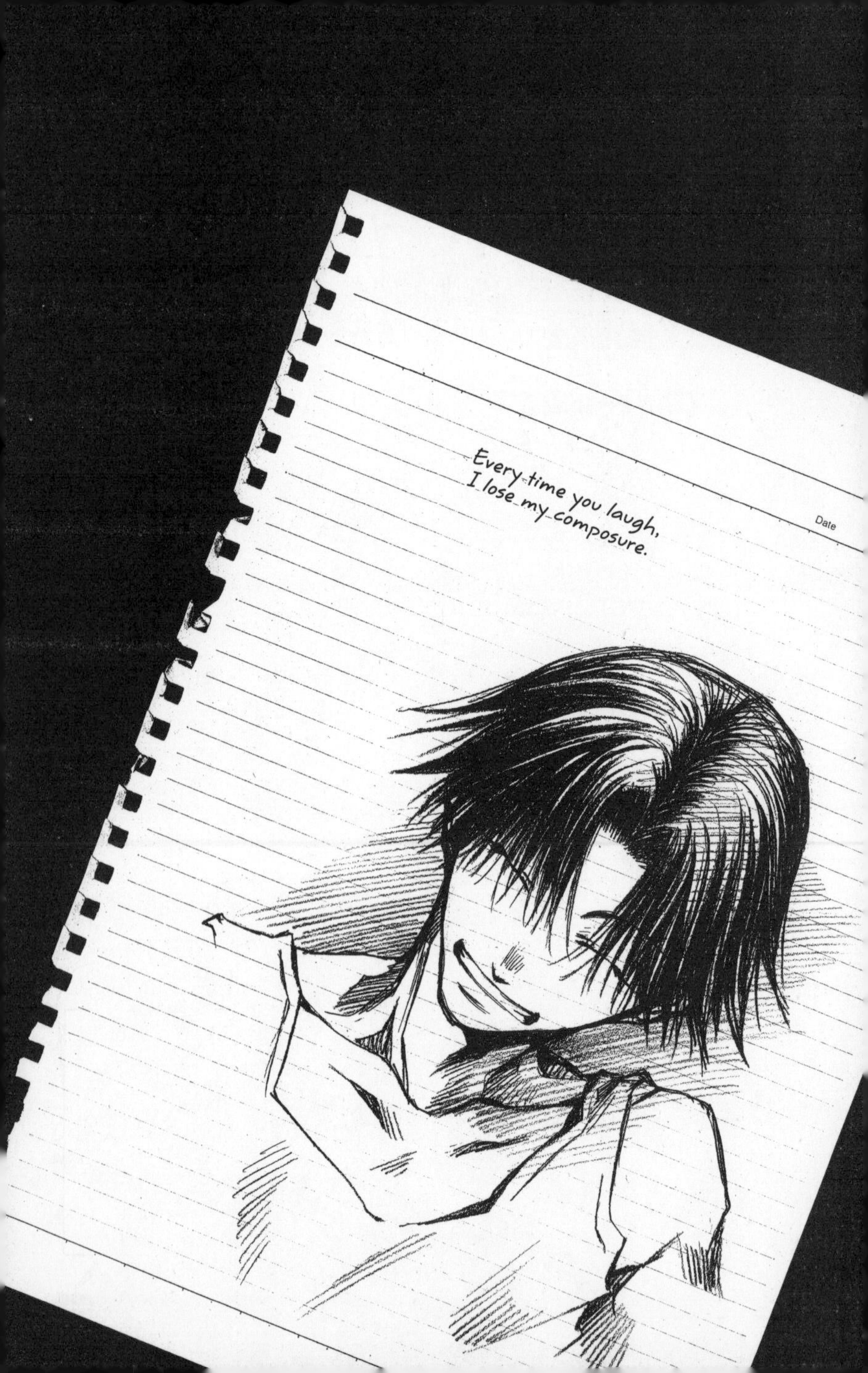
Every time you laugh,
I lose my composure.
Date

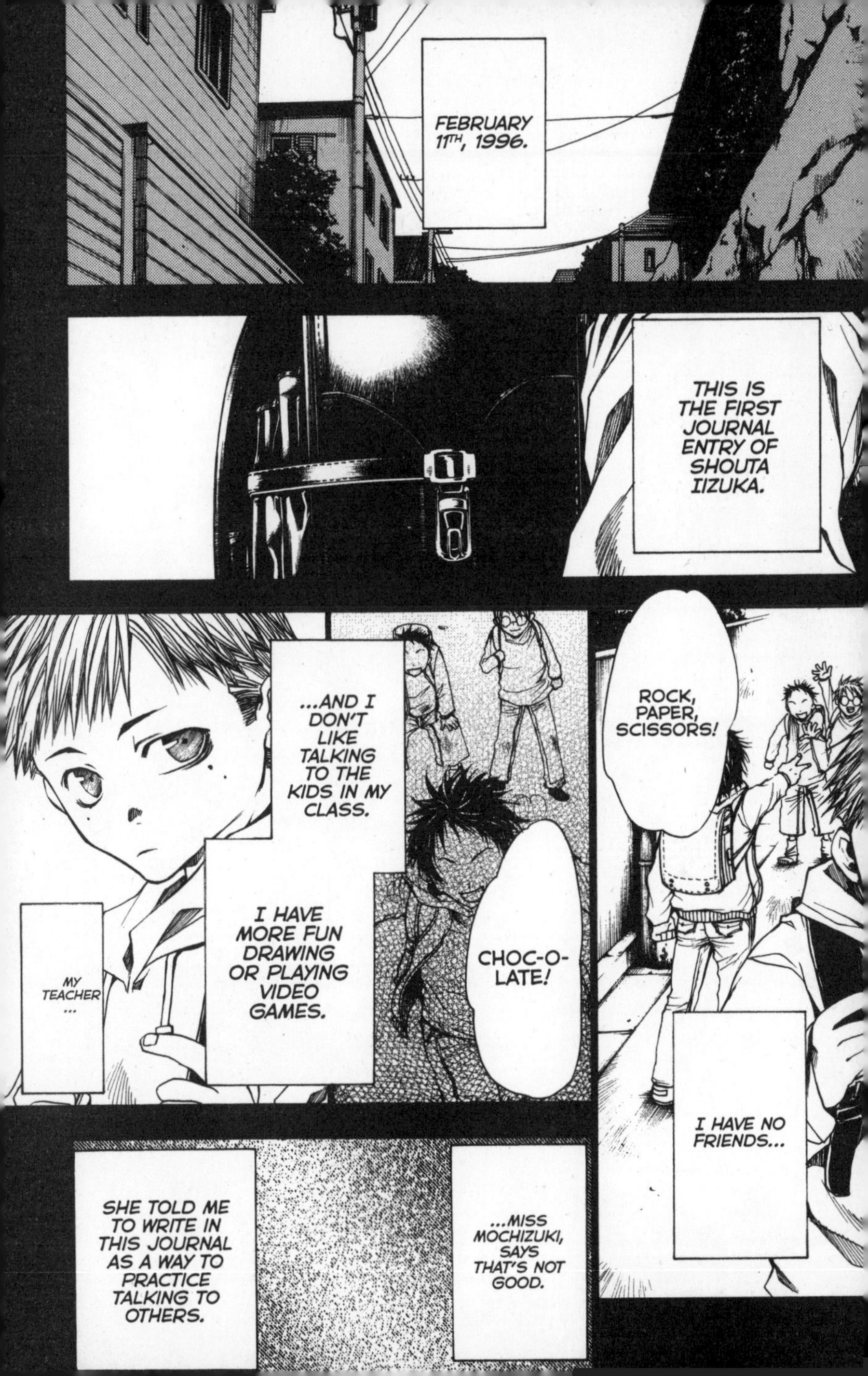
FEBRUARY 11TH, 1996.
THIS IS THE FIRST JOURNAL ENTRY OF SHOUTA IIZUKA.
ROCK, PAPER, SCISSORS!
I HAVE NO FRIENDS...
...AND I DON'T LIKE TALKING TO THE KIDS IN MY CLASS.
CHOC-O-LATE!
I HAVE MORE FUN DRAWING OR PLAYING VIDEO GAMES.
MY TEACHER...
...MISS MOCHIZUKI, SAYS THAT'S NOT GOOD.
SHE TOLD ME TO WRITE IN THIS JOURNAL AS A WAY TO PRACTICE TALKING TO OTHERS.

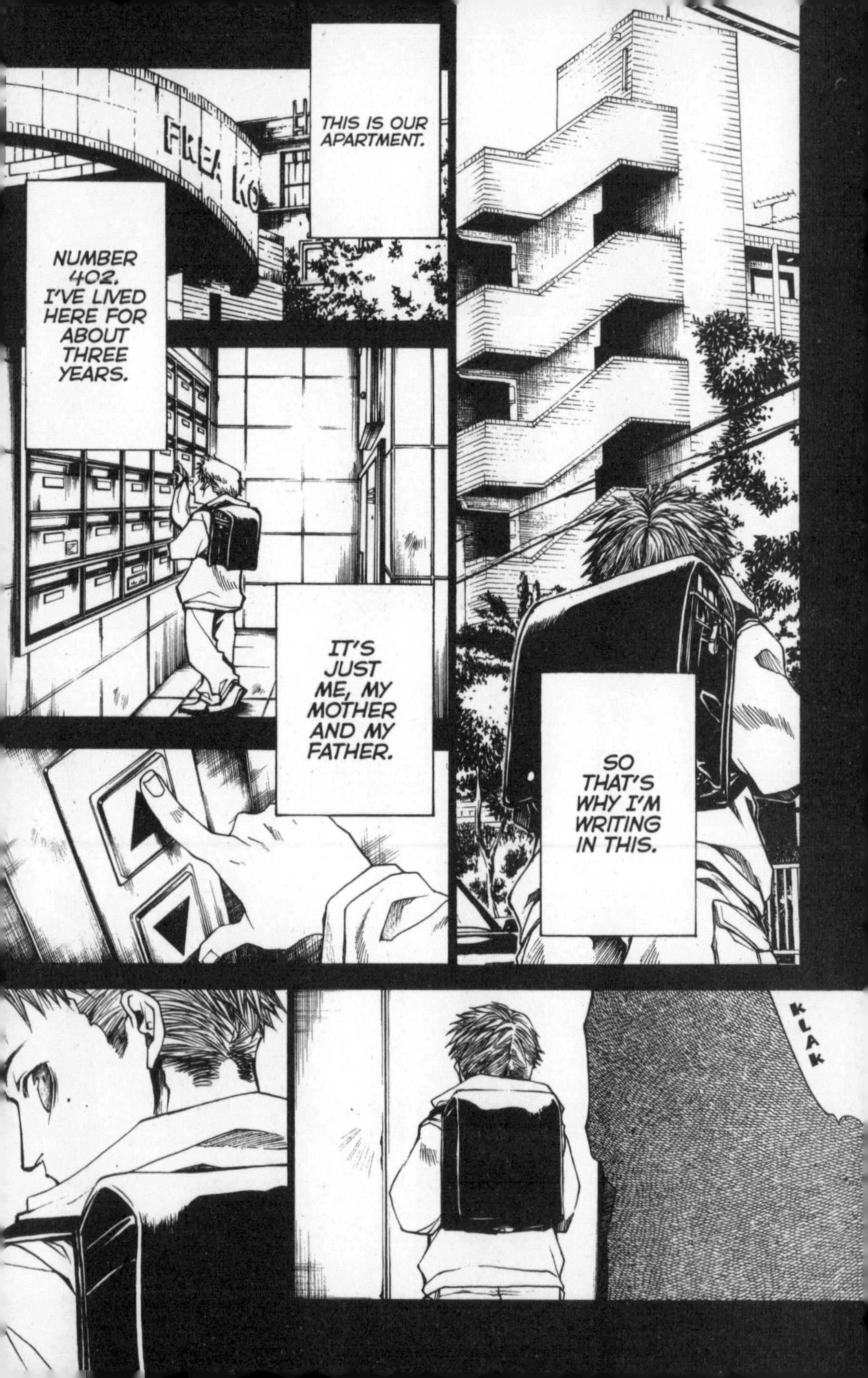
SO THAT'S WHY I'M WRITING IN THIS.
THIS IS OUR APARTMENT.
NUMBER 402. I'VE LIVED HERE FOR ABOUT THREE YEARS.
IT'S JUST ME, MY MOTHER AND MY FATHER.
KLAK

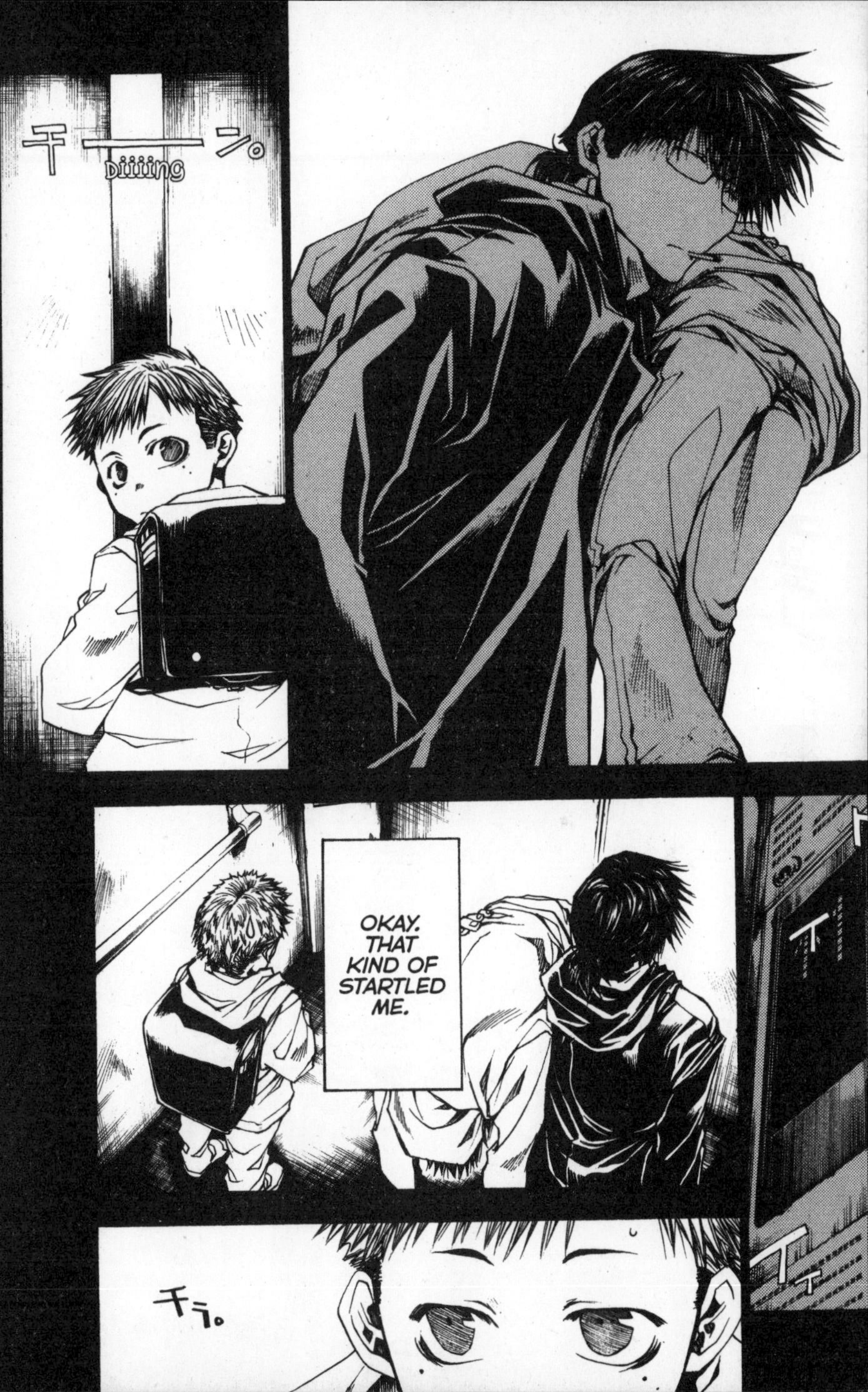
チーーン。
DIIIING
OKAY. THAT KIND OF STARTLED ME.
ドン
チラ。

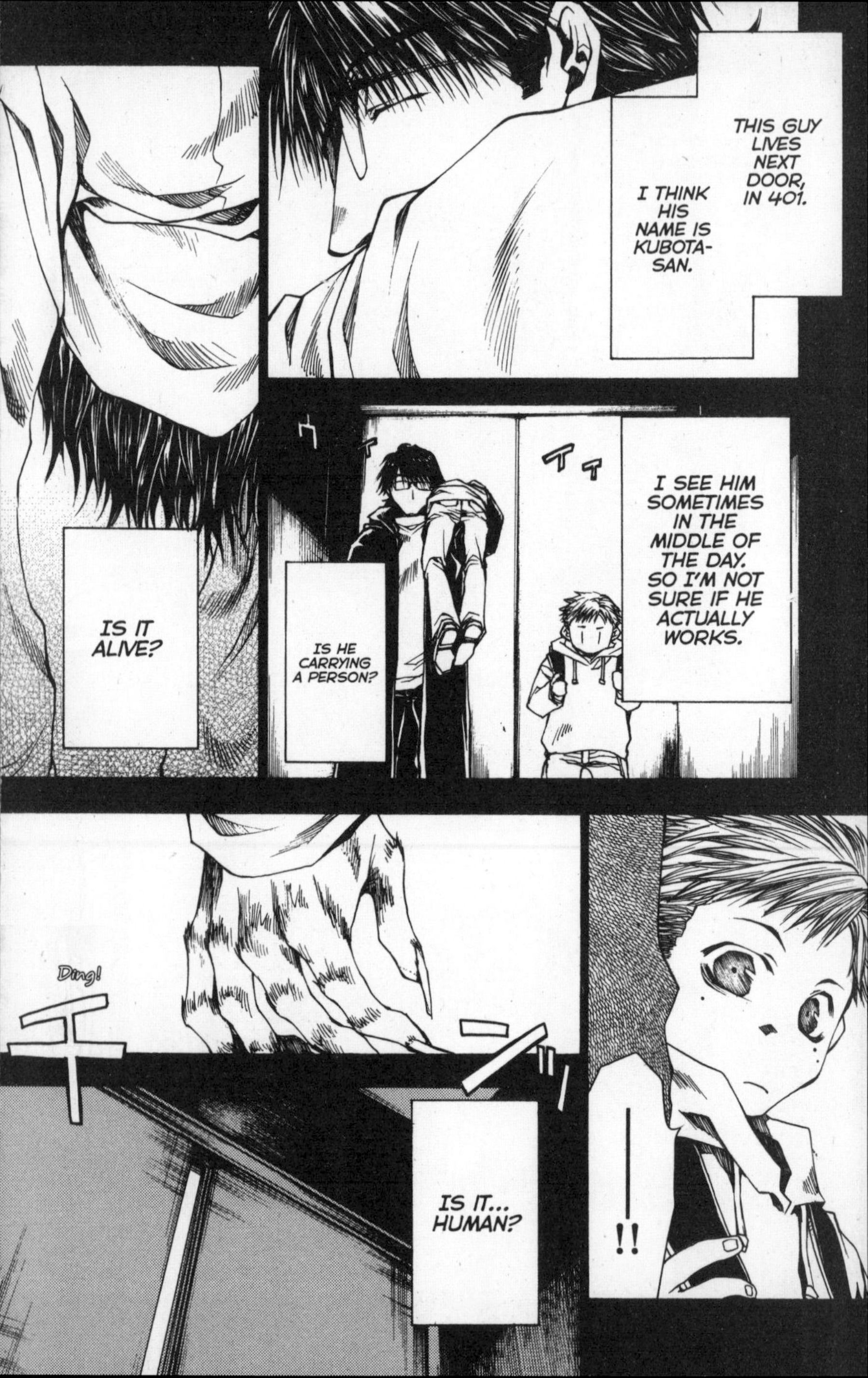
THIS GUY LIVES NEXT DOOR, IN 401.
I THINK HIS NAME IS KUBOTA-SAN.
I SEE HIM SOMETIMES IN THE MIDDLE OF THE DAY. SO I'M NOT SURE IF HE ACTUALLY WORKS.
IS HE CARRYING A PERSON?
IS IT ALIVE?
!!
Ding!
IS IT... HUMAN?

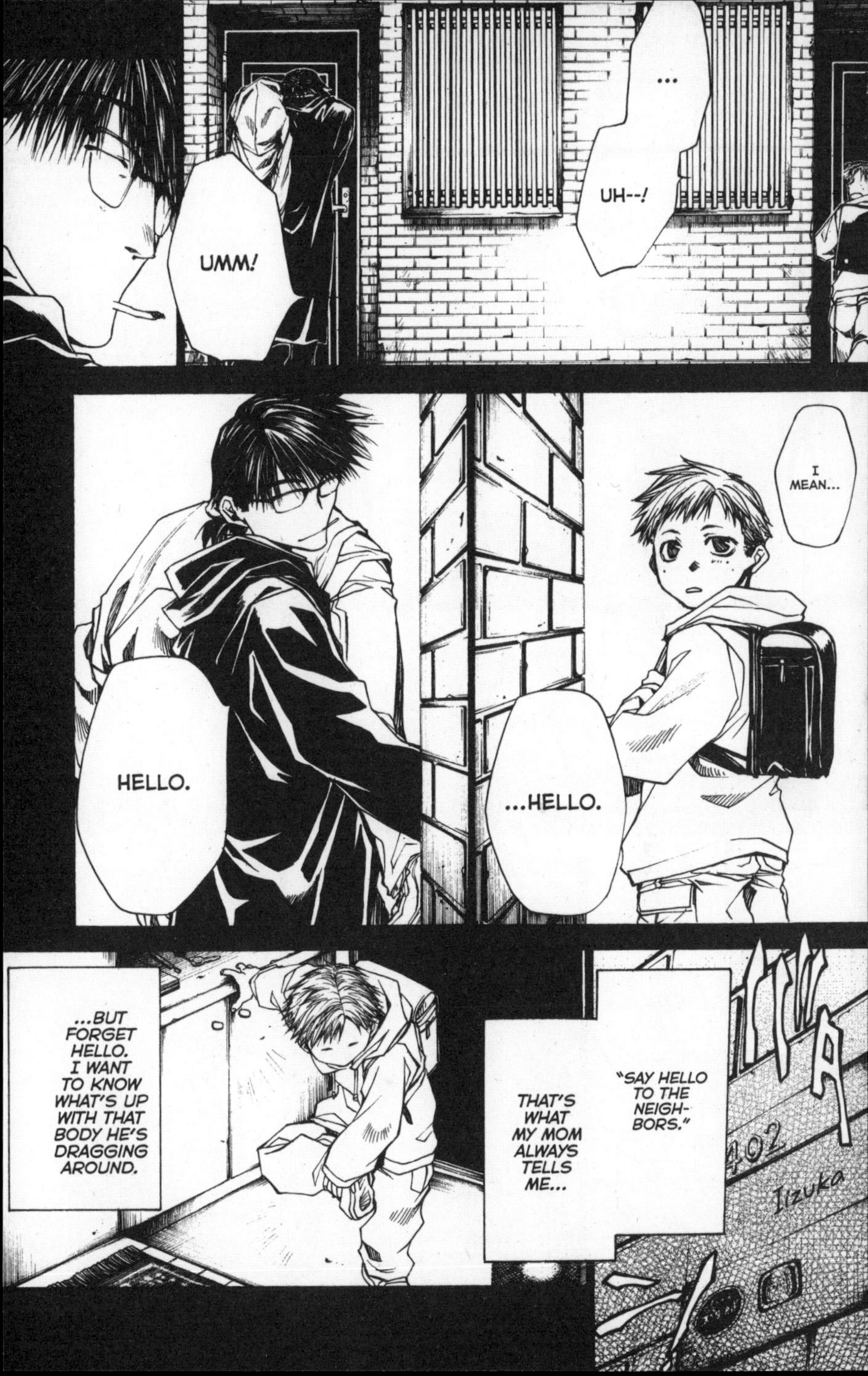
...
UH--!
UMM!
I MEAN...
...HELLO.
HELLO.
"SAY HELLO TO THE NEIGH-BORS."
THAT'S WHAT MY MOM ALWAYS TELLS ME...
402
Iizuka
...BUT FORGET HELLO. I WANT TO KNOW WHAT'S UP WITH THAT BODY HE'S DRAGGING AROUND.

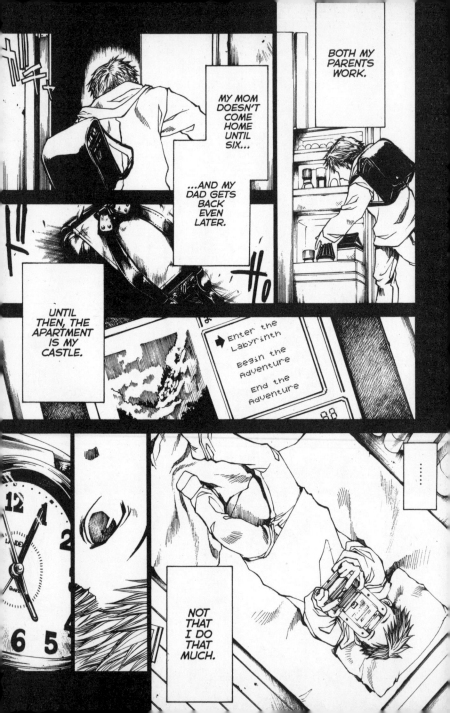

BOTH MY PARENTS WORK.

MY MOM DOESN'T COME HOME UNTIL SIX...

...AND MY DAD GETS BACK EVEN LATER.

UNTIL THEN, THE APARTMENT IS MY CASTLE.

▶ Enter the Labyrinth

Begin the Adventure

End the Adventure

NOT THAT I DO THAT MUCH.

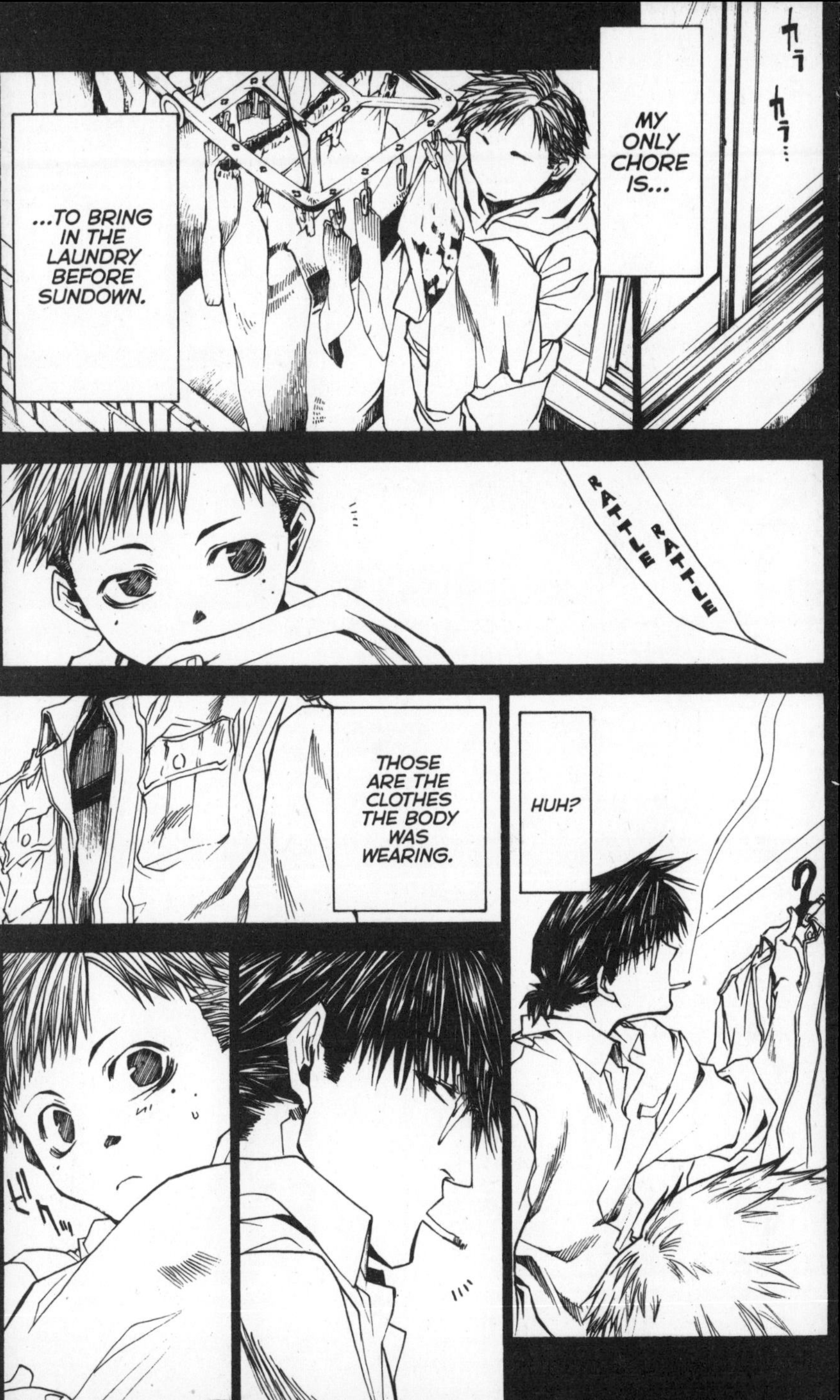

カラ
カラ…
MY ONLY CHORE IS...
...TO BRING IN THE LAUNDRY BEFORE SUNDOWN.
RATTLE RATTLE
HUH?
THOSE ARE THE CLOTHES THE BODY WAS WEARING.
ビクッ

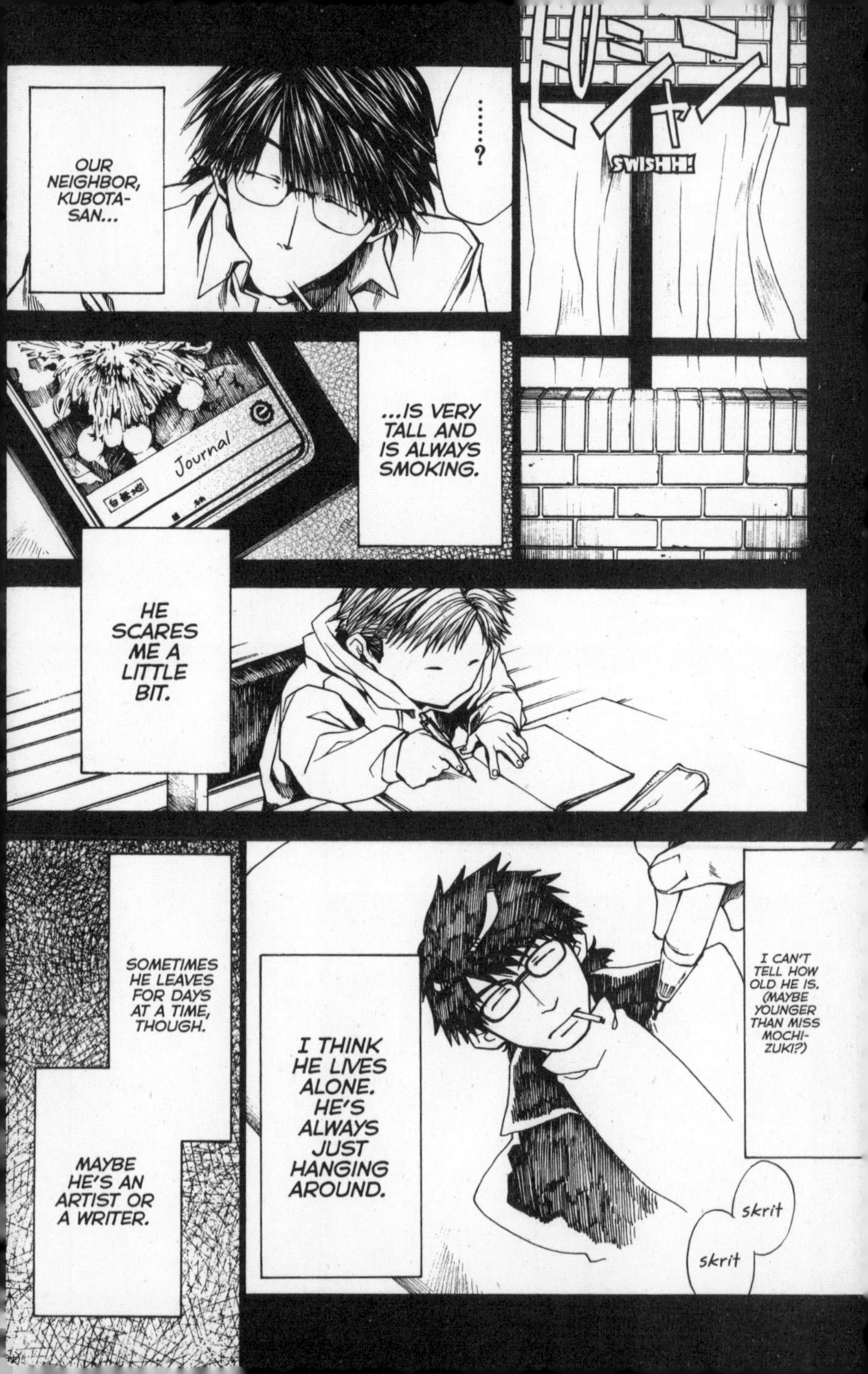
SWISHH!
......?
OUR NEIGHBOR, KUBOTA-SAN...
...IS VERY TALL AND IS ALWAYS SMOKING.
Journal
HE SCARES ME A LITTLE BIT.
I CAN'T TELL HOW OLD HE IS. (MAYBE YOUNGER THAN MISS MOCHI-ZUKI?)
I THINK HE LIVES ALONE. HE'S ALWAYS JUST HANGING AROUND.
skrit
skrit
SOMETIMES HE LEAVES FOR DAYS AT A TIME, THOUGH.
MAYBE HE'S AN ARTIST OR A WRITER.

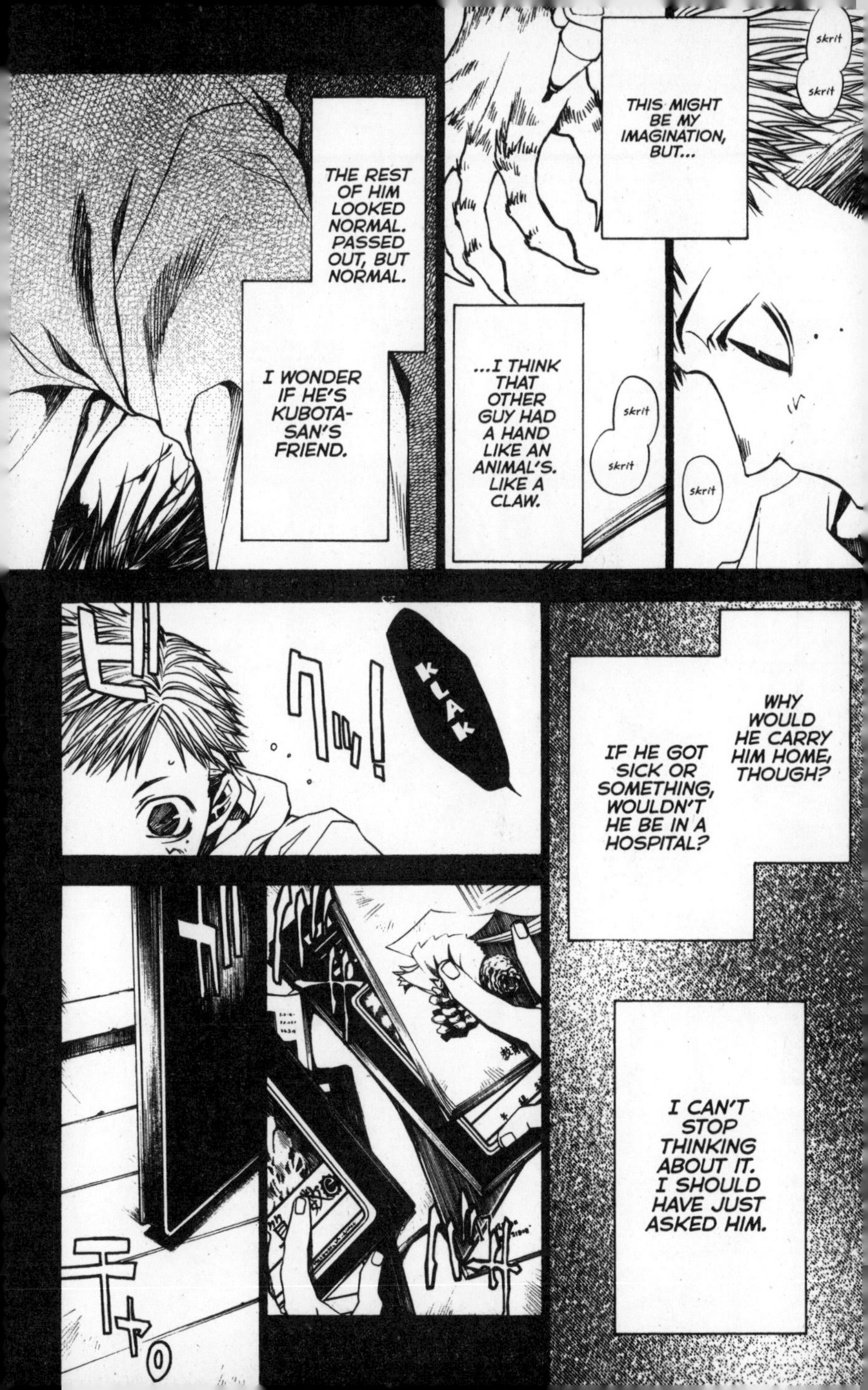
skrit
skrit
THIS MIGHT BE MY IMAGINATION, BUT...
skrit
skrit
skrit
...I THINK THAT OTHER GUY HAD A HAND LIKE AN ANIMAL'S. LIKE A CLAW.
THE REST OF HIM LOOKED NORMAL. PASSED OUT, BUT NORMAL.
I WONDER IF HE'S KUBOTA-SAN'S FRIEND.
WHY WOULD HE CARRY HIM HOME, THOUGH?
IF HE GOT SICK OR SOMETHING, WOULDN'T HE BE IN A HOSPITAL?
I CAN'T STOP THINKING ABOUT IT. I SHOULD HAVE JUST ASKED HIM.
KLAK

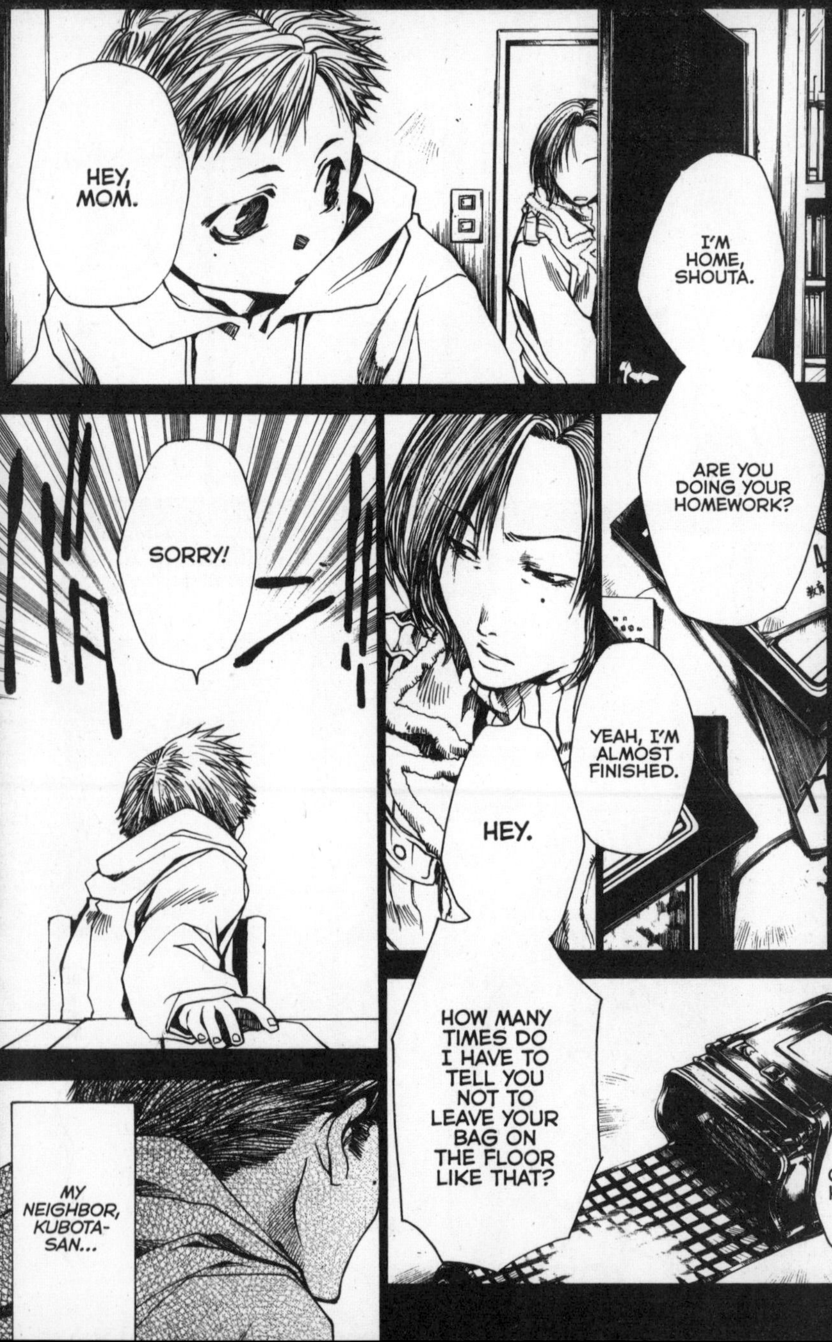
I'M HOME, SHOUTA.
HEY, MOM.
ARE YOU DOING YOUR HOMEWORK?
YEAH, I'M ALMOST FINISHED.
HEY.
HOW MANY TIMES DO I HAVE TO TELL YOU NOT TO LEAVE YOUR BAG ON THE FLOOR LIKE THAT?
OH.
SORRY!
MY NEIGHBOR, KUBOTA-SAN...

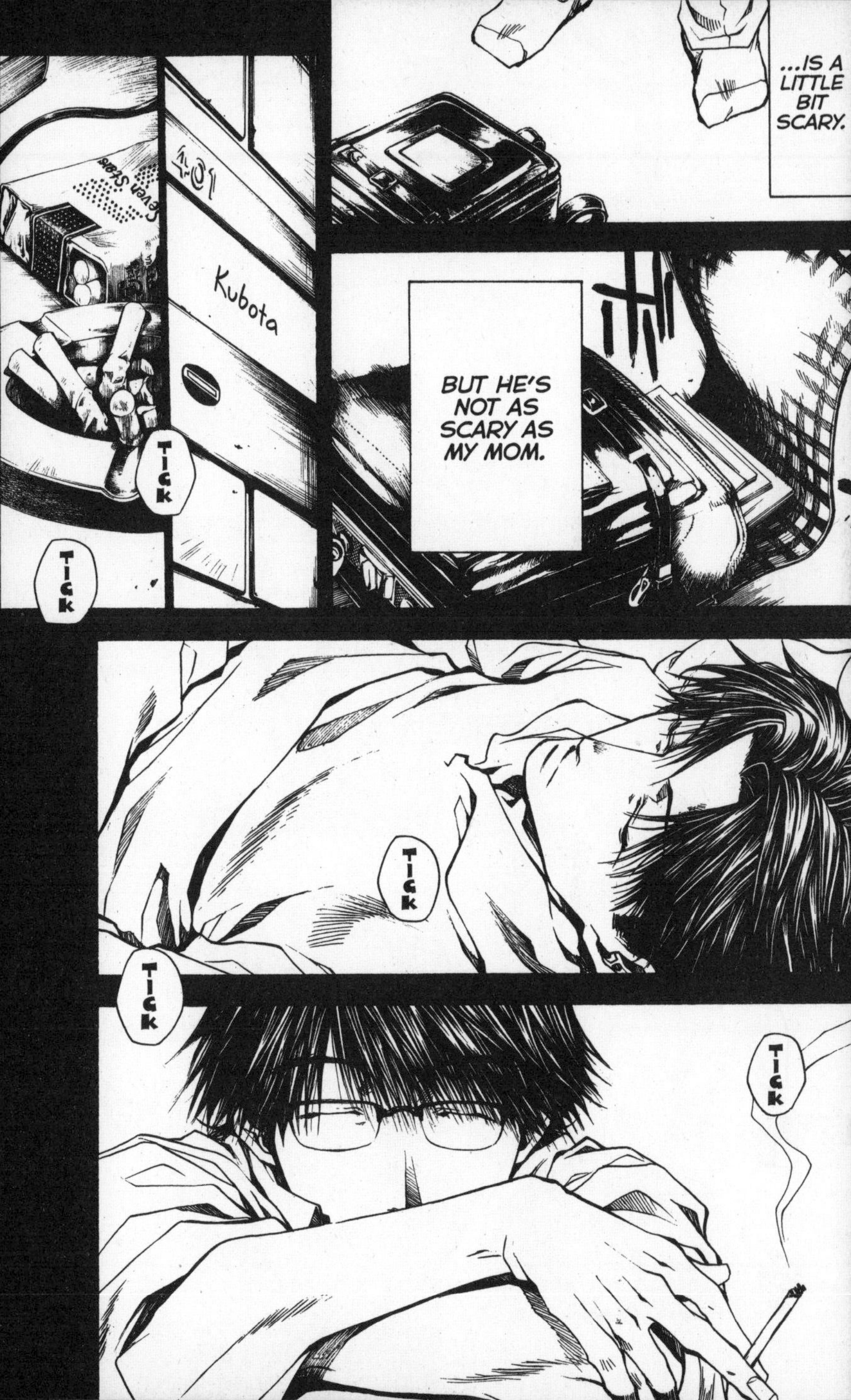

...IS A LITTLE BIT SCARY.
BUT HE'S NOT AS SCARY AS MY MOM.
Seven Stars
Kubota
TICK
TICK
TICK
TICK
TICK

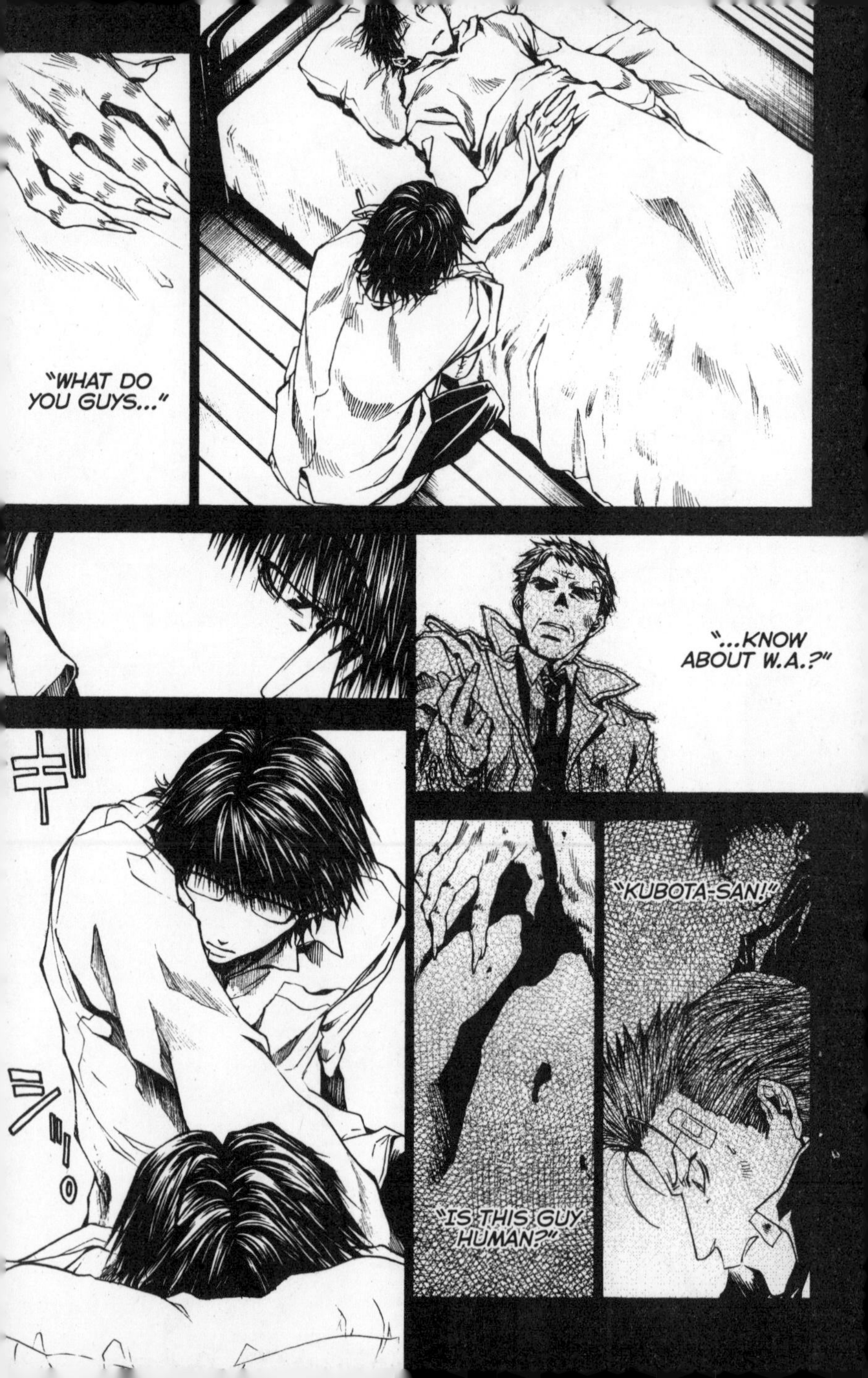
"WHAT DO YOU GUYS..."
"...KNOW ABOUT W.A.?"
"KUBOTA-SAN!"
"IS THIS GUY HUMAN?"

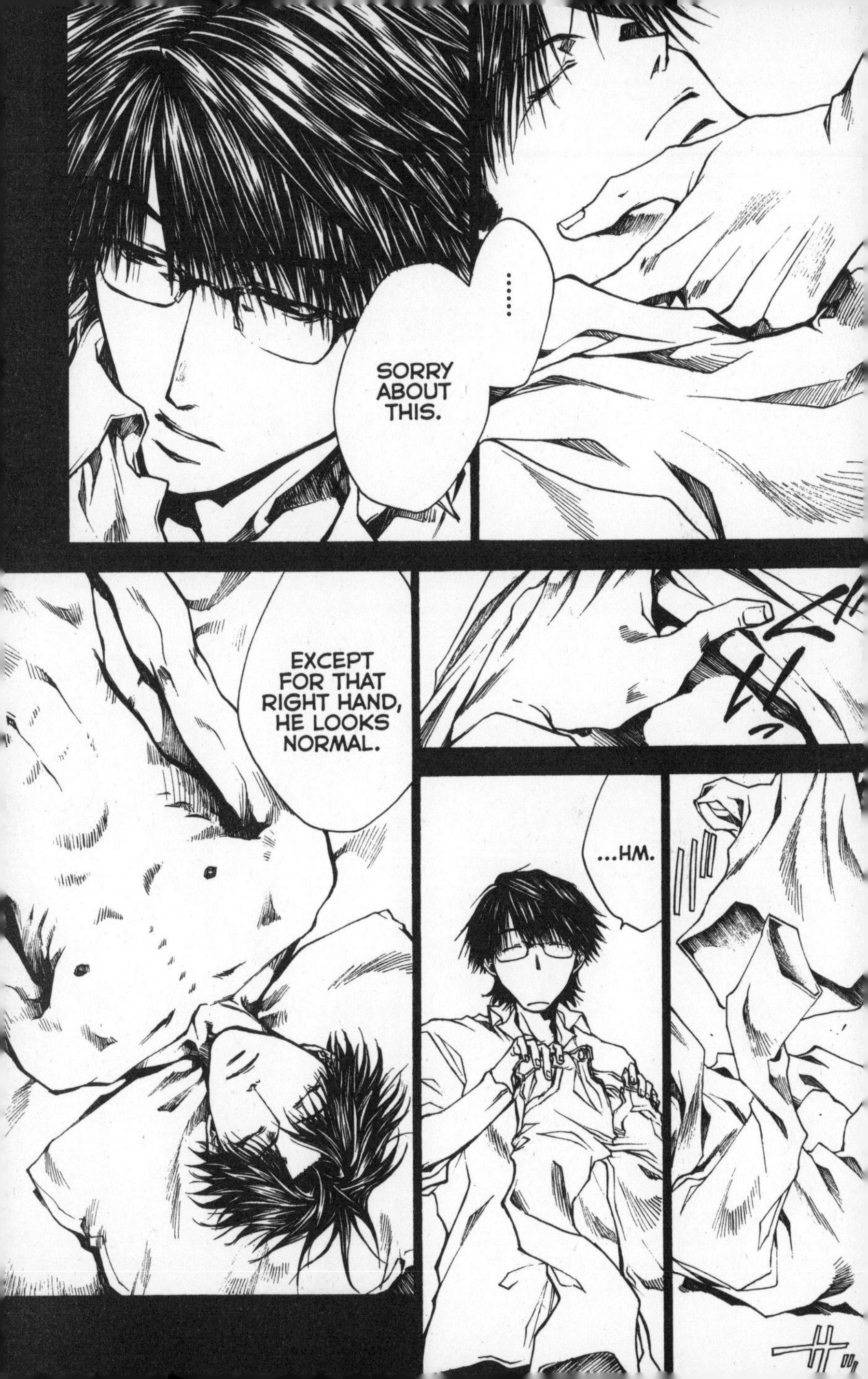
……
SORRY ABOUT THIS.
...HM.
EXCEPT FOR THAT RIGHT HAND, HE LOOKS NORMAL.

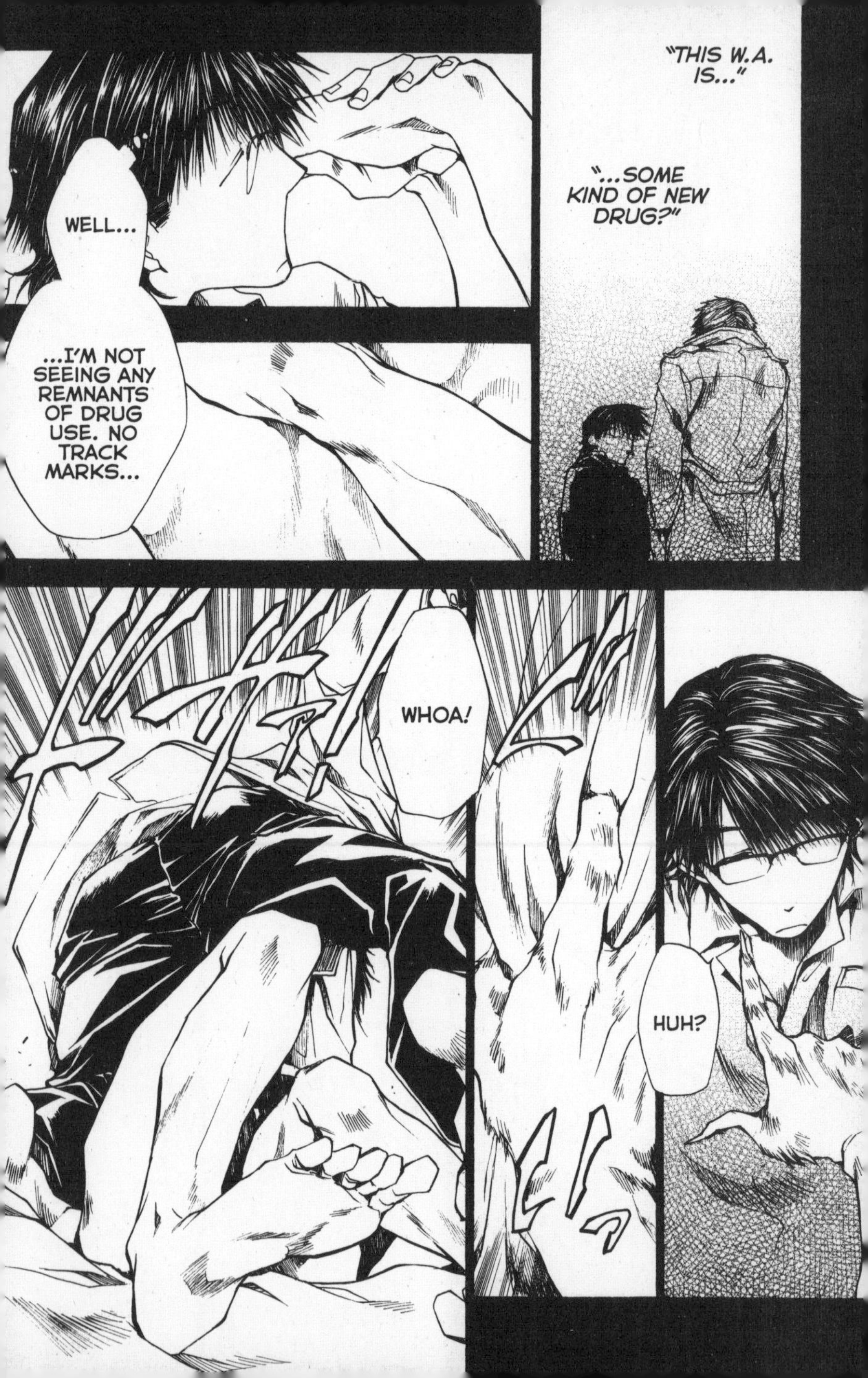
"THIS W.A. IS..."
"...SOME KIND OF NEW DRUG?"
WELL...
...I'M NOT SEEING ANY REMNANTS OF DRUG USE. NO TRACK MARKS...
HUH?
WHOA!

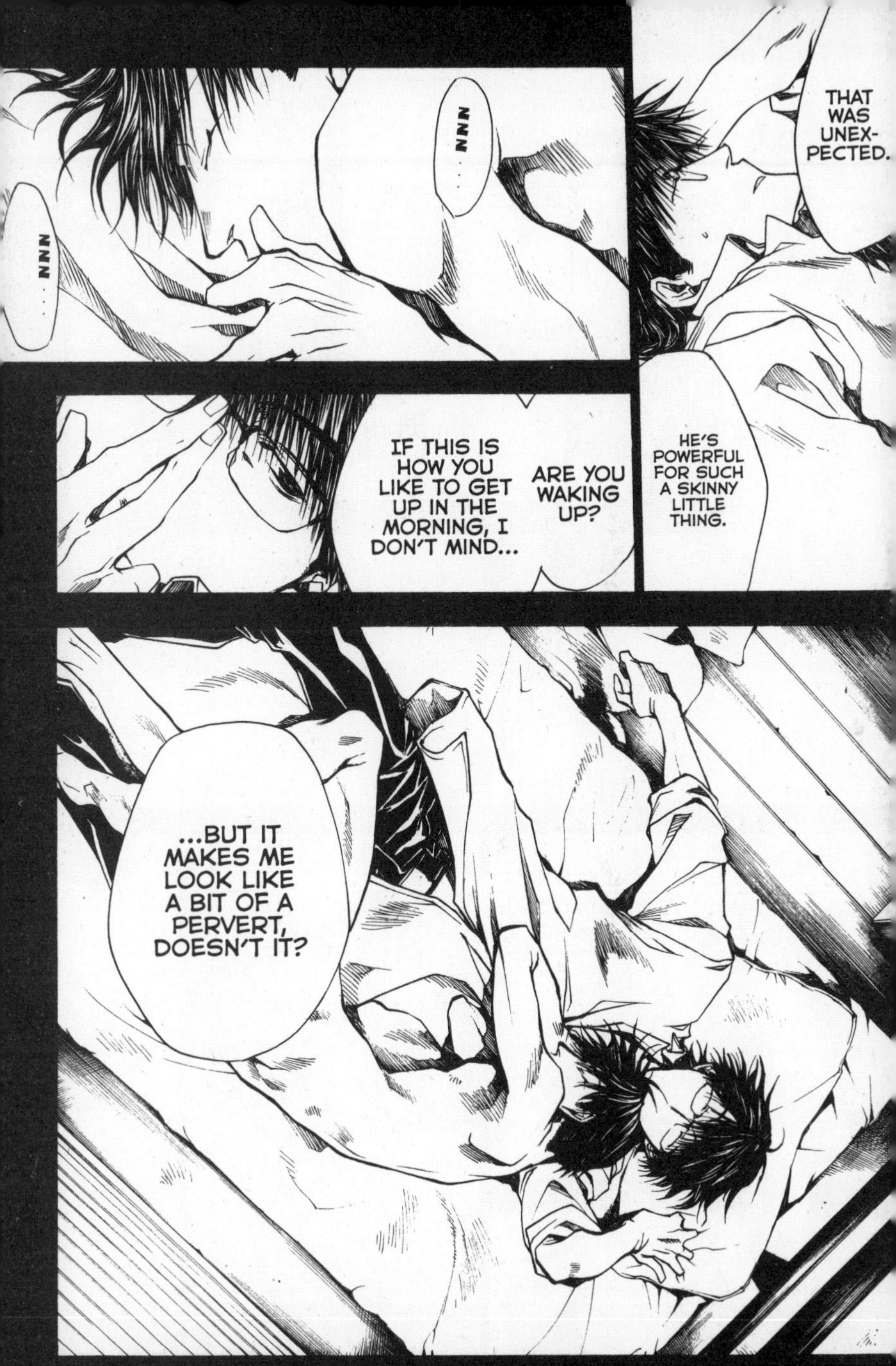
THAT WAS UNEXPECTED.
...NNN
...NNN
HE'S POWERFUL FOR SUCH A SKINNY LITTLE THING.
ARE YOU WAKING UP?
IF THIS IS HOW YOU LIKE TO GET UP IN THE MORNING, I DON'T MIND...
...BUT IT MAKES ME LOOK LIKE A BIT OF A PERVERT, DOESN'T IT?

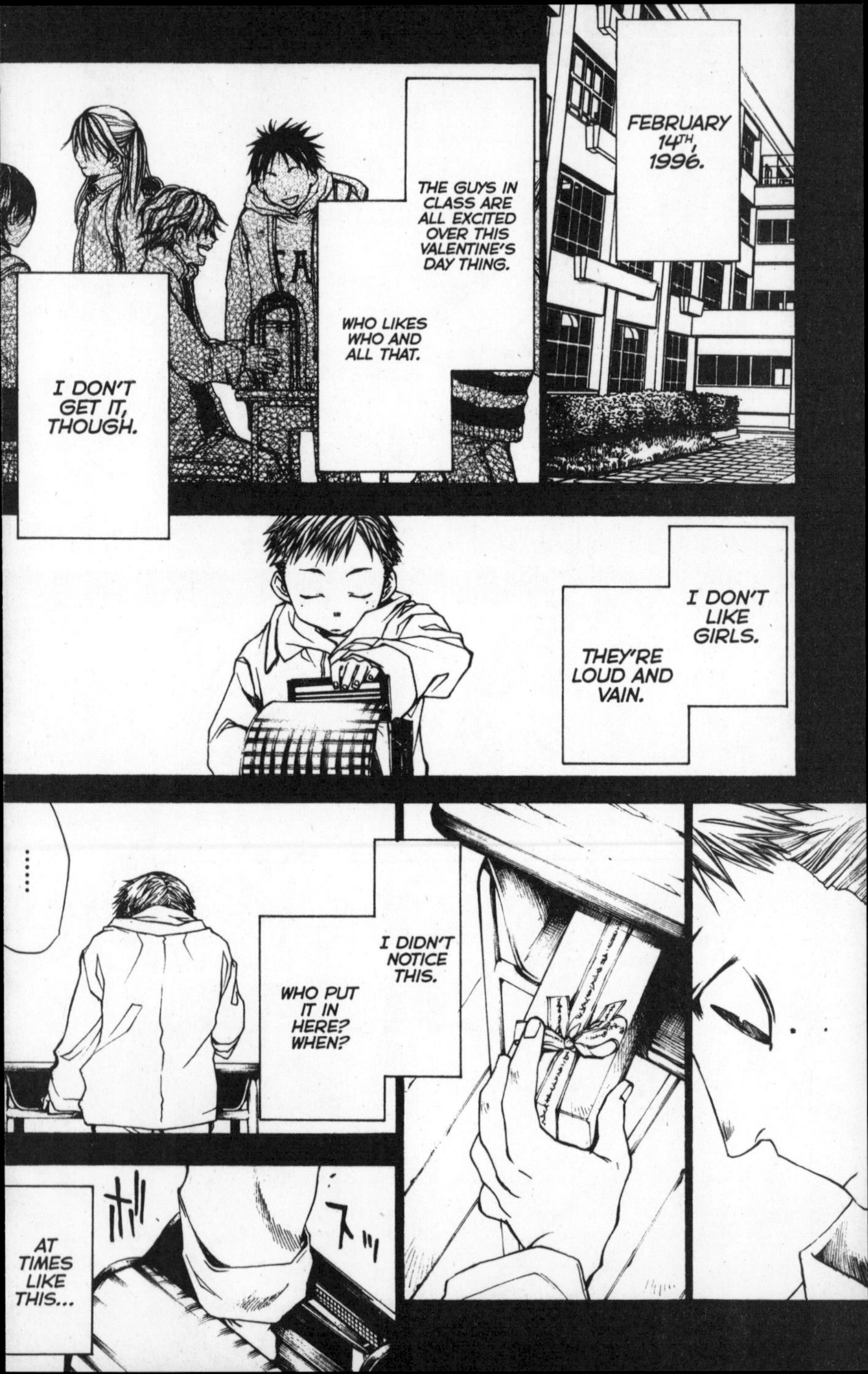
FEBRUARY 14TH, 1996.
THE GUYS IN CLASS ARE ALL EXCITED OVER THIS VALENTINE'S DAY THING.
WHO LIKES WHO AND ALL THAT.
I DON'T GET IT, THOUGH.
I DON'T LIKE GIRLS.
THEY'RE LOUD AND VAIN.
. . .
I DIDN'T NOTICE THIS.
WHO PUT IT IN HERE? WHEN?
......
AT TIMES LIKE THIS...

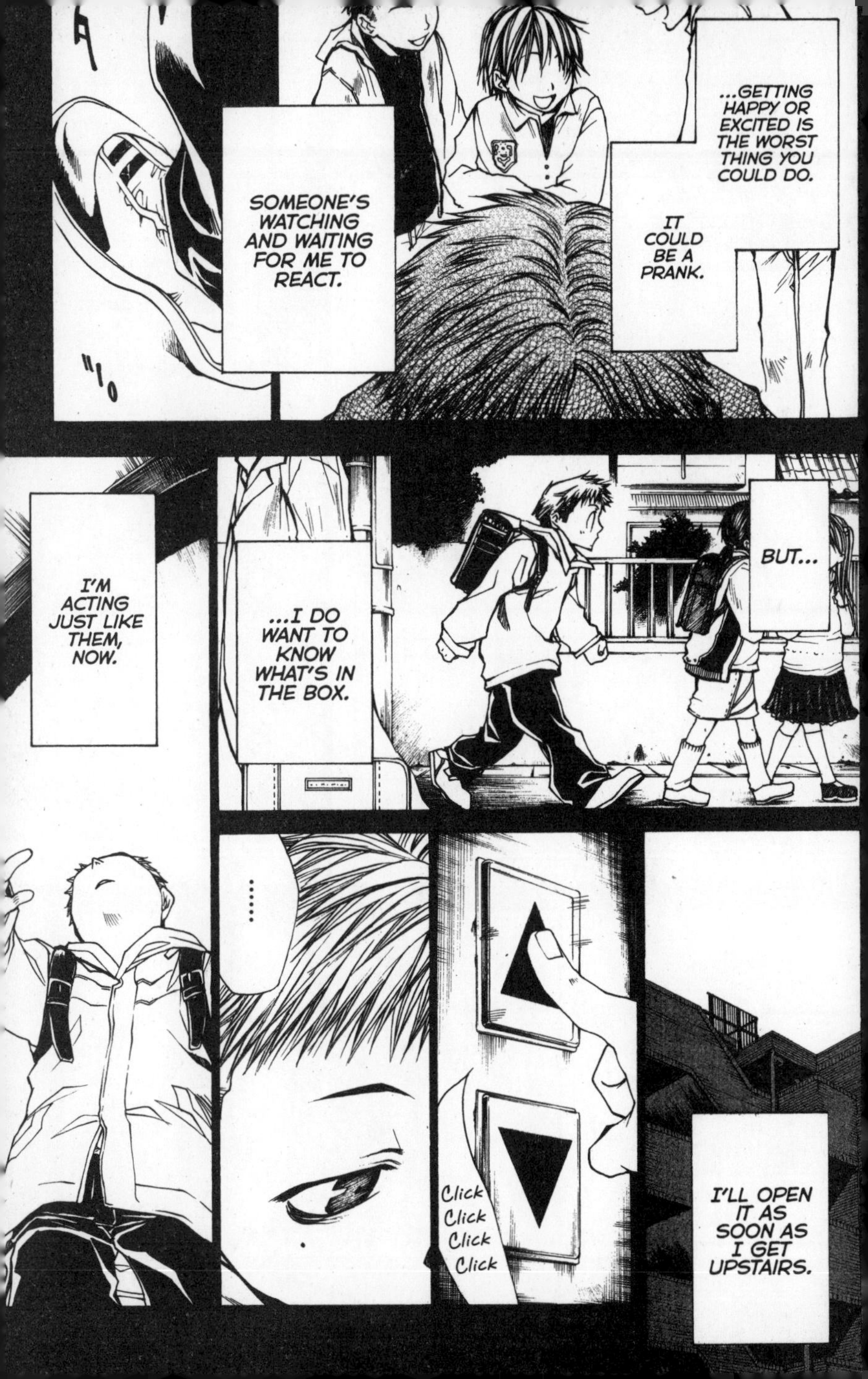
...GETTING HAPPY OR EXCITED IS THE WORST THING YOU COULD DO.
IT COULD BE A PRANK.
SOMEONE'S WATCHING AND WAITING FOR ME TO REACT.
BUT...
...I DO WANT TO KNOW WHAT'S IN THE BOX.
I'M ACTING JUST LIKE THEM, NOW.
I'LL OPEN IT AS SOON AS I GET UPSTAIRS.
Click
Click
Click
Click
......

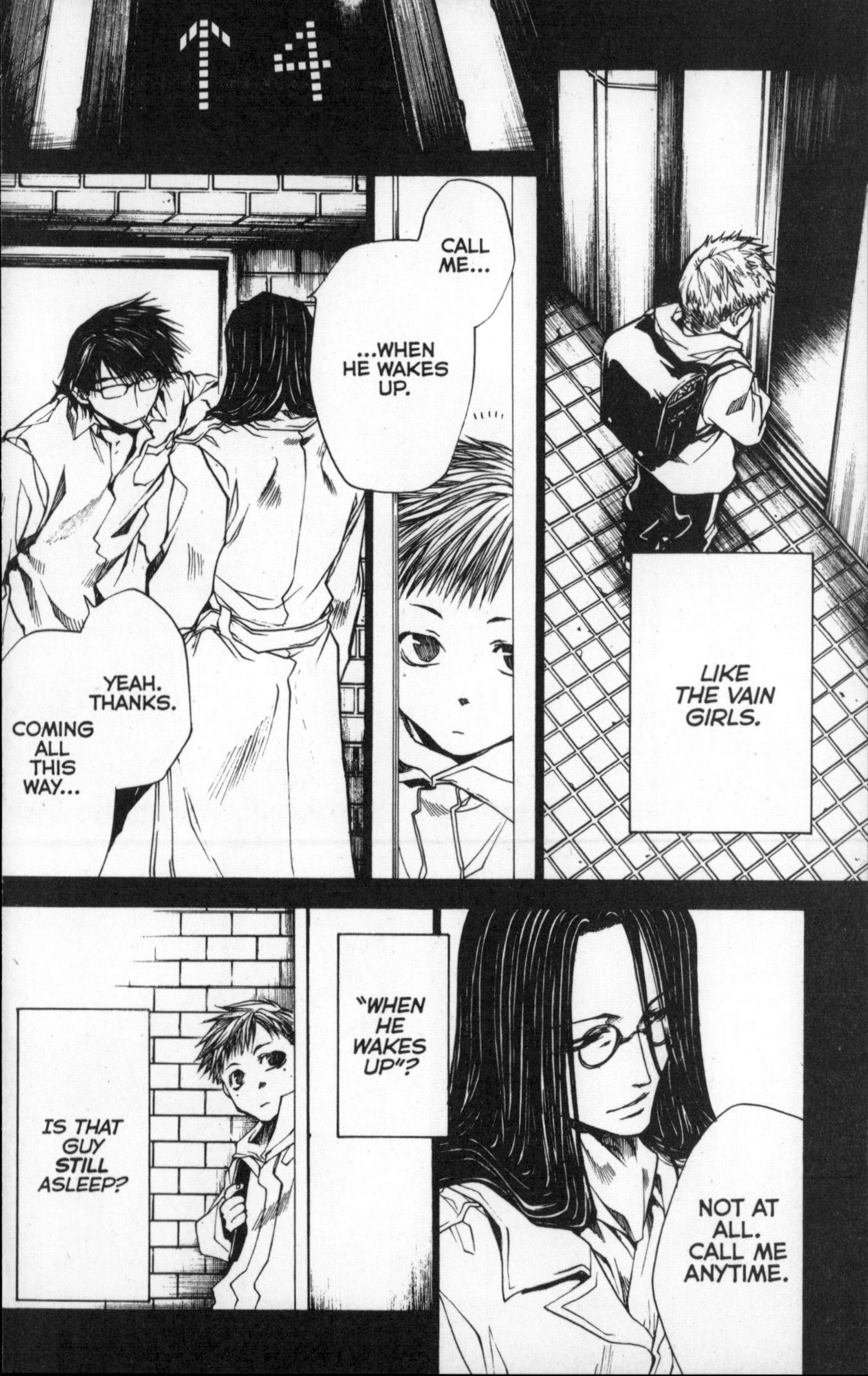
LIKE THE VAIN GIRLS.
CALL ME...
...WHEN HE WAKES UP.
YEAH. THANKS.
COMING ALL THIS WAY...
NOT AT ALL. CALL ME ANYTIME.
"WHEN HE WAKES UP"?
IS THAT GUY STILL ASLEEP?

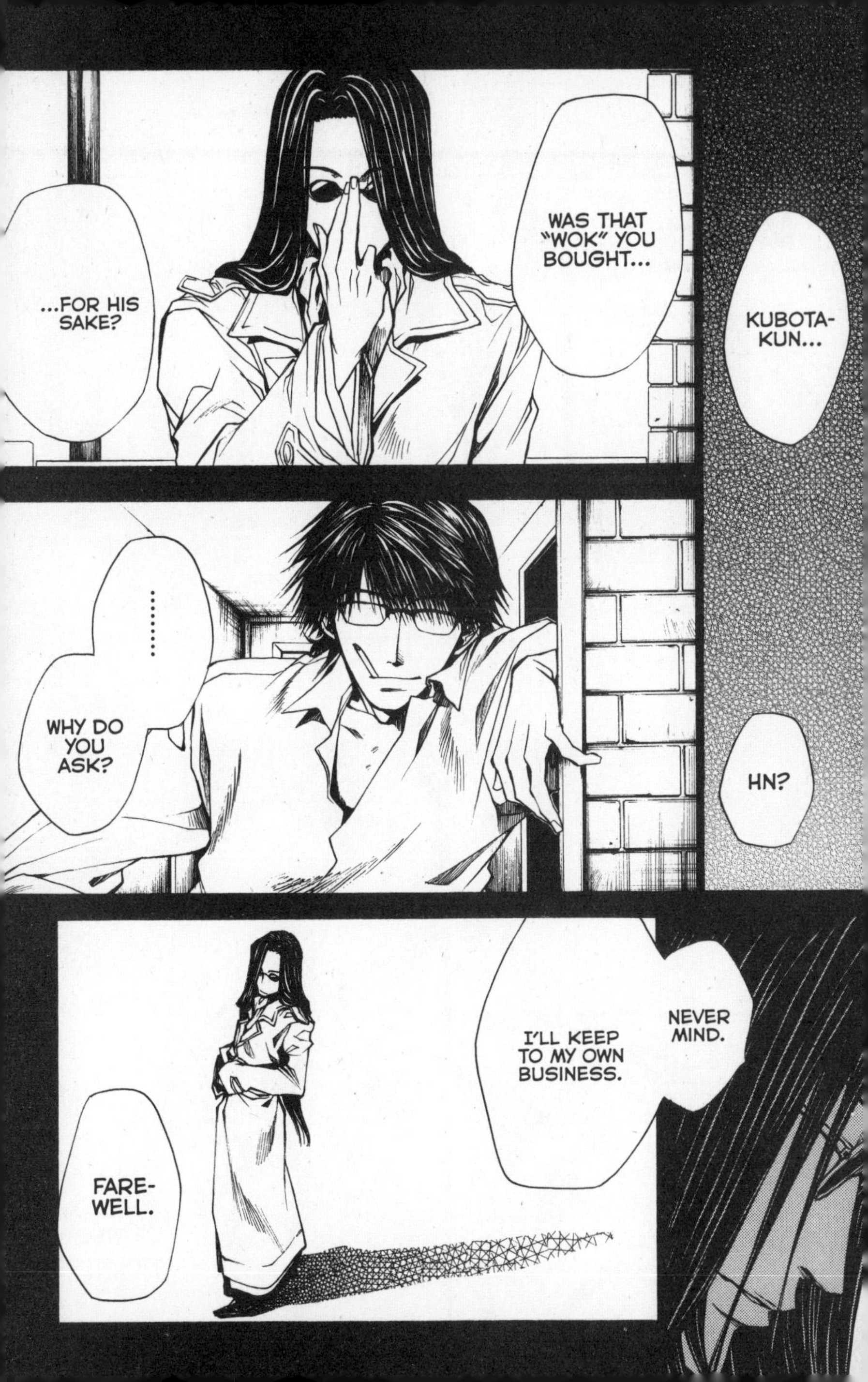
KUBOTA-KUN...
HN?
WAS THAT "WOK" YOU BOUGHT...
...FOR HIS SAKE?
......
WHY DO YOU ASK?
NEVER MIND.
I'LL KEEP TO MY OWN BUSINESS.
FARE-WELL.

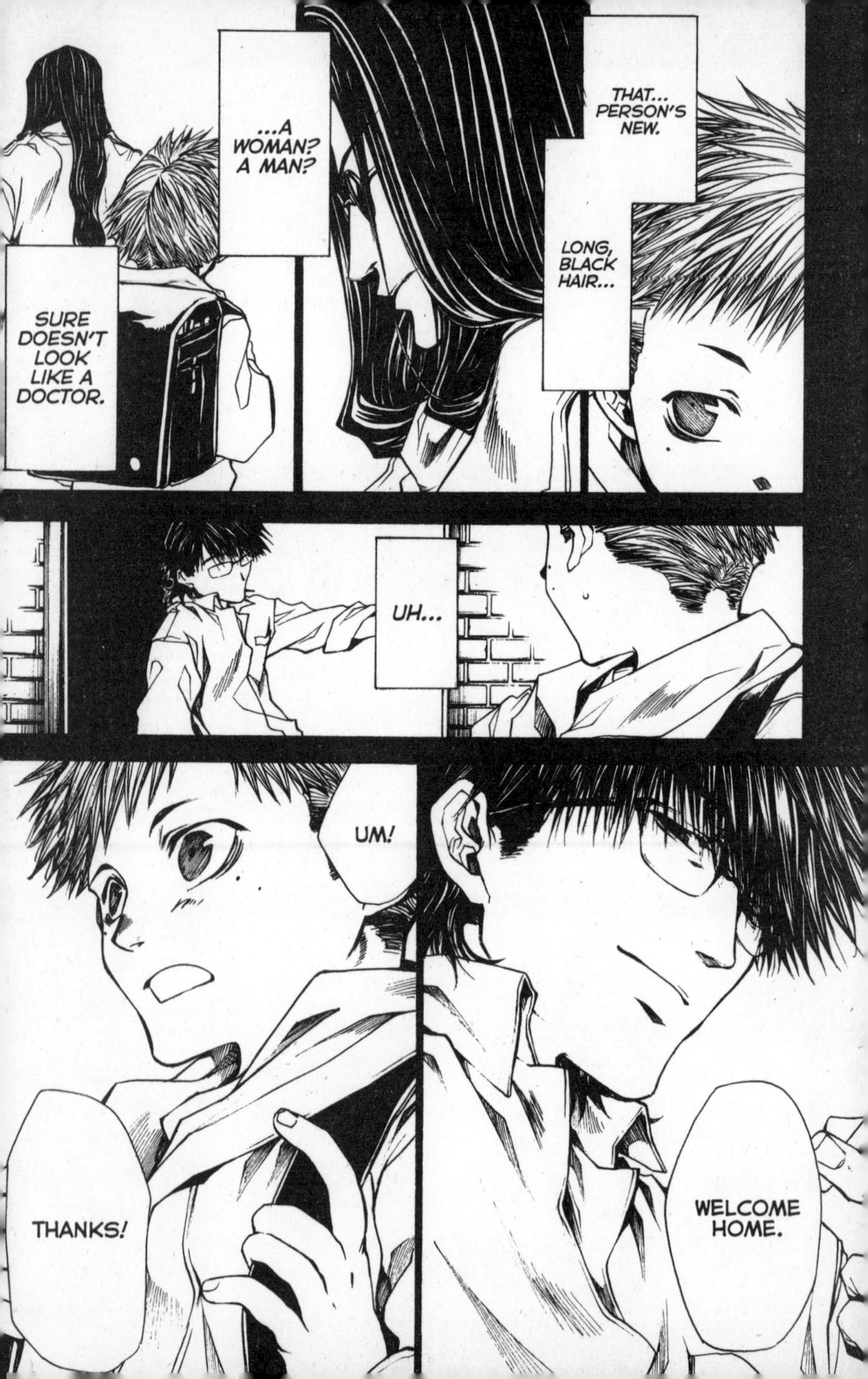
THAT... PERSON'S NEW.
LONG, BLACK HAIR...
...A WOMAN? A MAN?
SURE DOESN'T LOOK LIKE A DOCTOR.
UH...
WELCOME HOME.
UM!
THANKS!

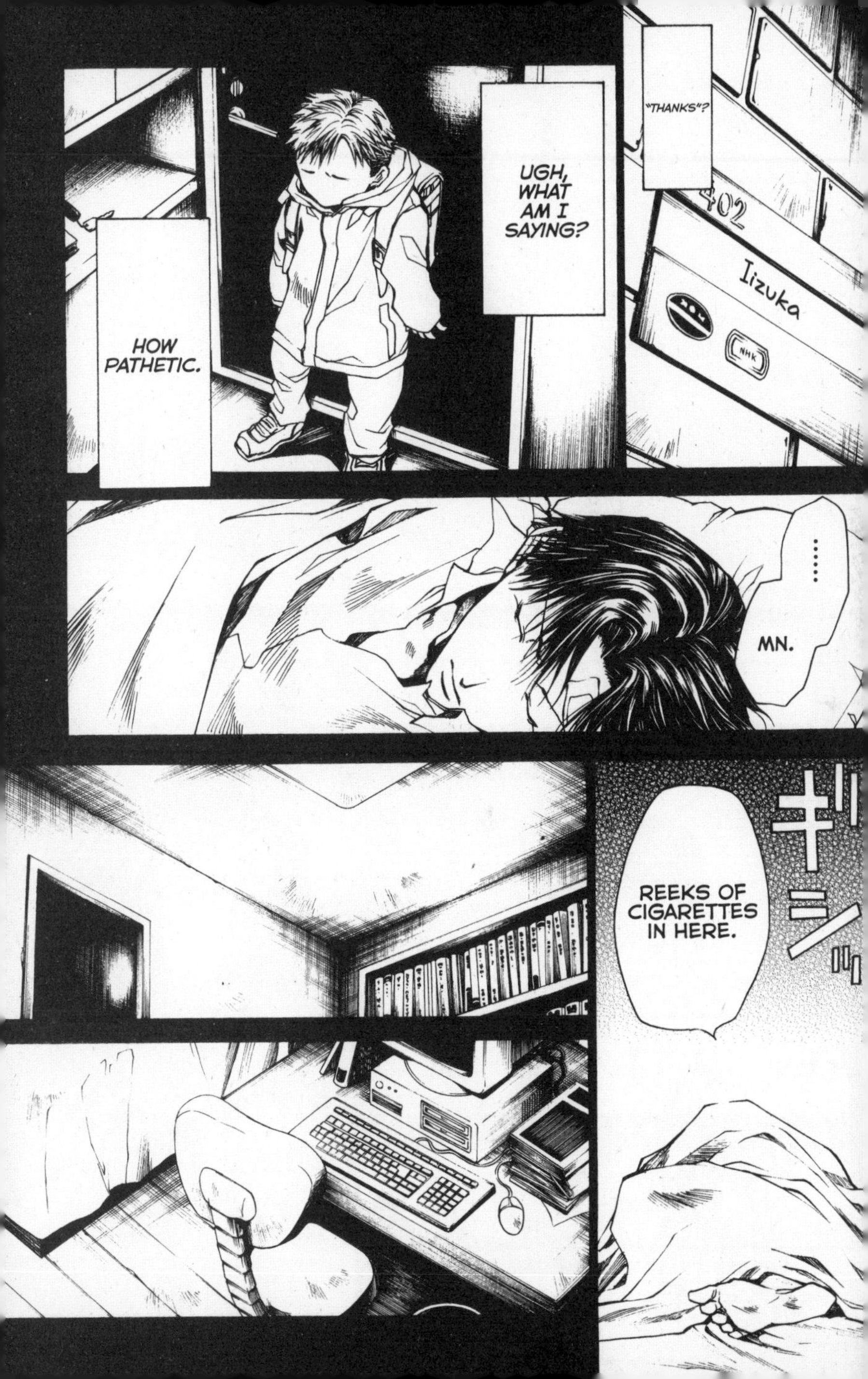
"THANKS"?
402
Iizuka
NHK
UGH, WHAT AM I SAYING?
HOW PATHETIC.
......
MN.
REEKS OF CIGARETTES IN HERE.

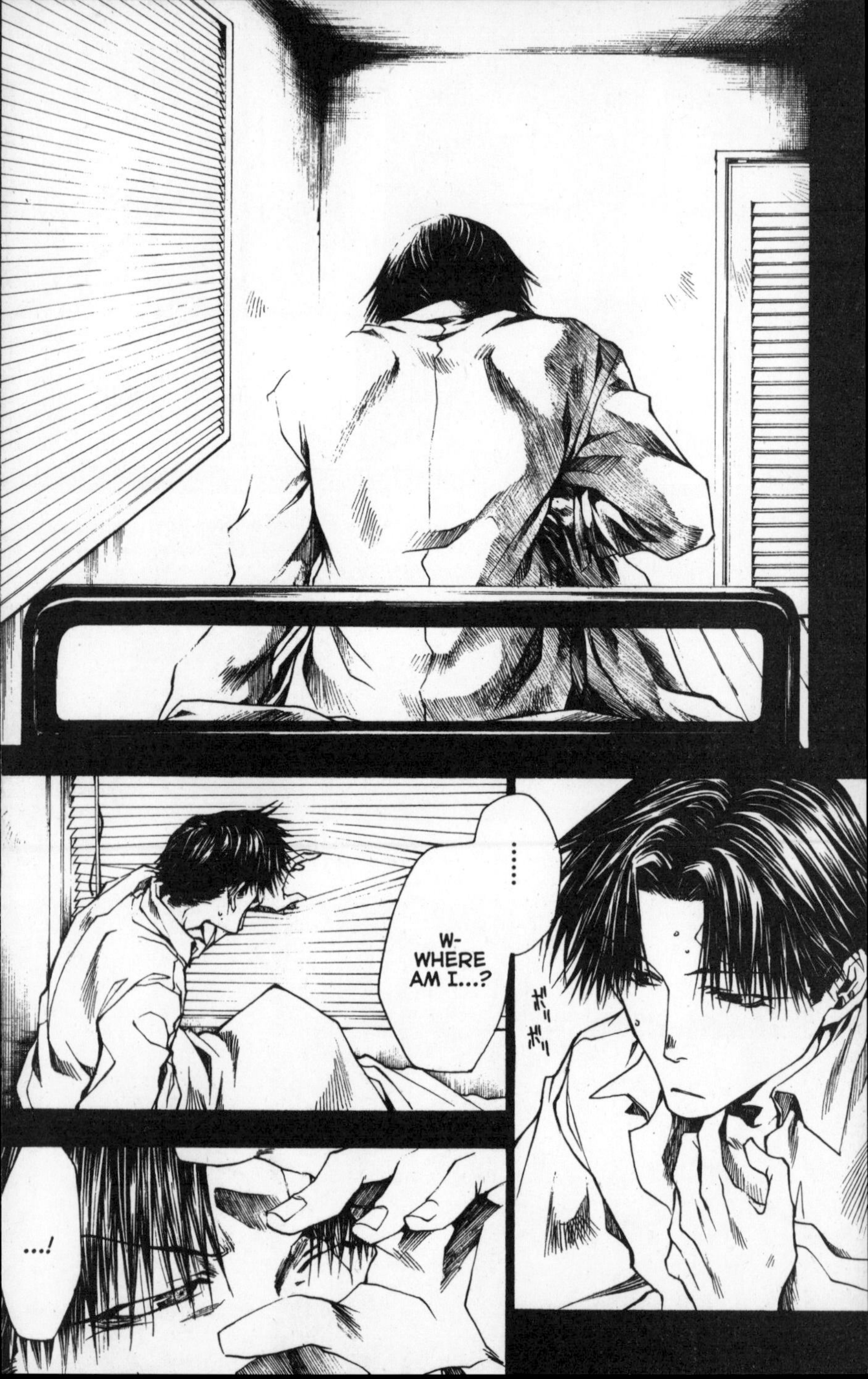
......
W- WHERE AM I...?
ボリ ボリ
...!

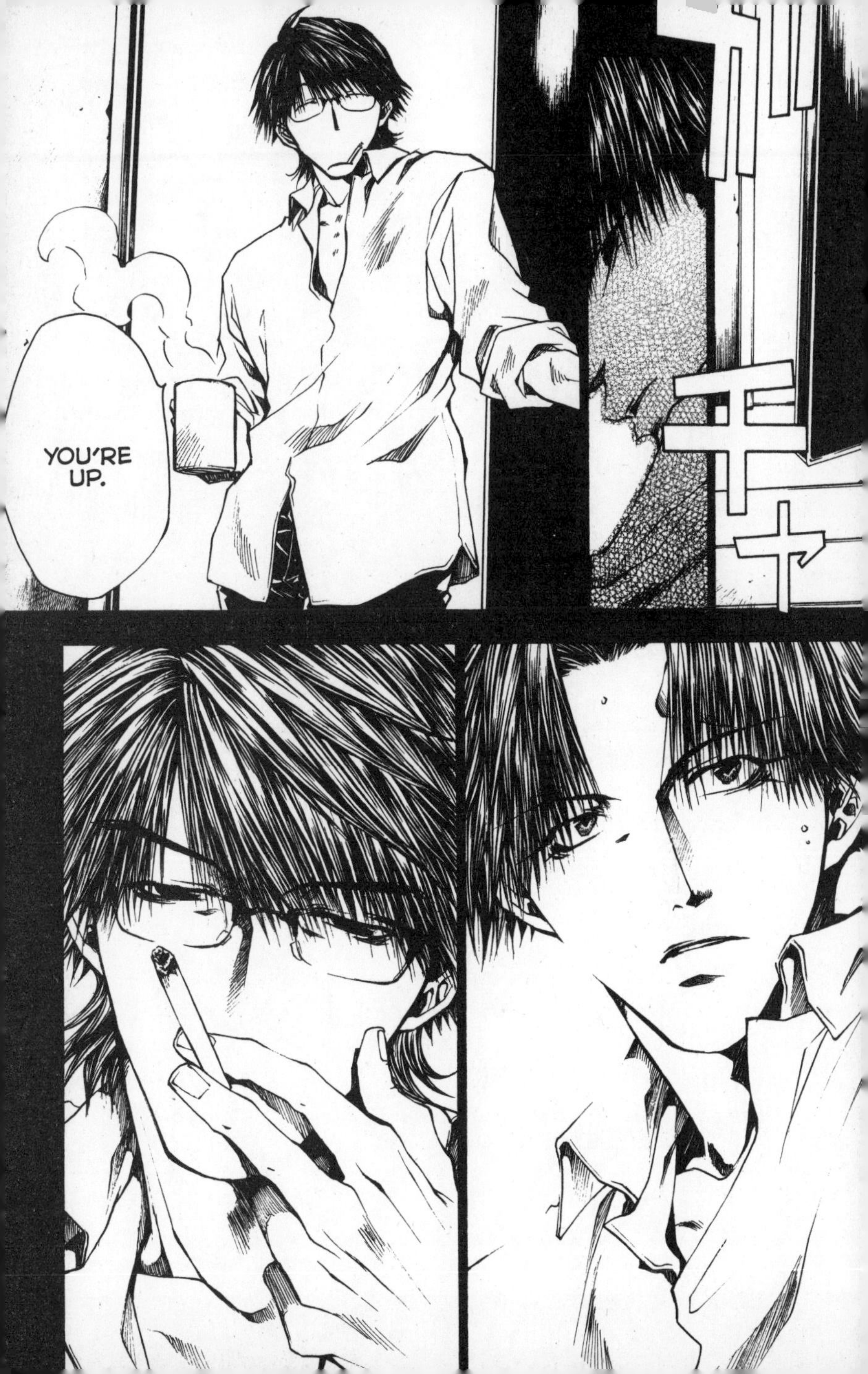
YOU'RE UP.

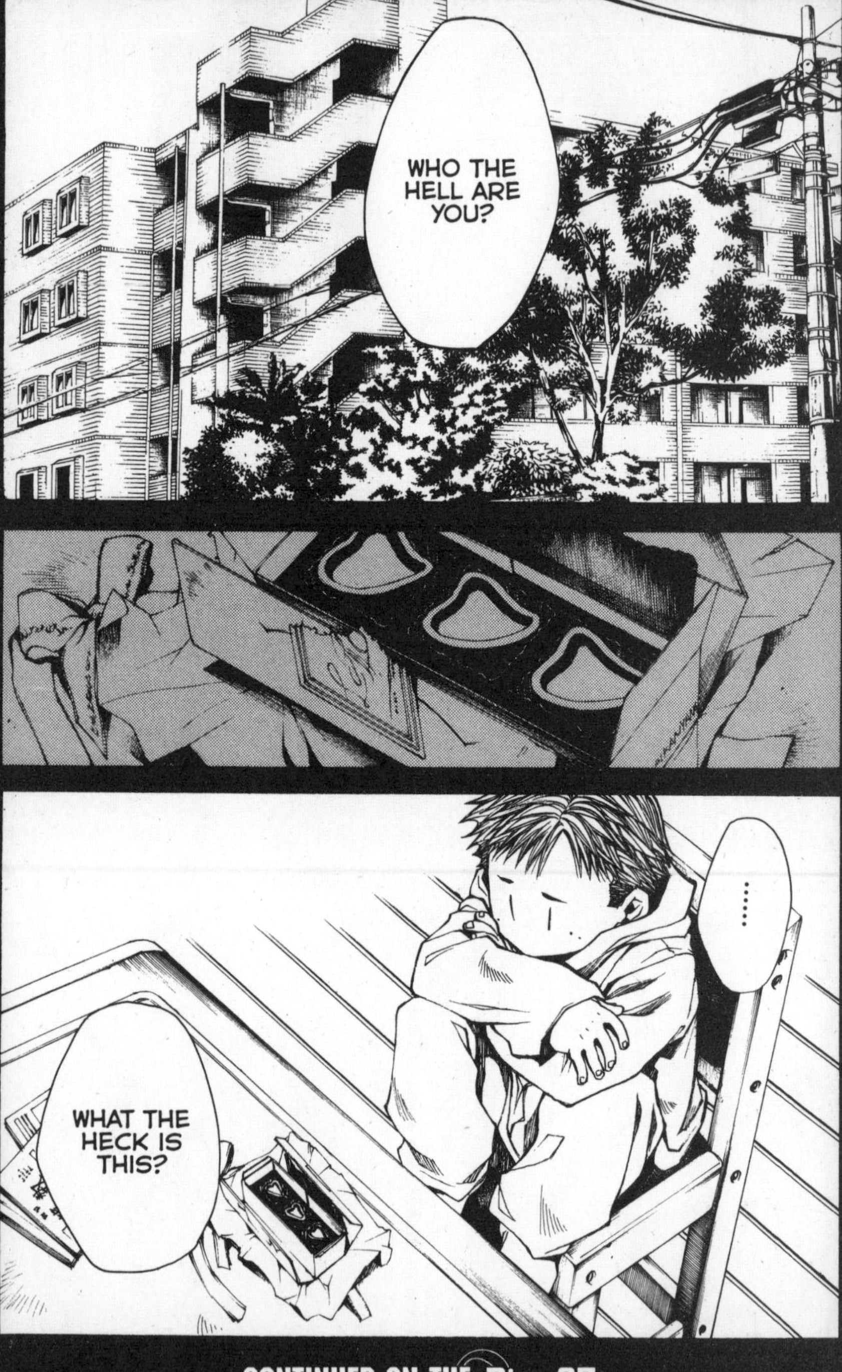
WHO THE HELL ARE YOU?
......
WHAT THE HECK IS THIS?

CONTINUED ON THE Dice:27

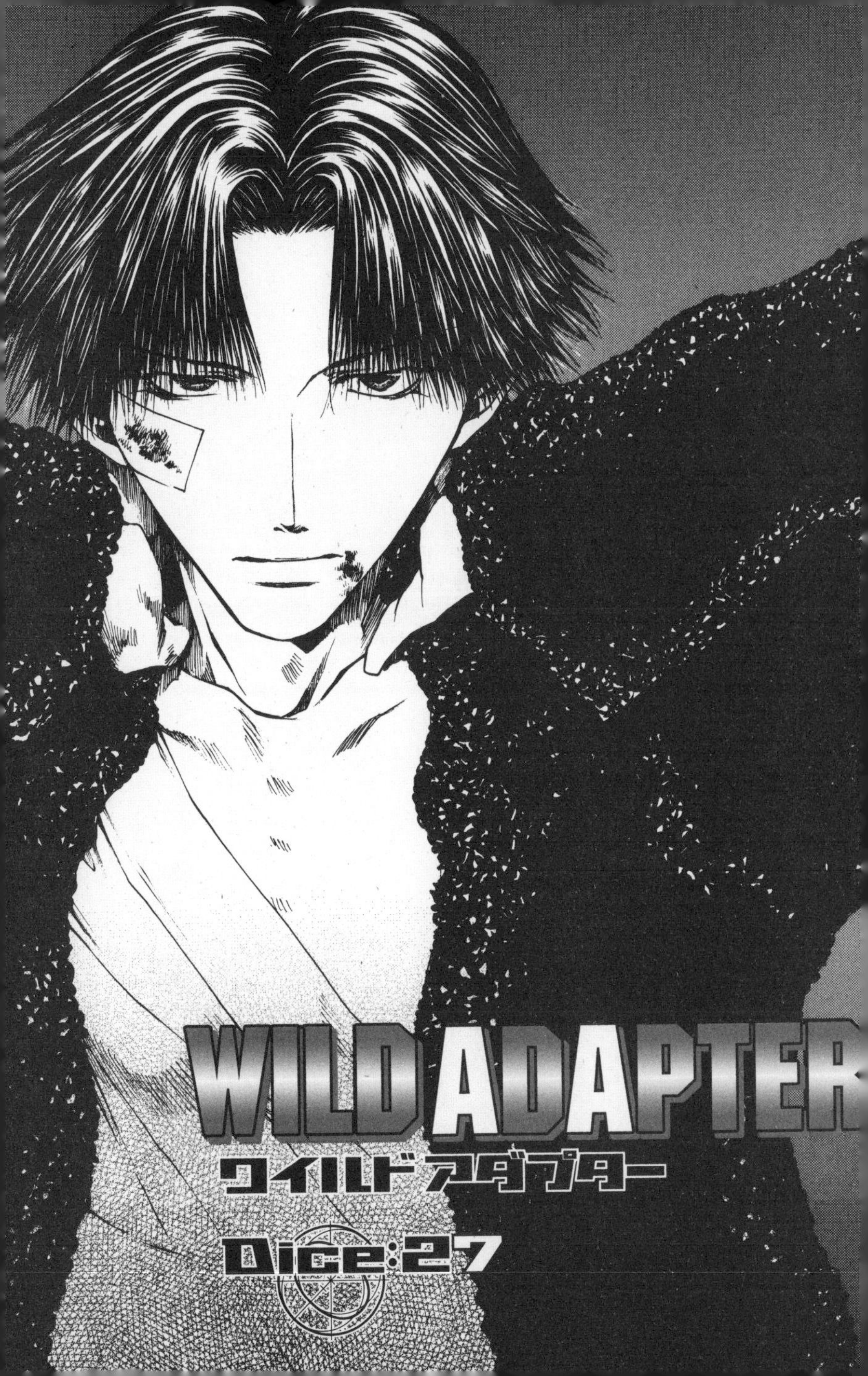
WILD ADAPTER
ワイルドアダプター
Dice:27

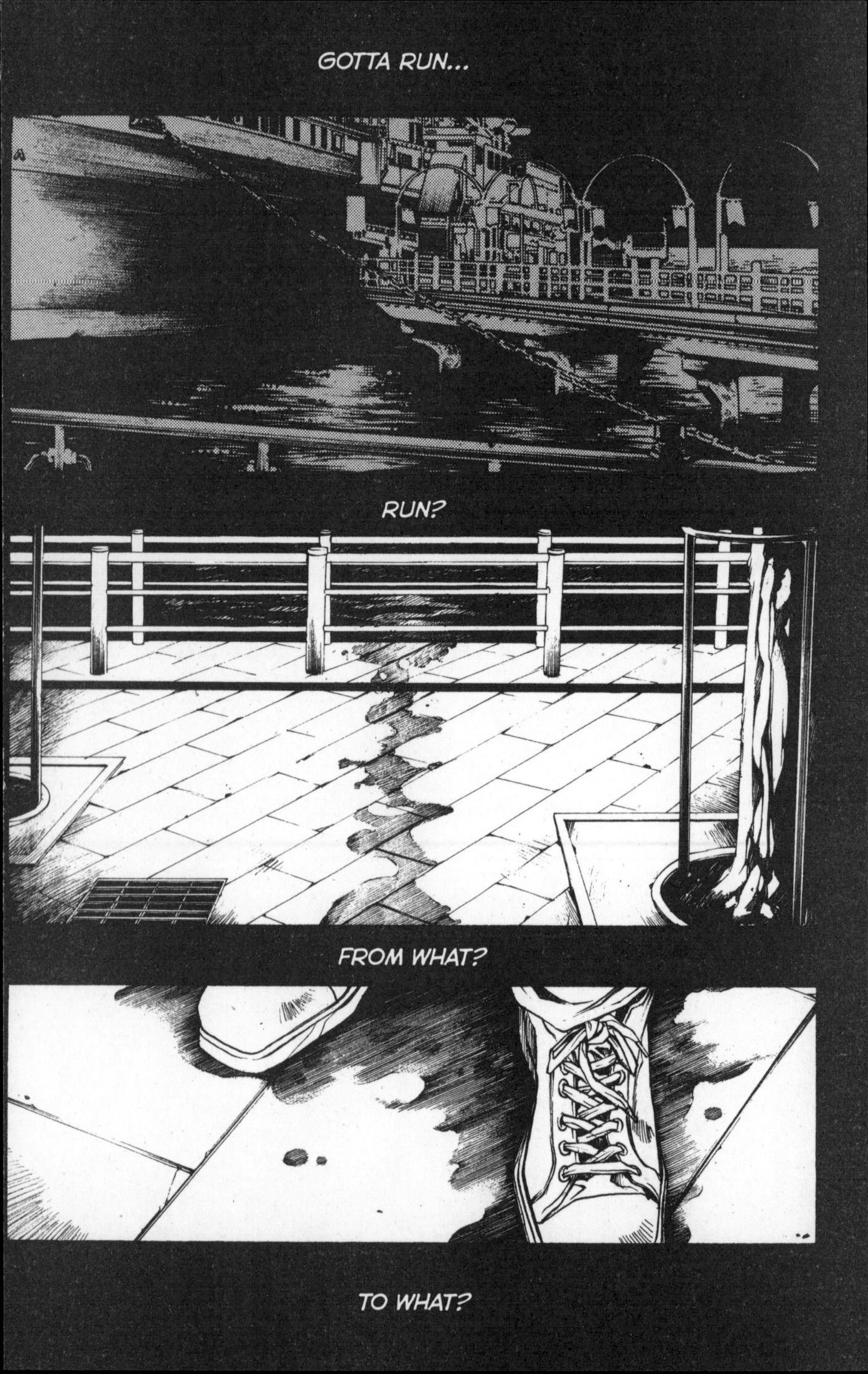
GOTTA RUN...
RUN?
FROM WHAT?
TO WHAT?

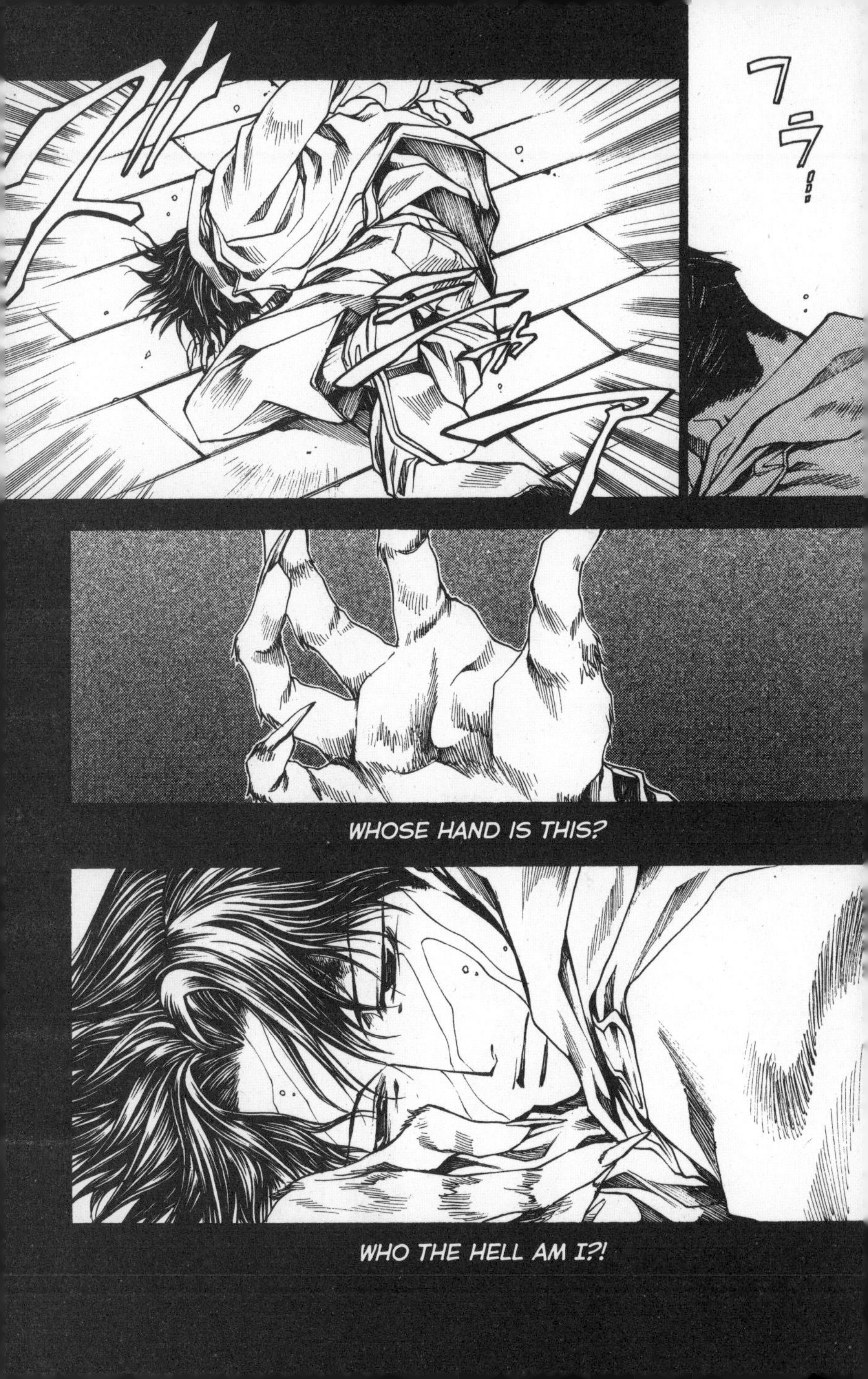
フラ…!
WHOSE HAND IS THIS?
WHO THE HELL AM I?!

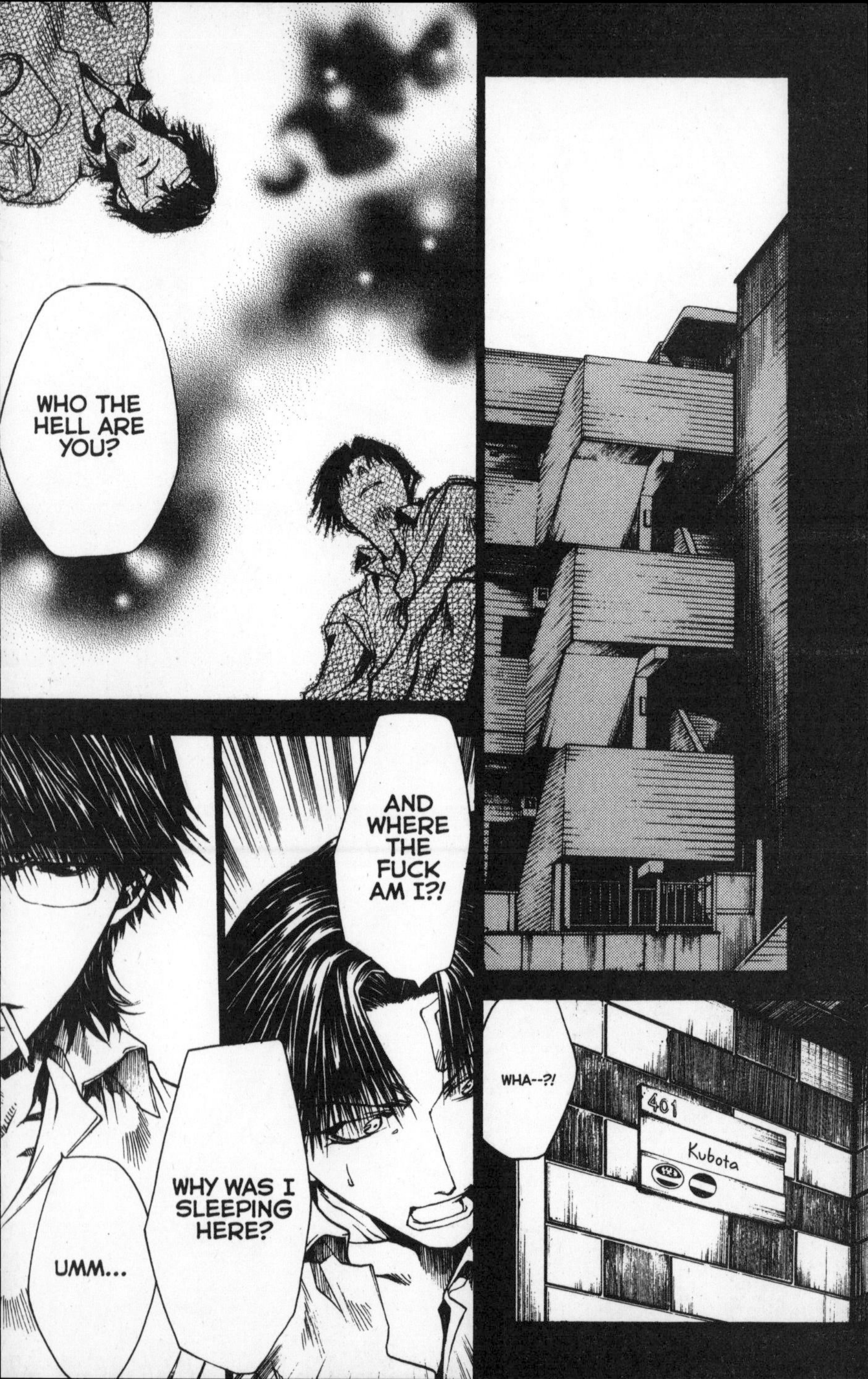
WHA--?!
401
Kubota
WHO THE HELL ARE YOU?
AND WHERE THE FUCK AM I?!
WHY WAS I SLEEPING HERE?
UMM...

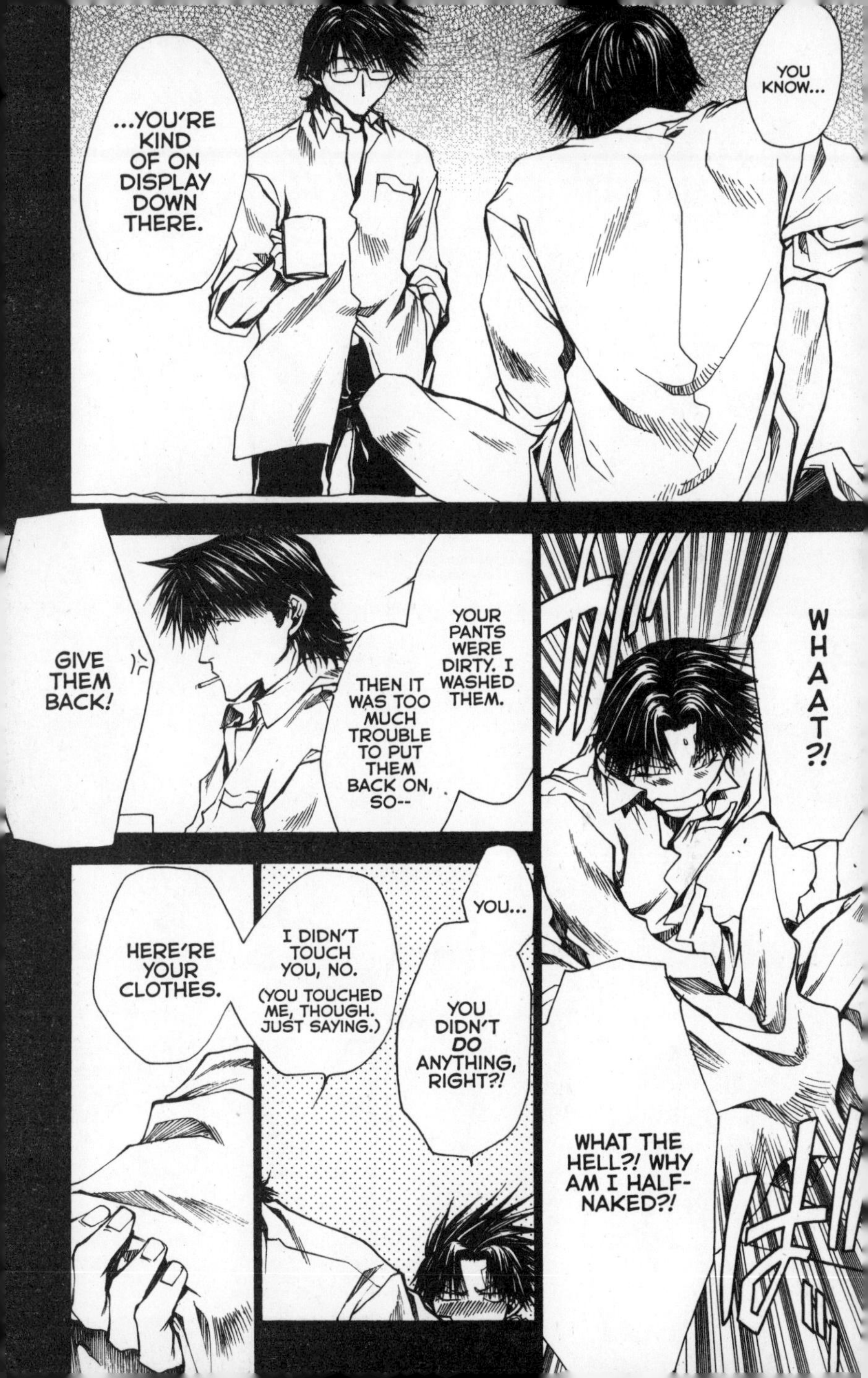
YOU KNOW...
...YOU'RE KIND OF ON DISPLAY DOWN THERE.
WHAAT?!
WHAT THE HELL?! WHY AM I HALF-NAKED?!
YOUR PANTS WERE DIRTY. I WASHED THEM.
THEN IT WAS TOO MUCH TROUBLE TO PUT THEM BACK ON, SO--
GIVE THEM BACK!
YOU...
YOU DIDN'T *DO* ANYTHING, RIGHT?!
I DIDN'T TOUCH YOU, NO.
(YOU TOUCHED ME, THOUGH. JUST SAYING.)
HERE'RE YOUR CLOTHES.

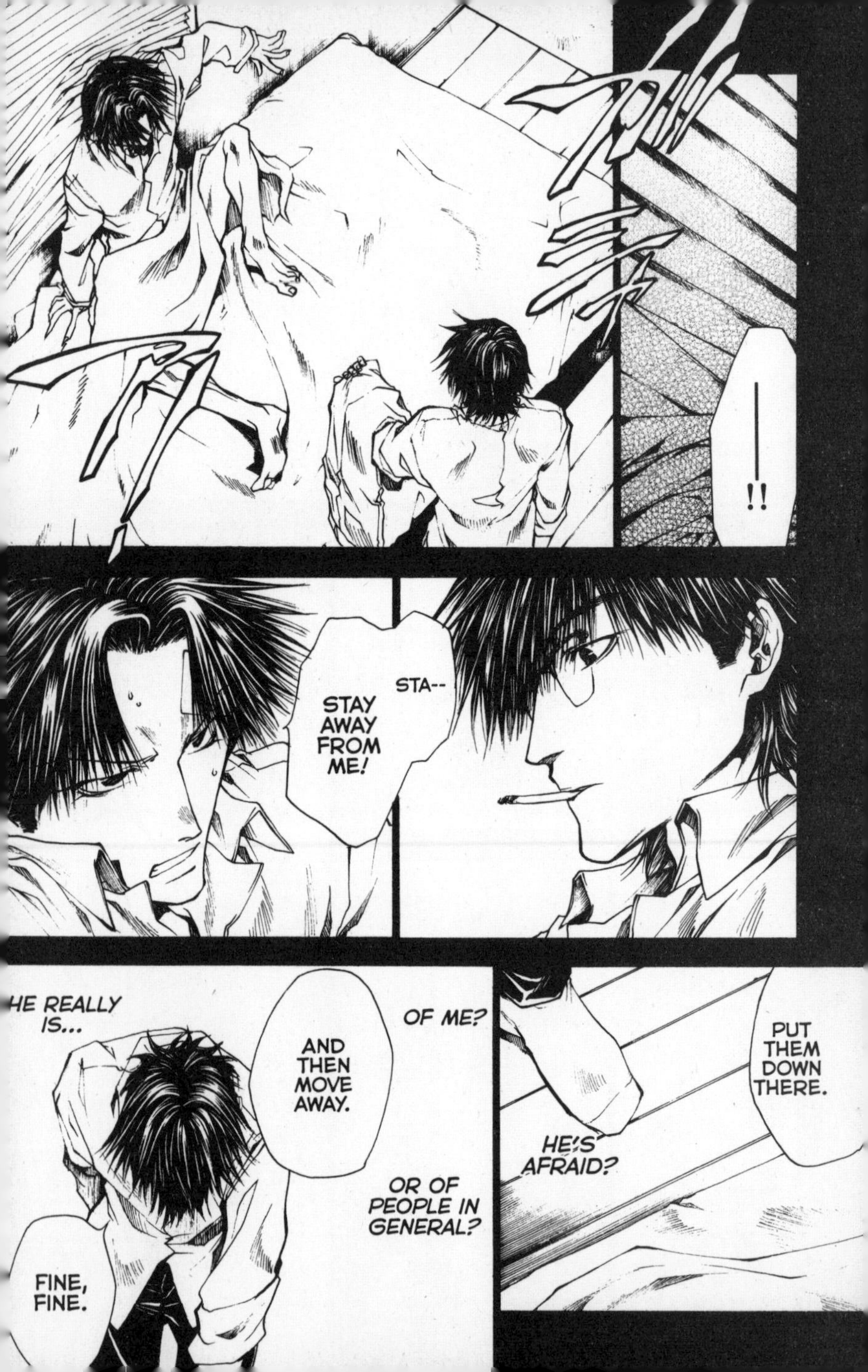
——
!!
STA--
STAY AWAY FROM ME!
PUT THEM DOWN THERE.
HE'S AFRAID?
OF ME?
AND THEN MOVE AWAY.
HE REALLY IS...
OR OF PEOPLE IN GENERAL?
FINE, FINE.

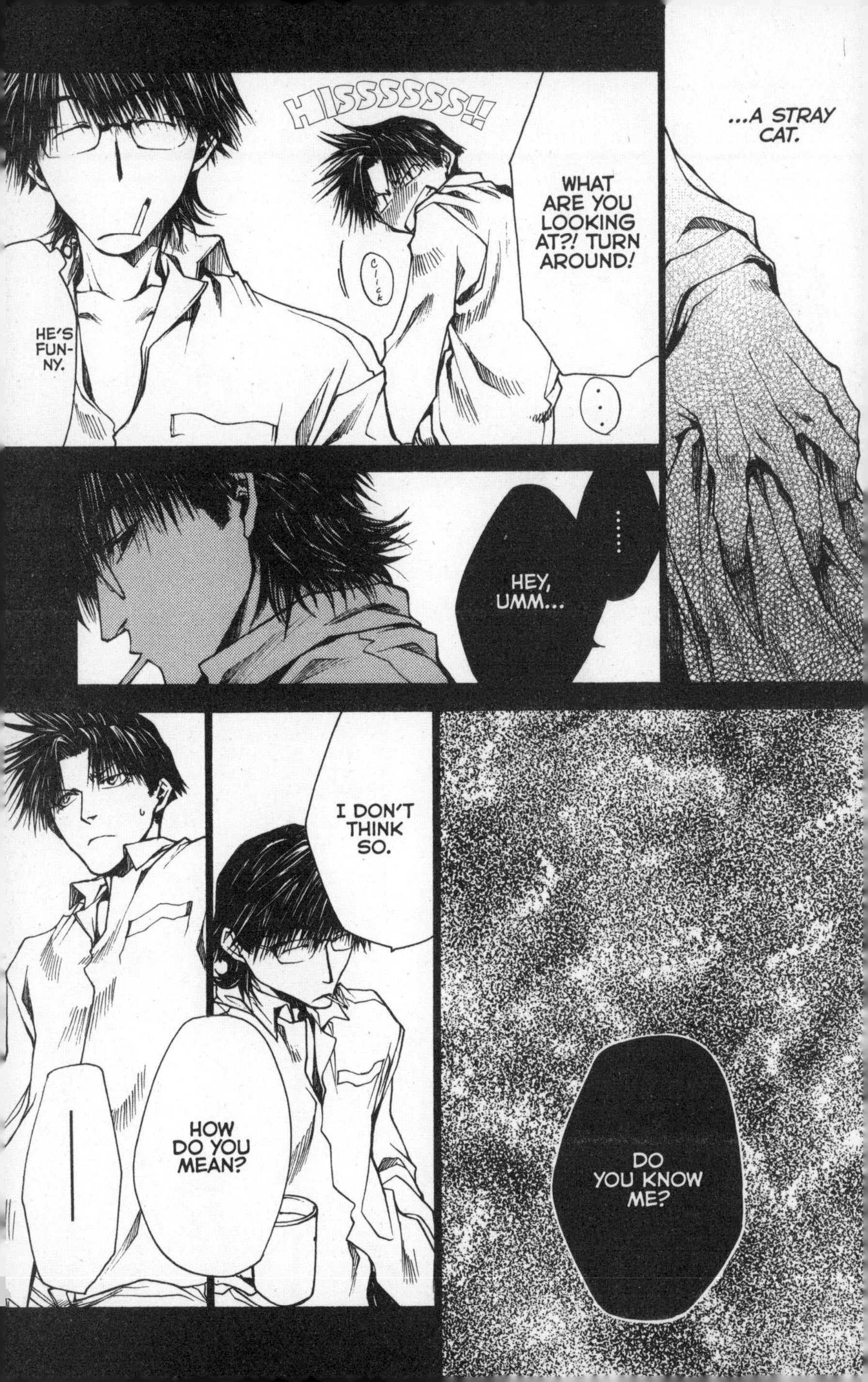
...A STRAY CAT.
WHAT ARE YOU LOOKING AT?! TURN AROUND!
HISSSSSS!!
Click
...
HE'S FUN-NY.
......
HEY, UMM...
DO YOU KNOW ME?
I DON'T THINK SO.
HOW DO YOU MEAN?

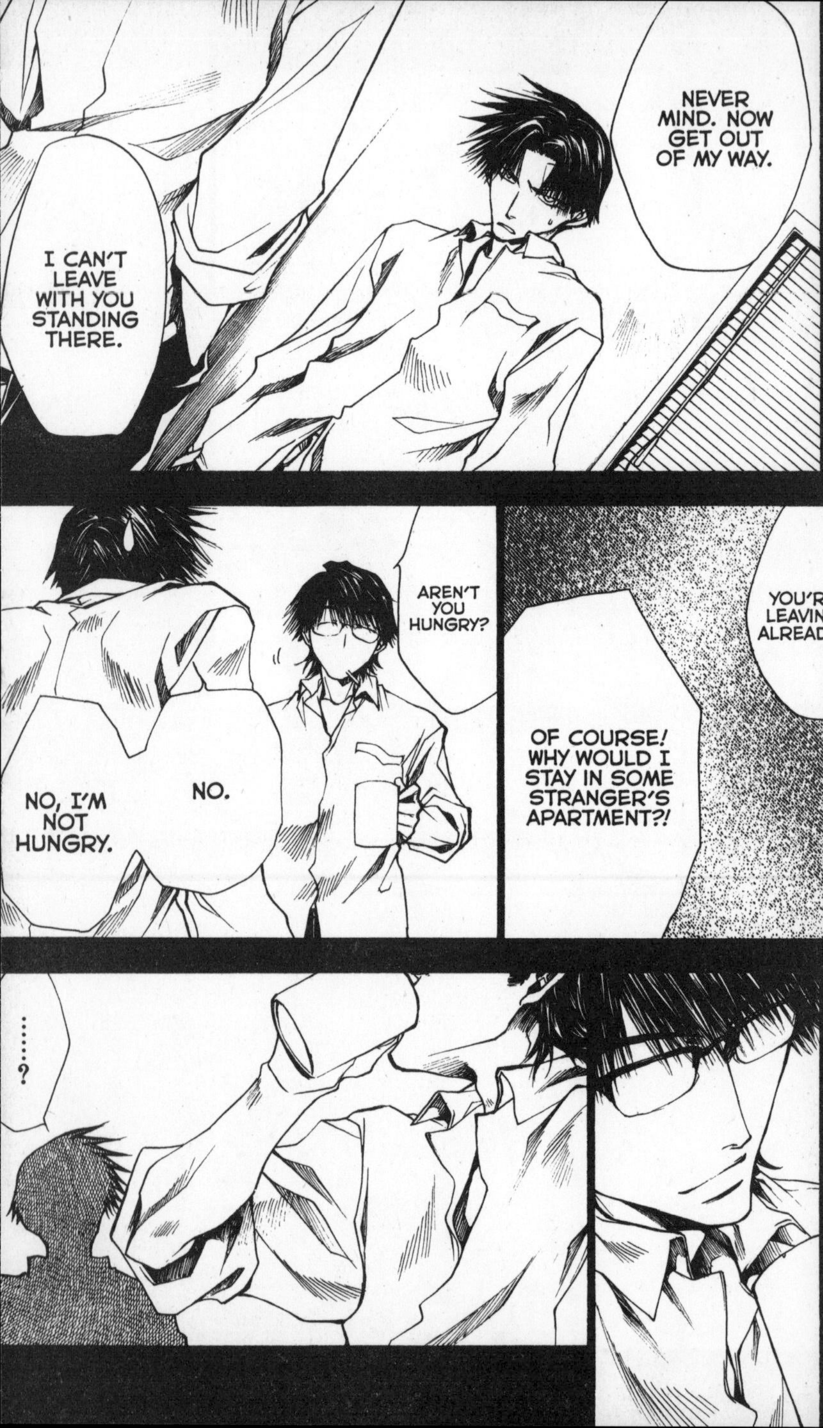
NEVER MIND. NOW GET OUT OF MY WAY.
I CAN'T LEAVE WITH YOU STANDING THERE.
YOU'RE LEAVING ALREADY?
OF COURSE! WHY WOULD I STAY IN SOME STRANGER'S APARTMENT?!
AREN'T YOU HUNGRY?
NO.
NO, I'M NOT HUNGRY.
......?

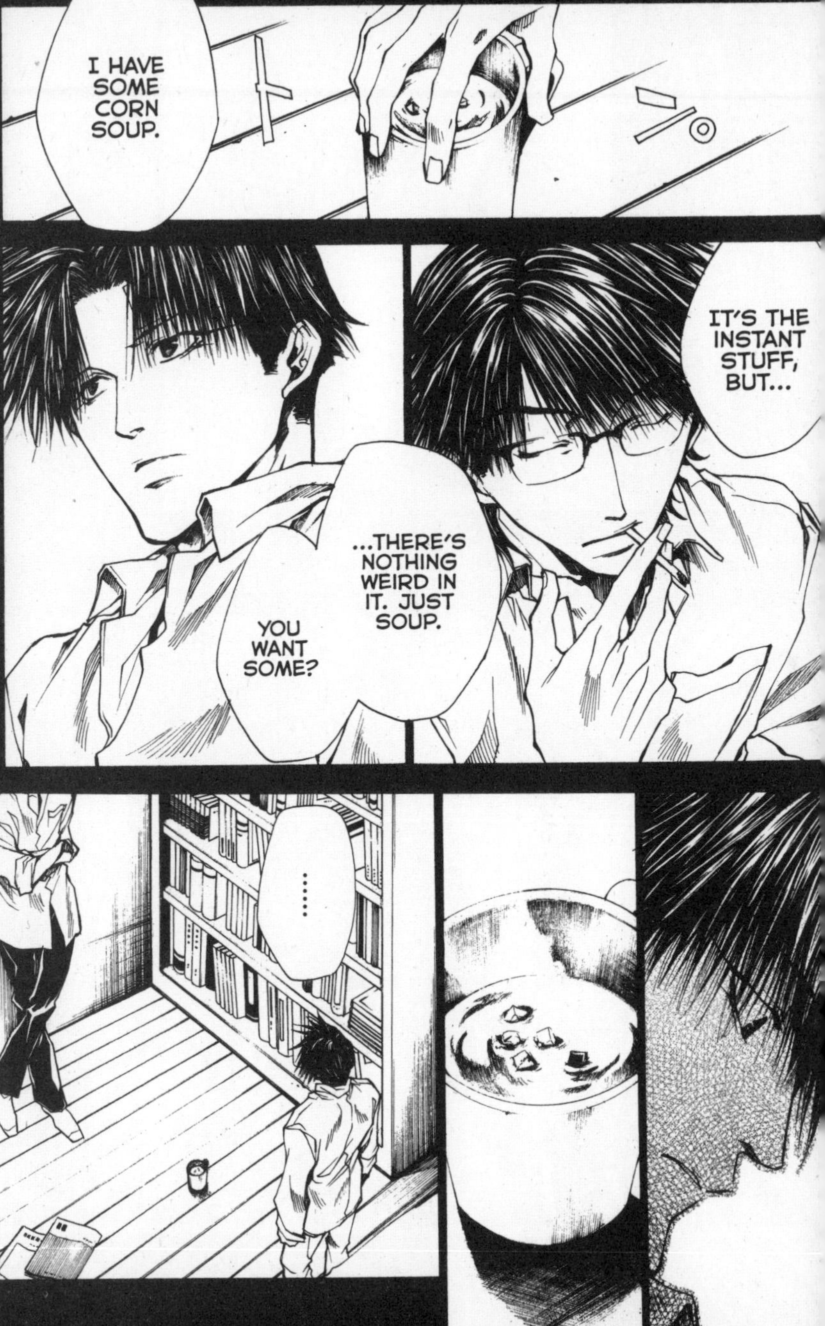
I HAVE SOME CORN SOUP.
IT'S THE INSTANT STUFF, BUT...
...THERE'S NOTHING WEIRD IN IT. JUST SOUP.
YOU WANT SOME?
......

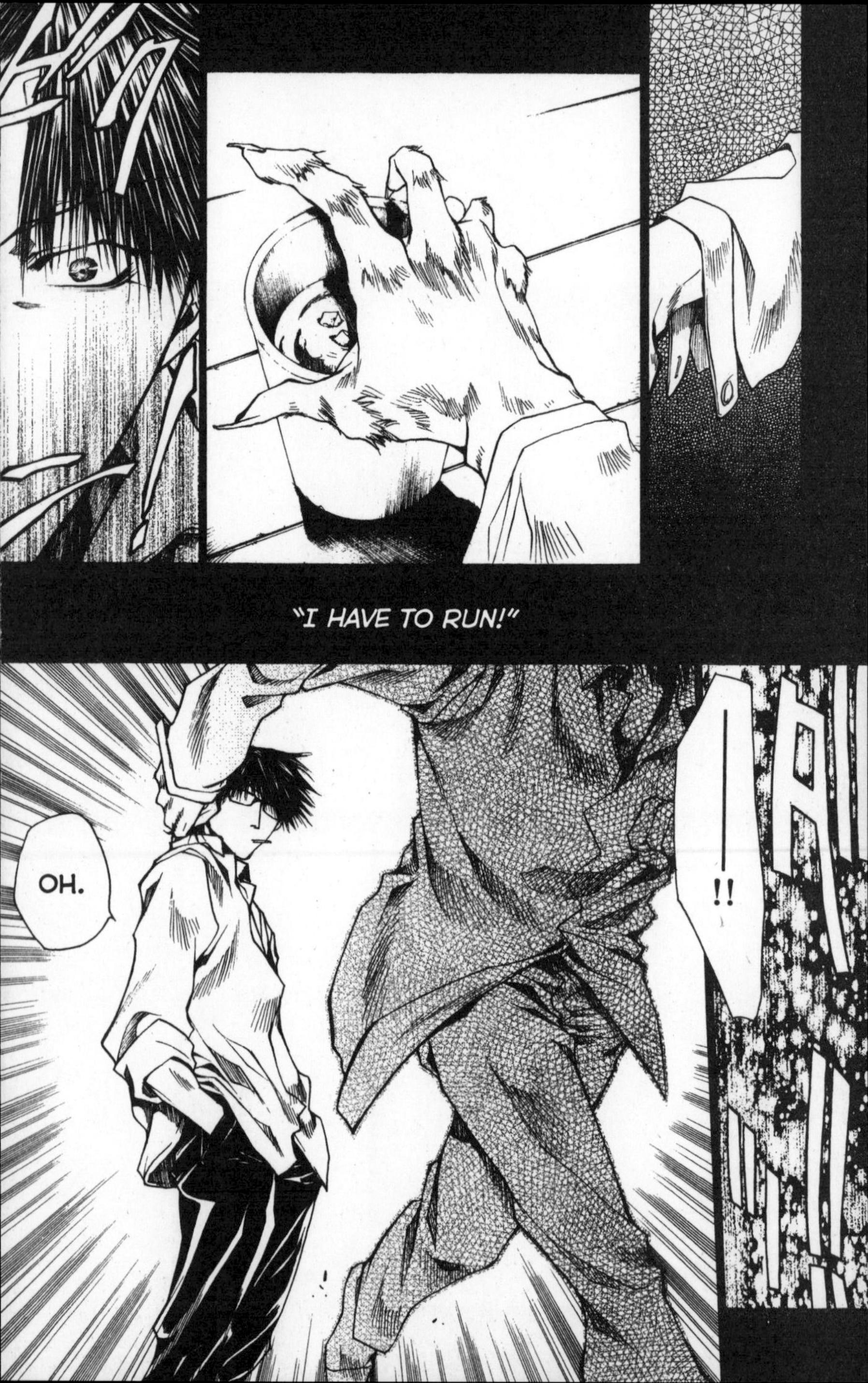
"I HAVE TO RUN!"
—!!
OH.

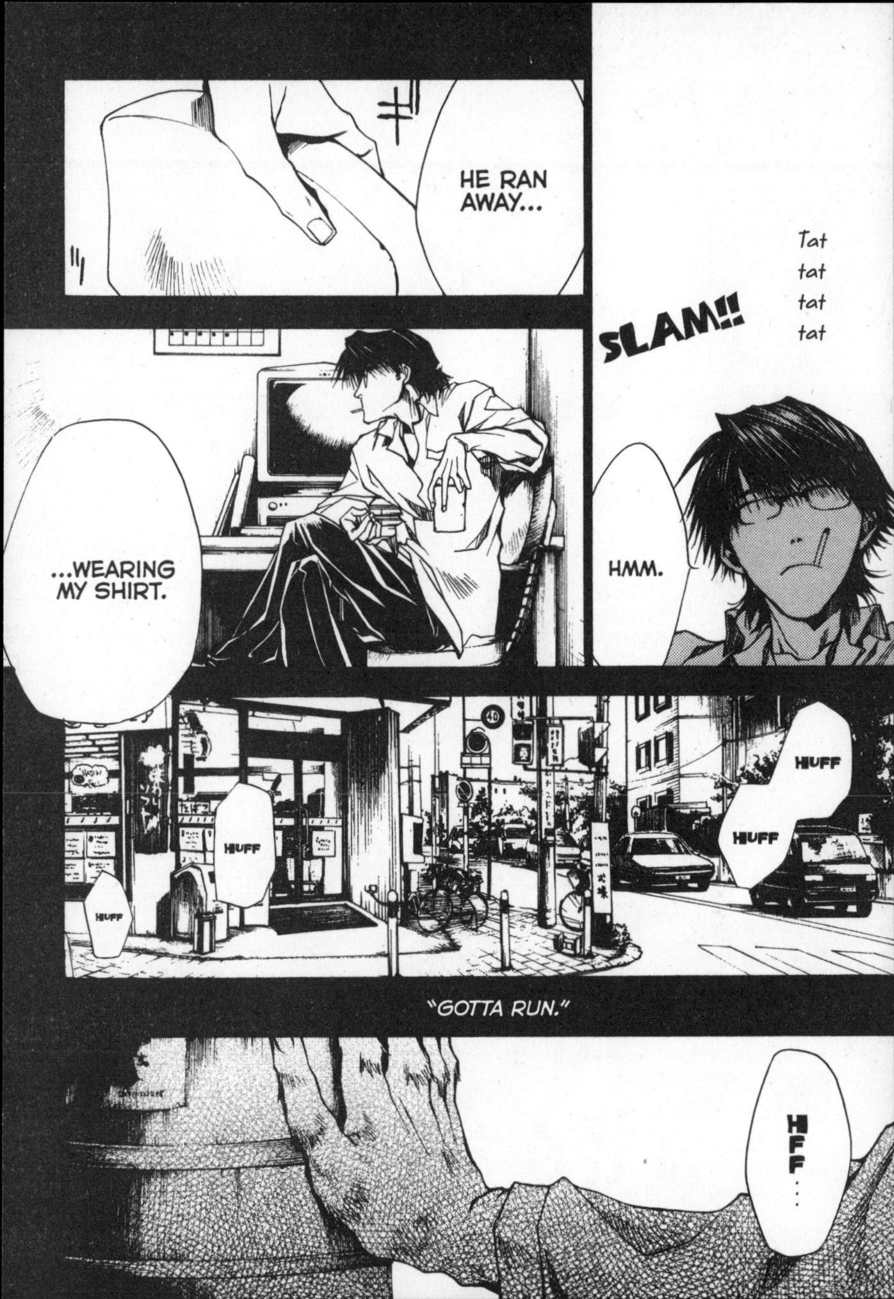
Tat
tat
tat
tat
SLAM!!
HMM.
HE RAN AWAY...
...WEARING MY SHIRT.
HUFF
HUFF
HUFF
HUFF
"GOTTA RUN."
HFF...

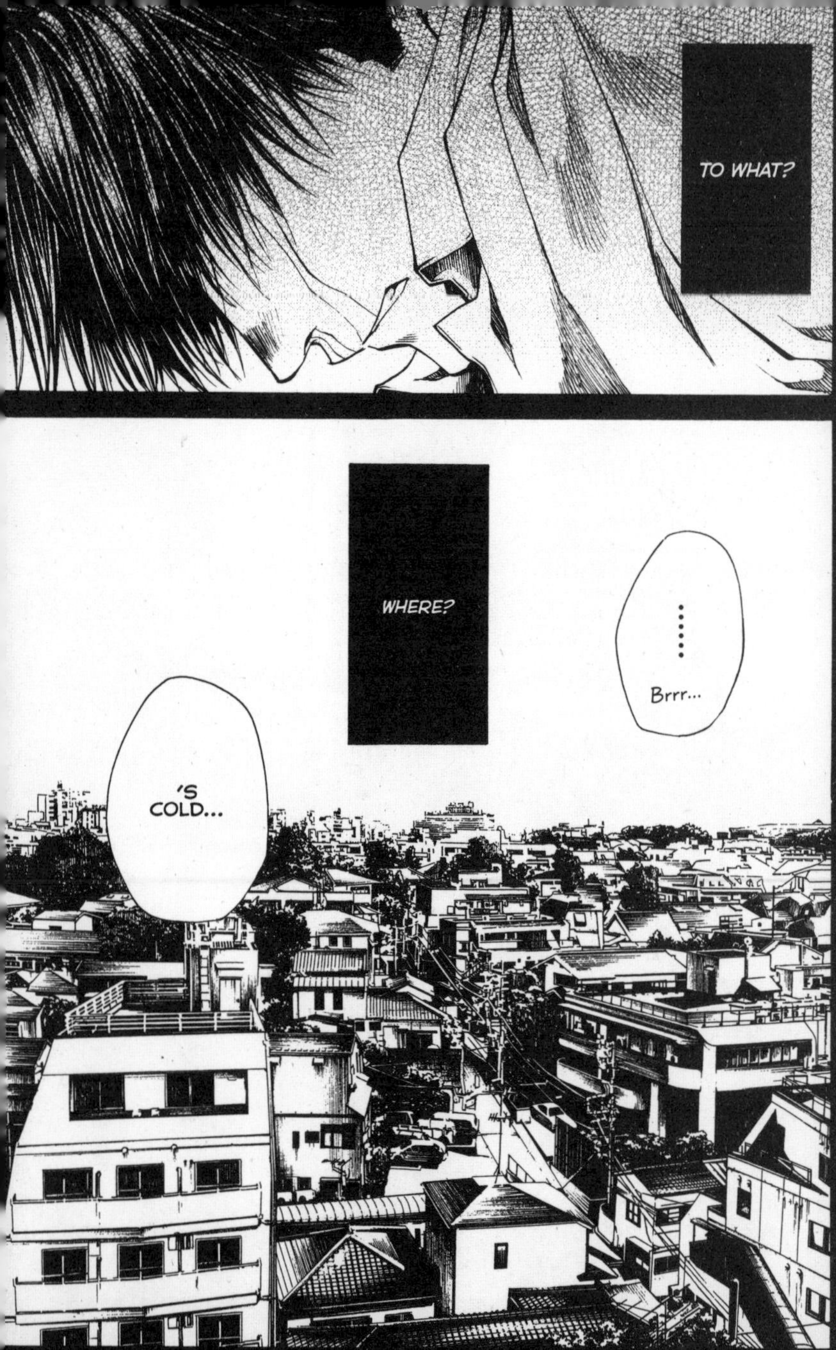
TO WHAT?
......
Brrr...
WHERE?
'S COLD...

CONTINUED ON THE Dice:28

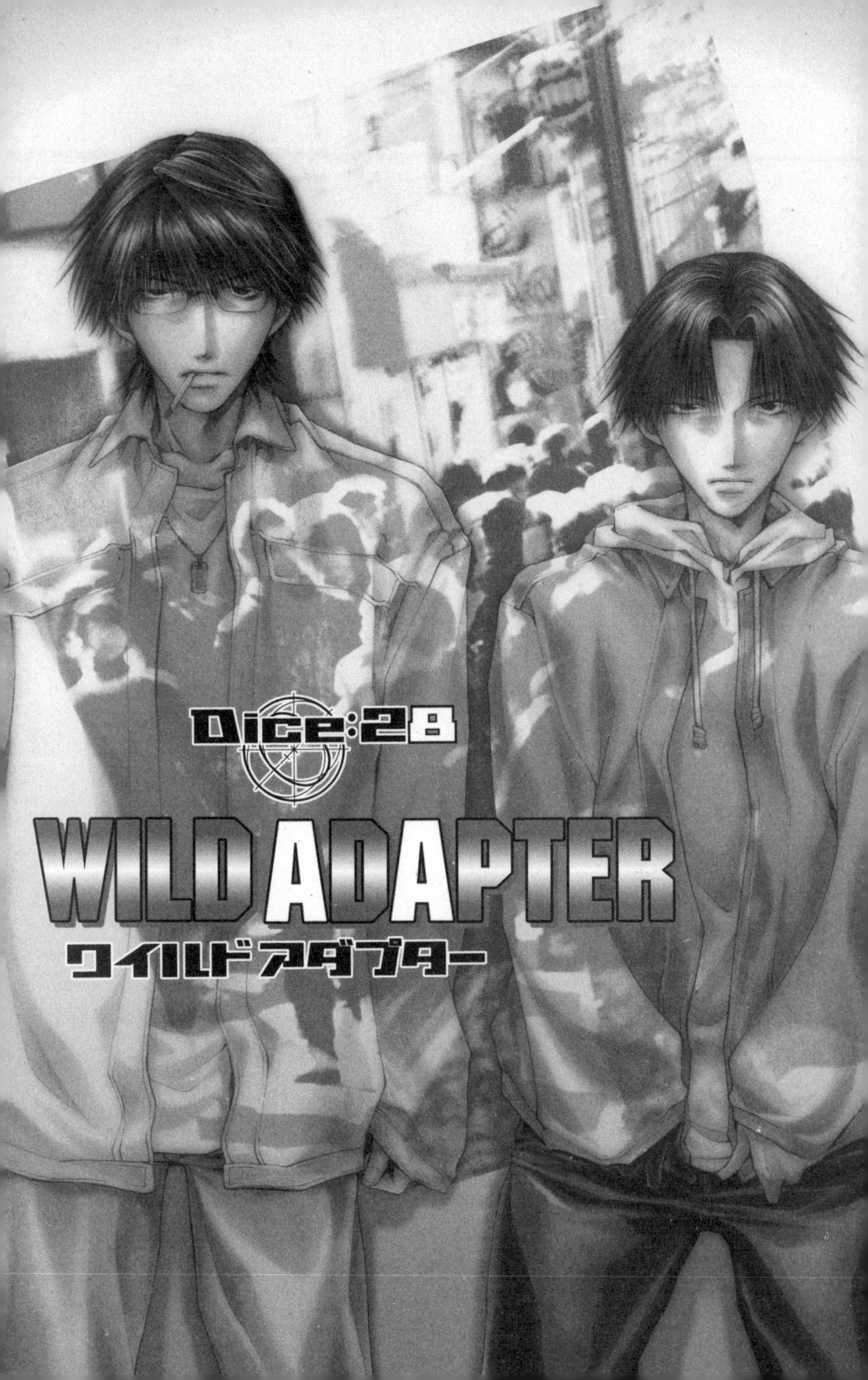
Dice:28
WILD ADAPTER
ワイルドアダプター

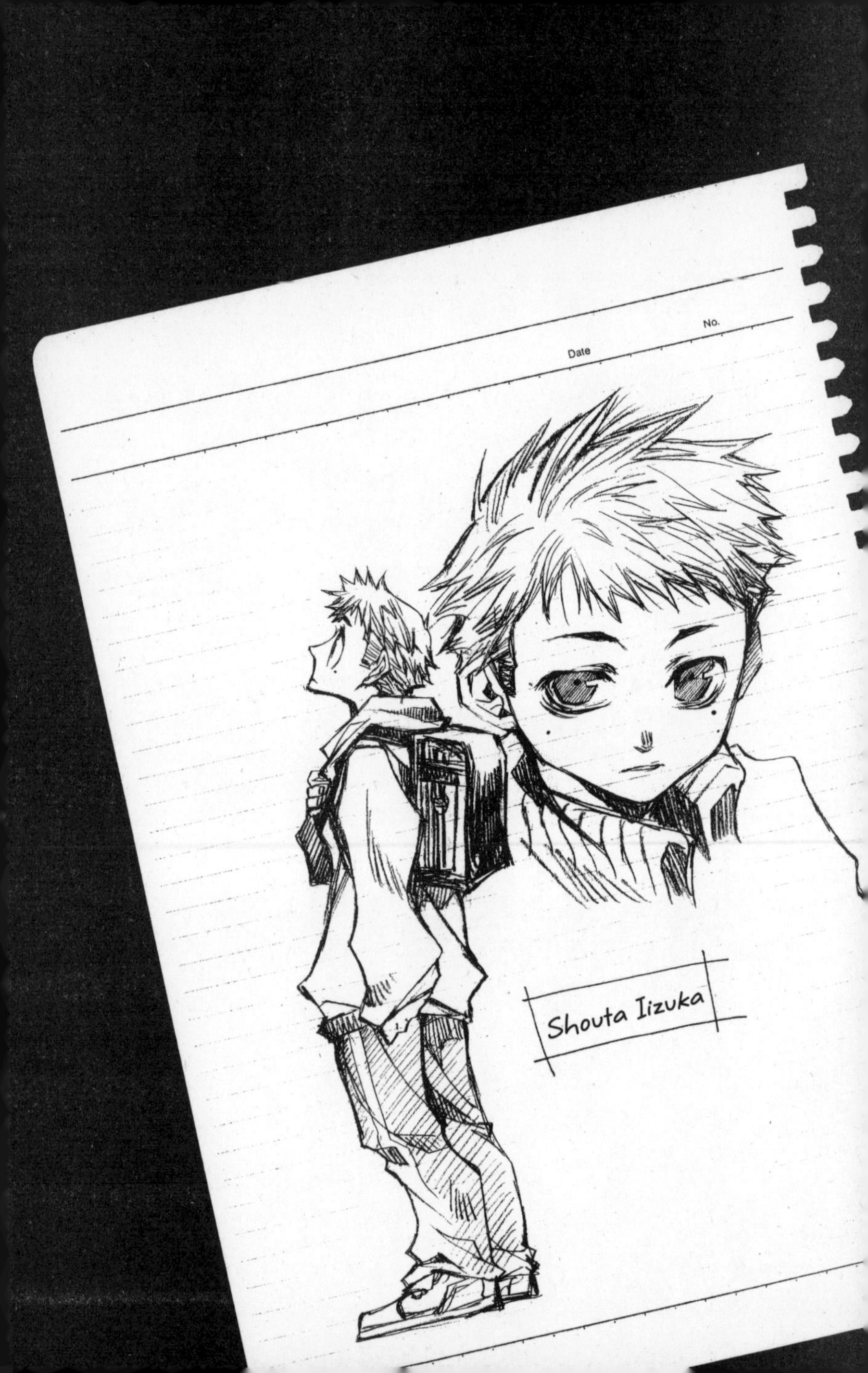
No.
Date
Shouta Iizuka

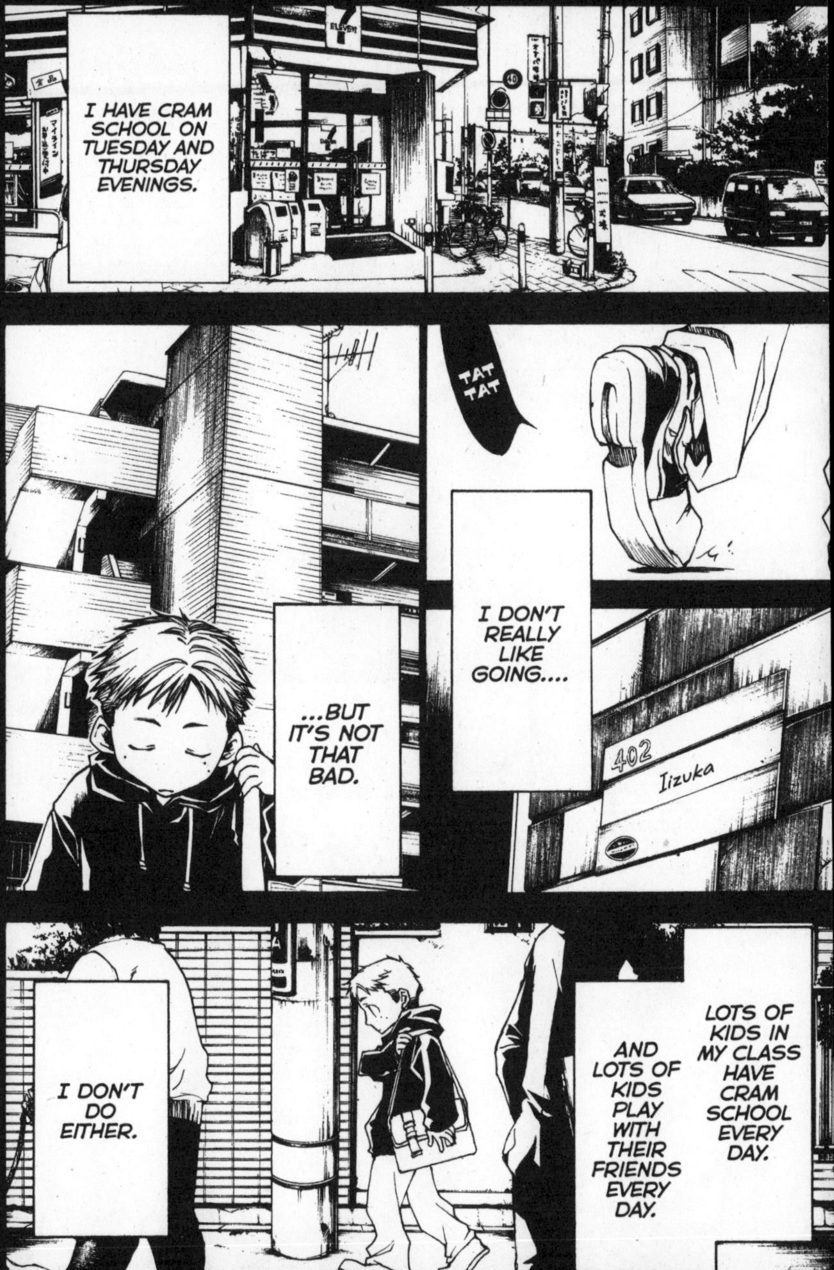
I HAVE CRAM SCHOOL ON TUESDAY AND THURSDAY EVENINGS.
TAT TAT
I DON'T REALLY LIKE GOING....
402
Iizuka
...BUT IT'S NOT THAT BAD.
LOTS OF KIDS IN MY CLASS HAVE CRAM SCHOOL EVERY DAY.
AND LOTS OF KIDS PLAY WITH THEIR FRIENDS EVERY DAY.
I DON'T DO EITHER.

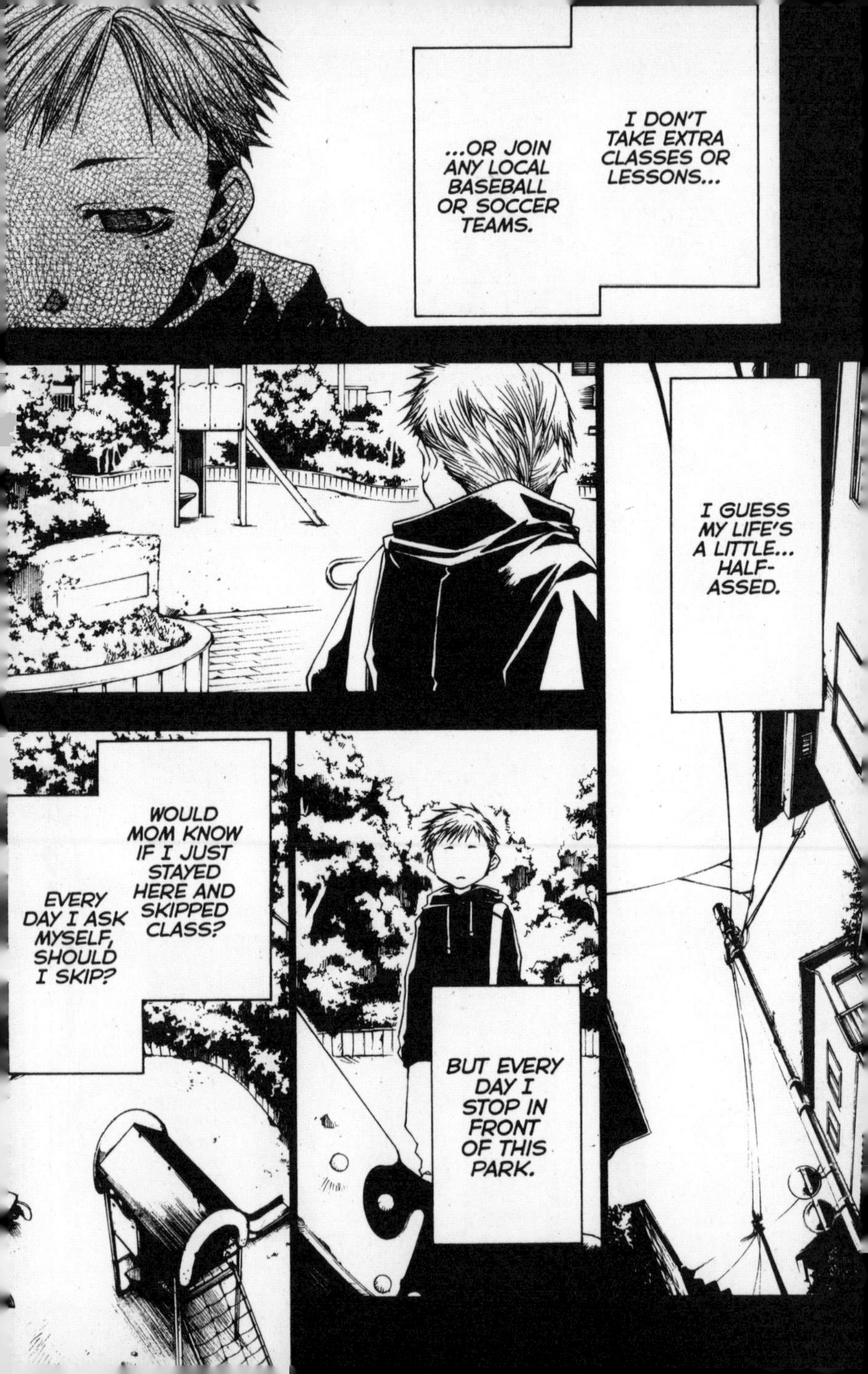
I DON'T TAKE EXTRA CLASSES OR LESSONS...
...OR JOIN ANY LOCAL BASEBALL OR SOCCER TEAMS.
I GUESS MY LIFE'S A LITTLE... HALF-ASSED.
BUT EVERY DAY I STOP IN FRONT OF THIS PARK.
WOULD MOM KNOW IF I JUST STAYED HERE AND SKIPPED CLASS?
EVERY DAY I ASK MYSELF, SHOULD I SKIP?

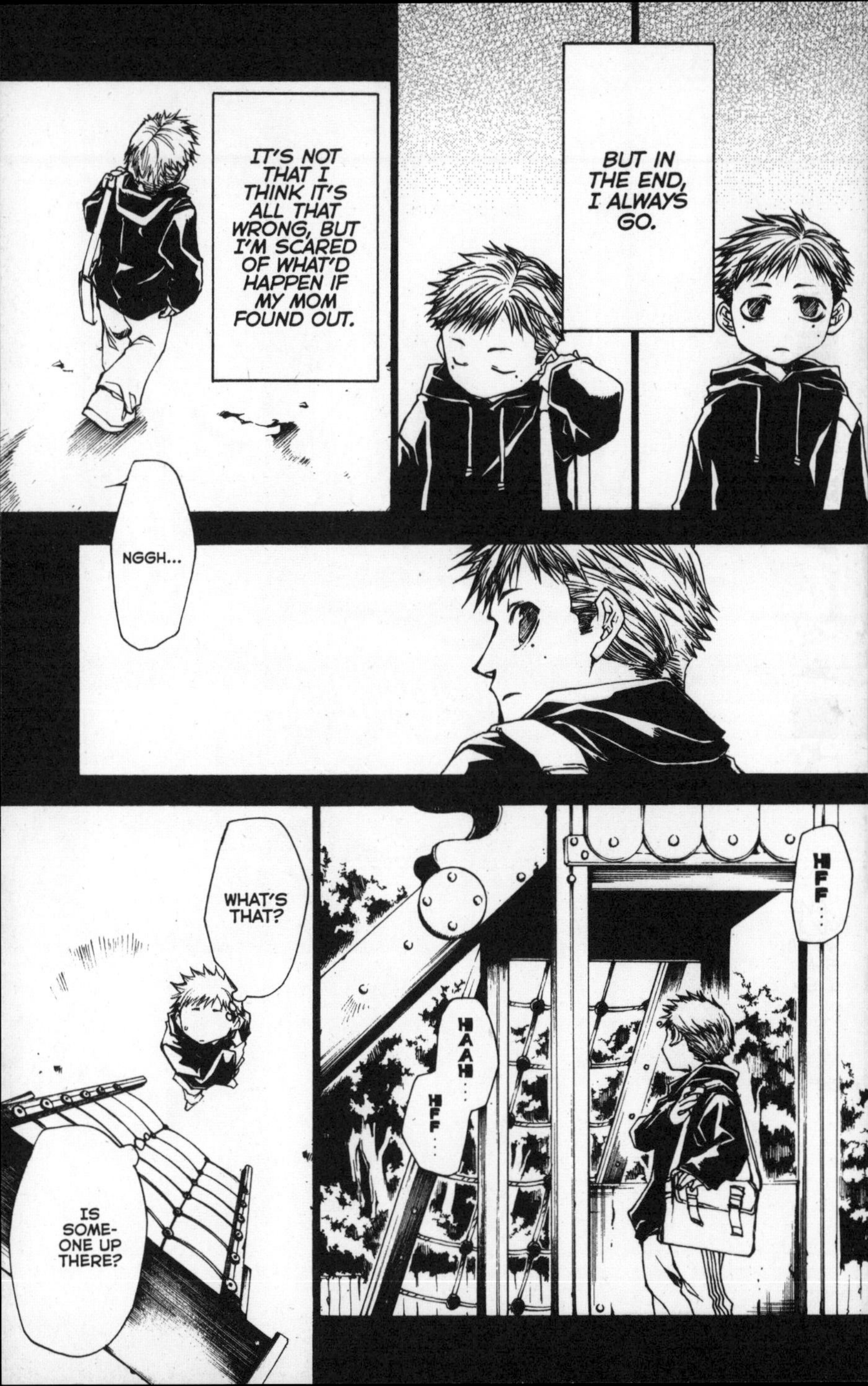
BUT IN THE END, I ALWAYS GO.
IT'S NOT THAT I THINK IT'S ALL THAT WRONG, BUT I'M SCARED OF WHAT'D HAPPEN IF MY MOM FOUND OUT.
NGGH...
HFF...
HAAH... HFF...
WHAT'S THAT?
IS SOME-ONE UP THERE?

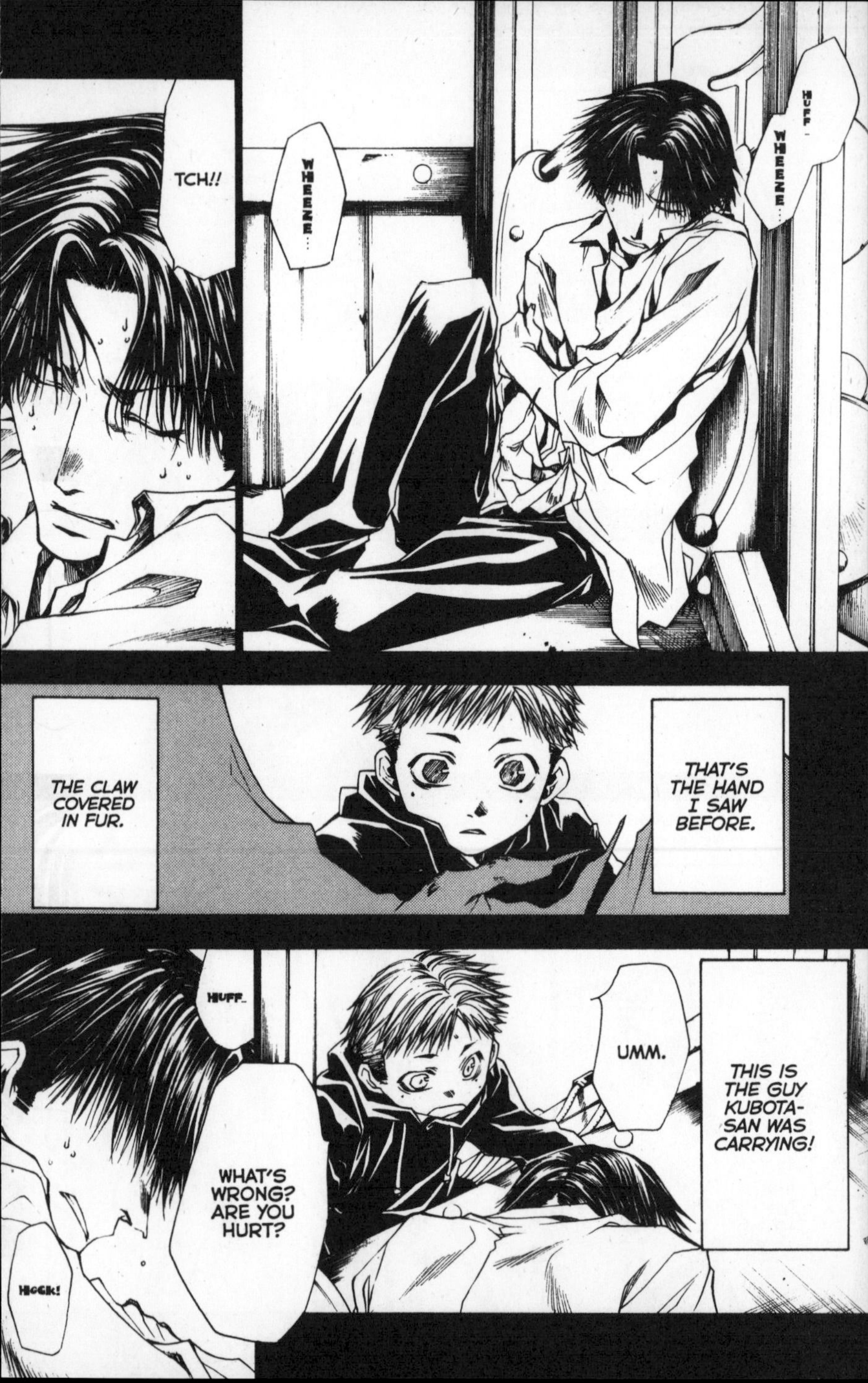
HUFF... WHEEZE...
WHEEZE...
TCH!!
THAT'S THE HAND I SAW BEFORE.
THE CLAW COVERED IN FUR.
THIS IS THE GUY KUBOTA-SAN WAS CARRYING!
UMM.
HUFF...
WHAT'S WRONG? ARE YOU HURT?
HGGK!

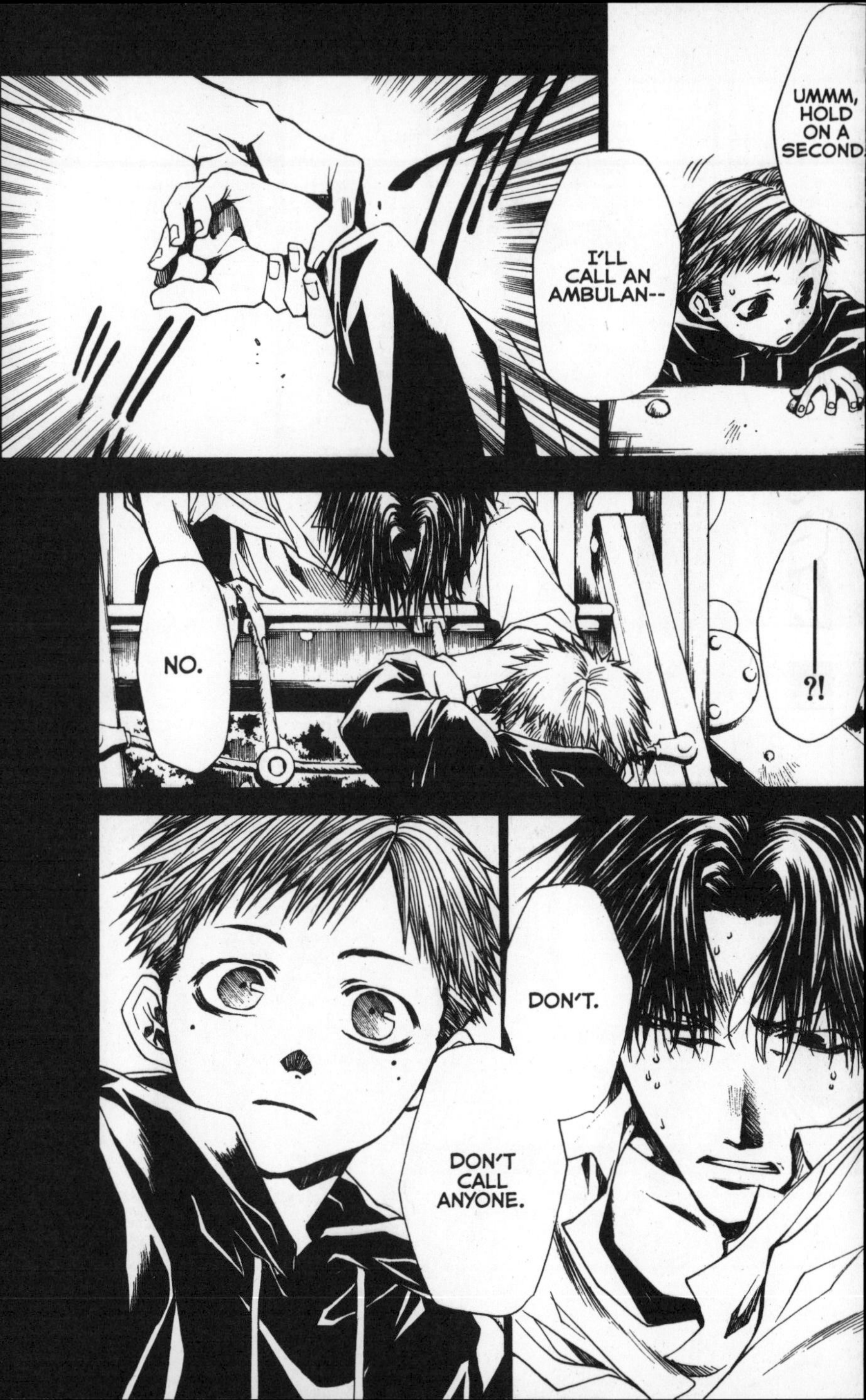
UMMM, HOLD ON A SECOND.
I'LL CALL AN AMBULAN--
?!
NO.
DON'T.
DON'T CALL ANYONE.

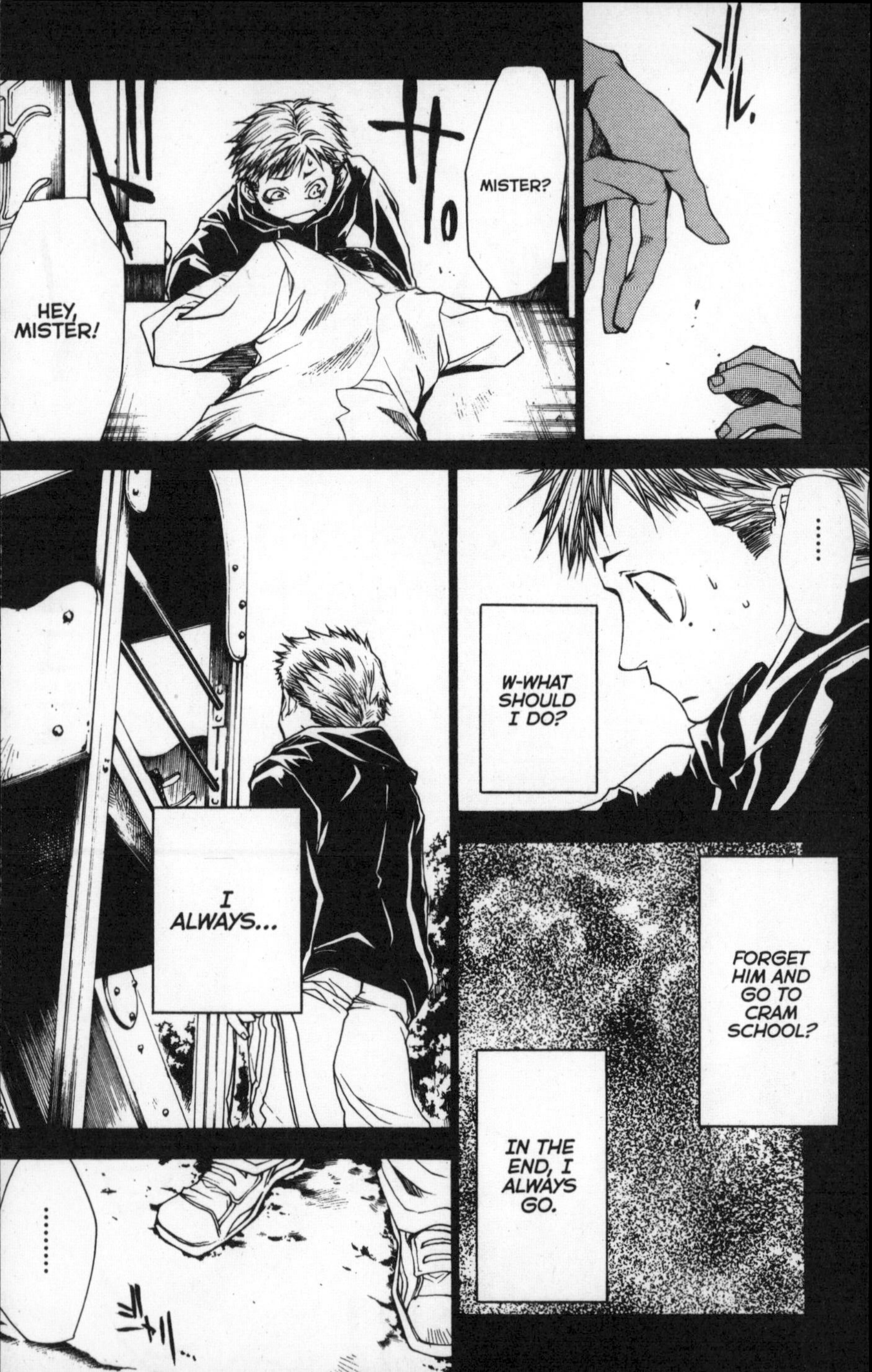
MISTER?
HEY, MISTER!
......
W-WHAT SHOULD I DO?
FORGET HIM AND GO TO CRAM SCHOOL?
IN THE END, I ALWAYS GO.
I ALWAYS...
......

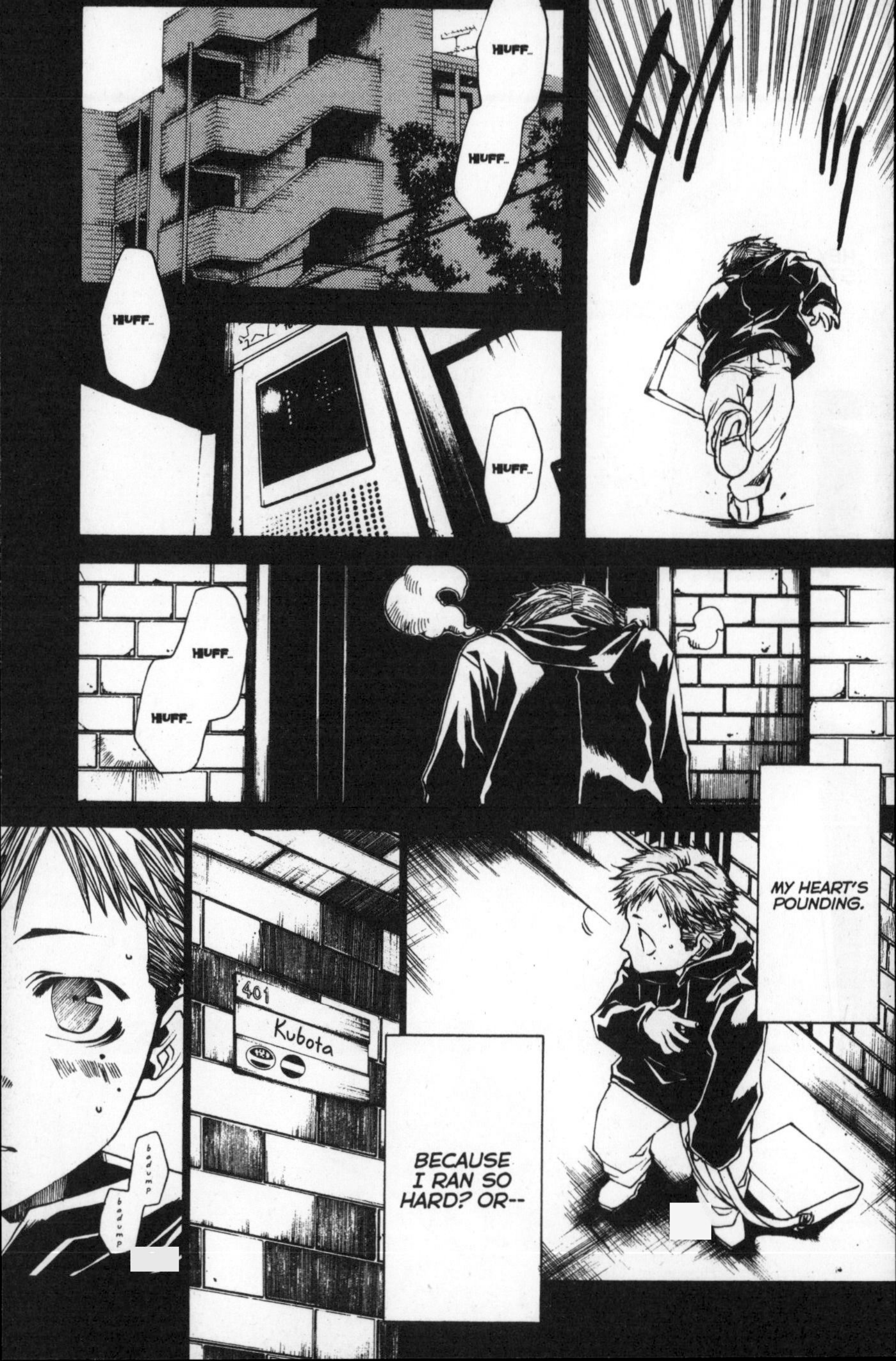
HUFF...
HUFF...
HUFF...
HUFF...
HUFF...
HUFF...
MY HEART'S POUNDING.
BECAUSE I RAN SO HARD? OR--
401
Kubota
badump
badump

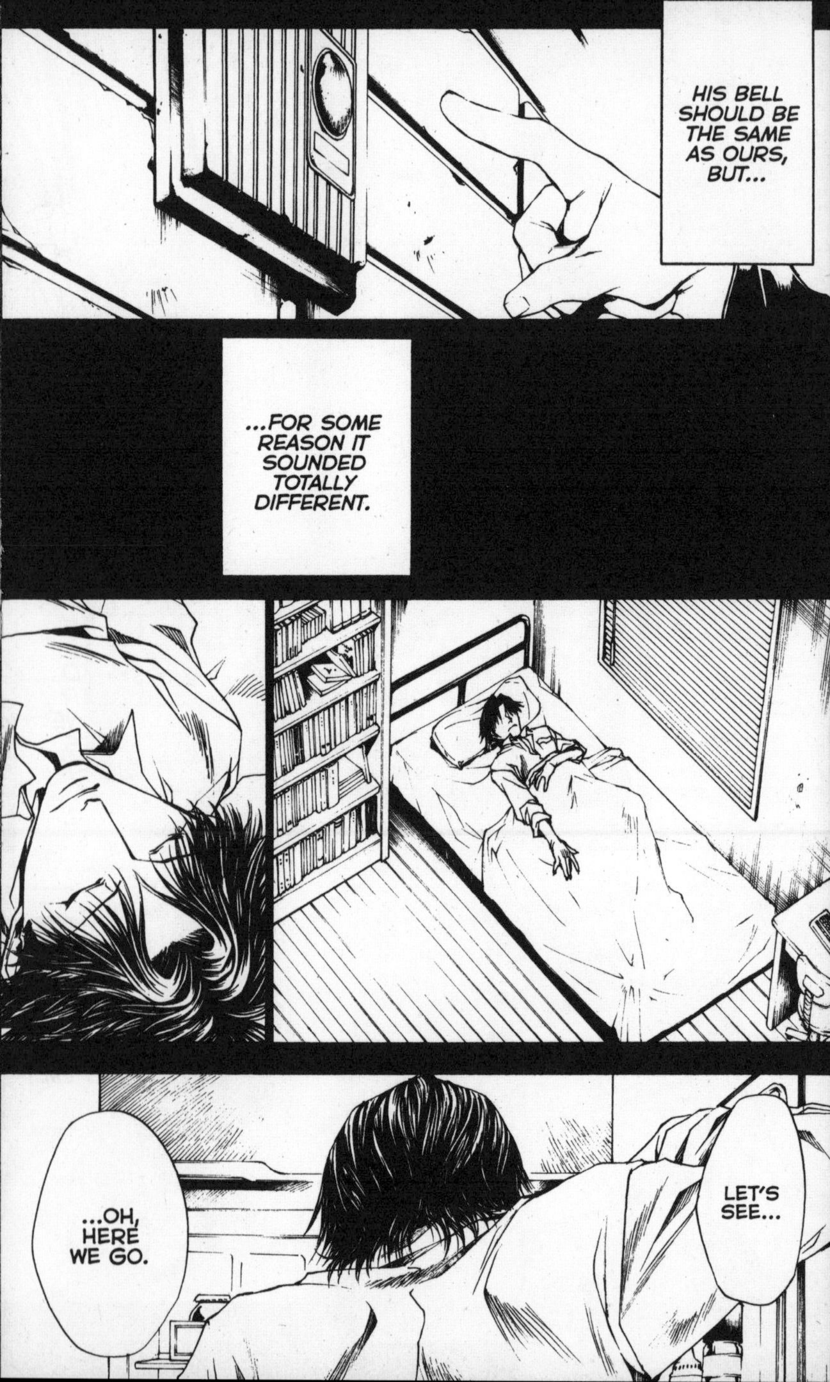
HIS BELL SHOULD BE THE SAME AS OURS, BUT...
...FOR SOME REASON IT SOUNDED TOTALLY DIFFERENT.
LET'S SEE...
...OH, HERE WE GO.

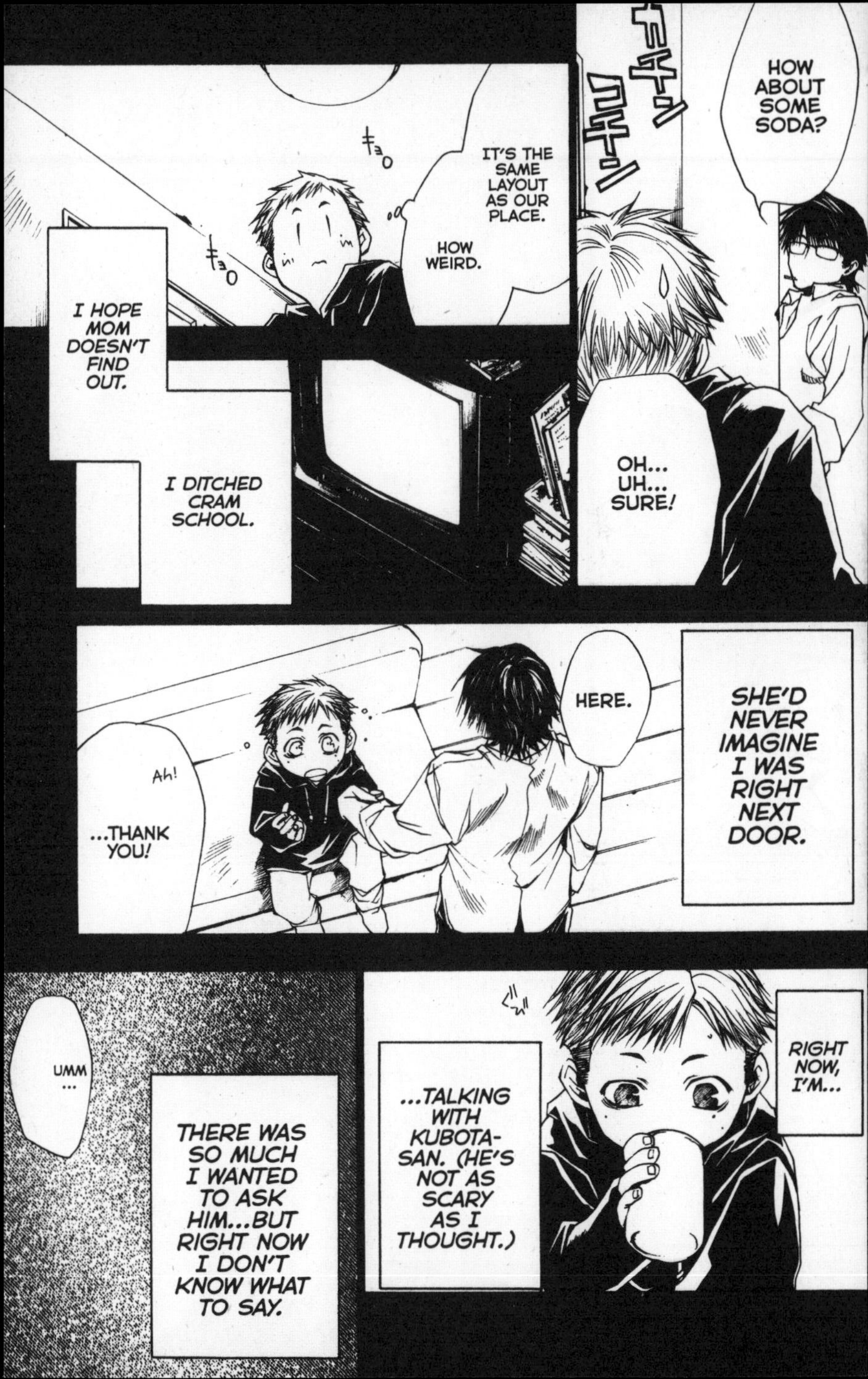
HOW ABOUT SOME SODA?
OH... UH... SURE!
IT'S THE SAME LAYOUT AS OUR PLACE.
HOW WEIRD.
I DITCHED CRAM SCHOOL.
I HOPE MOM DOESN'T FIND OUT.
SHE'D NEVER IMAGINE I WAS RIGHT NEXT DOOR.
HERE.
Ah!
...THANK YOU!
RIGHT NOW, I'M...
...TALKING WITH KUBOTA-SAN. (HE'S NOT AS SCARY AS I THOUGHT.)
THERE WAS SO MUCH I WANTED TO ASK HIM...BUT RIGHT NOW I DON'T KNOW WHAT TO SAY.
UMM ...

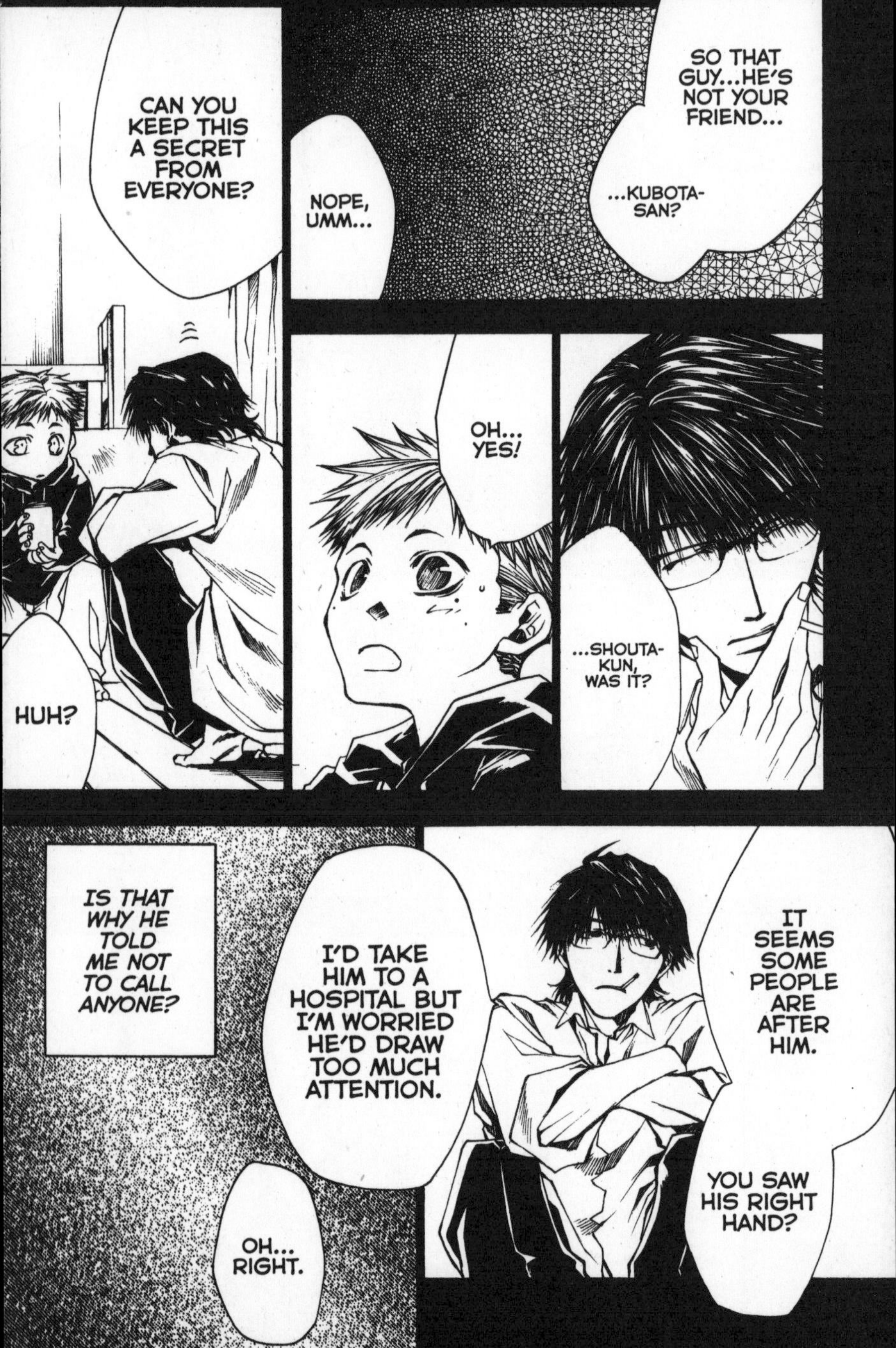
SO THAT GUY...HE'S NOT YOUR FRIEND...
...KUBOTA-SAN?
NOPE, UMM...
...SHOUTA-KUN, WAS IT?
OH... YES!
CAN YOU KEEP THIS A SECRET FROM EVERYONE?
HUH?
IT SEEMS SOME PEOPLE ARE AFTER HIM.
I'D TAKE HIM TO A HOSPITAL BUT I'M WORRIED HE'D DRAW TOO MUCH ATTENTION.
YOU SAW HIS RIGHT HAND?
OH... RIGHT.
IS THAT WHY HE TOLD ME NOT TO CALL ANYONE?

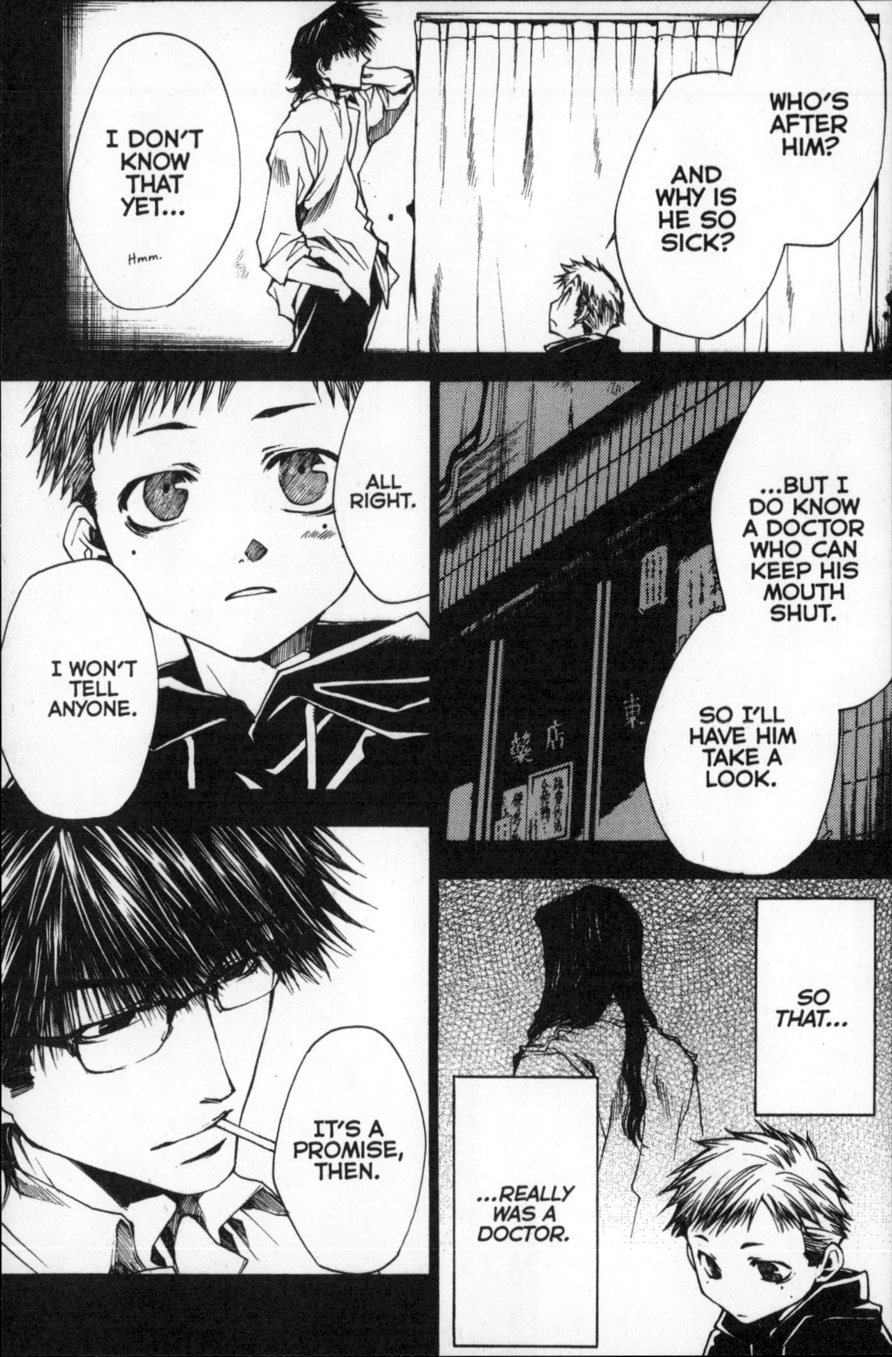
WHO'S AFTER HIM?
AND WHY IS HE SO SICK?
I DON'T KNOW THAT YET...
Hmm.
...BUT I DO KNOW A DOCTOR WHO CAN KEEP HIS MOUTH SHUT.
SO I'LL HAVE HIM TAKE A LOOK.
ALL RIGHT.
I WON'T TELL ANYONE.
SO THAT...
...REALLY WAS A DOCTOR.
IT'S A PROMISE, THEN.

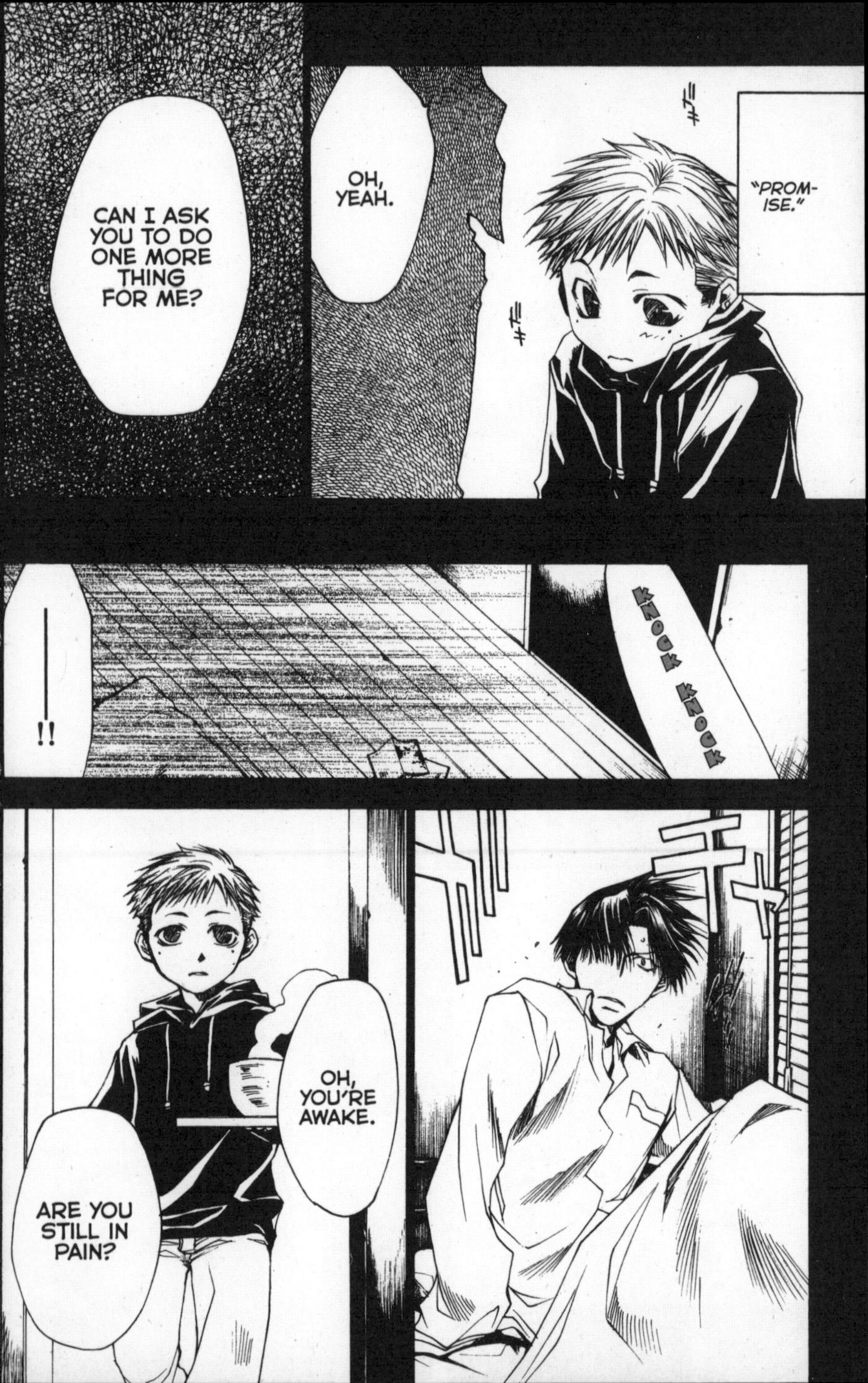
"PROM-
ISE."
OH,
YEAH.
CAN I ASK
YOU TO DO
ONE MORE
THING
FOR ME?
KNOCK KNOCK
—!!
OH,
YOU'RE
AWAKE.
ARE YOU
STILL IN
PAIN?

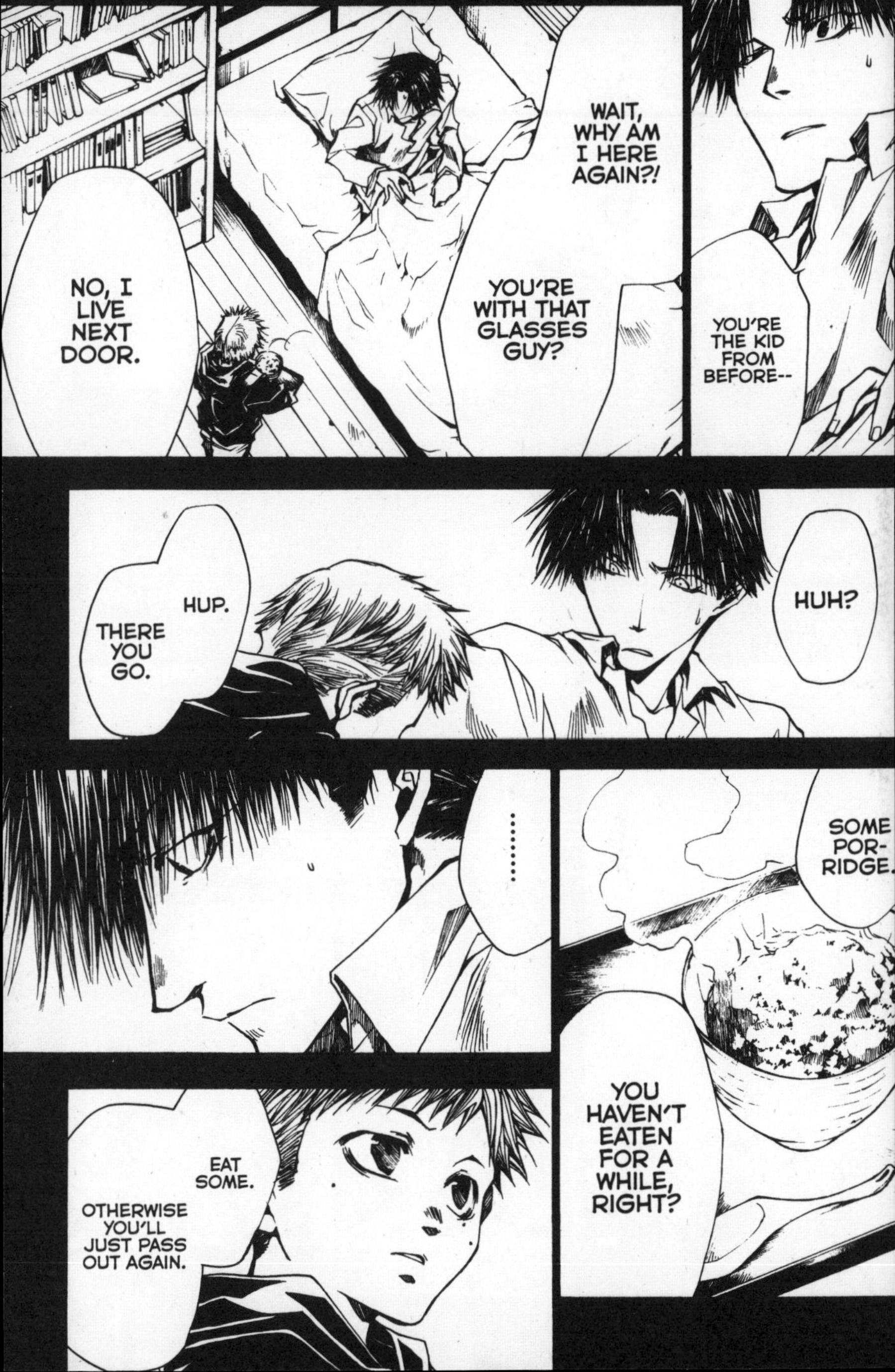
YOU'RE THE KID FROM BEFORE--
WAIT, WHY AM I HERE AGAIN?!
YOU'RE WITH THAT GLASSES GUY?
NO, I LIVE NEXT DOOR.
HUH?
HUP.
THERE YOU GO.
SOME POR-RIDGE.
YOU HAVEN'T EATEN FOR A WHILE, RIGHT?
......
EAT SOME.
OTHERWISE YOU'LL JUST PASS OUT AGAIN.

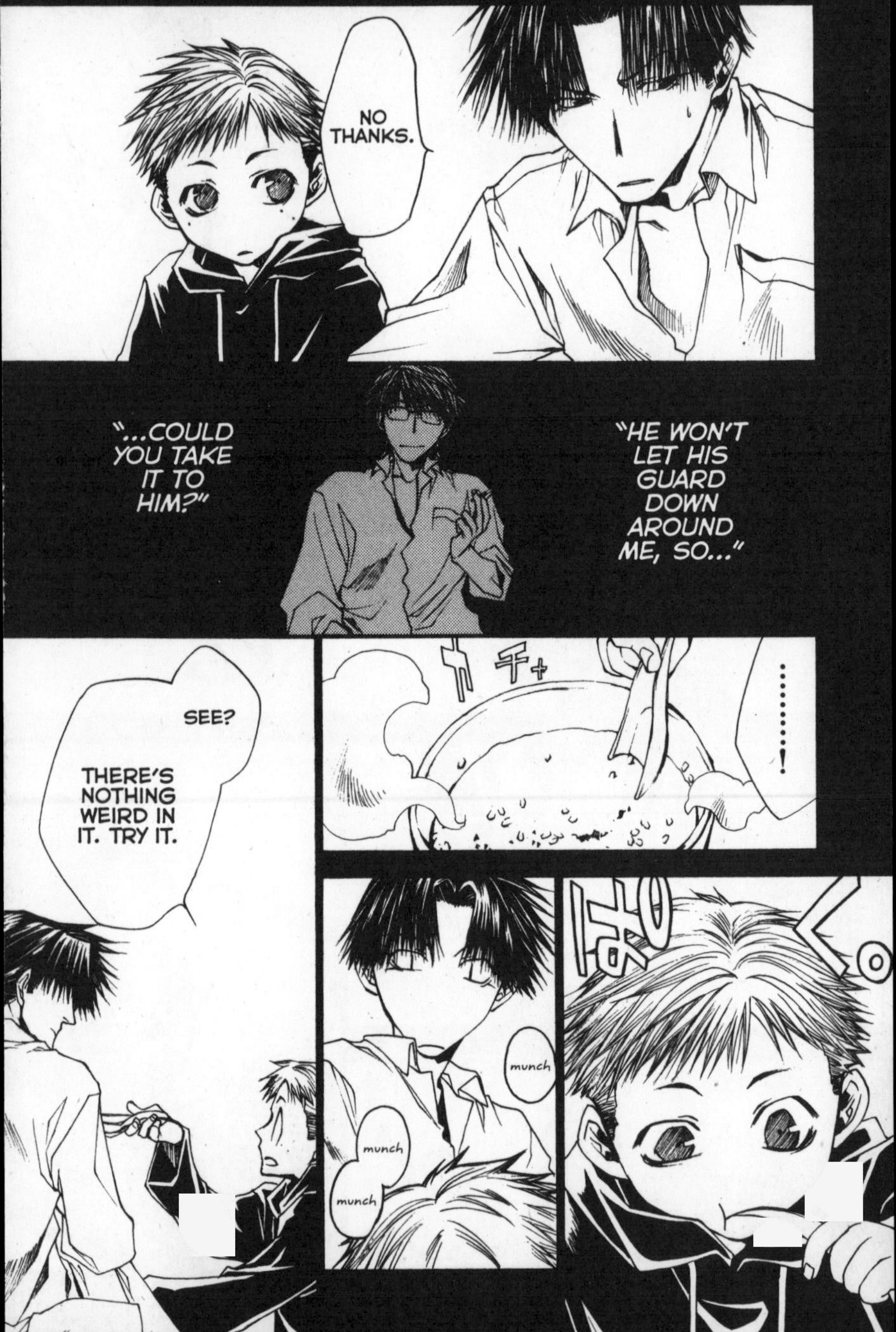
NO THANKS.
"HE WON'T LET HIS GUARD DOWN AROUND ME, SO..."
"...COULD YOU TAKE IT TO HIM?"
カチ
......!
ぱく
munch
munch
munch
SEE?
THERE'S NOTHING WEIRD IN IT. TRY IT.

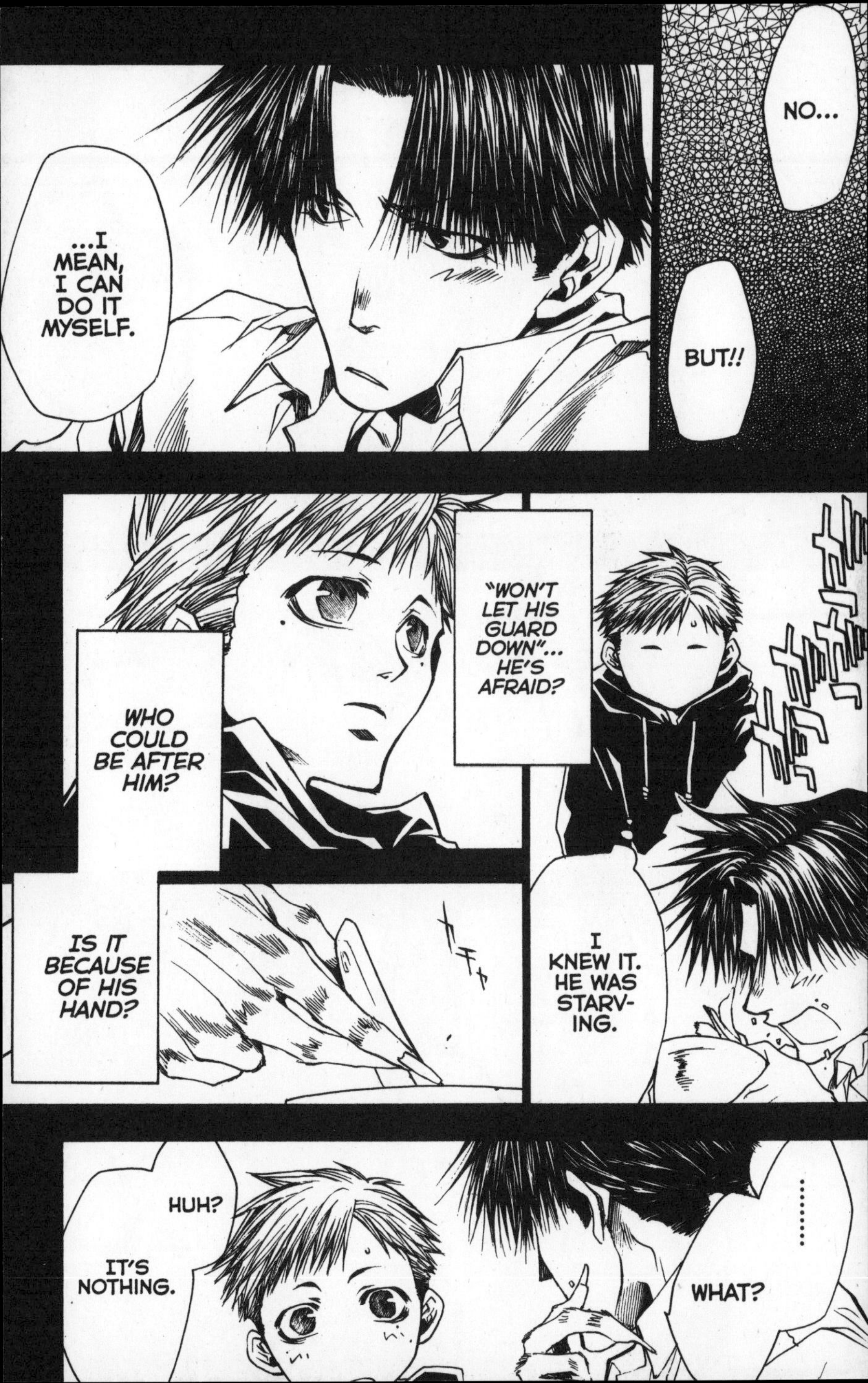
NO...
BUT!!
...I MEAN, I CAN DO IT MYSELF.
"WON'T LET HIS GUARD DOWN"... HE'S AFRAID?
I KNEW IT. HE WAS STARV-ING.
WHO COULD BE AFTER HIM?
IS IT BECAUSE OF HIS HAND?
......
WHAT?
HUH?
IT'S NOTHING.

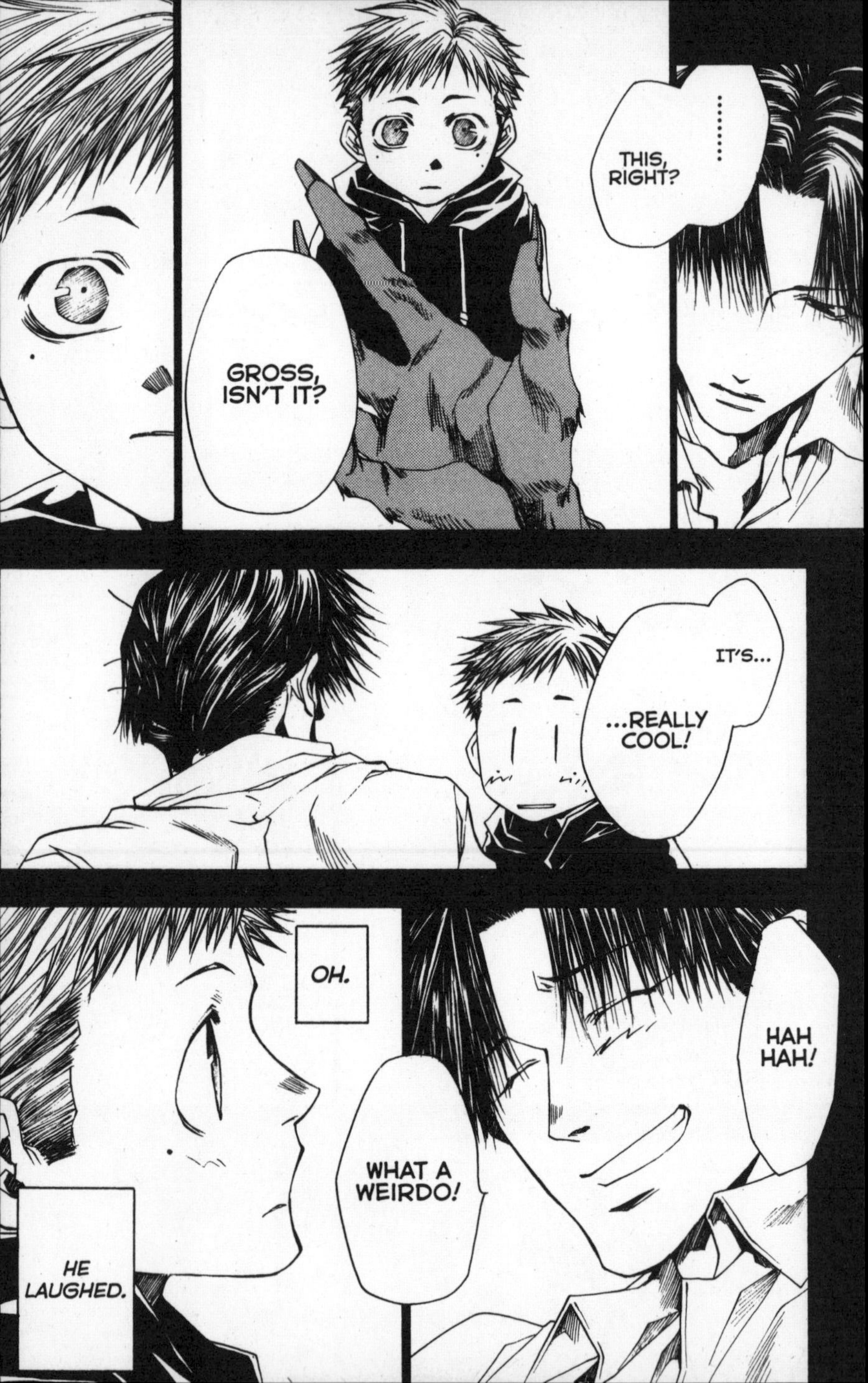
......
THIS, RIGHT?
GROSS, ISN'T IT?
IT'S...
...REALLY COOL!
HAH HAH!
WHAT A WEIRDO!
OH.
HE LAUGHED.

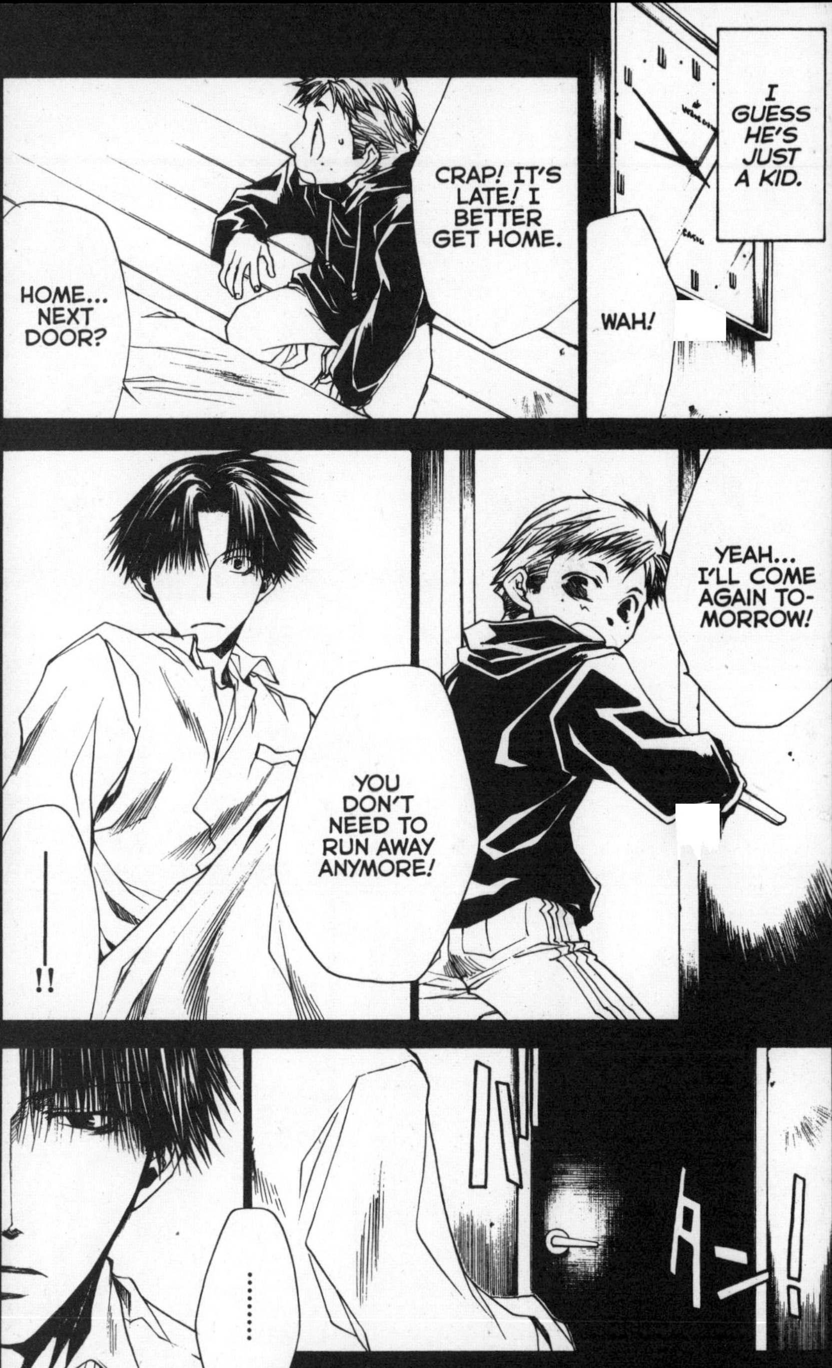
I GUESS HE'S JUST A KID.
WAH!
CRAP! IT'S LATE! I BETTER GET HOME.
HOME... NEXT DOOR?
YEAH... I'LL COME AGAIN TO-MORROW!
YOU DON'T NEED TO RUN AWAY ANYMORE!
!!
....

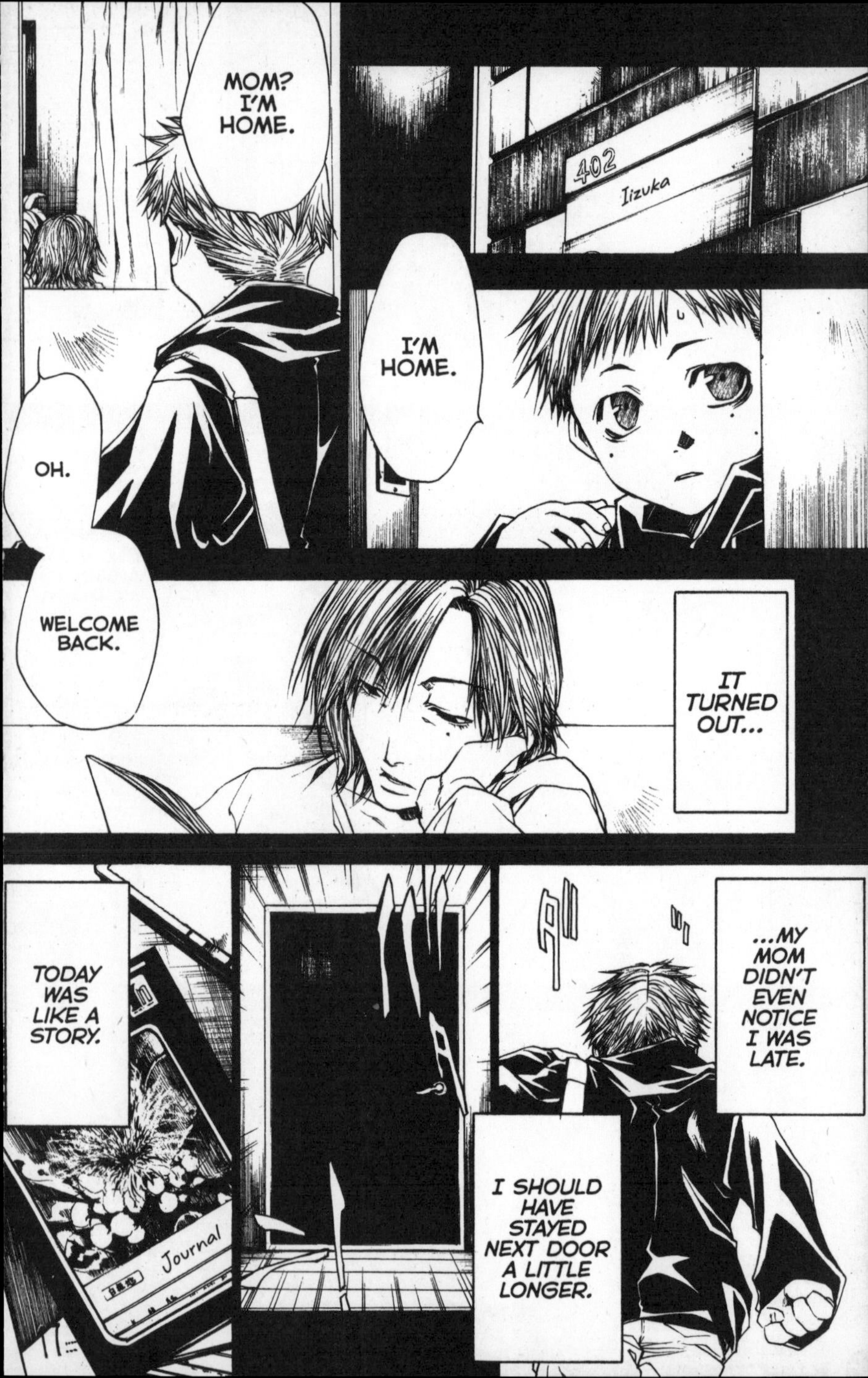
402
Iizuka
MOM? I'M HOME.
I'M HOME.
OH.
WELCOME BACK.
IT TURNED OUT...
...MY MOM DIDN'T EVEN NOTICE I WAS LATE.
I SHOULD HAVE STAYED NEXT DOOR A LITTLE LONGER.
TODAY WAS LIKE A STORY.
Journal

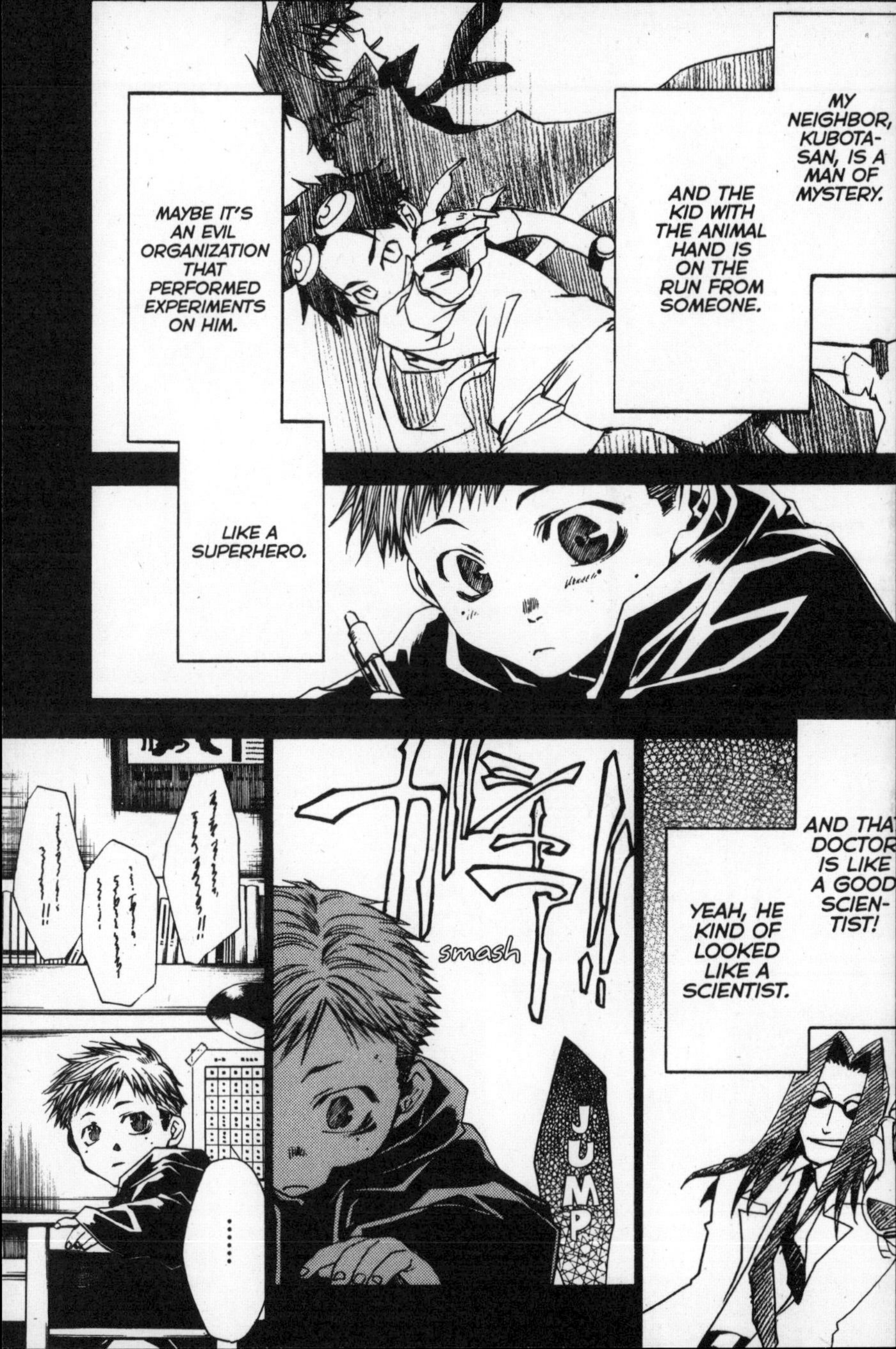
MY NEIGHBOR, KUBOTA-SAN, IS A MAN OF MYSTERY.
AND THE KID WITH THE ANIMAL HAND IS ON THE RUN FROM SOMEONE.
MAYBE IT'S AN EVIL ORGANIZATION THAT PERFORMED EXPERIMENTS ON HIM.
LIKE A SUPERHERO.
AND THA DOCTOR IS LIKE A GOOD SCIEN-TIST!
YEAH, HE KIND OF LOOKED LIKE A SCIENTIST.
smash
JUMP
......

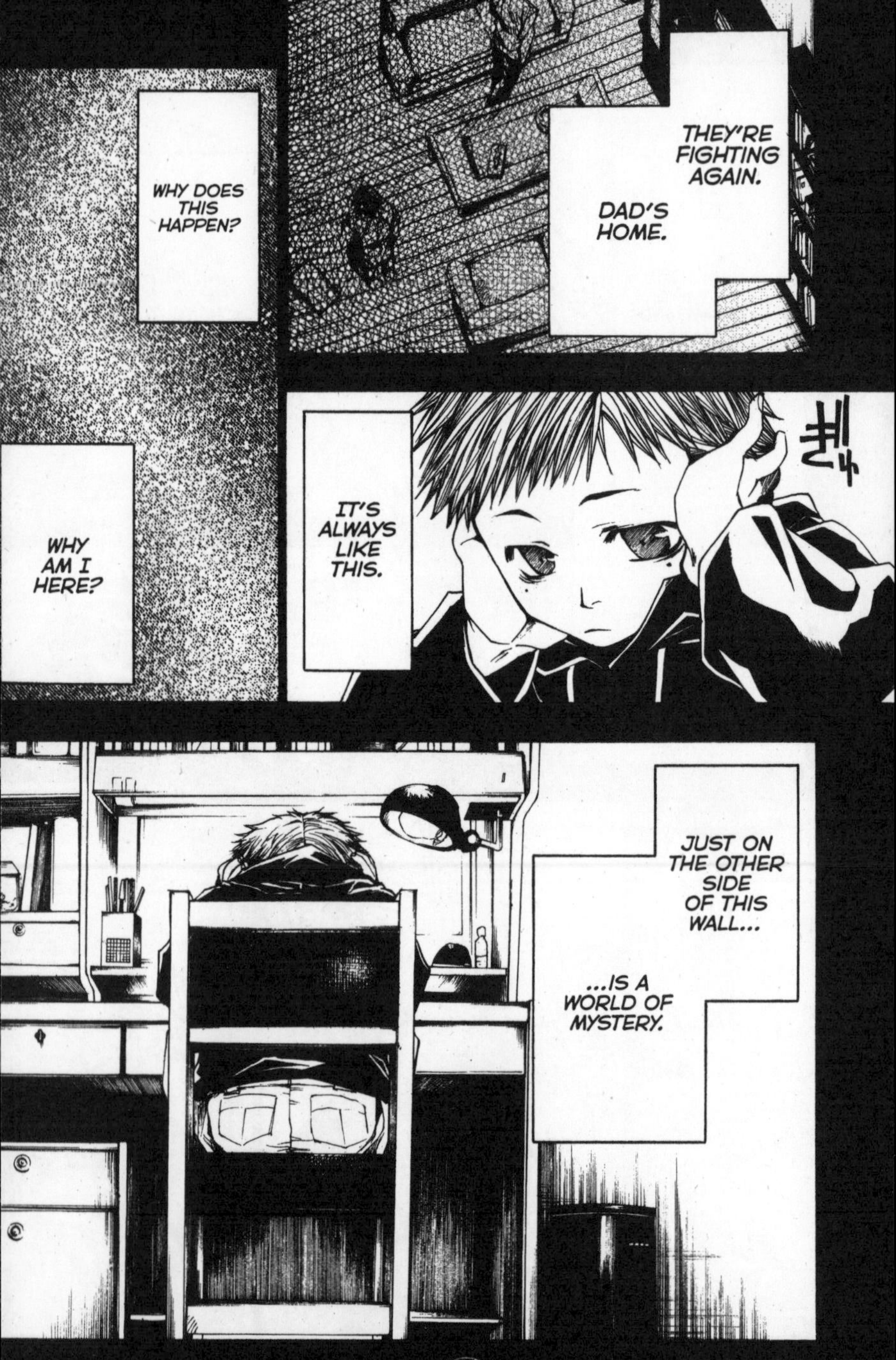
THEY'RE FIGHTING AGAIN.
DAD'S HOME.
WHY DOES THIS HAPPEN?
IT'S ALWAYS LIKE THIS.
WHY AM I HERE?
JUST ON THE OTHER SIDE OF THIS WALL...
...IS A WORLD OF MYSTERY.

CONTINUED ON THE Dice:29

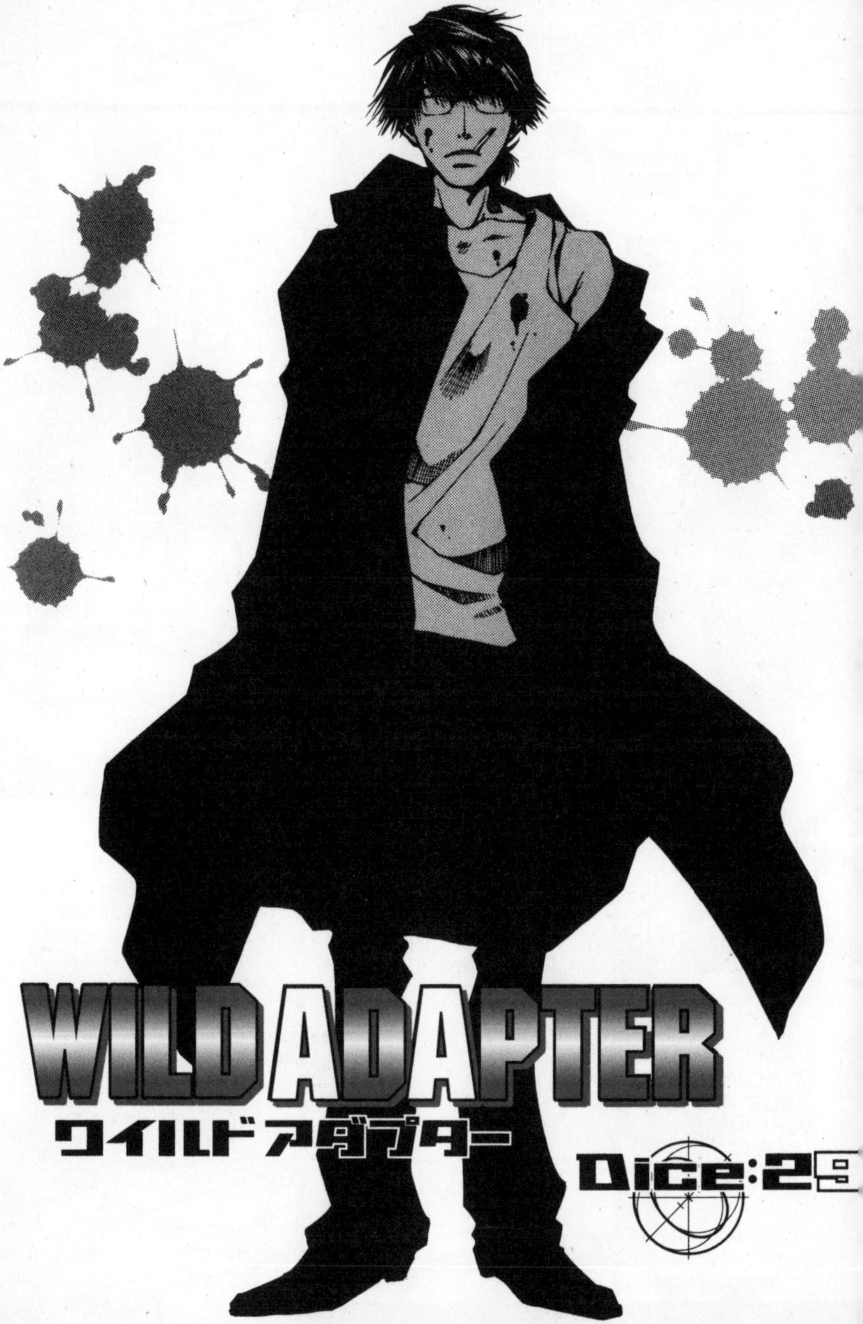
WILD ADAPTER
ワイルドアダプター
Dice:2

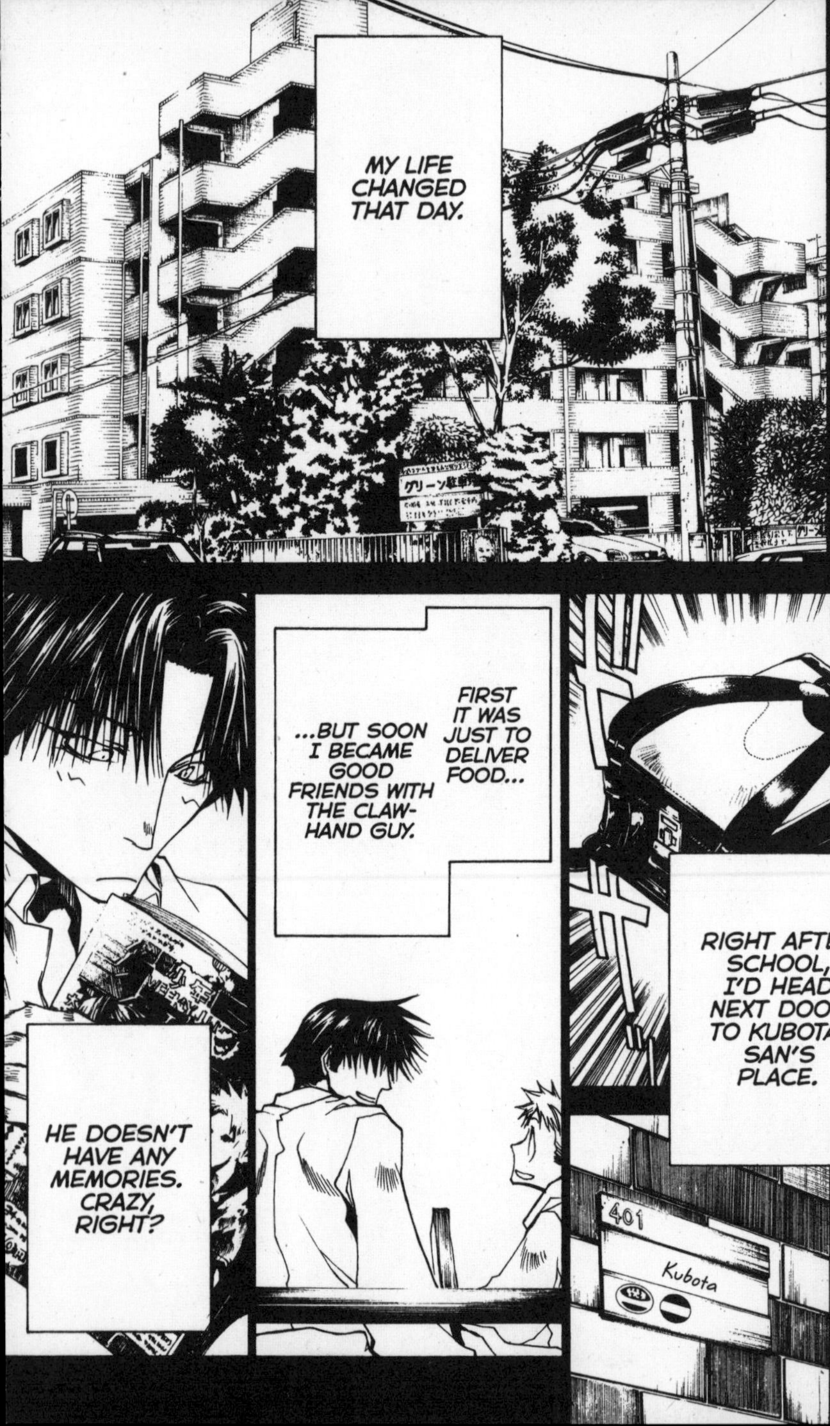
MY LIFE CHANGED THAT DAY.
RIGHT AFTER SCHOOL, I'D HEAD NEXT DOOR TO KUBOTA-SAN'S PLACE.
401
Kubota
FIRST IT WAS JUST TO DELIVER FOOD...
...BUT SOON I BECAME GOOD FRIENDS WITH THE CLAW-HAND GUY.
HE DOESN'T HAVE ANY MEMORIES. CRAZY, RIGHT?

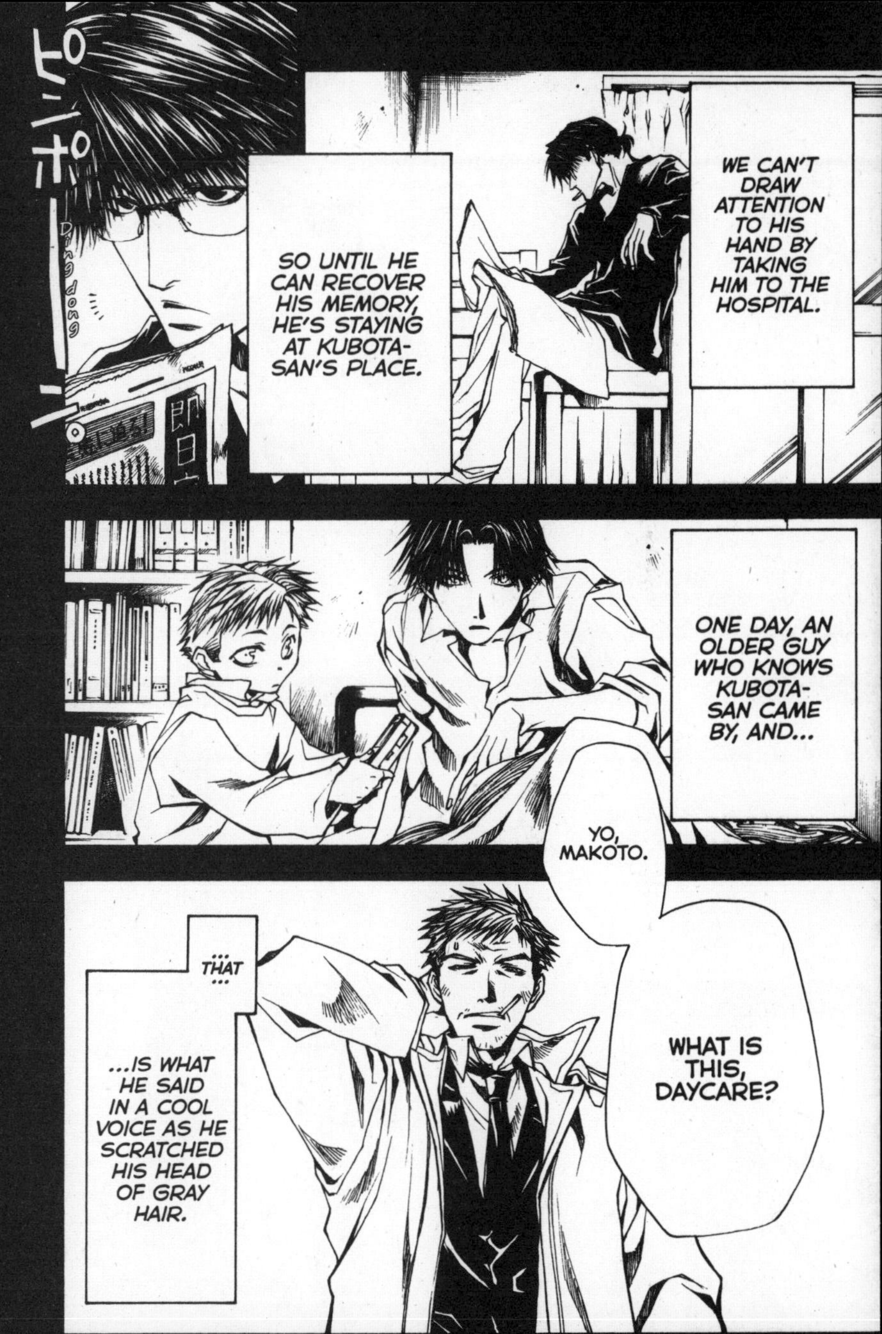

WE CAN'T DRAW ATTENTION TO HIS HAND BY TAKING HIM TO THE HOSPITAL.
SO UNTIL HE CAN RECOVER HIS MEMORY, HE'S STAYING AT KUBOTA-SAN'S PLACE.
ピンポーン
Ding dong
ONE DAY, AN OLDER GUY WHO KNOWS KUBOTA-SAN CAME BY, AND...
YO, MAKOTO.
WHAT IS THIS, DAYCARE?
...THAT...
...IS WHAT HE SAID IN A COOL VOICE AS HE SCRATCHED HIS HEAD OF GRAY HAIR.

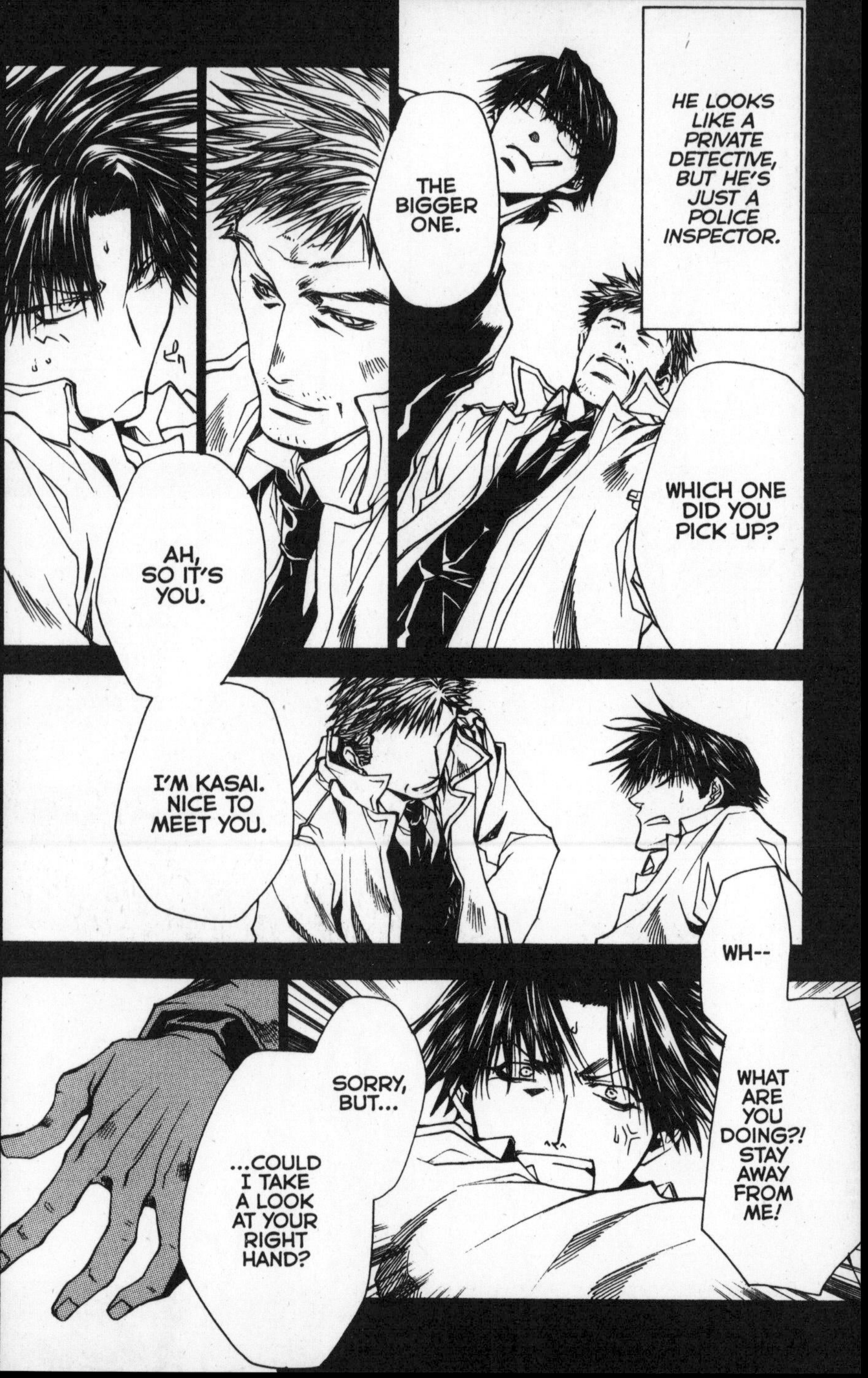
HE LOOKS LIKE A PRIVATE DETECTIVE, BUT HE'S JUST A POLICE INSPECTOR.
WHICH ONE DID YOU PICK UP?
THE BIGGER ONE.
AH, SO IT'S YOU.
I'M KASAI. NICE TO MEET YOU.
WH--
WHAT ARE YOU DOING?! STAY AWAY FROM ME!
SORRY, BUT...
...COULD I TAKE A LOOK AT YOUR RIGHT HAND?

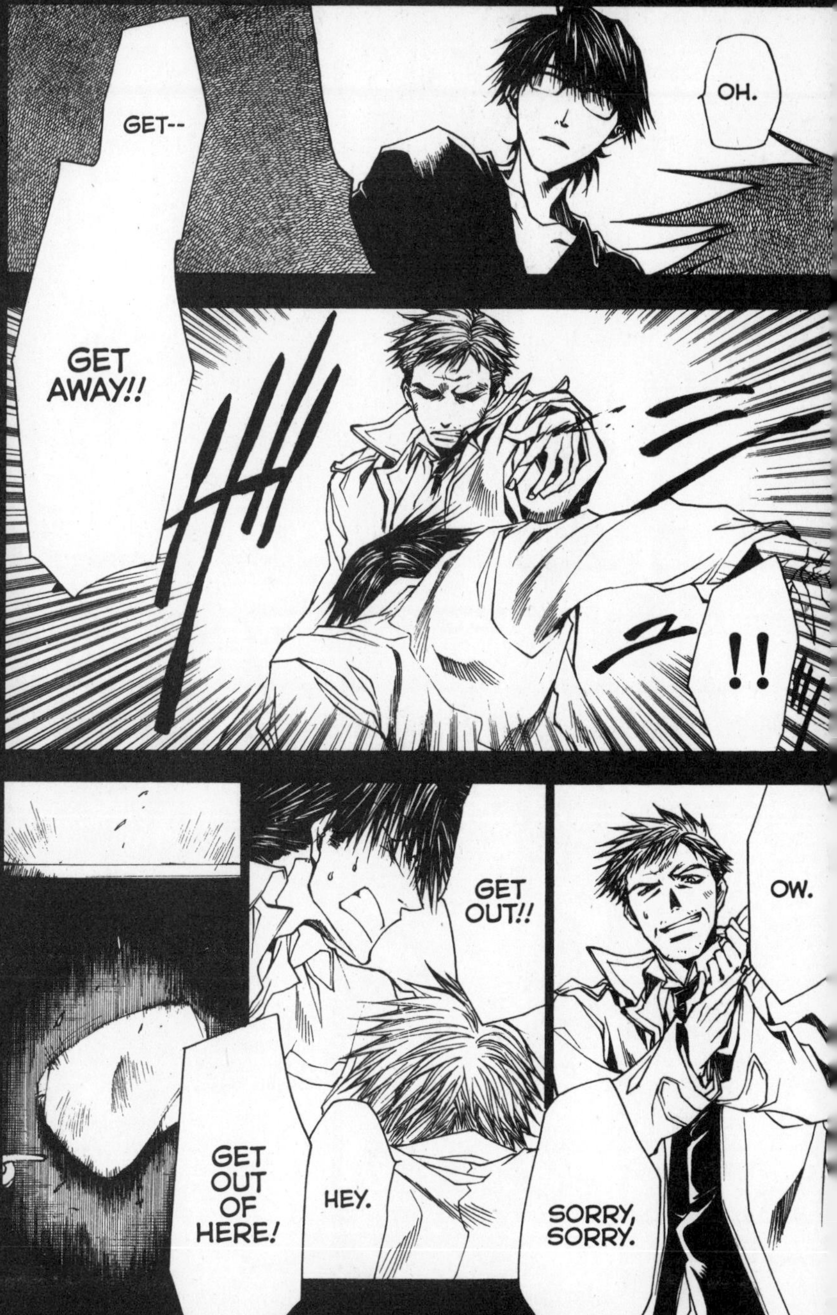
OH.
GET--
GET AWAY!!
!!
OW.
SORRY, SORRY.
GET OUT!!
HEY.
GET OUT OF HERE!

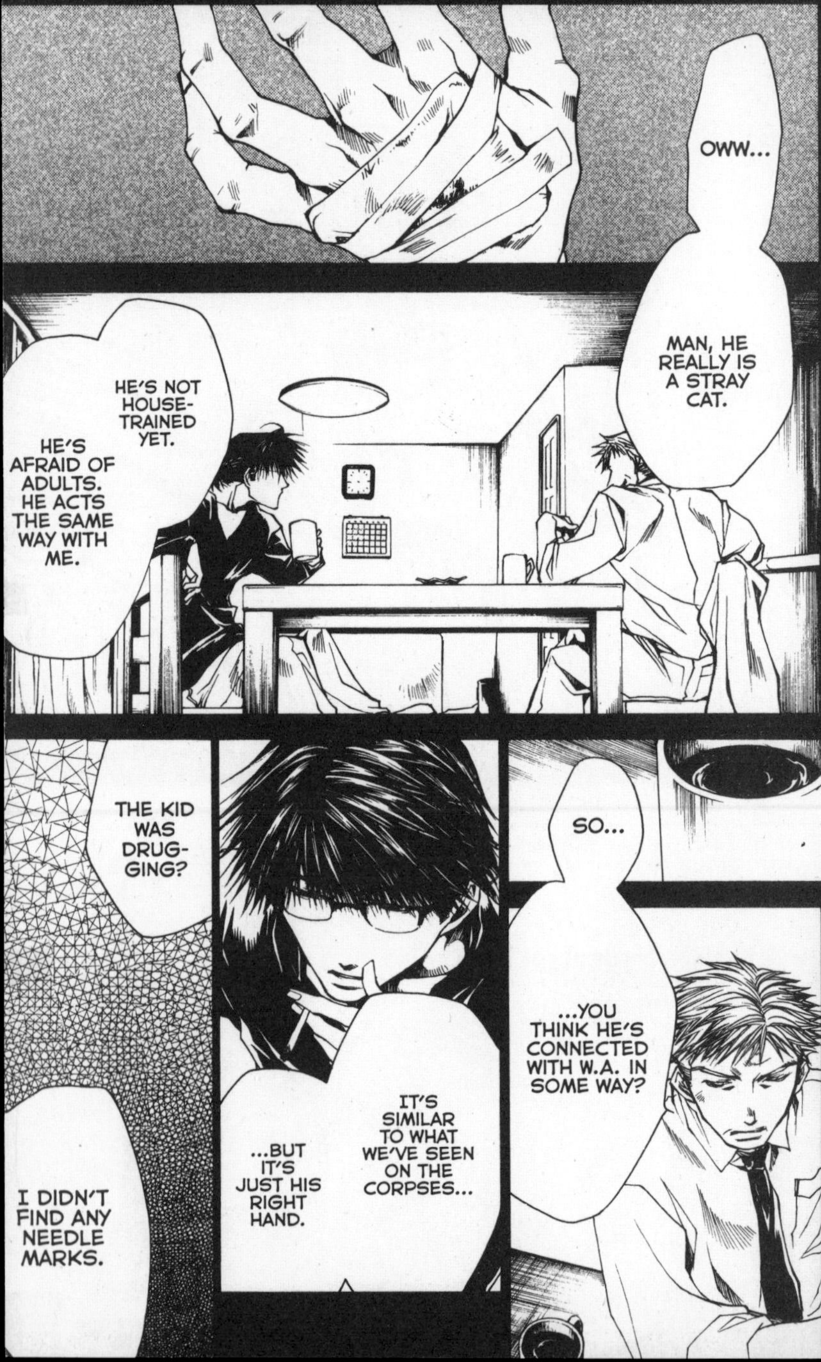
OWW...
MAN, HE REALLY IS A STRAY CAT.
HE'S NOT HOUSE-TRAINED YET.
HE'S AFRAID OF ADULTS. HE ACTS THE SAME WAY WITH ME.
SO...
...YOU THINK HE'S CONNECTED WITH W.A. IN SOME WAY?
IT'S SIMILAR TO WHAT WE'VE SEEN ON THE CORPSES...
...BUT IT'S JUST HIS RIGHT HAND.
THE KID WAS DRUGGING?
I DIDN'T FIND ANY NEEDLE MARKS.

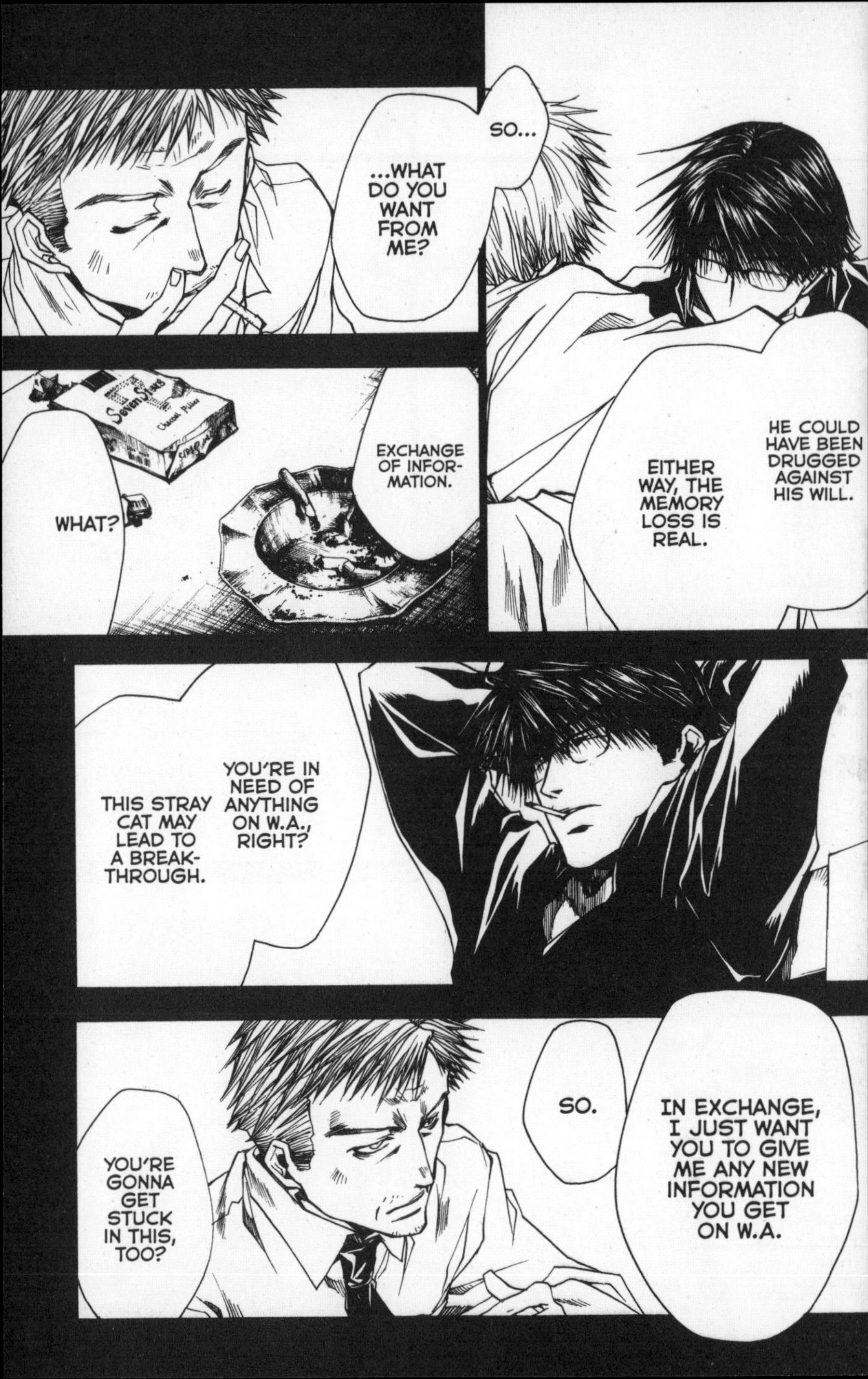
HE COULD HAVE BEEN DRUGGED AGAINST HIS WILL.
EITHER WAY, THE MEMORY LOSS IS REAL.
SO...
...WHAT DO YOU WANT FROM ME?
EXCHANGE OF INFORMATION.
Seven Stars
WHAT?
YOU'RE IN NEED OF ANYTHING ON W.A., RIGHT?
THIS STRAY CAT MAY LEAD TO A BREAK-THROUGH.
IN EXCHANGE, I JUST WANT YOU TO GIVE ME ANY NEW INFORMATION YOU GET ON W.A.
SO.
YOU'RE GONNA GET STUCK IN THIS, TOO?

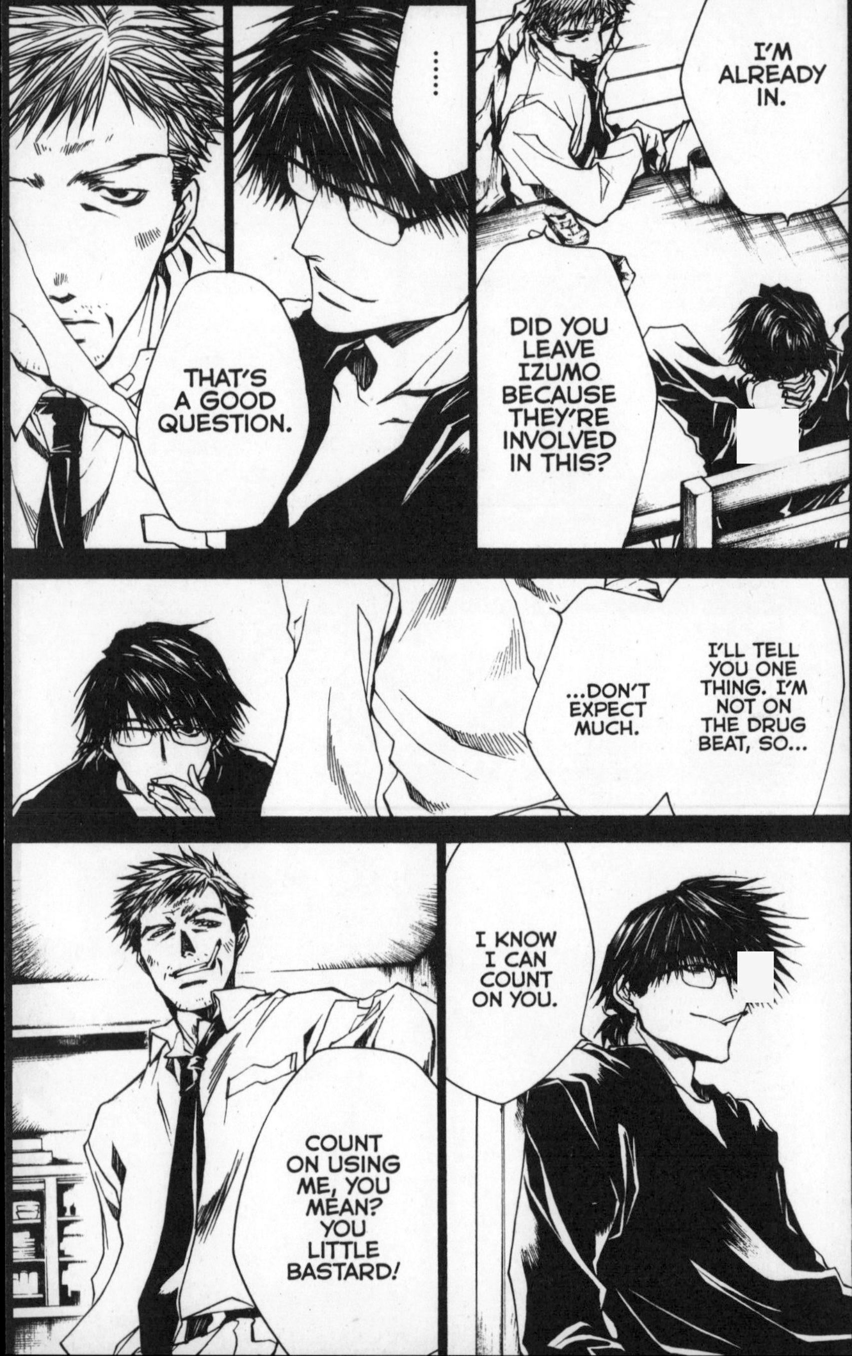
I'M ALREADY IN.
DID YOU LEAVE IZUMO BECAUSE THEY'RE INVOLVED IN THIS?
......
THAT'S A GOOD QUESTION.
I'LL TELL YOU ONE THING. I'M NOT ON THE DRUG BEAT, SO...
...DON'T EXPECT MUCH.
I KNOW I CAN COUNT ON YOU.
COUNT ON USING ME, YOU MEAN? YOU LITTLE BASTARD!

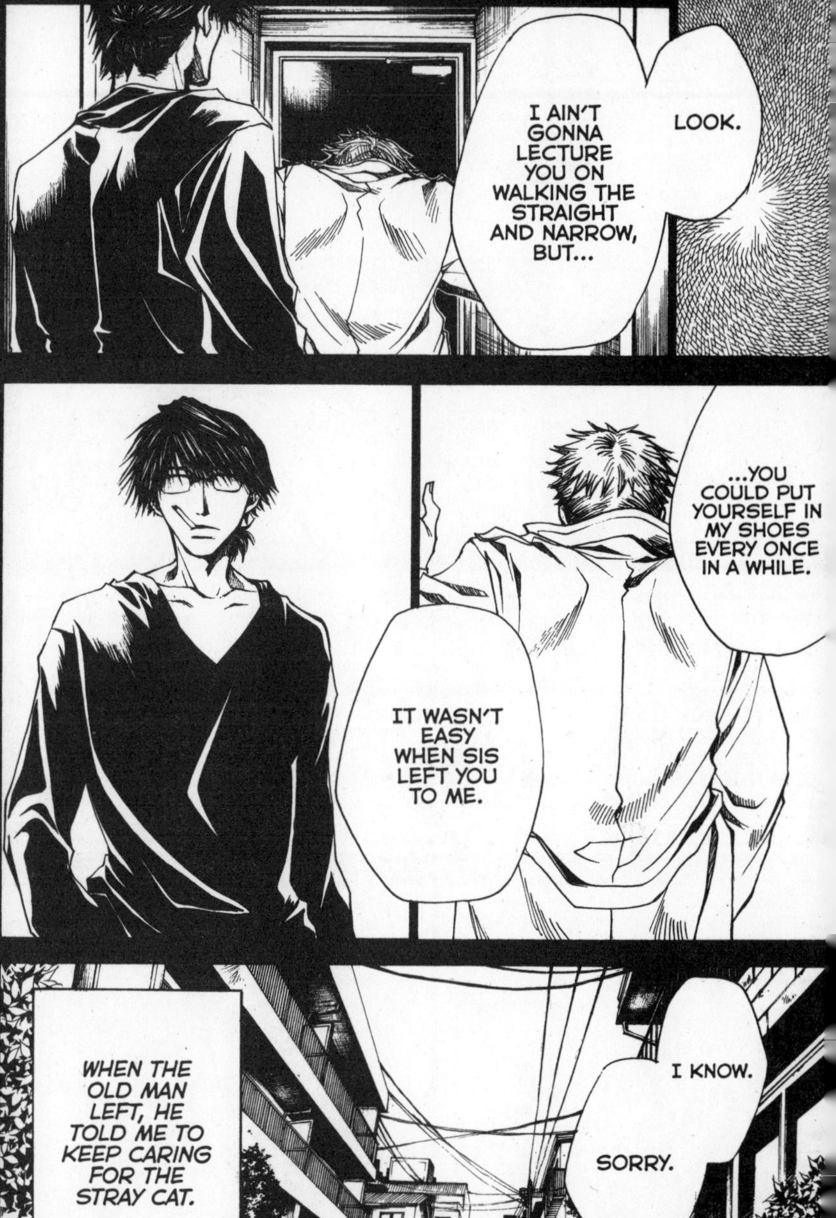
LOOK.
I AIN'T GONNA LECTURE YOU ON WALKING THE STRAIGHT AND NARROW, BUT...
...YOU COULD PUT YOURSELF IN MY SHOES EVERY ONCE IN A WHILE.
IT WASN'T EASY WHEN SIS LEFT YOU TO ME.
I KNOW.
SORRY.
WHEN THE OLD MAN LEFT, HE TOLD ME TO KEEP CARING FOR THE STRAY CAT.

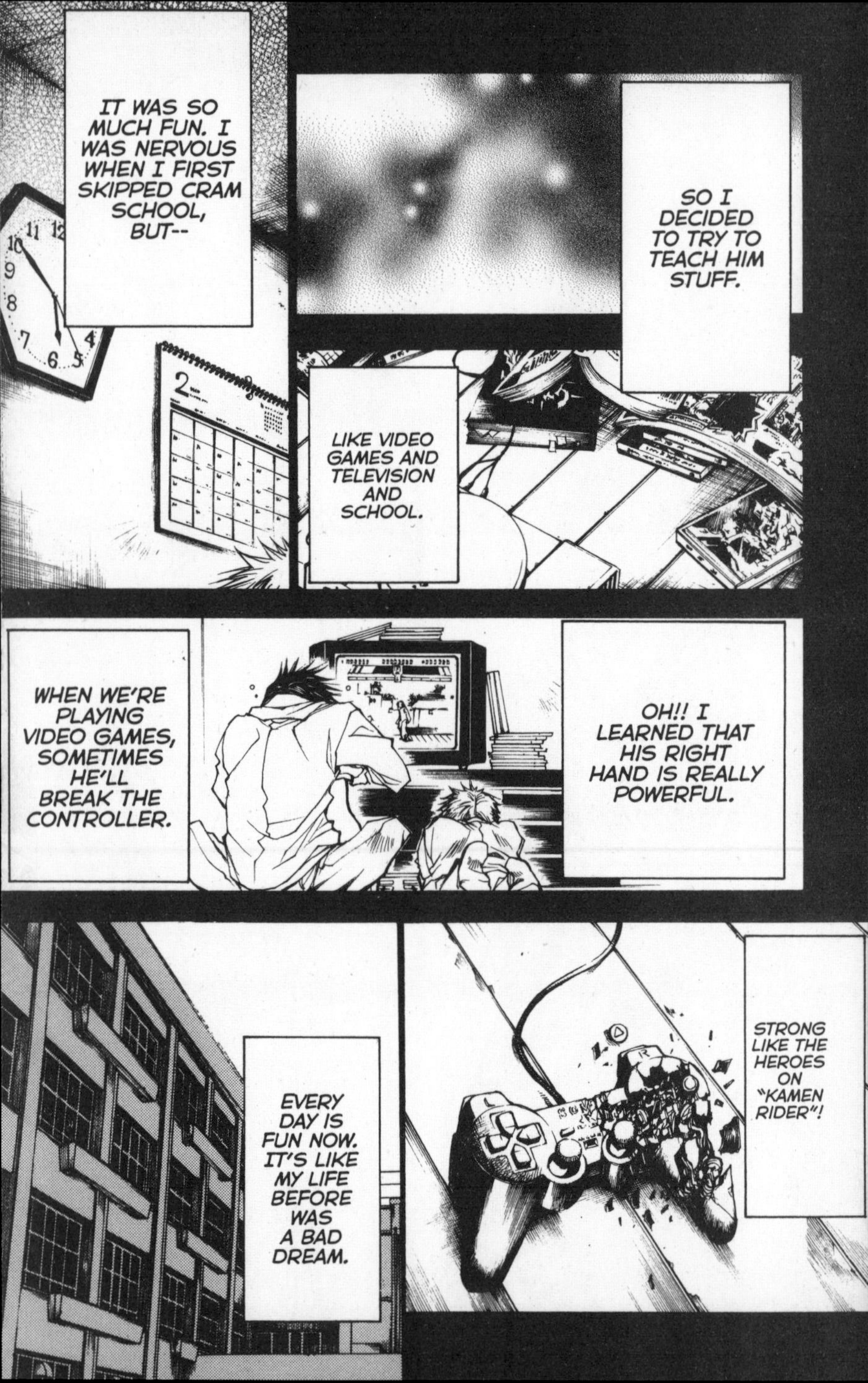
SO I DECIDED TO TRY TO TEACH HIM STUFF.
LIKE VIDEO GAMES AND TELEVISION AND SCHOOL.
IT WAS SO MUCH FUN. I WAS NERVOUS WHEN I FIRST SKIPPED CRAM SCHOOL, BUT--
OH!! I LEARNED THAT HIS RIGHT HAND IS REALLY POWERFUL.
WHEN WE'RE PLAYING VIDEO GAMES, SOMETIMES HE'LL BREAK THE CONTROLLER.
STRONG LIKE THE HEROES ON "KAMEN RIDER"!
EVERY DAY IS FUN NOW. IT'S LIKE MY LIFE BEFORE WAS A BAD DREAM.

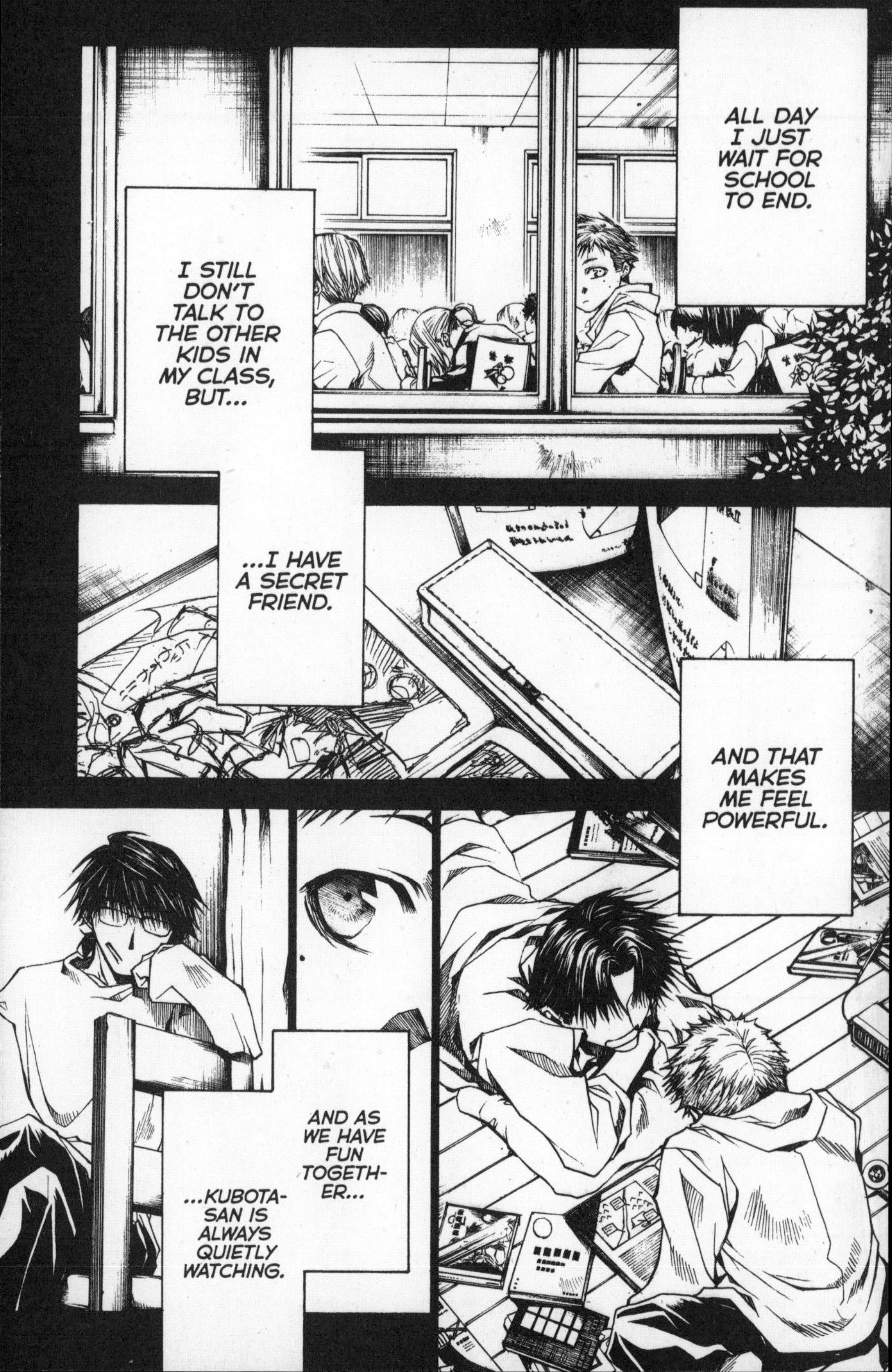
ALL DAY I JUST WAIT FOR SCHOOL TO END.
I STILL DON'T TALK TO THE OTHER KIDS IN MY CLASS, BUT...
...I HAVE A SECRET FRIEND.
AND THAT MAKES ME FEEL POWERFUL.
AND AS WE HAVE FUN TOGETH-ER...
...KUBOTA-SAN IS ALWAYS QUIETLY WATCHING.

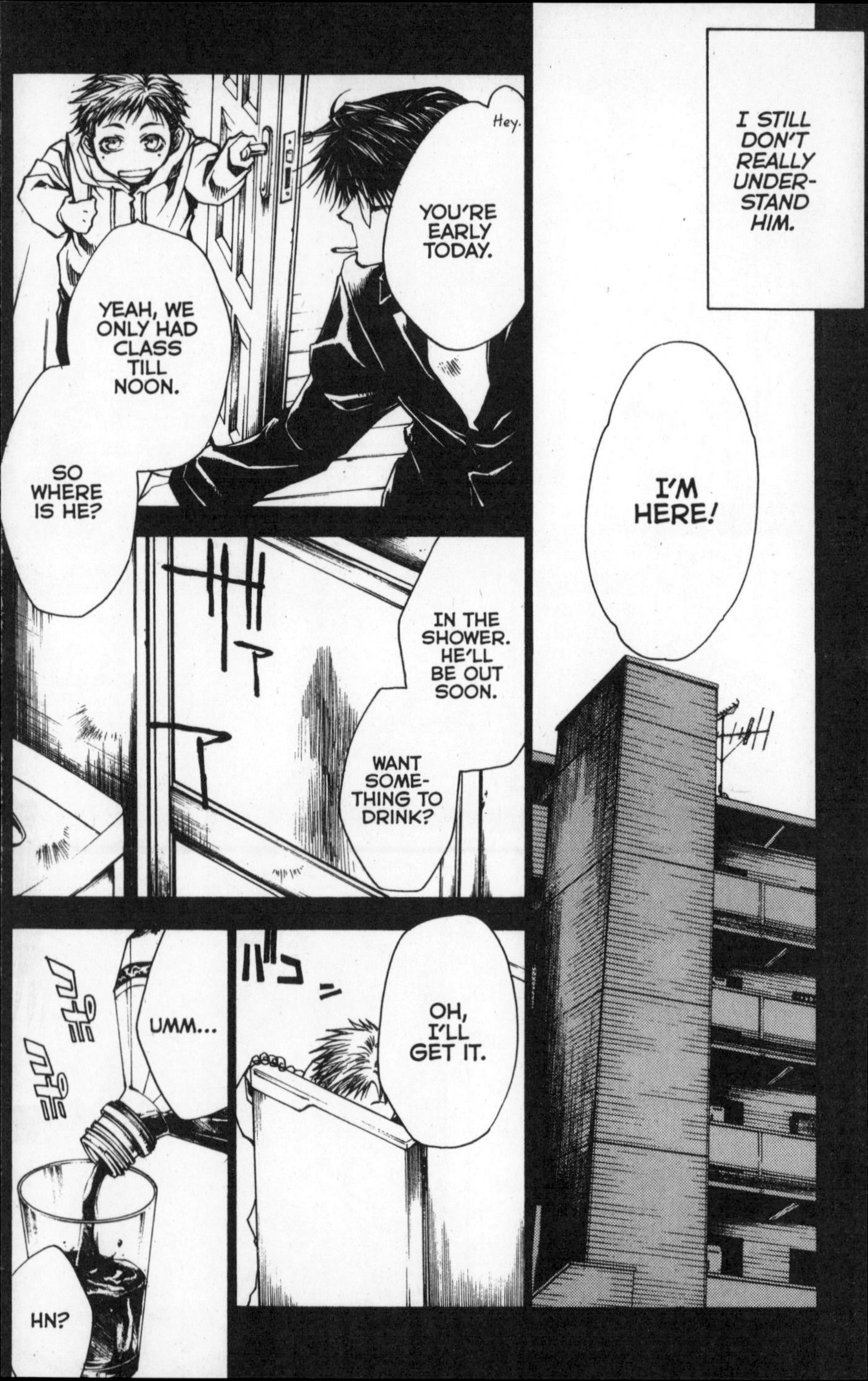
I STILL DON'T REALLY UNDER-STAND HIM.
I'M HERE!
Hey.
YOU'RE EARLY TODAY.
YEAH, WE ONLY HAD CLASS TILL NOON.
SO WHERE IS HE?
IN THE SHOWER. HE'LL BE OUT SOON.
WANT SOME-THING TO DRINK?
OH, I'LL GET IT.
UMM...
HN?

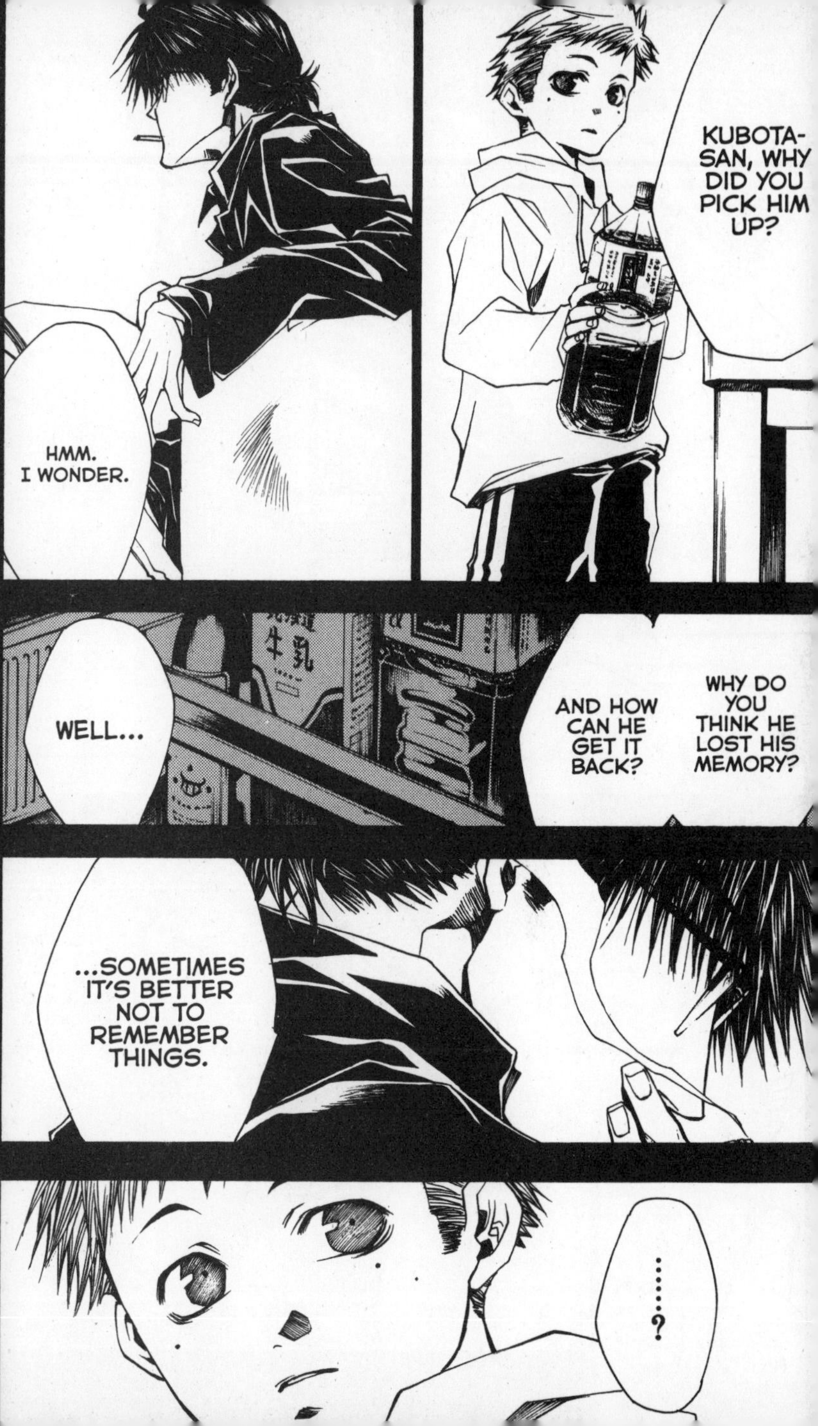
KUBOTA-SAN, WHY DID YOU PICK HIM UP?
HMM. I WONDER.
WHY DO YOU THINK HE LOST HIS MEMORY?
AND HOW CAN HE GET IT BACK?
WELL...
...SOMETIMES IT'S BETTER NOT TO REMEMBER THINGS.
.....?

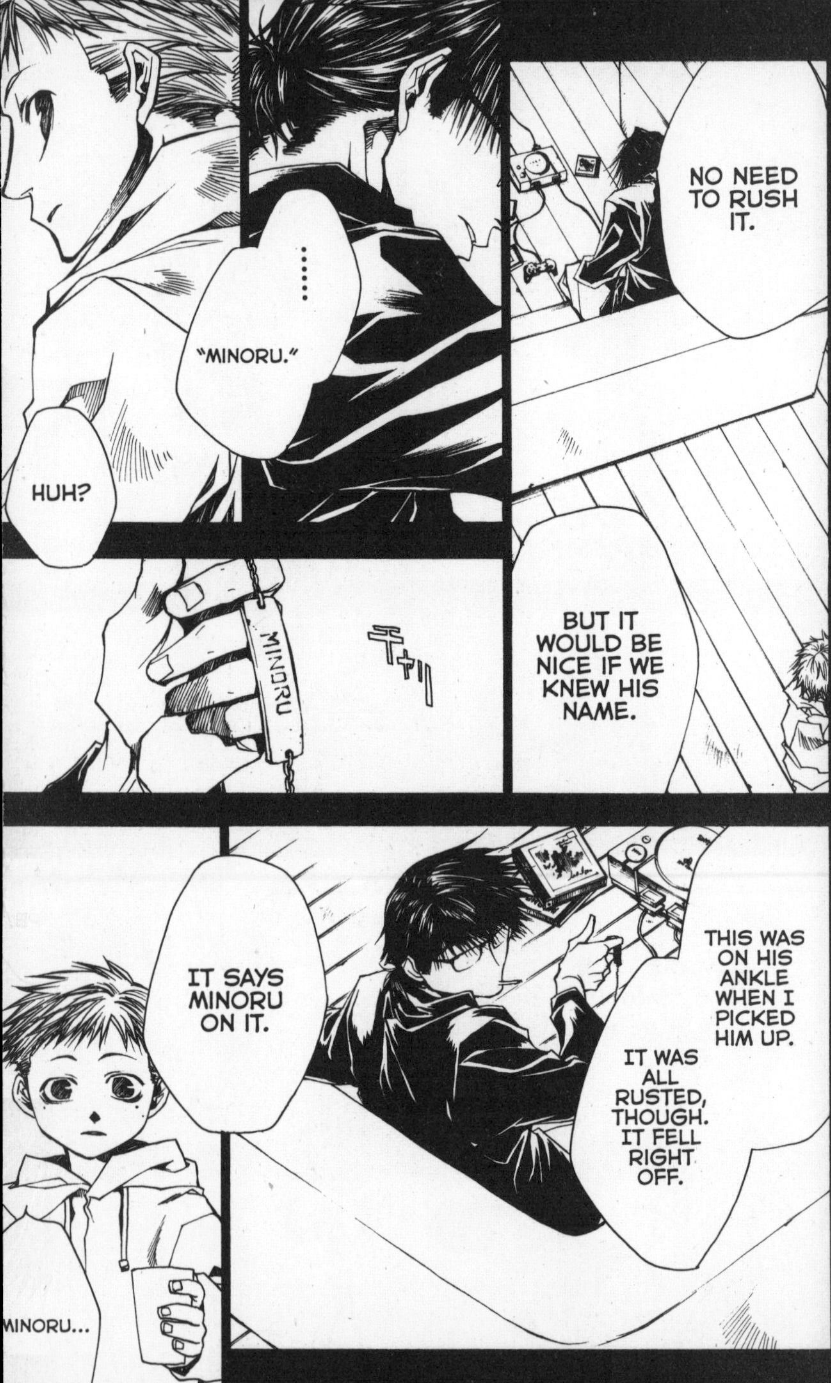
NO NEED TO RUSH IT.
BUT IT WOULD BE NICE IF WE KNEW HIS NAME.
......
“MINORU.”
HUH?
MINORU
チャリ
THIS WAS ON HIS ANKLE WHEN I PICKED HIM UP.
IT WAS ALL RUSTED, THOUGH. IT FELL RIGHT OFF.
IT SAYS MINORU ON IT.
MINORU...

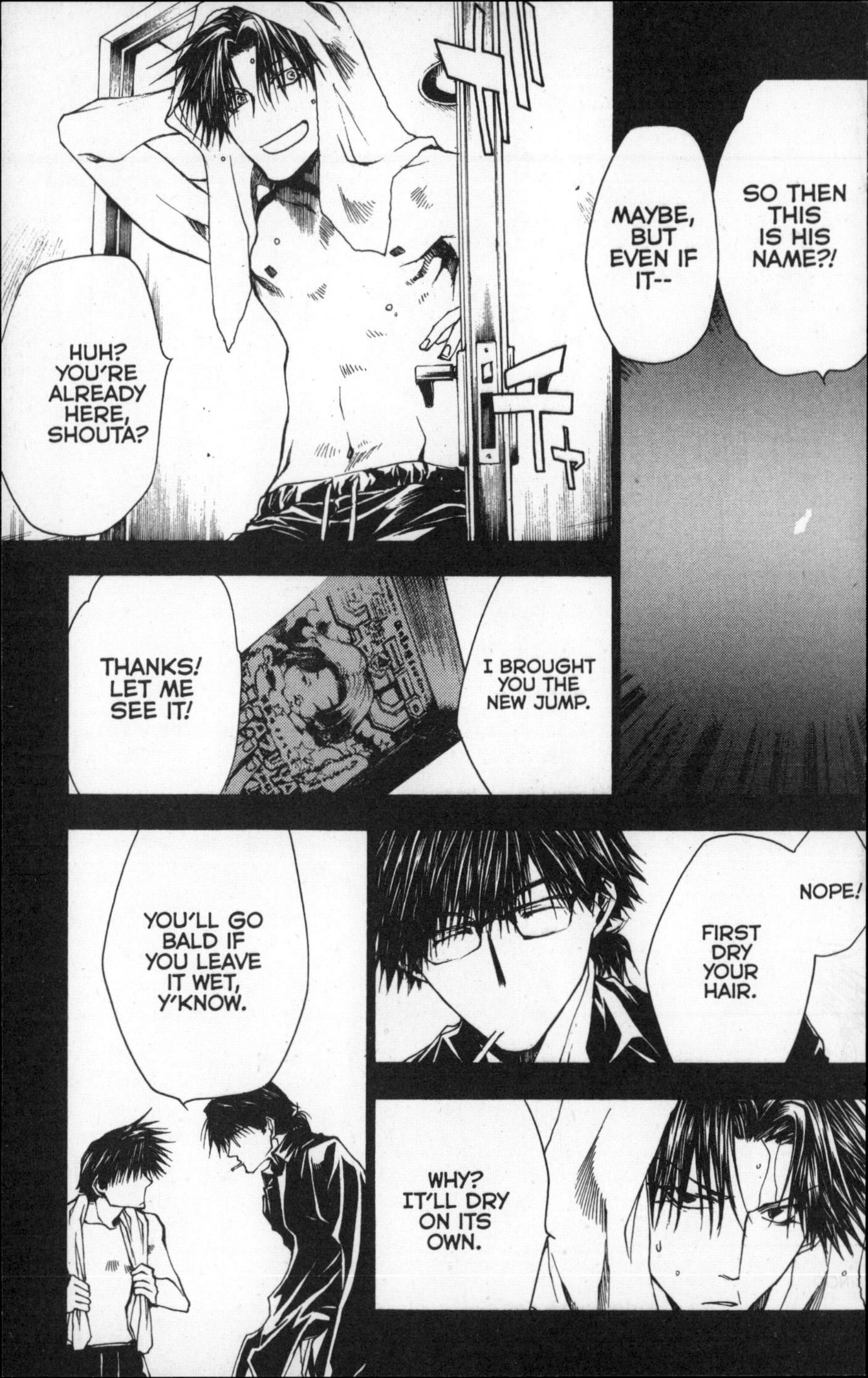
SO THEN THIS IS HIS NAME?!
MAYBE, BUT EVEN IF IT--
HUH? YOU'RE ALREADY HERE, SHOUTA?
I BROUGHT YOU THE NEW JUMP.
THANKS! LET ME SEE IT!
NOPE!
FIRST DRY YOUR HAIR.
WHY? IT'LL DRY ON ITS OWN.
YOU'LL GO BALD IF YOU LEAVE IT WET, Y'KNOW.

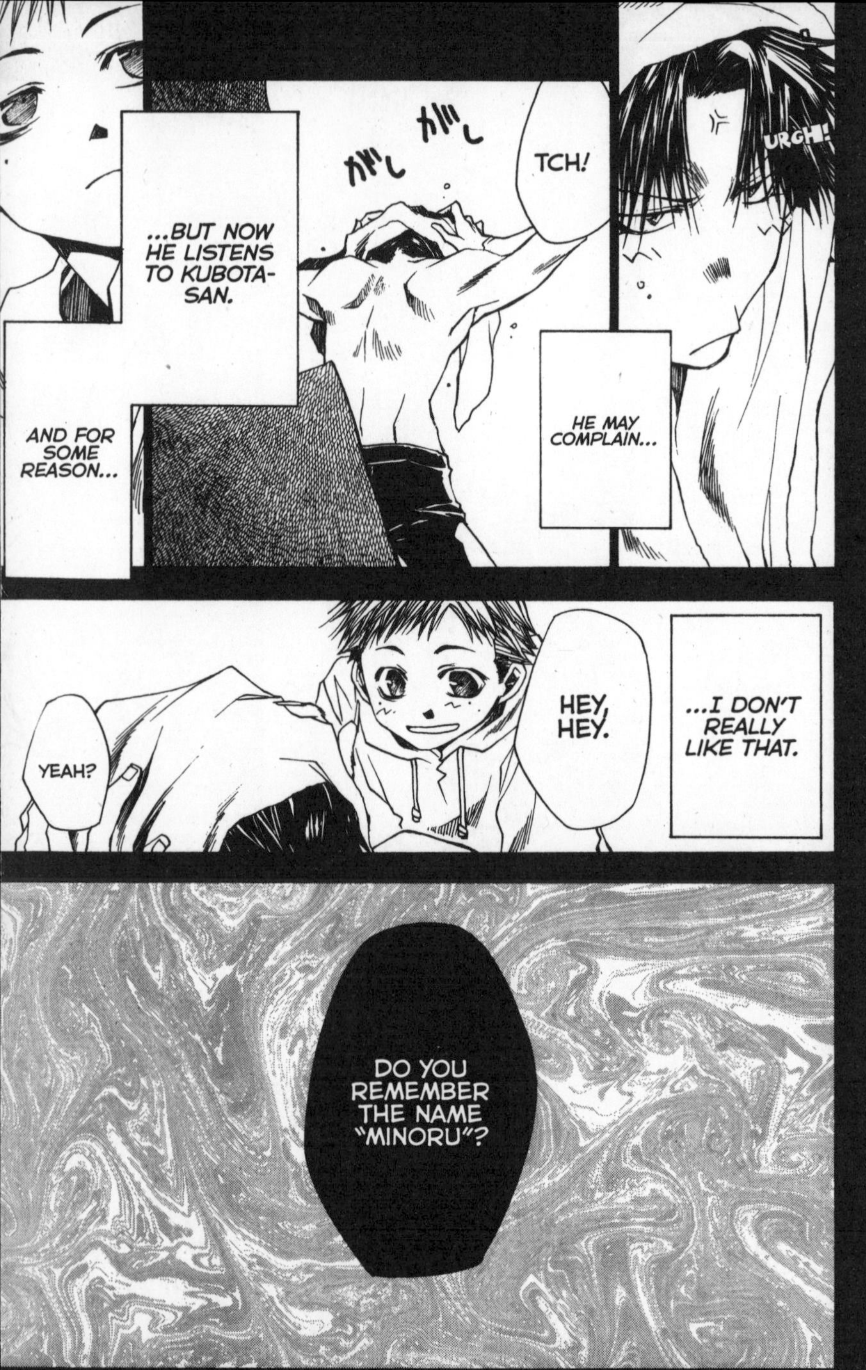
URGH!
HE MAY COMPLAIN...
TCH!
がし
がし
...BUT NOW HE LISTENS TO KUBOTA-SAN.
AND FOR SOME REASON...
...I DON'T REALLY LIKE THAT.
HEY, HEY.
YEAH?
DO YOU REMEMBER THE NAME "MINORU"?

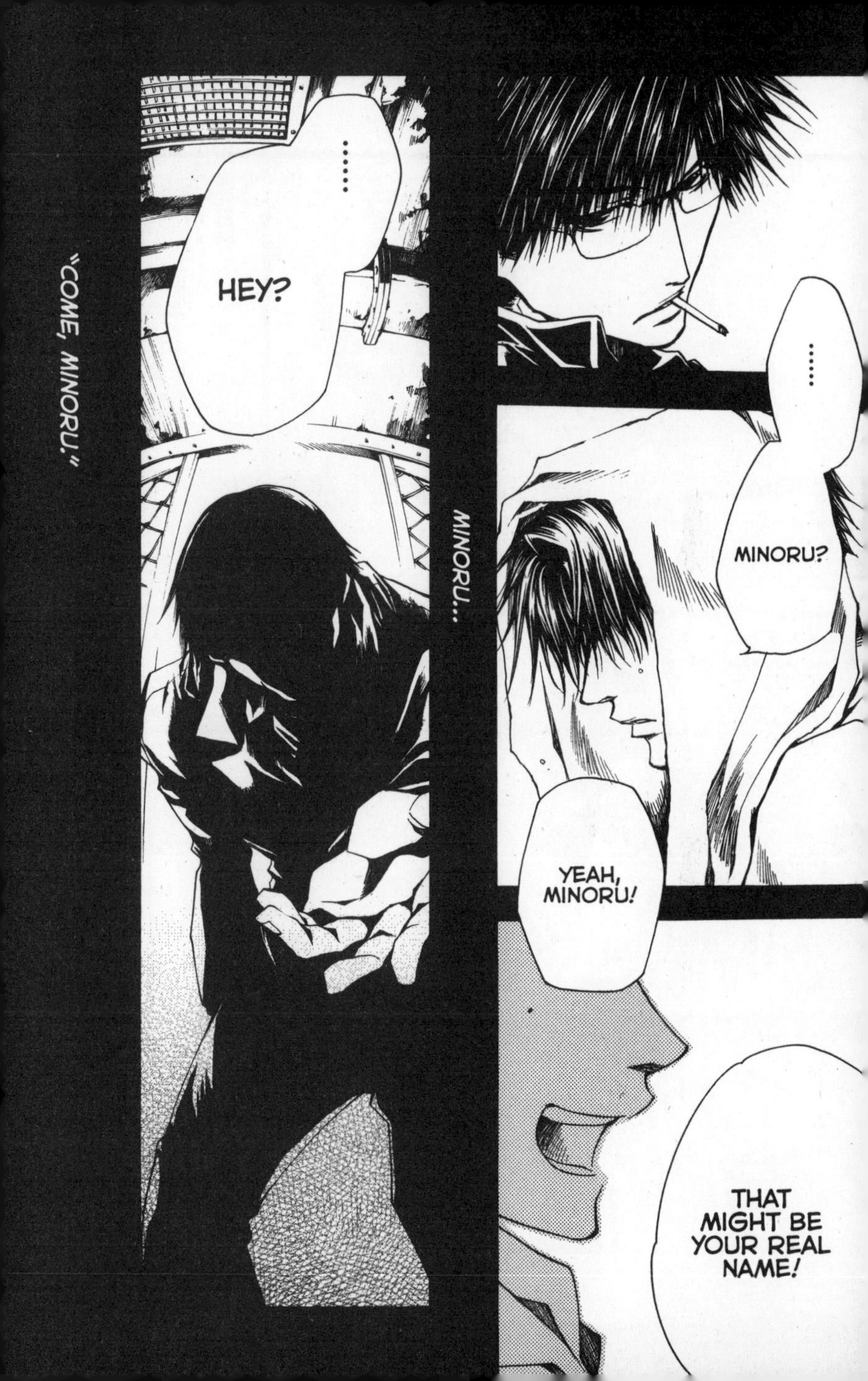
......
MINORU?
YEAH, MINORU!
THAT MIGHT BE YOUR REAL NAME!
MINORU...
......
HEY?
"COME, MINORU."

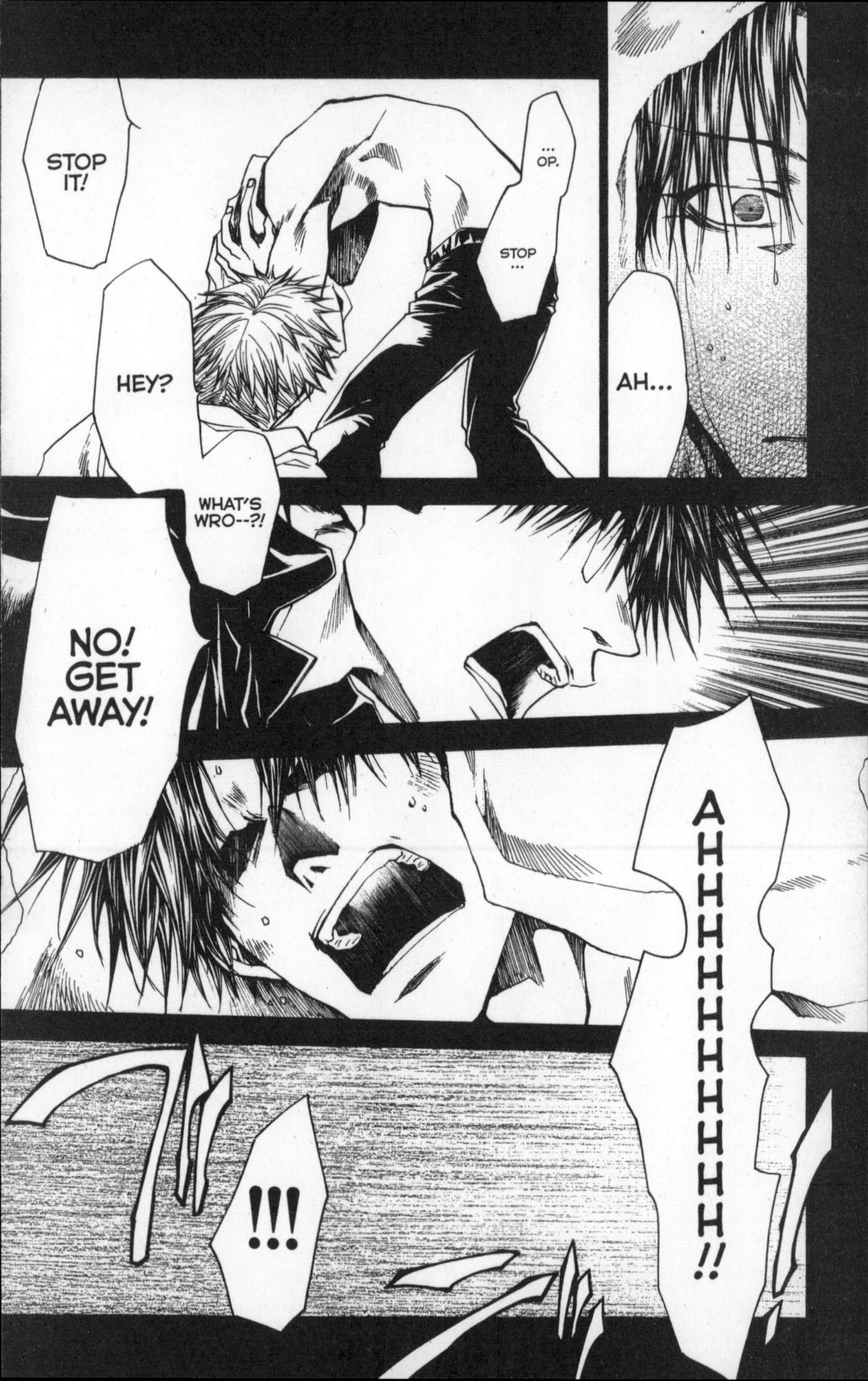
AH...
... OP.
STOP ...
STOP IT!
HEY?
WHAT'S WRO--?!
NO! GET AWAY!
AHHHHHHHHHHHHH!!
!!!

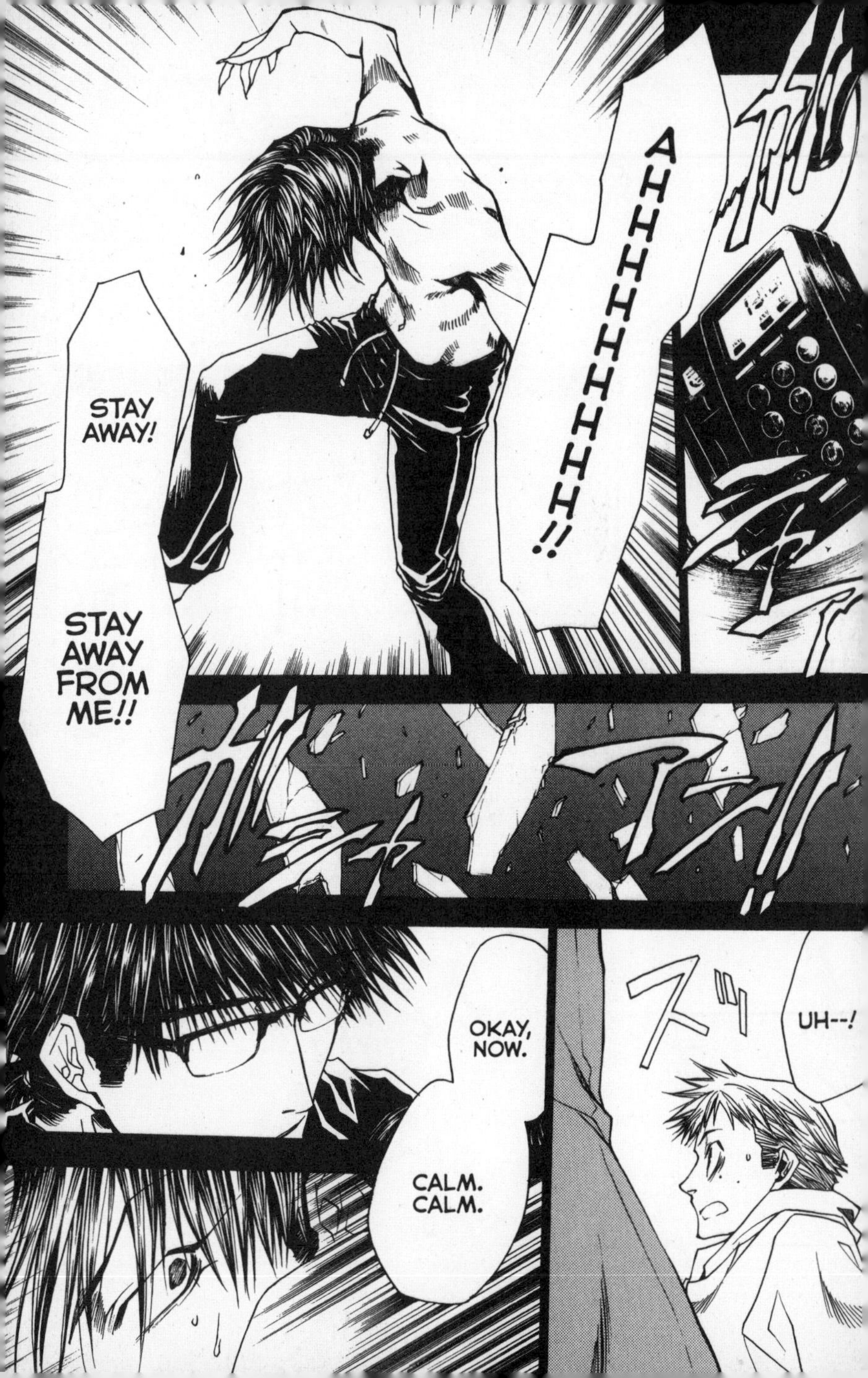
AHHHHHHHHHHH!!
STAY AWAY!
STAY AWAY FROM ME!!
UH--!
OKAY, NOW.
CALM. CALM.

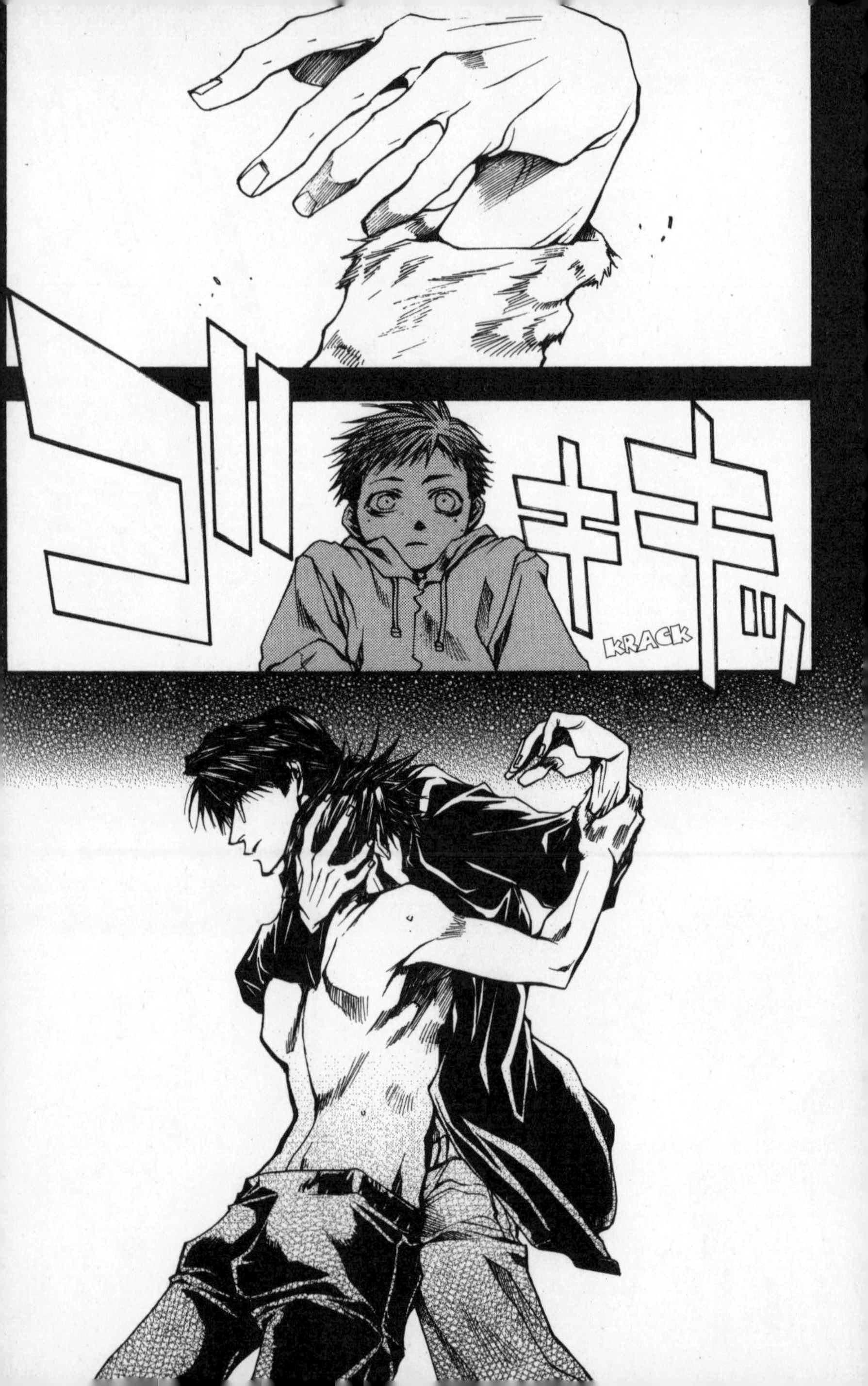
ゴキキッ
KRACK

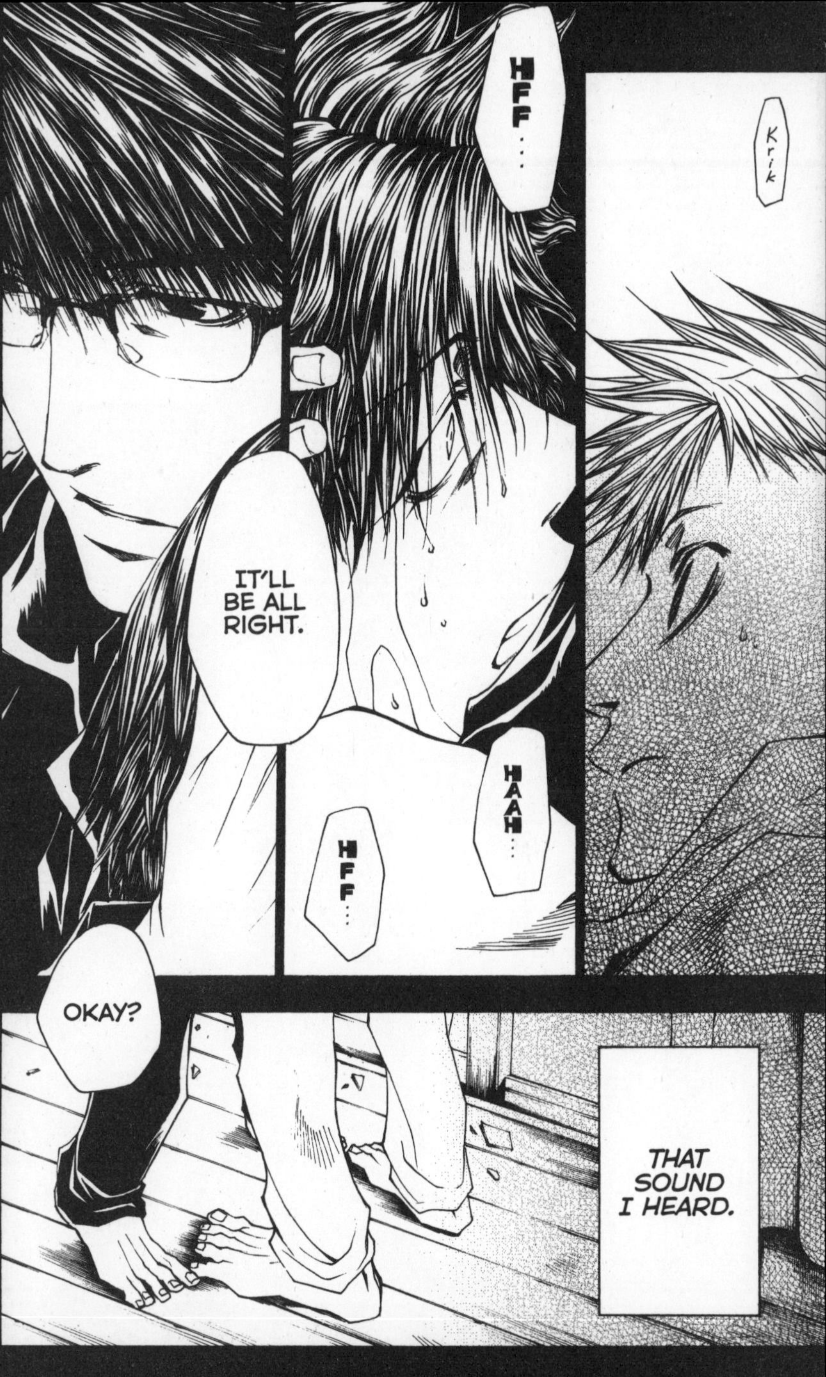
Krik
HFF...
HAAH...
HFF...
IT'LL BE ALL RIGHT.
OKAY?
THAT SOUND I HEARD.

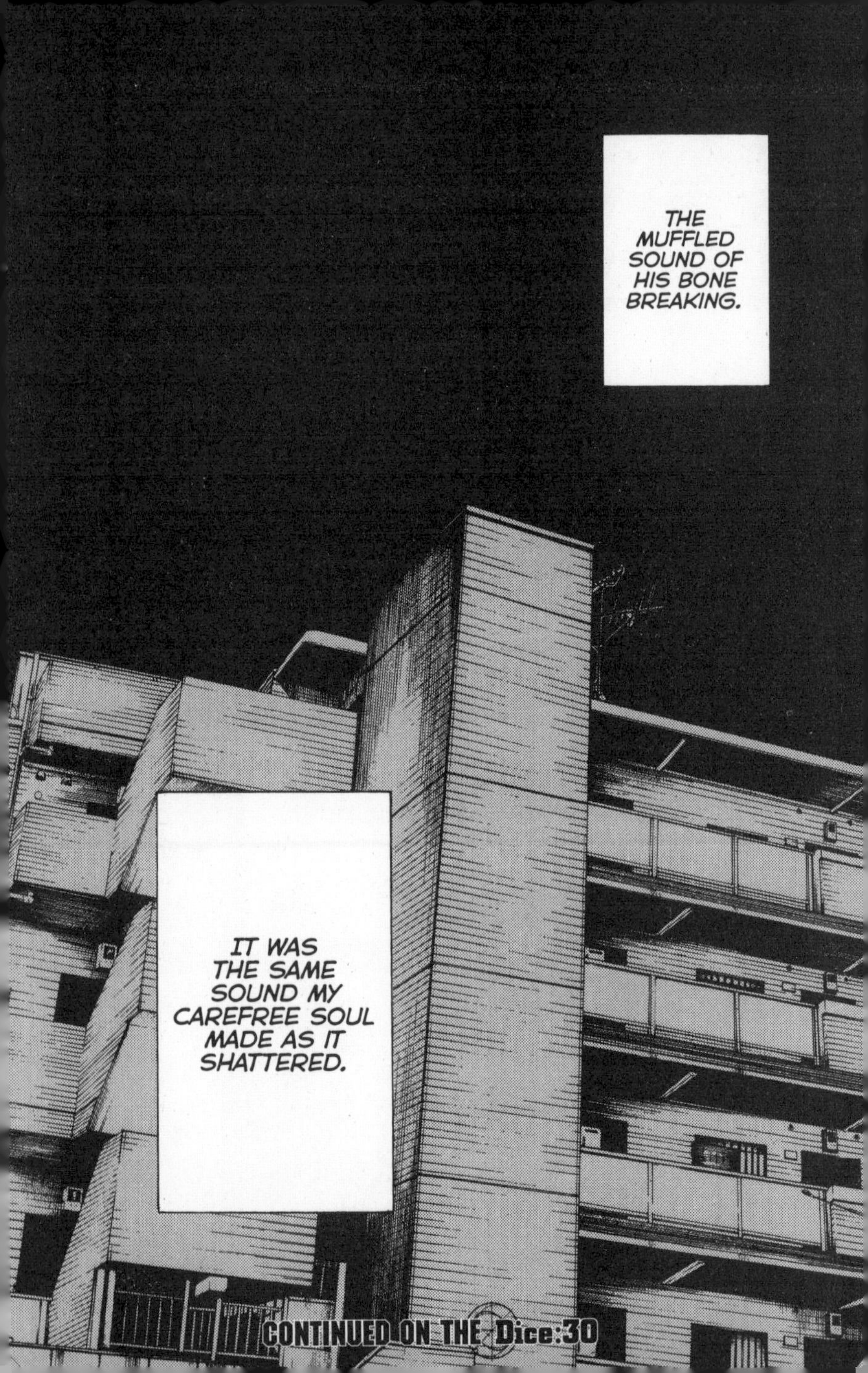
THE MUFFLED SOUND OF HIS BONE BREAKING.
IT WAS THE SAME SOUND MY CAREFREE SOUL MADE AS IT SHATTERED.
CONTINUED ON THE Dice:30

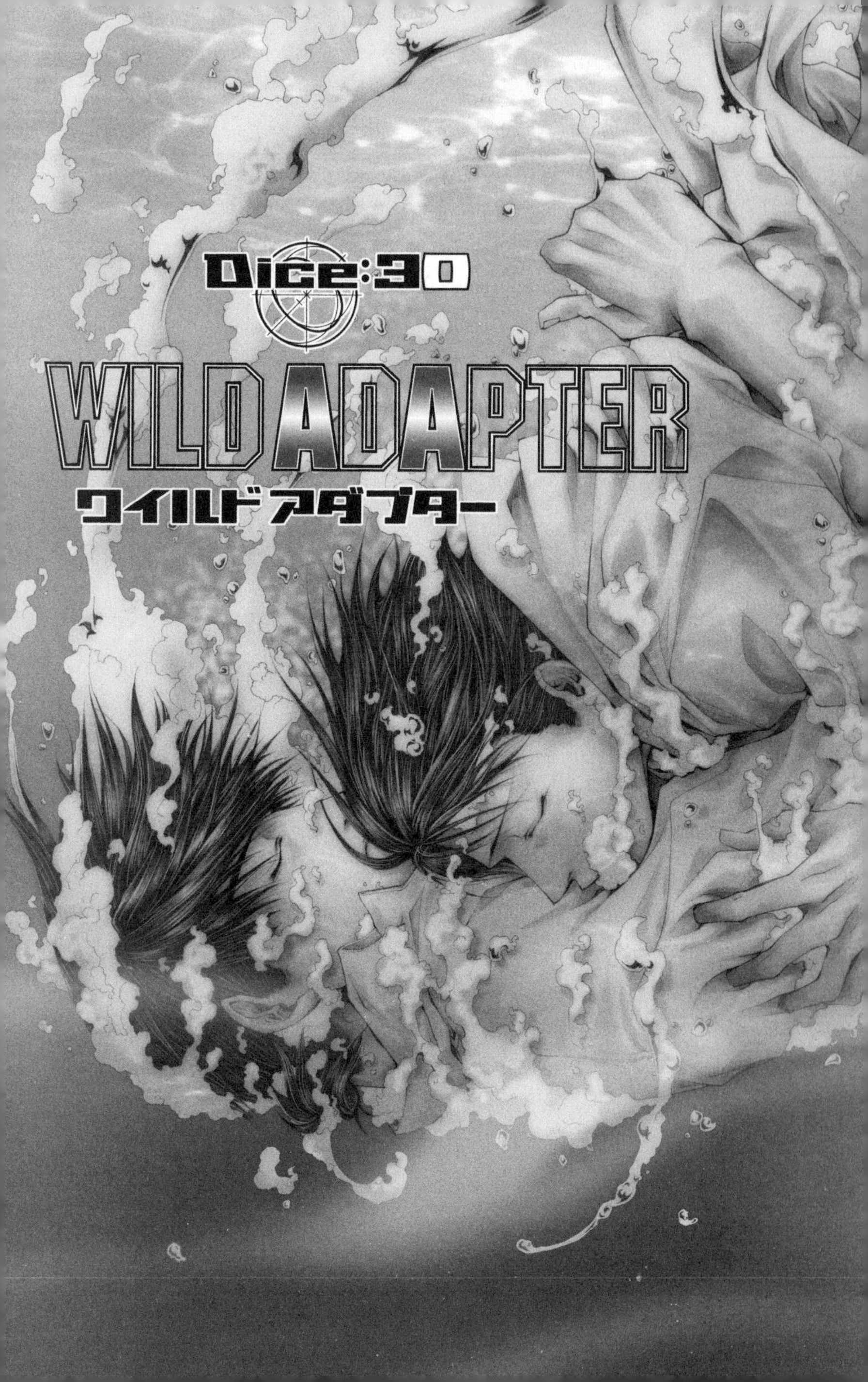
Dice:30
WILD ADAPTER
ワイルドアダプター

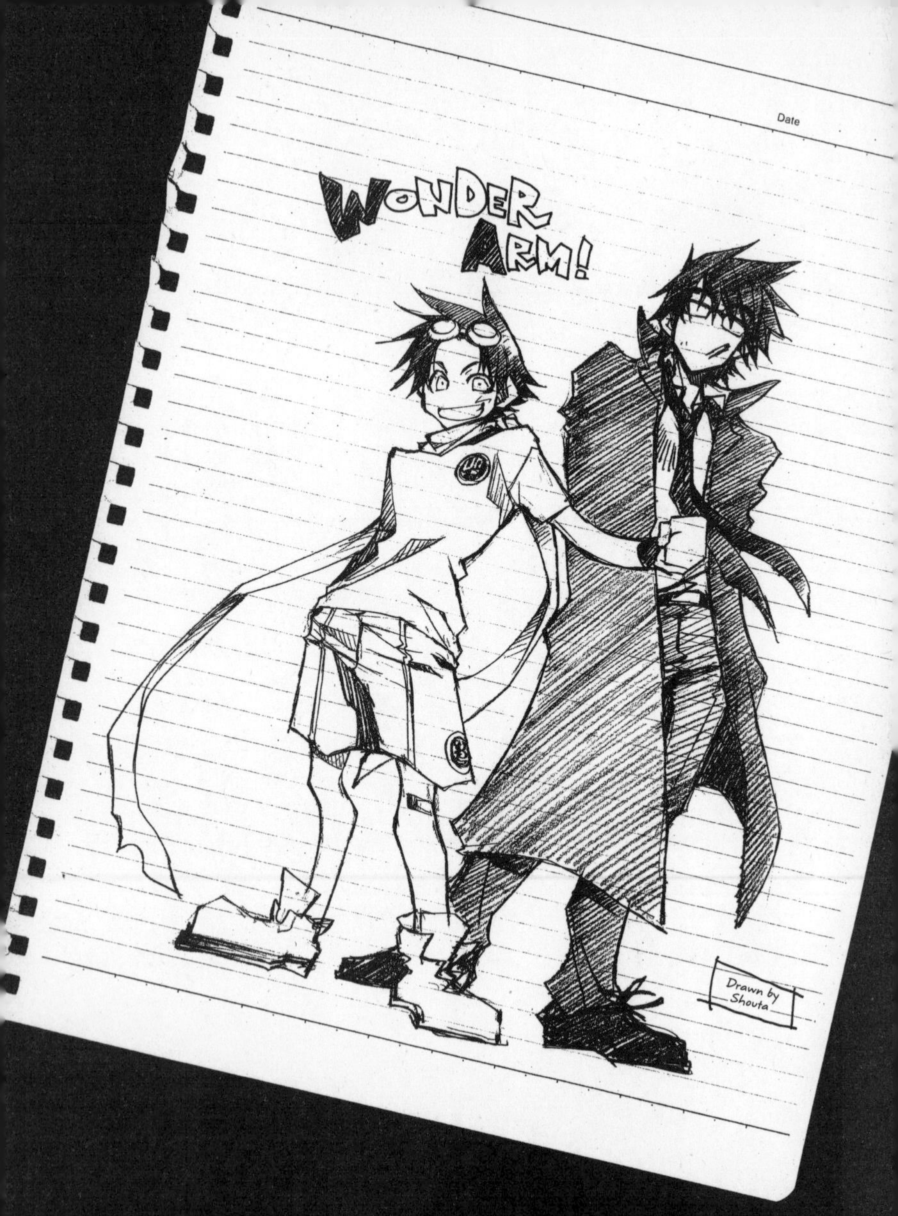
Date
WONDER ARM!
Drawn by Shouta

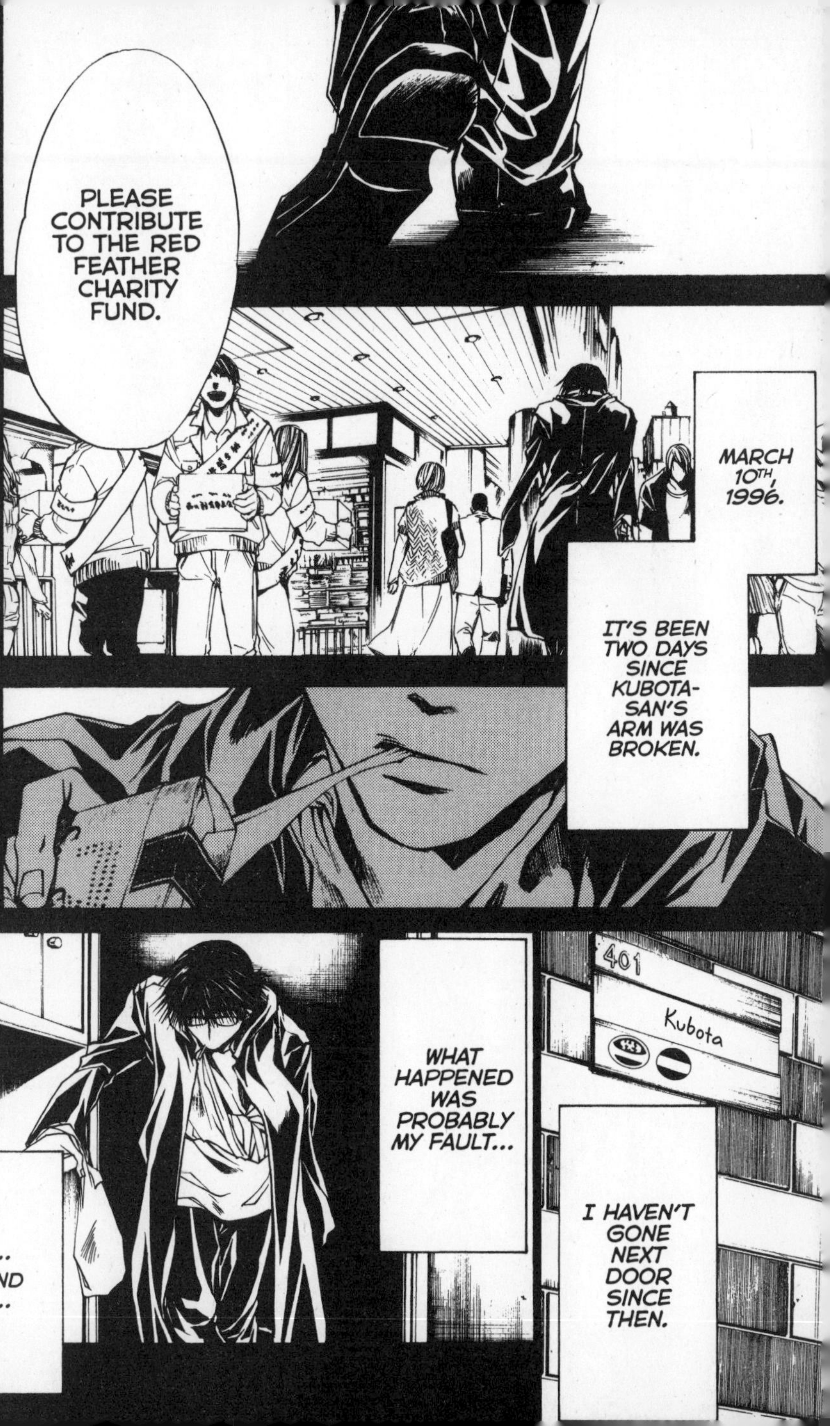
PLEASE CONTRIBUTE TO THE RED FEATHER CHARITY FUND.
MARCH 10TH, 1996.
IT'S BEEN TWO DAYS SINCE KUBOTA-SAN'S ARM WAS BROKEN.
401
Kubota
I HAVEN'T GONE NEXT DOOR SINCE THEN.
WHAT HAPPENED WAS PROBABLY MY FAULT...
... AND ...

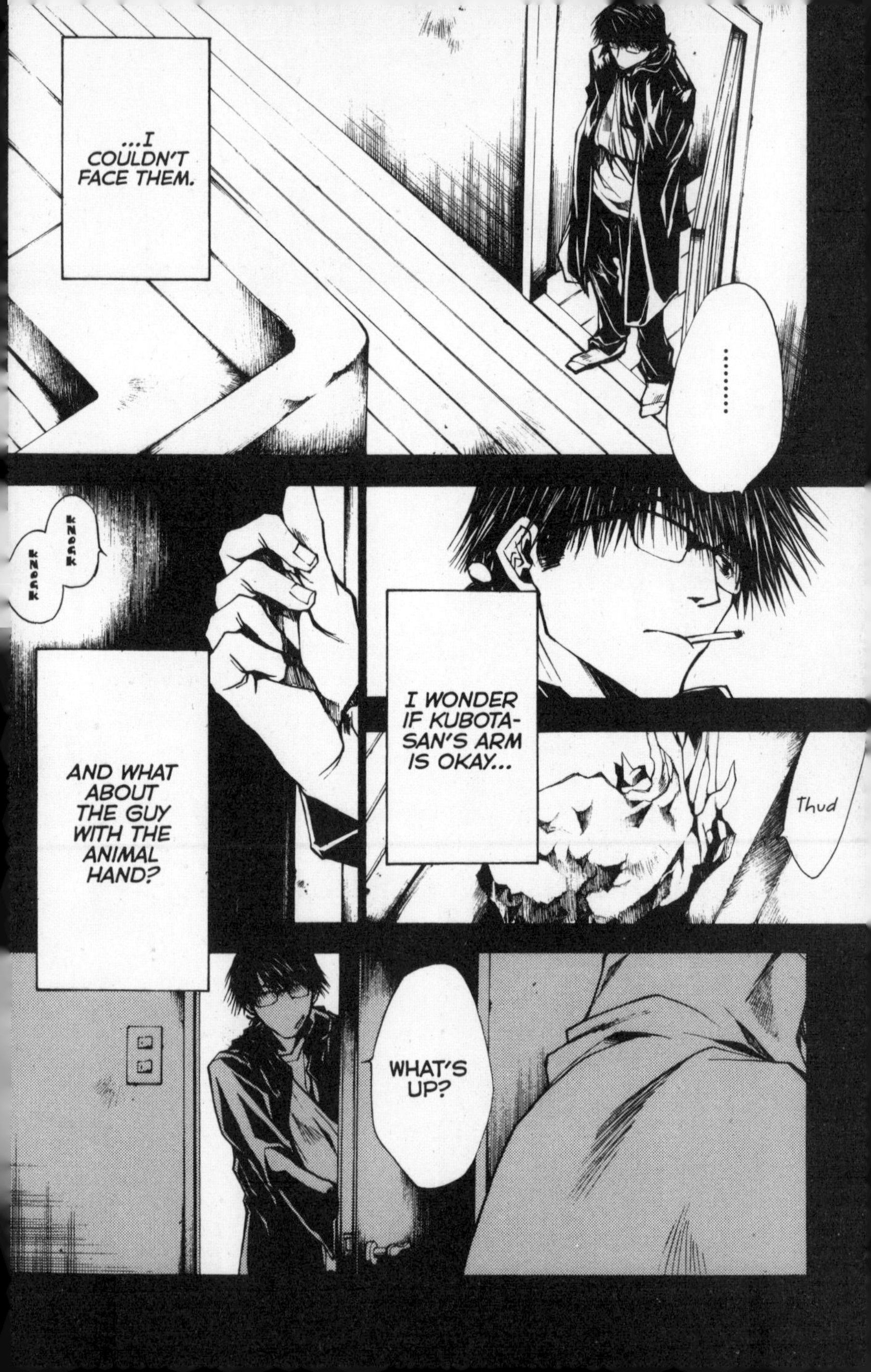
...I COULDN'T FACE THEM.
......
I WONDER IF KUBOTA-SAN'S ARM IS OKAY...
Thud
knock knock
AND WHAT ABOUT THE GUY WITH THE ANIMAL HAND?
WHAT'S UP?

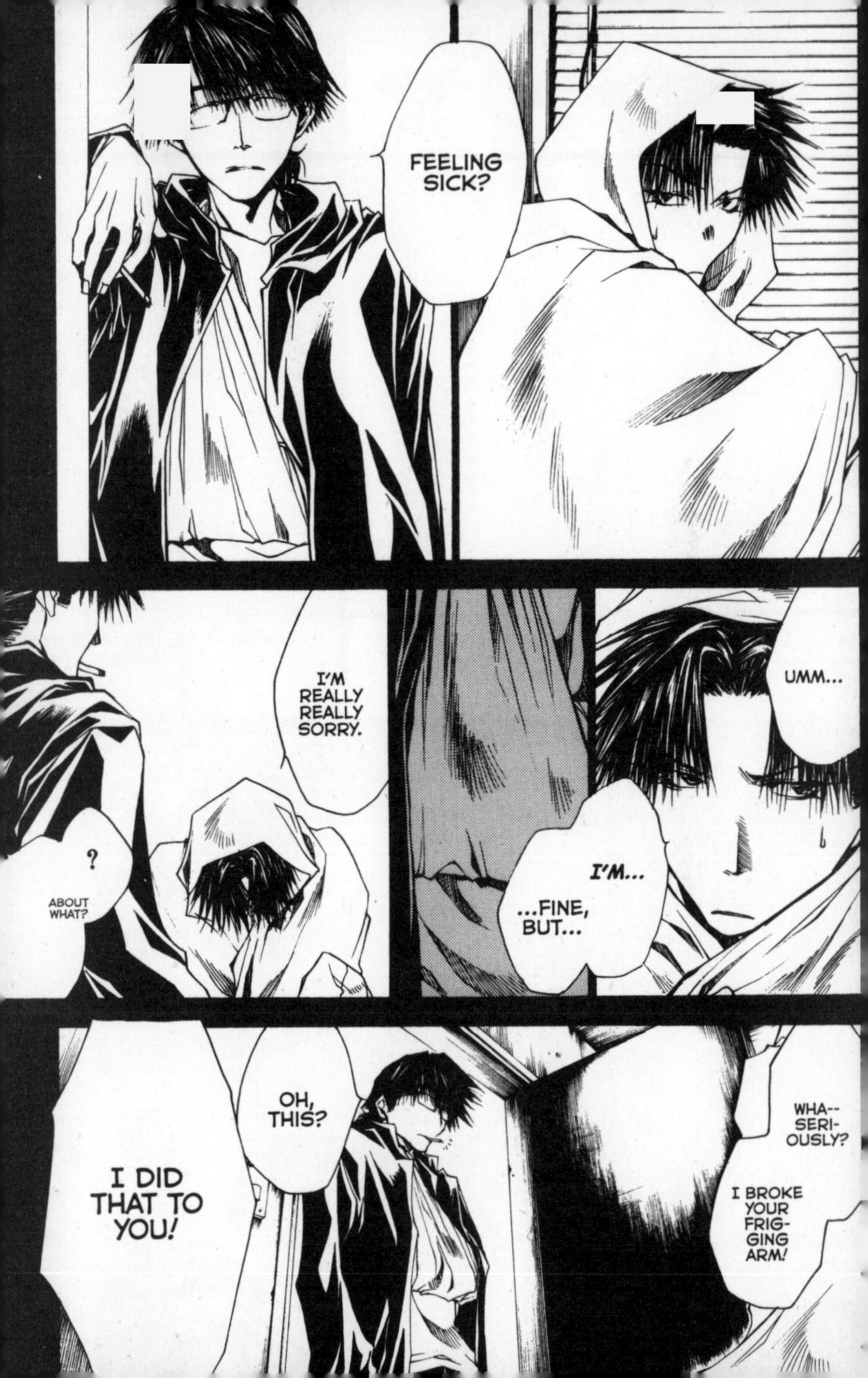
FEELING SICK?
UMM...
I'M...
...FINE, BUT...
I'M REALLY REALLY SORRY.
?
ABOUT WHAT?
WHA-- SERIOUSLY?
OH, THIS?
I BROKE YOUR FRIG- GING ARM!
I DID THAT TO YOU!

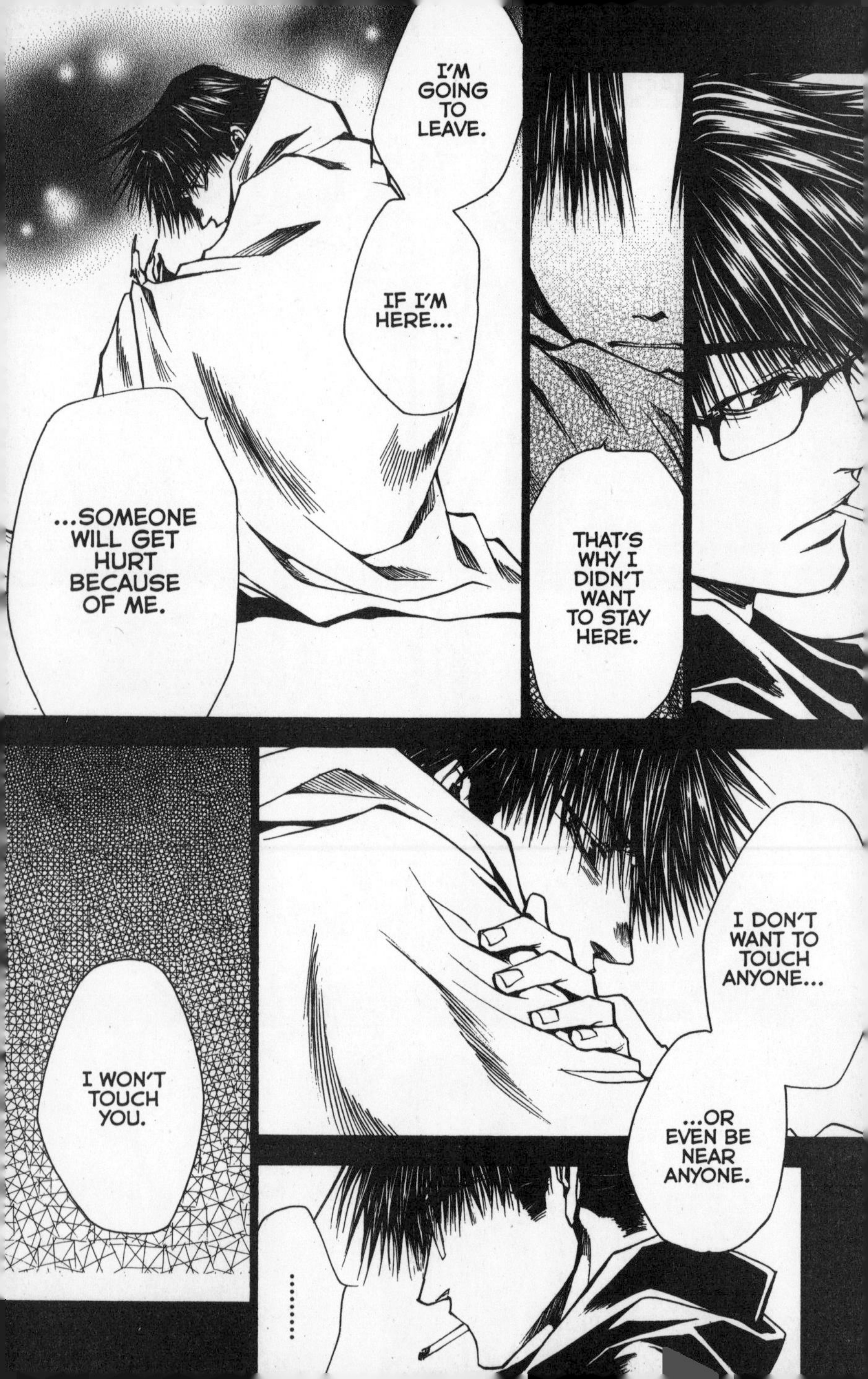
THAT'S WHY I DIDN'T WANT TO STAY HERE.
I'M GOING TO LEAVE.
IF I'M HERE...
...SOMEONE WILL GET HURT BECAUSE OF ME.
I DON'T WANT TO TOUCH ANYONE...
...OR EVEN BE NEAR ANYONE.
......
I WON'T TOUCH YOU.

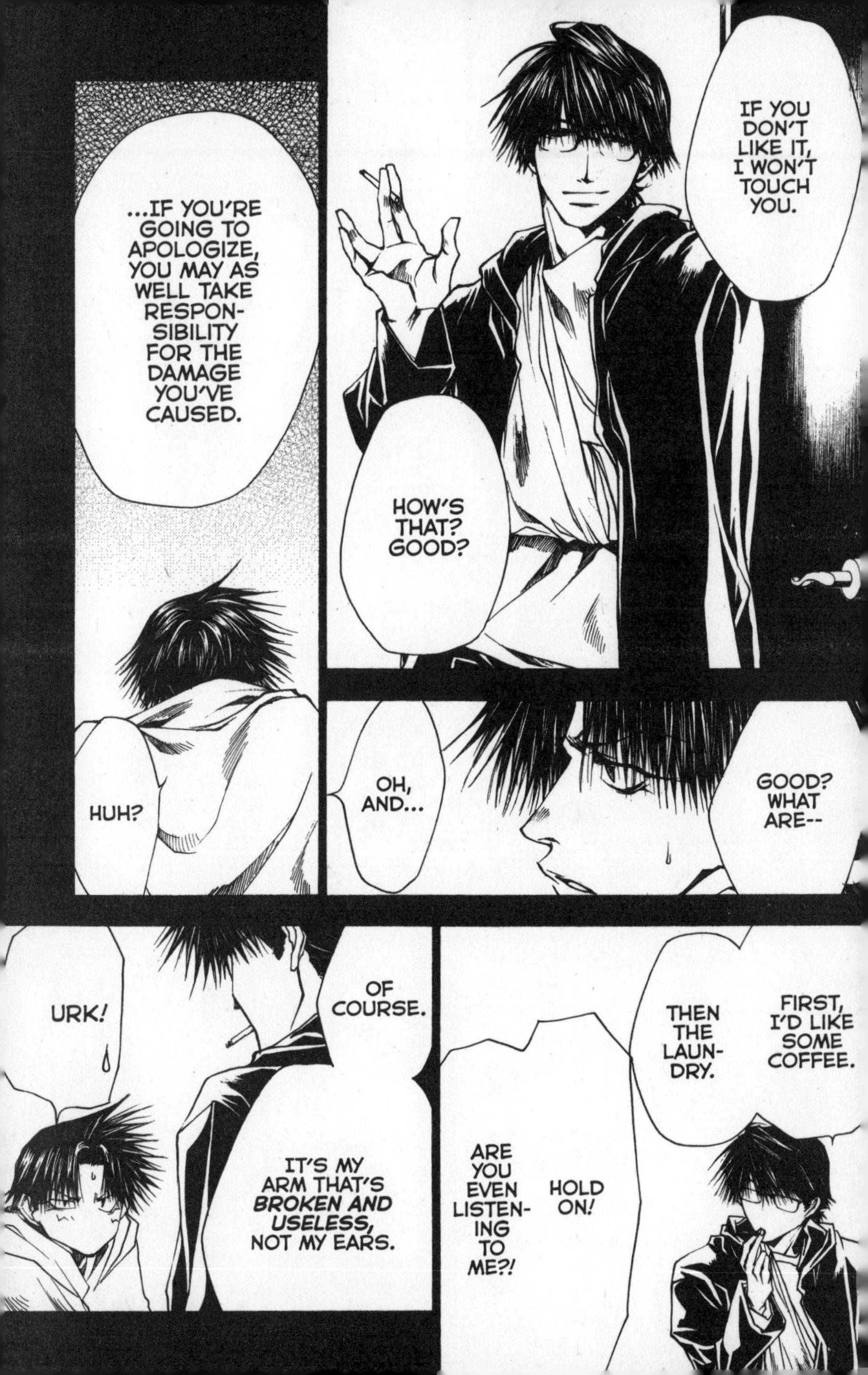
IF YOU DON'T LIKE IT, I WON'T TOUCH YOU.
HOW'S THAT? GOOD?
GOOD? WHAT ARE--
OH, AND...
...IF YOU'RE GOING TO APOLOGIZE, YOU MAY AS WELL TAKE RESPON-SIBILITY FOR THE DAMAGE YOU'VE CAUSED.
HUH?
FIRST, I'D LIKE SOME COFFEE.
THEN THE LAUN-DRY.
HOLD ON!
ARE YOU EVEN LISTEN-ING TO ME?!
OF COURSE.
IT'S MY ARM THAT'S *BROKEN AND USELESS,* NOT MY EARS.
URK!

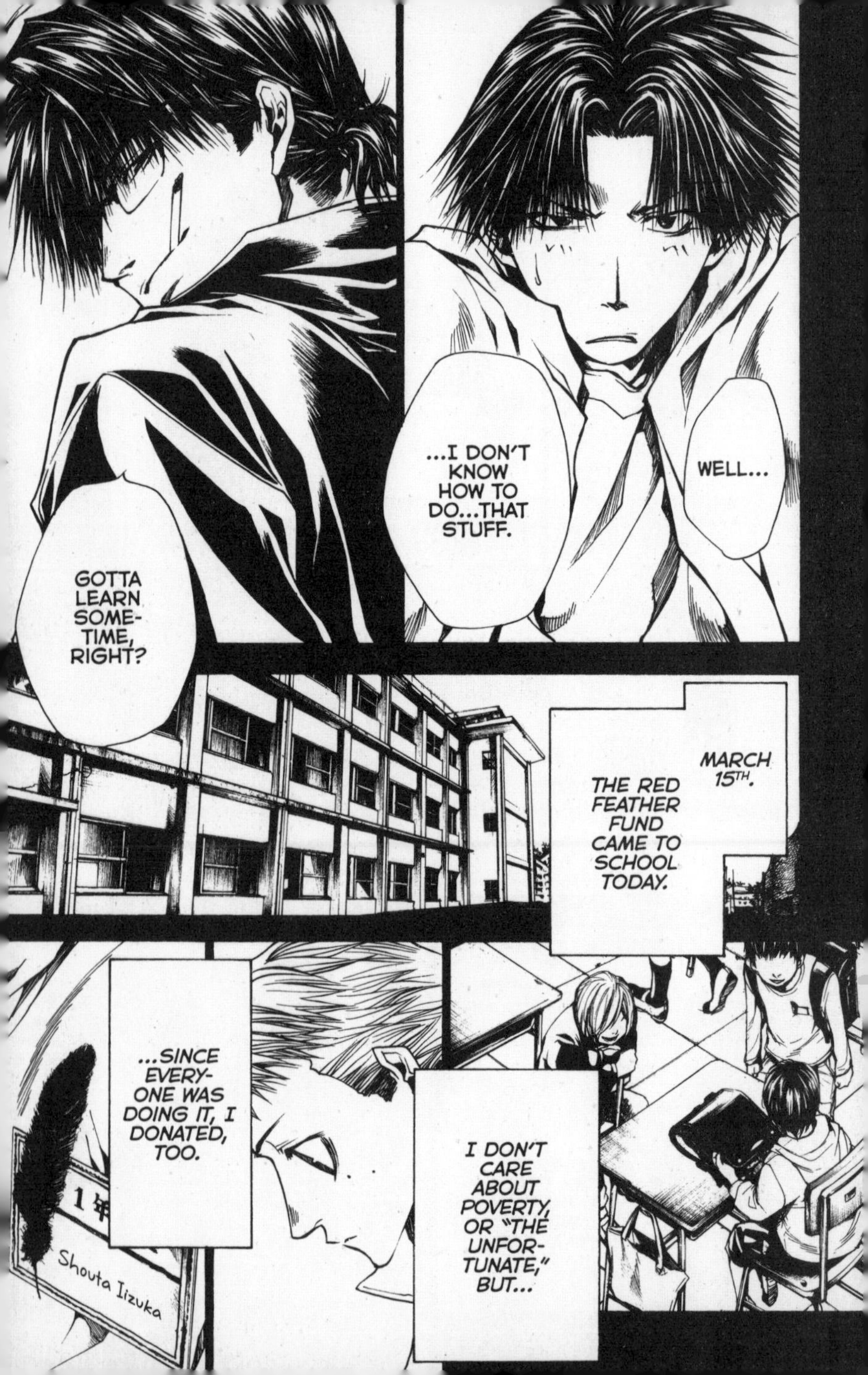
WELL...
...I DON'T KNOW HOW TO DO...THAT STUFF.
GOTTA LEARN SOME-TIME, RIGHT?
MARCH 15TH.
THE RED FEATHER FUND CAME TO SCHOOL TODAY.
I DON'T CARE ABOUT POVERTY, OR "THE UNFORTU-NATE," BUT...
...SINCE EVERY-ONE WAS DOING IT, I DONATED, TOO.
1年
Shouta Iizuka

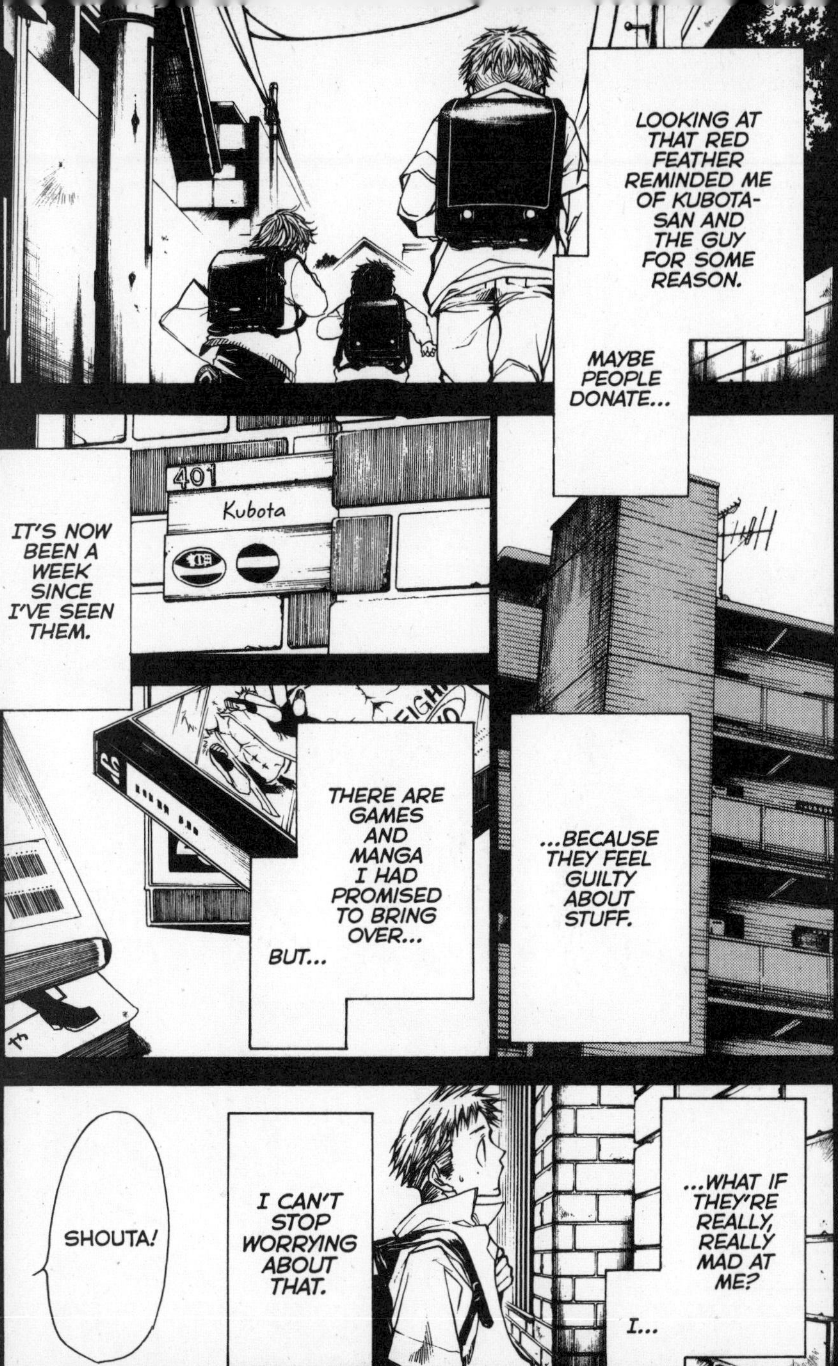
LOOKING AT THAT RED FEATHER REMINDED ME OF KUBOTA-SAN AND THE GUY FOR SOME REASON.
MAYBE PEOPLE DONATE...
...BECAUSE THEY FEEL GUILTY ABOUT STUFF.
IT'S NOW BEEN A WEEK SINCE I'VE SEEN THEM.
401
Kubota
THERE ARE GAMES AND MANGA I HAD PROMISED TO BRING OVER...
BUT...
...WHAT IF THEY'RE REALLY, REALLY MAD AT ME?
I...
I CAN'T STOP WORRYING ABOUT THAT.
SHOUTA!

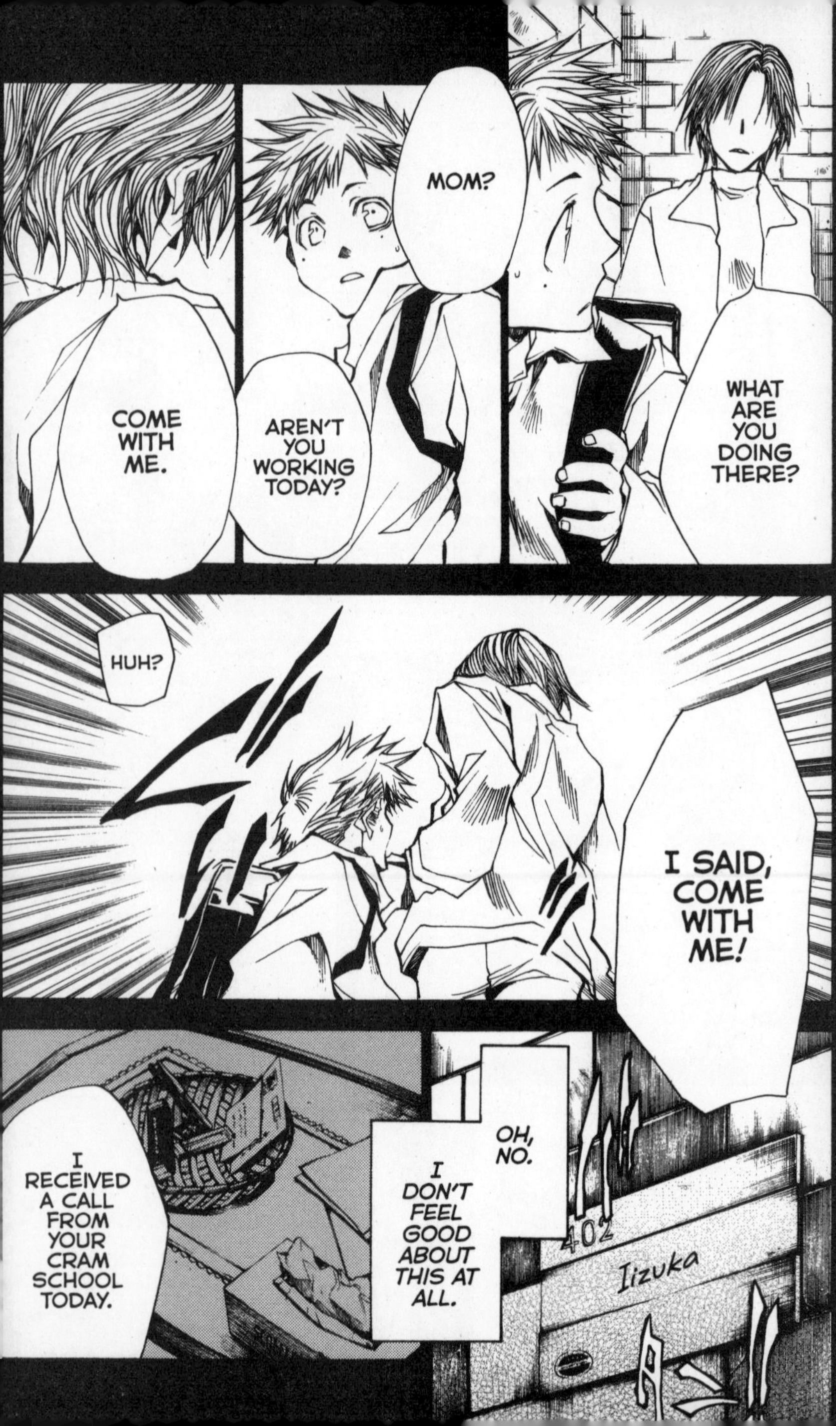
WHAT ARE YOU DOING THERE?
MOM?
AREN'T YOU WORKING TODAY?
COME WITH ME.
I SAID, COME WITH ME!
HUH?
OH, NO.
I DON'T FEEL GOOD ABOUT THIS AT ALL.
402
Iizuka
I RECEIVED A CALL FROM YOUR CRAM SCHOOL TODAY.

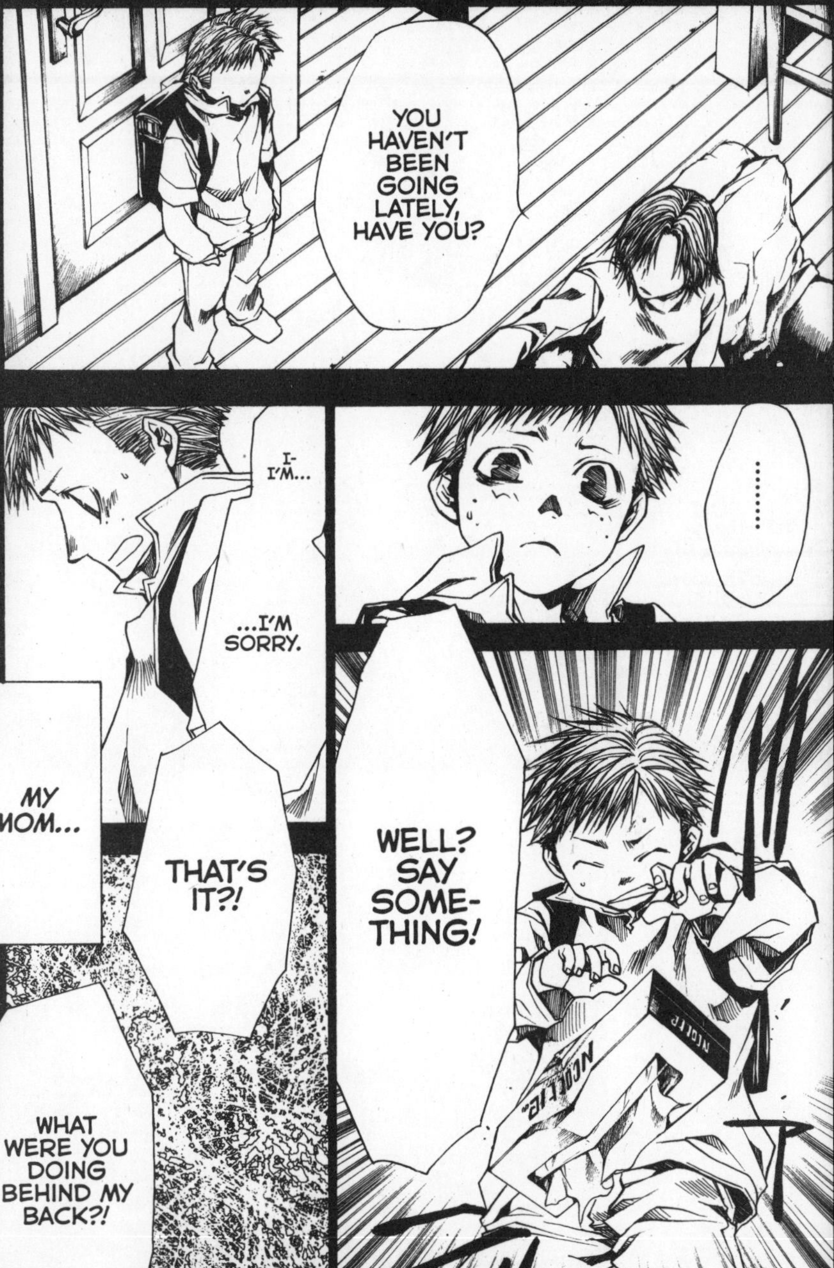
YOU HAVEN'T BEEN GOING LATELY, HAVE YOU?
......
I- I'M...
...I'M SORRY.
WELL? SAY SOME-THING!
THAT'S IT?!
MY MOM...
WHAT WERE YOU DOING BEHIND MY BACK?!

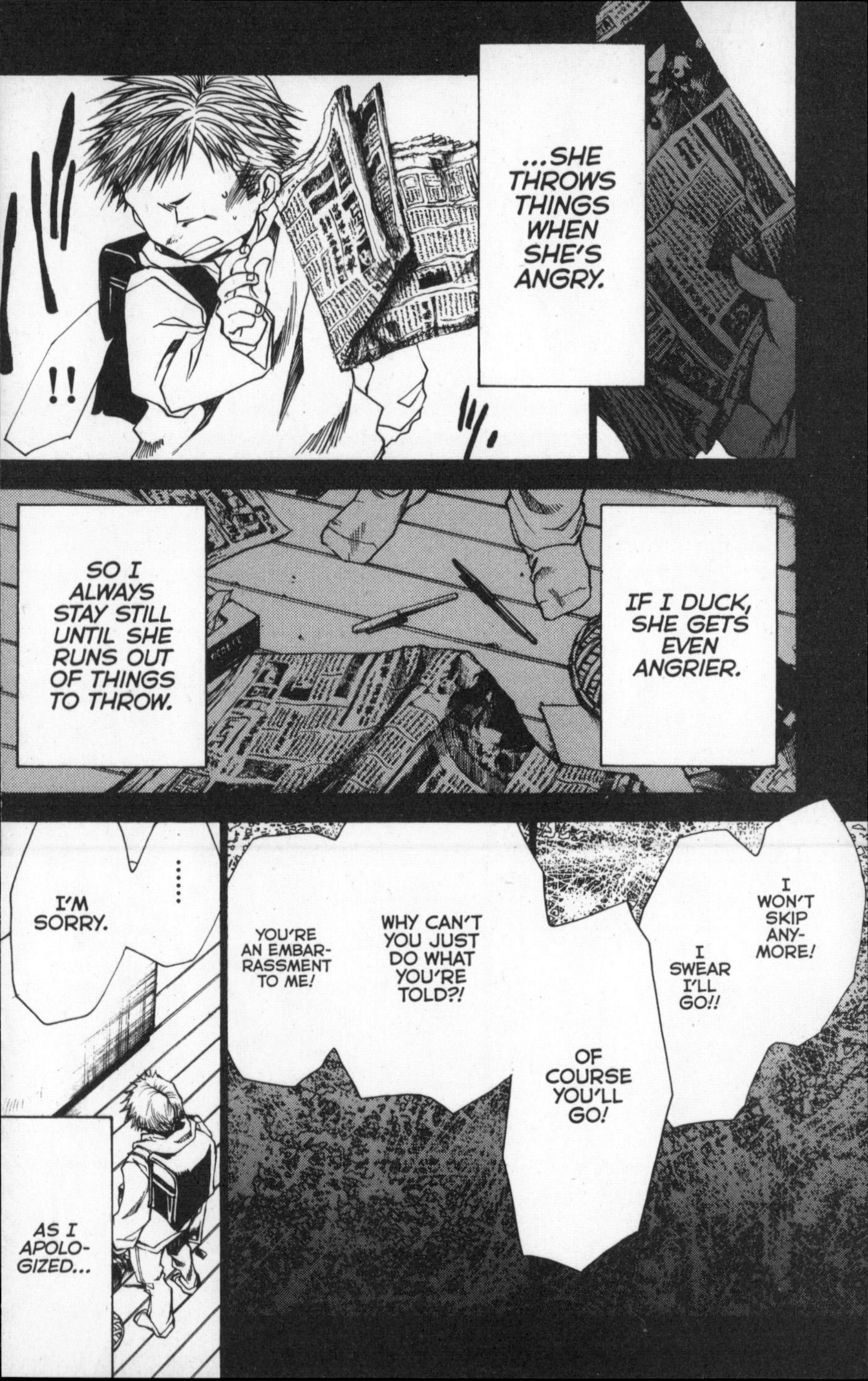
...SHE THROWS THINGS WHEN SHE'S ANGRY.
!!
IF I DUCK, SHE GETS EVEN ANGRIER.
SO I ALWAYS STAY STILL UNTIL SHE RUNS OUT OF THINGS TO THROW.
I WON'T SKIP ANYMORE!
I SWEAR I'LL GO!!
WHY CAN'T YOU JUST DO WHAT YOU'RE TOLD?!
YOU'RE AN EMBARRASSMENT TO ME!
OF COURSE YOU'LL GO!
......
I'M SORRY.
AS I APOLOGIZED...

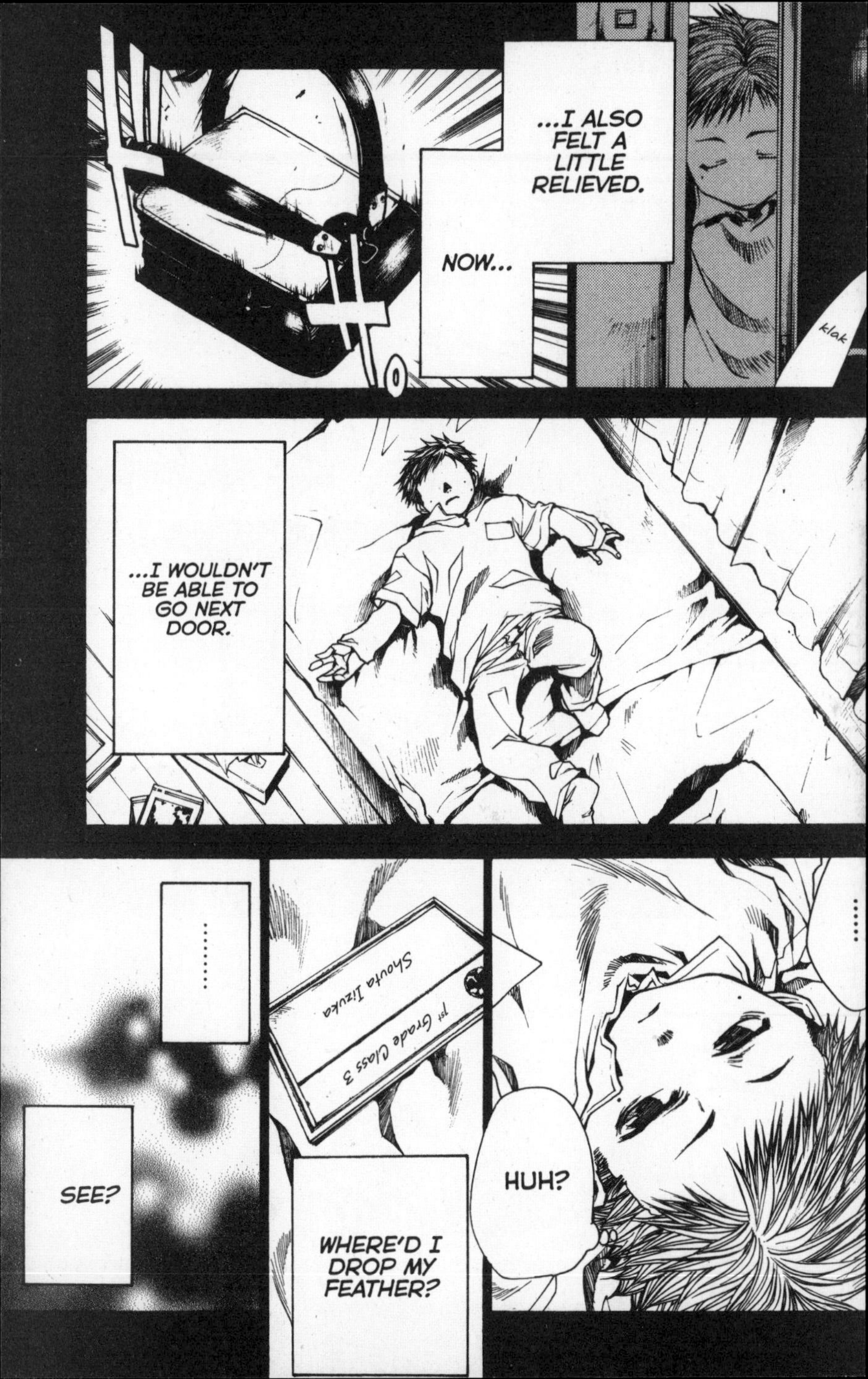
...I ALSO FELT A LITTLE RELIEVED.
klak
NOW...
...I WOULDN'T BE ABLE TO GO NEXT DOOR.
...
HUH?
1st Grade Class 3
Shouta Iizuka
WHERE'D I DROP MY FEATHER?
......
SEE?

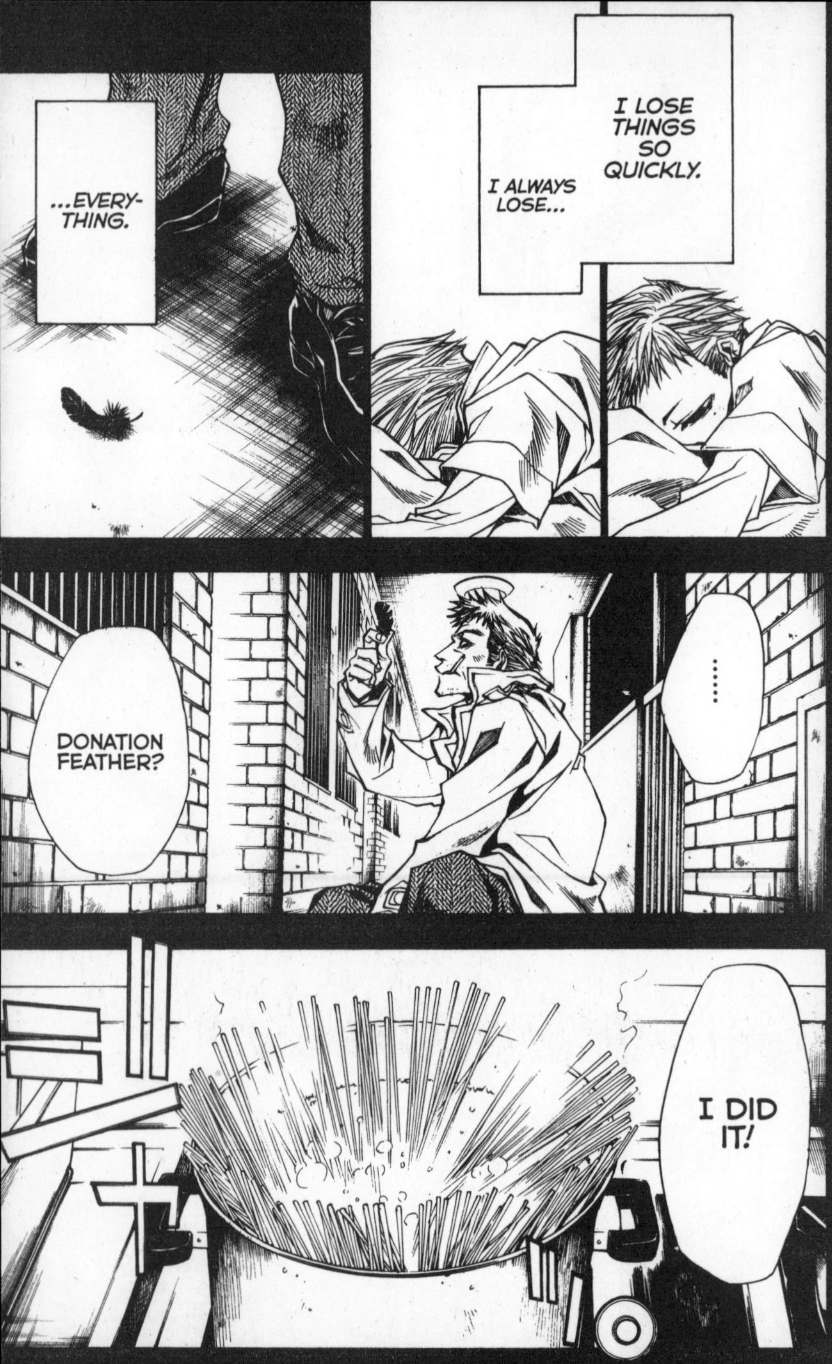
I LOSE THINGS SO QUICKLY.
I ALWAYS LOSE...
...EVERY-THING.
......
DONATION FEATHER?
I DID IT!

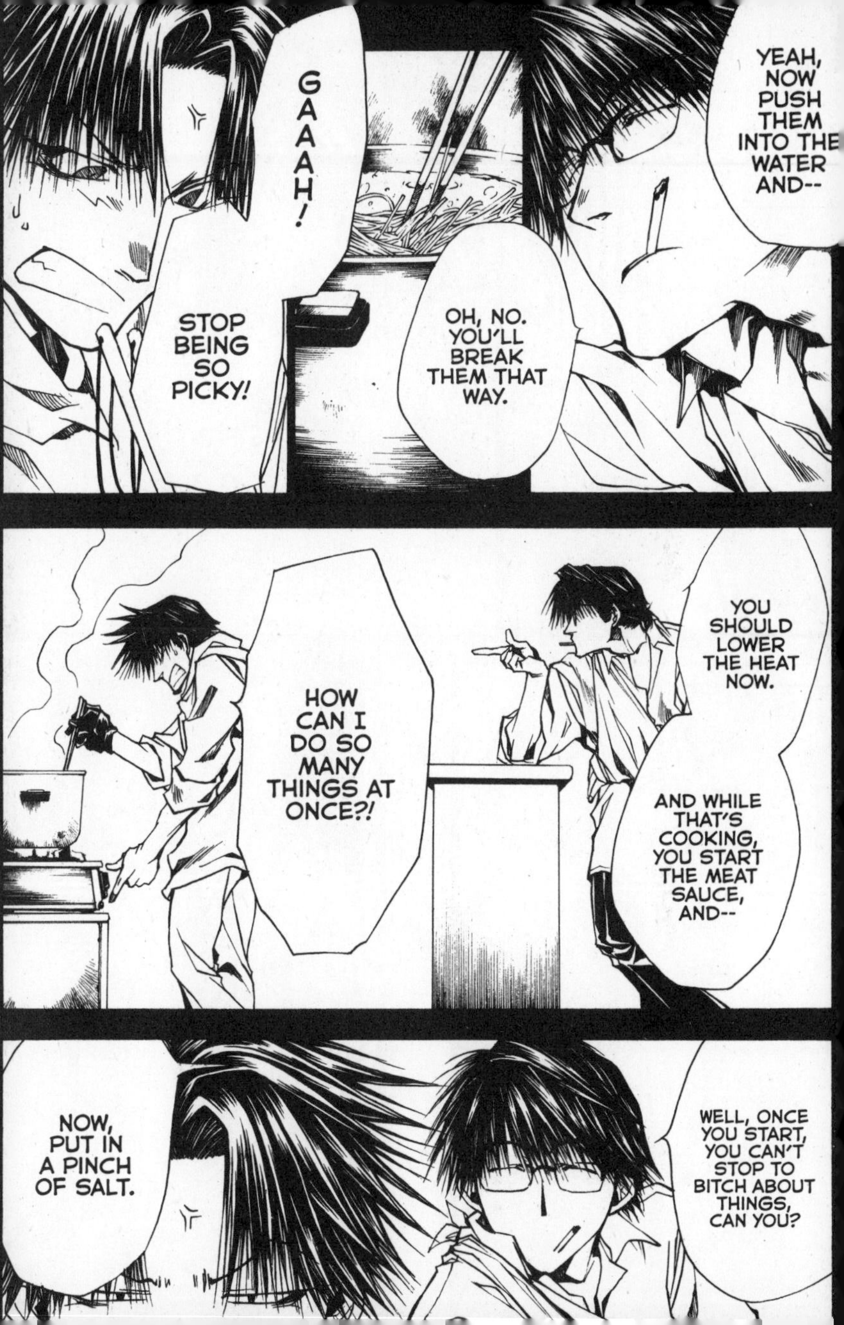
YEAH, NOW PUSH THEM INTO THE WATER AND--
OH, NO. YOU'LL BREAK THEM THAT WAY.
GAAAH!
STOP BEING SO PICKY!
YOU SHOULD LOWER THE HEAT NOW.
AND WHILE THAT'S COOKING, YOU START THE MEAT SAUCE, AND--
HOW CAN I DO SO MANY THINGS AT ONCE?!
WELL, ONCE YOU START, YOU CAN'T STOP TO BITCH ABOUT THINGS, CAN YOU?
NOW, PUT IN A PINCH OF SALT.

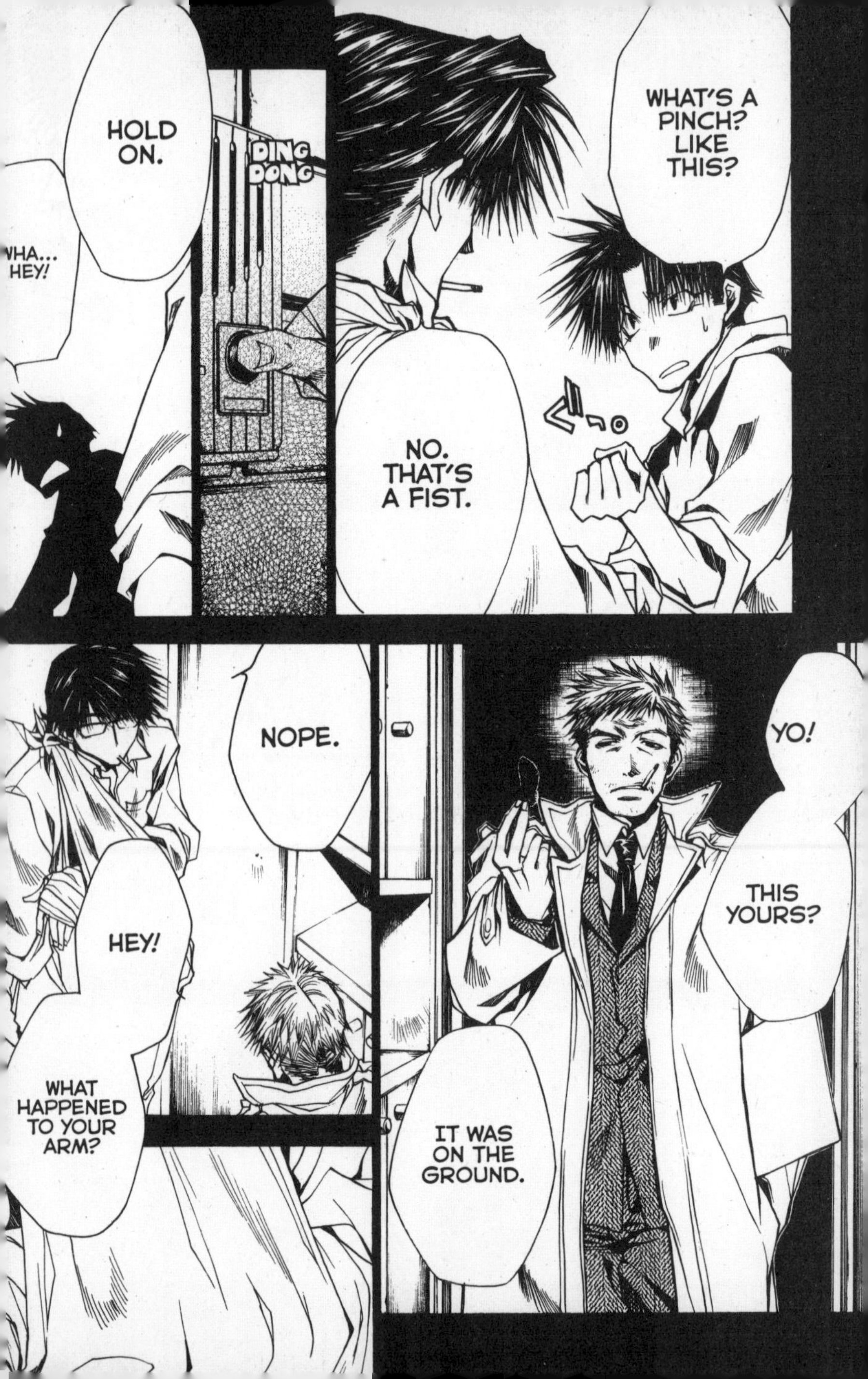
WHAT'S A PINCH? LIKE THIS?
NO. THAT'S A FIST.
DING DONG
HOLD ON.
WHA... HEY!
YO!
THIS YOURS?
IT WAS ON THE GROUND.
NOPE.
HEY!
WHAT HAPPENED TO YOUR ARM?

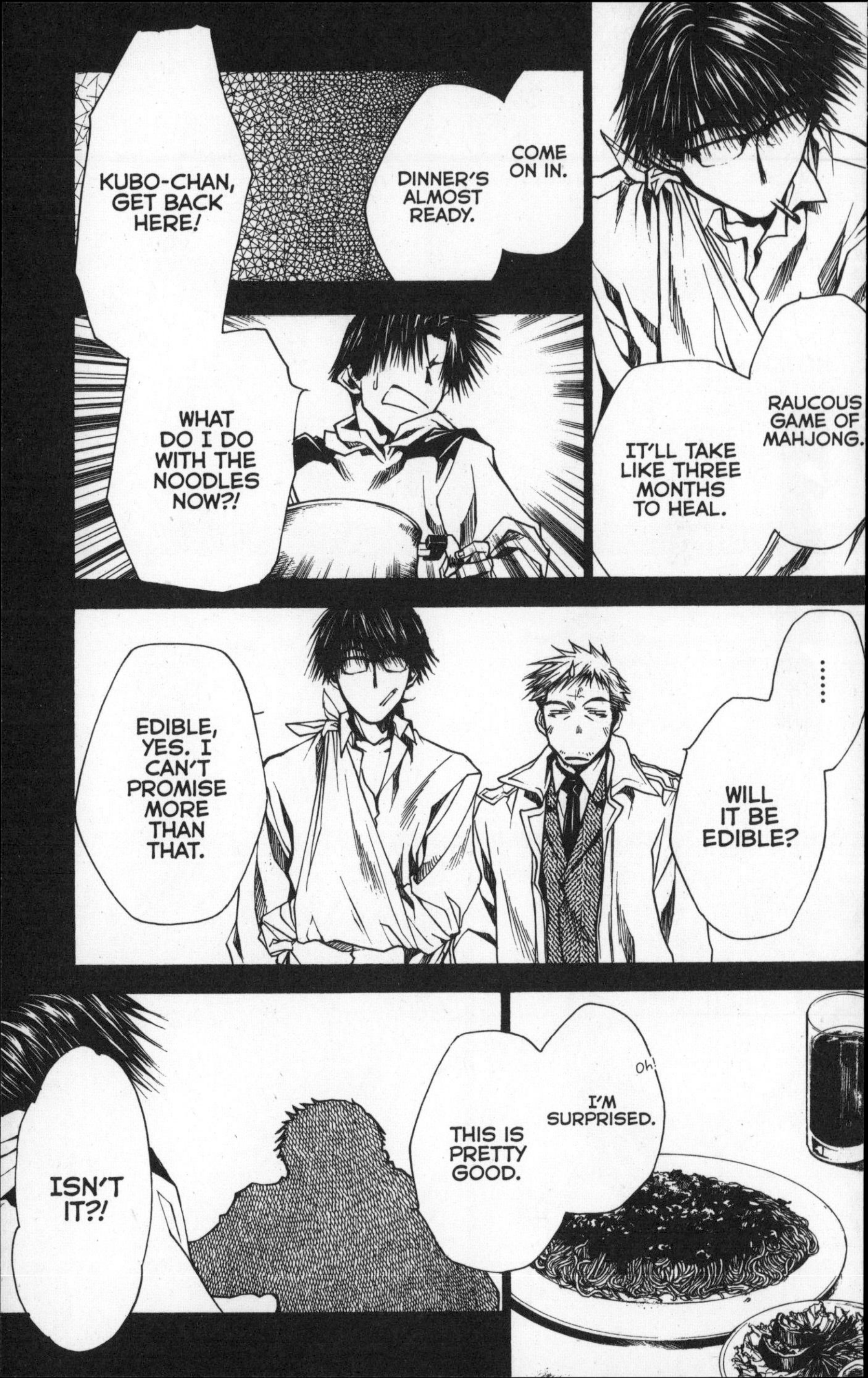
RAUCOUS GAME OF MAHJONG.
IT'LL TAKE LIKE THREE MONTHS TO HEAL.
COME ON IN.
DINNER'S ALMOST READY.
KUBO-CHAN, GET BACK HERE!
WHAT DO I DO WITH THE NOODLES NOW?!
......
WILL IT BE EDIBLE?
EDIBLE, YES. I CAN'T PROMISE MORE THAN THAT.
Oh!
I'M SURPRISED.
THIS IS PRETTY GOOD.
ISN'T IT?!

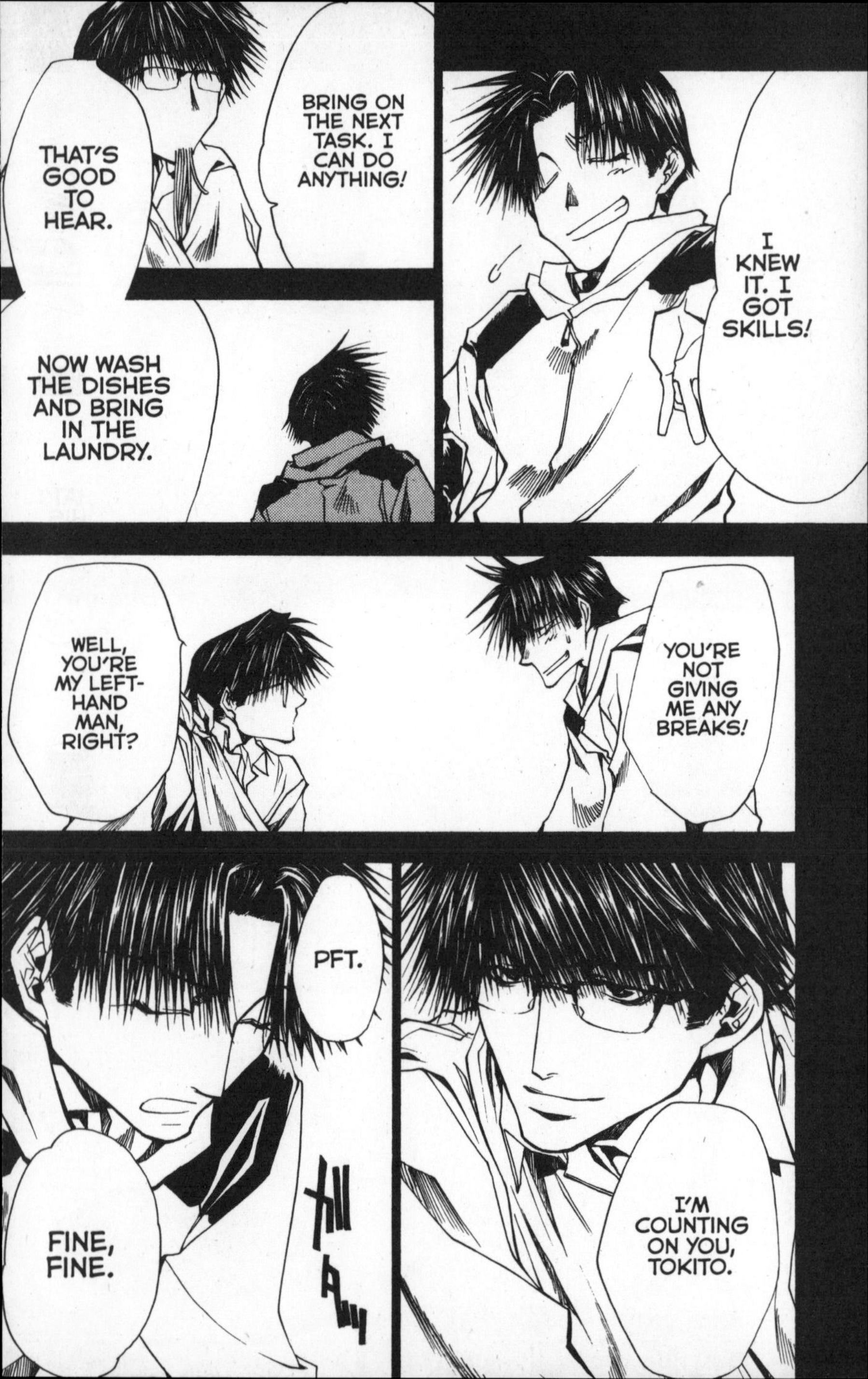
I KNEW IT. I GOT SKILLS!
BRING ON THE NEXT TASK. I CAN DO ANYTHING!
THAT'S GOOD TO HEAR.
NOW WASH THE DISHES AND BRING IN THE LAUNDRY.
YOU'RE NOT GIVING ME ANY BREAKS!
WELL, YOU'RE MY LEFT-HAND MAN, RIGHT?
I'M COUNTING ON YOU, TOKITO.
PFT.
FINE, FINE.

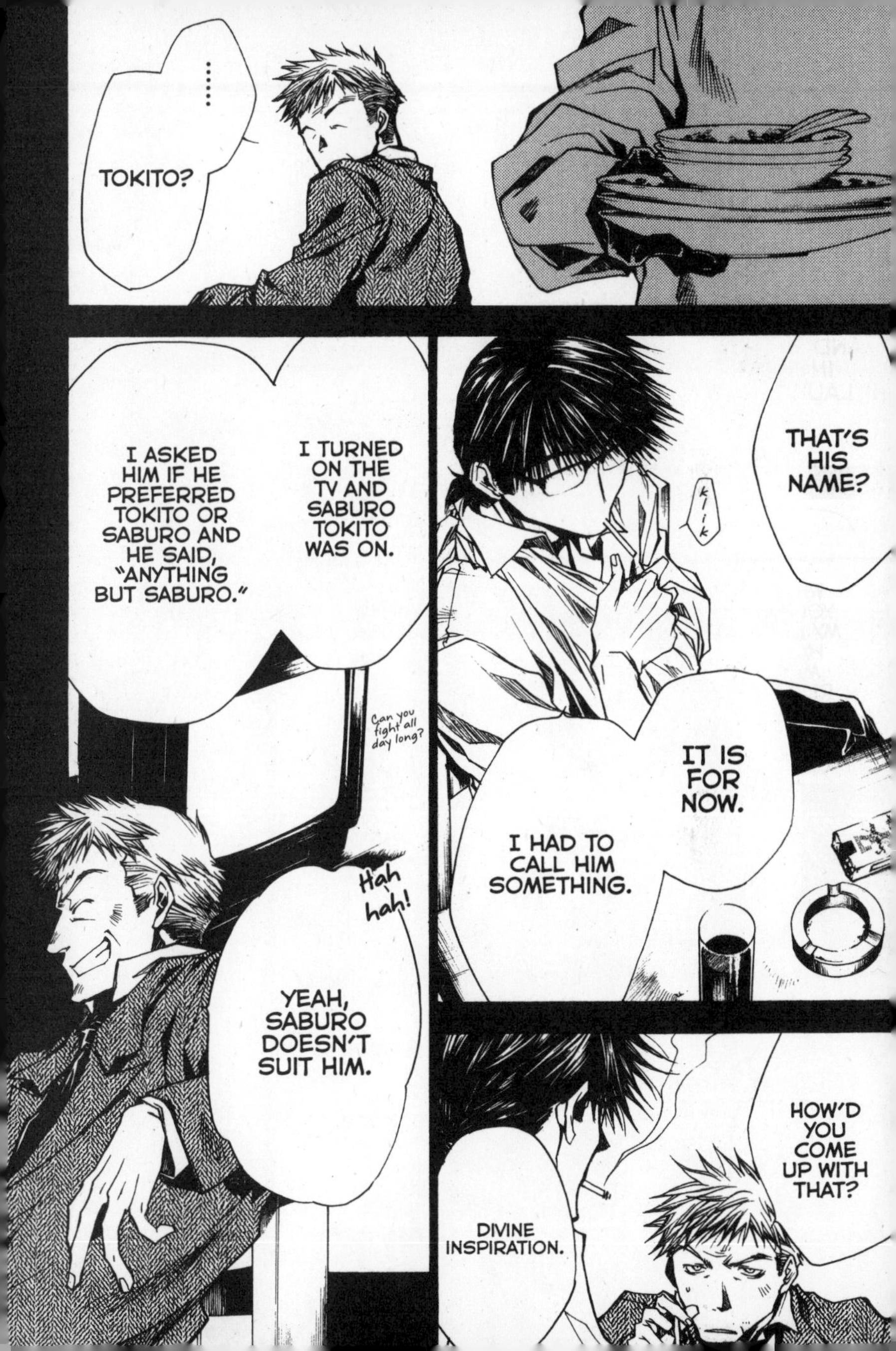
......
TOKITO?
THAT'S HIS NAME?
klik
IT IS FOR NOW.
I HAD TO CALL HIM SOMETHING.
HOW'D YOU COME UP WITH THAT?
DIVINE INSPIRATION.
I TURNED ON THE TV AND SABURO TOKITO WAS ON.
I ASKED HIM IF HE PREFERRED TOKITO OR SABURO AND HE SAID, "ANYTHING BUT SABURO."
Can you fight all day long?
Hah hah!
YEAH, SABURO DOESN'T SUIT HIM.

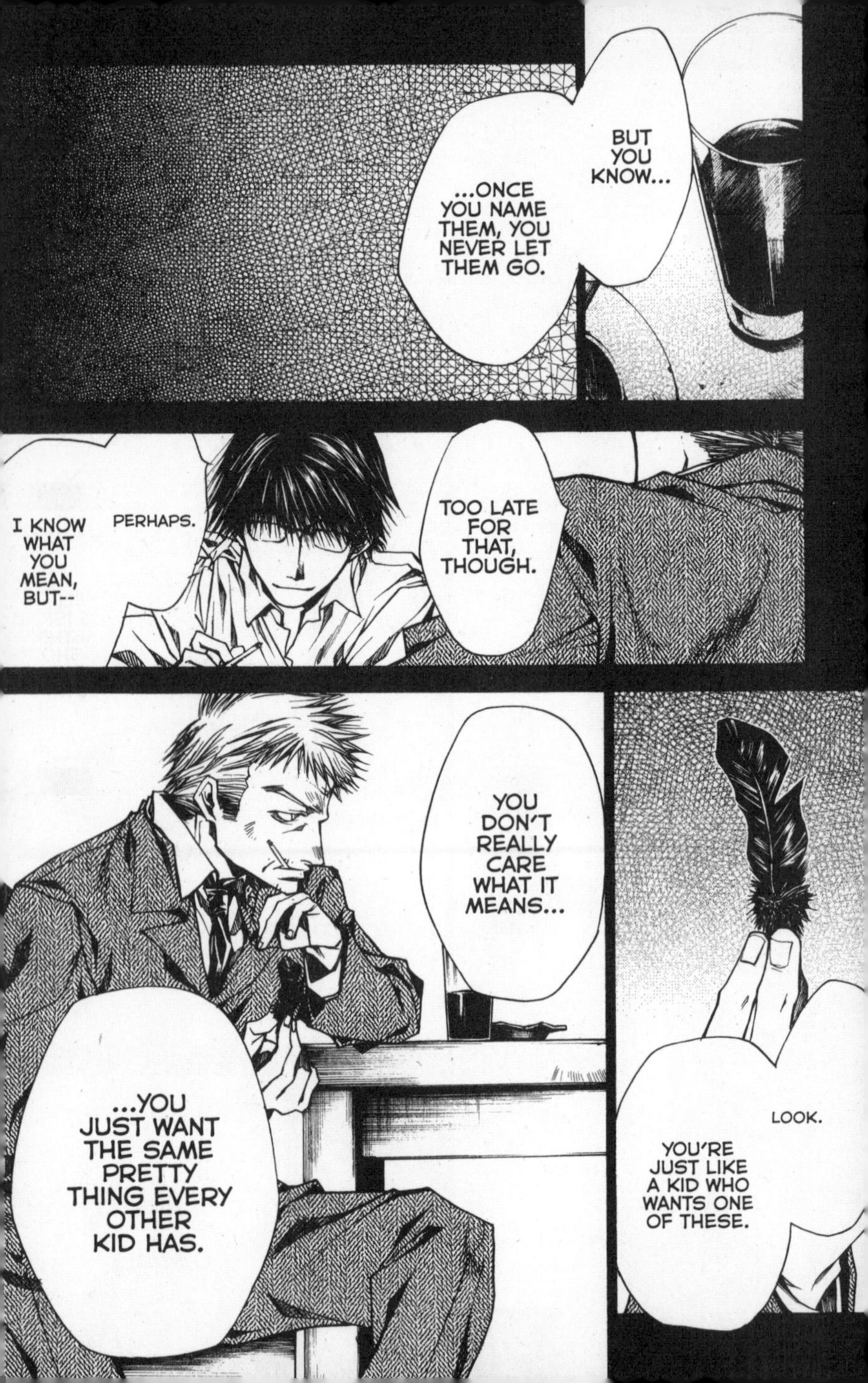
BUT YOU KNOW...
...ONCE YOU NAME THEM, YOU NEVER LET THEM GO.
TOO LATE FOR THAT, THOUGH.
PERHAPS.
I KNOW WHAT YOU MEAN, BUT--
LOOK.
YOU'RE JUST LIKE A KID WHO WANTS ONE OF THESE.
YOU DON'T REALLY CARE WHAT IT MEANS...
...YOU JUST WANT THE SAME PRETTY THING EVERY OTHER KID HAS.

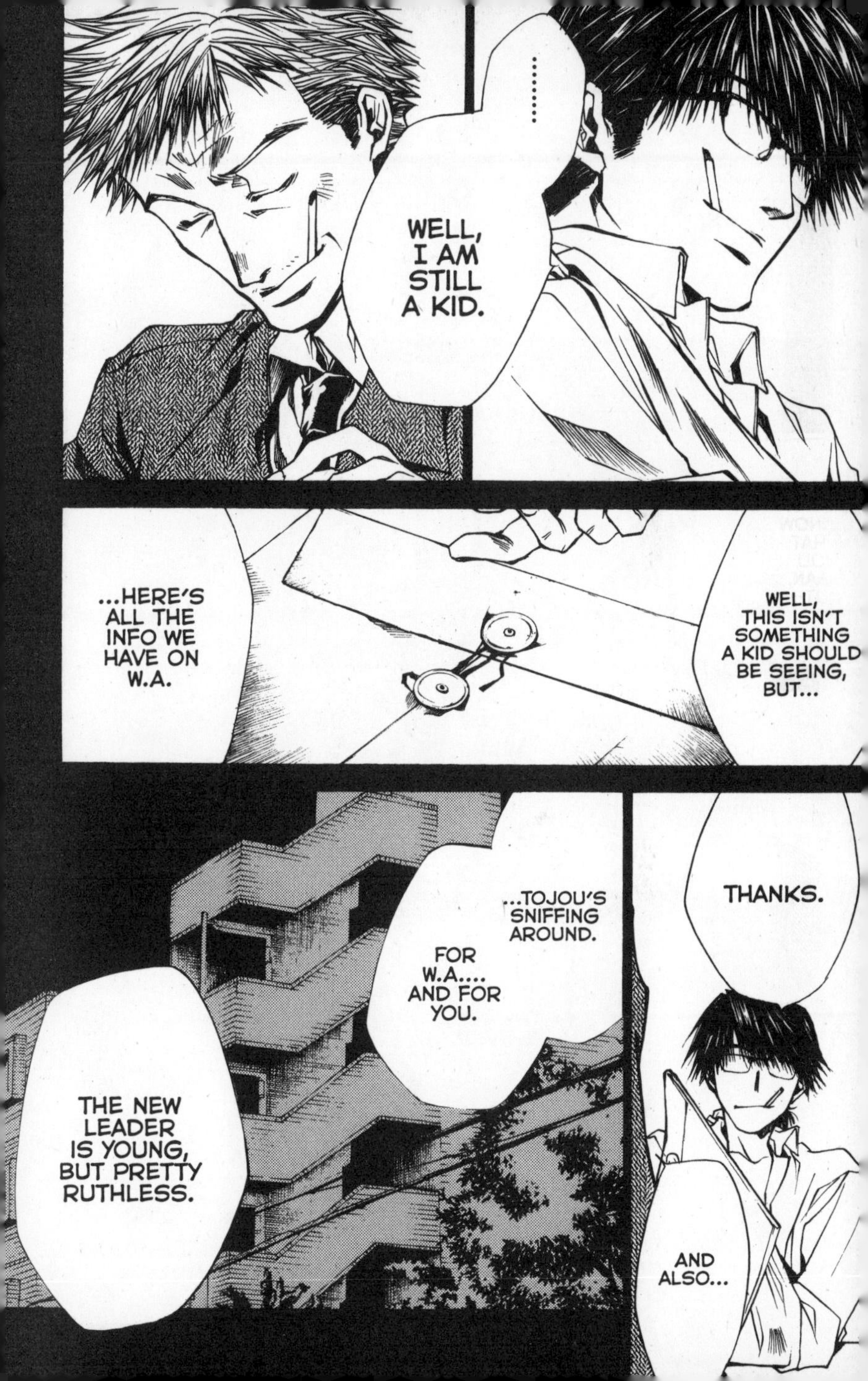
......
WELL, I AM STILL A KID.
WELL, THIS ISN'T SOMETHING A KID SHOULD BE SEEING, BUT...
...HERE'S ALL THE INFO WE HAVE ON W.A.
THANKS.
AND ALSO...
...TOJOU'S SNIFFING AROUND.
FOR W.A.... AND FOR YOU.
THE NEW LEADER IS YOUNG, BUT PRETTY RUTHLESS.

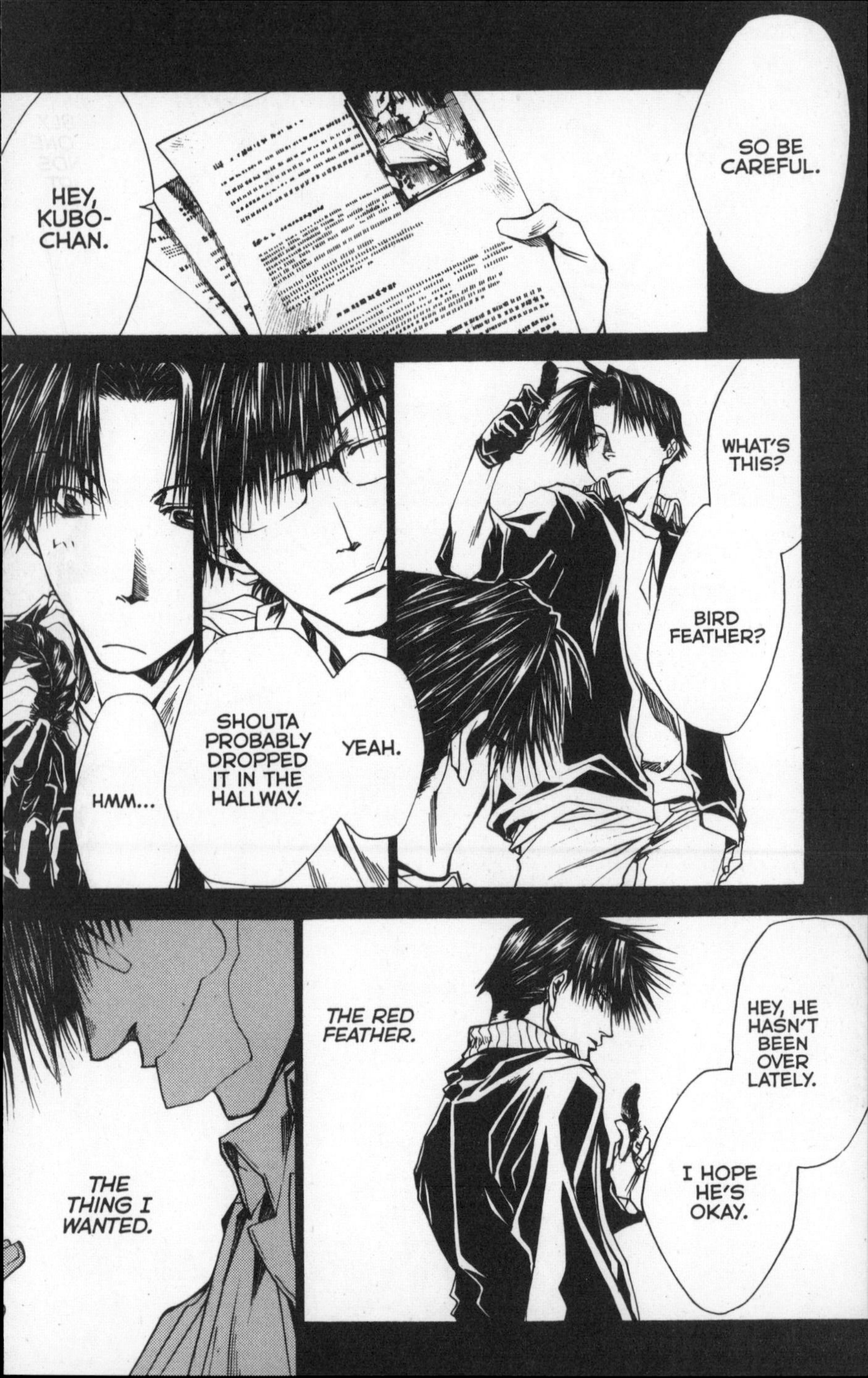
SO BE CAREFUL.
HEY, KUBO-CHAN.
WHAT'S THIS?
BIRD FEATHER?
YEAH.
SHOUTA PROBABLY DROPPED IT IN THE HALLWAY.
HMM...
HEY, HE HASN'T BEEN OVER LATELY.
I HOPE HE'S OKAY.
THE RED FEATHER.
THE THING I WANTED.

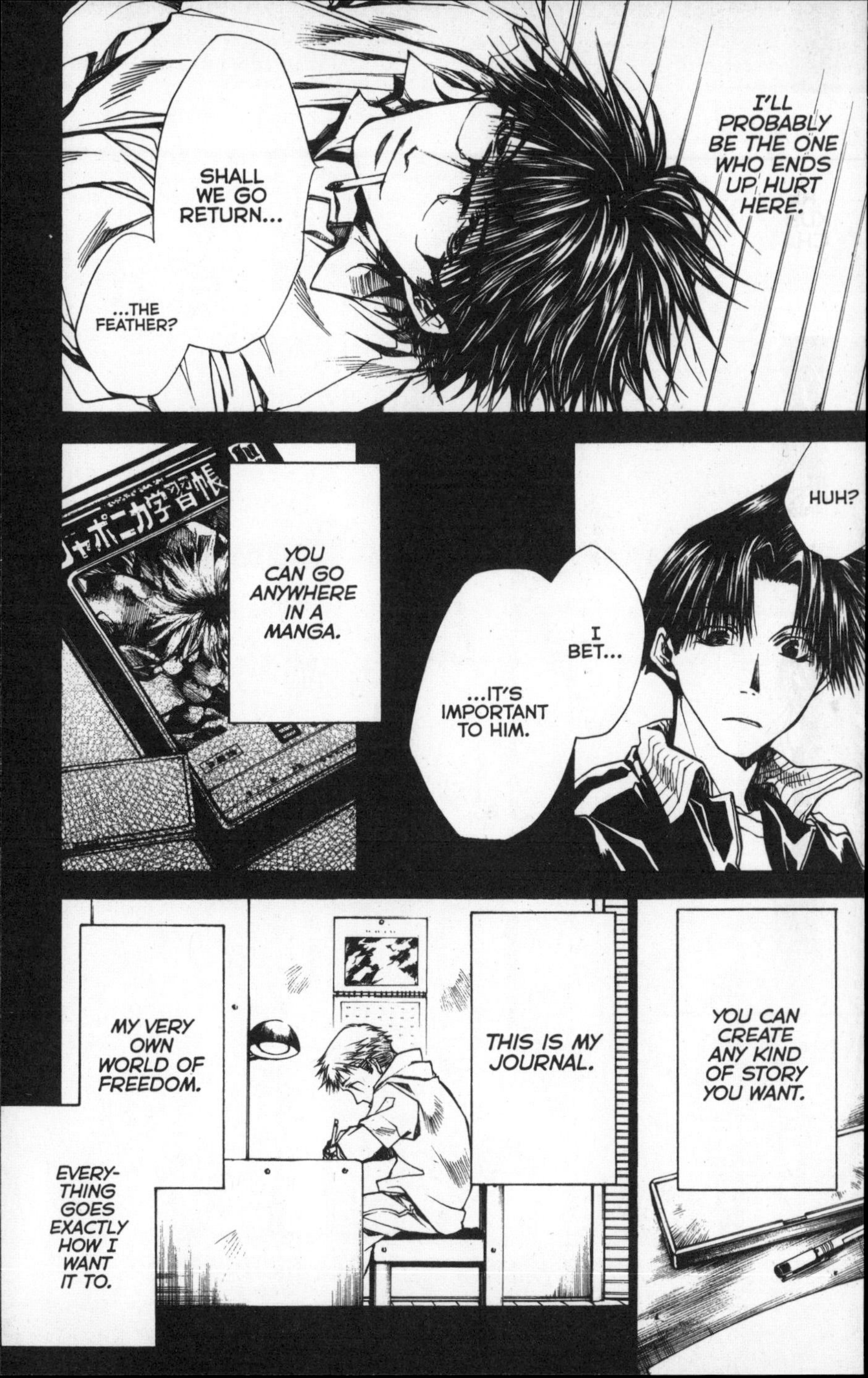

I'LL PROBABLY BE THE ONE WHO ENDS UP HURT HERE.
SHALL WE GO RETURN...
...THE FEATHER?
HUH?
I BET...
...IT'S IMPORTANT TO HIM.
ャポニカ学習帳
YOU CAN GO ANYWHERE IN A MANGA.
YOU CAN CREATE ANY KIND OF STORY YOU WANT.
THIS IS MY JOURNAL.
MY VERY OWN WORLD OF FREEDOM.
EVERYTHING GOES EXACTLY HOW I WANT IT TO.

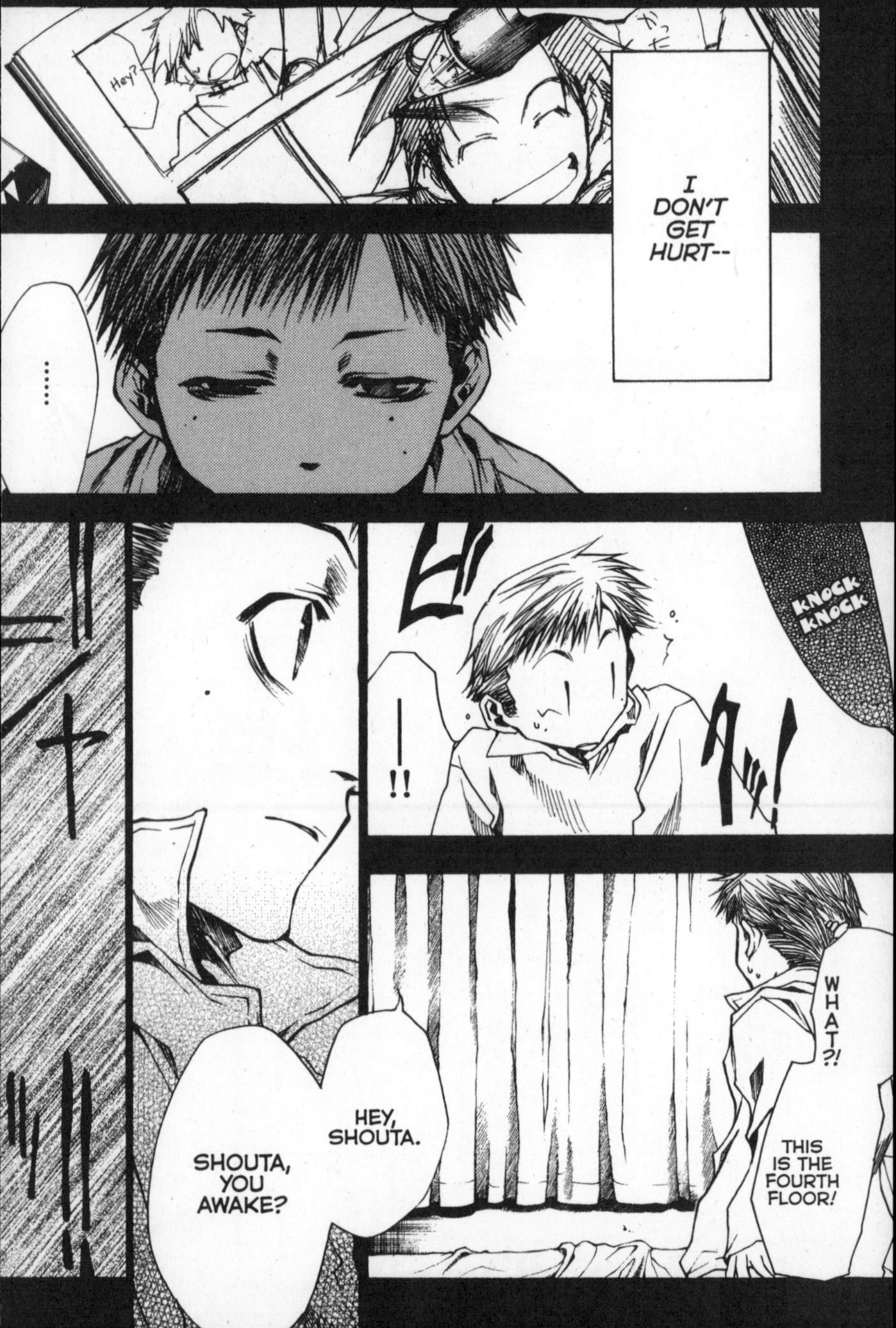
I DON'T GET HURT--
Hey?
.....
KNOCK KNOCK
--!!
WHAT?!
THIS IS THE FOURTH FLOOR!
HEY, SHOUTA.
SHOUTA, YOU AWAKE?

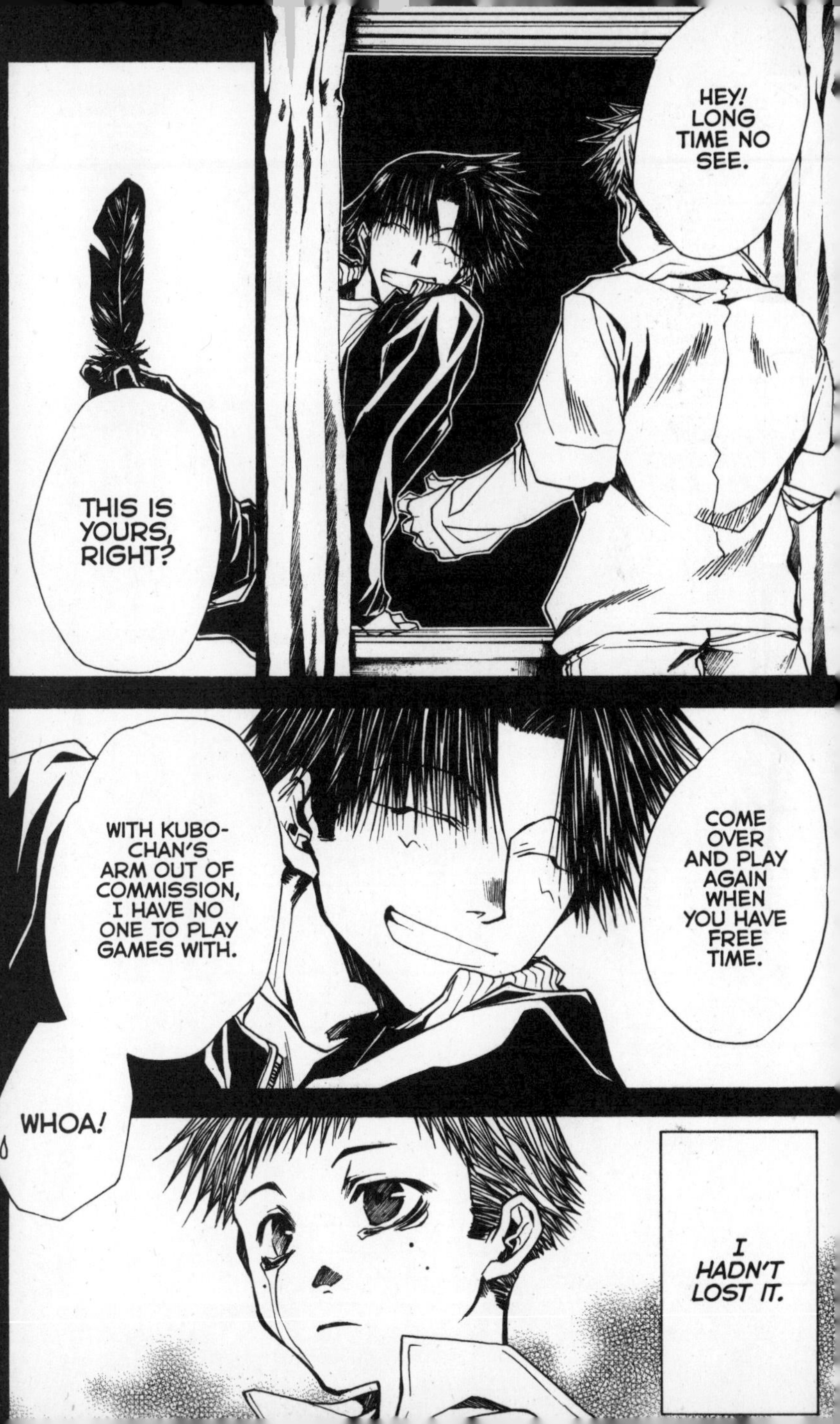
HEY! LONG TIME NO SEE.
THIS IS YOURS, RIGHT?
COME OVER AND PLAY AGAIN WHEN YOU HAVE FREE TIME.
WITH KUBO-CHAN'S ARM OUT OF COMMISSION, I HAVE NO ONE TO PLAY GAMES WITH.
WHOA!
I HADN'T LOST IT.

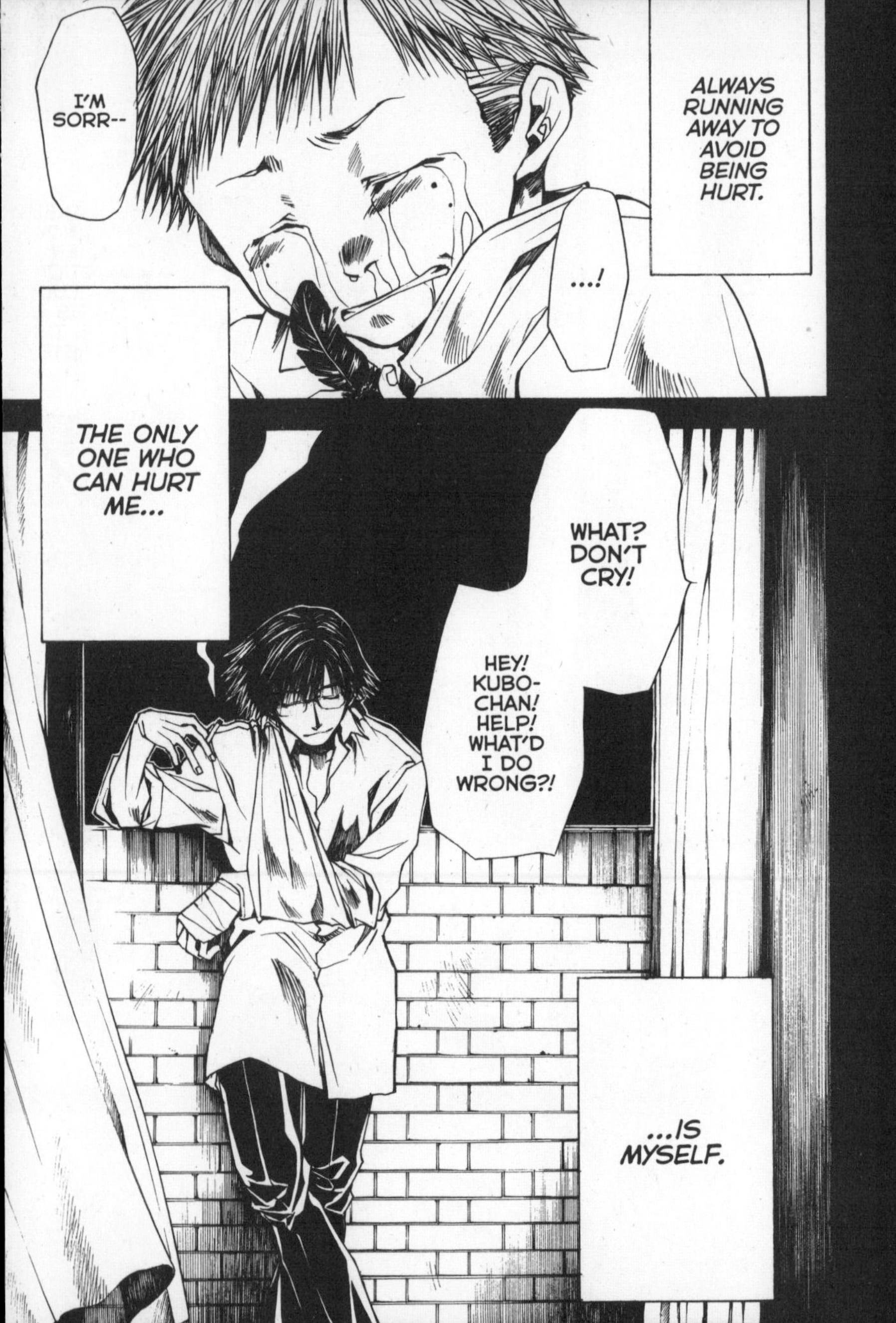
ALWAYS RUNNING AWAY TO AVOID BEING HURT.
...!
I'M SORR--
THE ONLY ONE WHO CAN HURT ME...
WHAT? DON'T CRY!
HEY! KUBO-CHAN! HELP! WHAT'D I DO WRONG?!
...IS MYSELF.

CONTINUED ON THE Dice:31

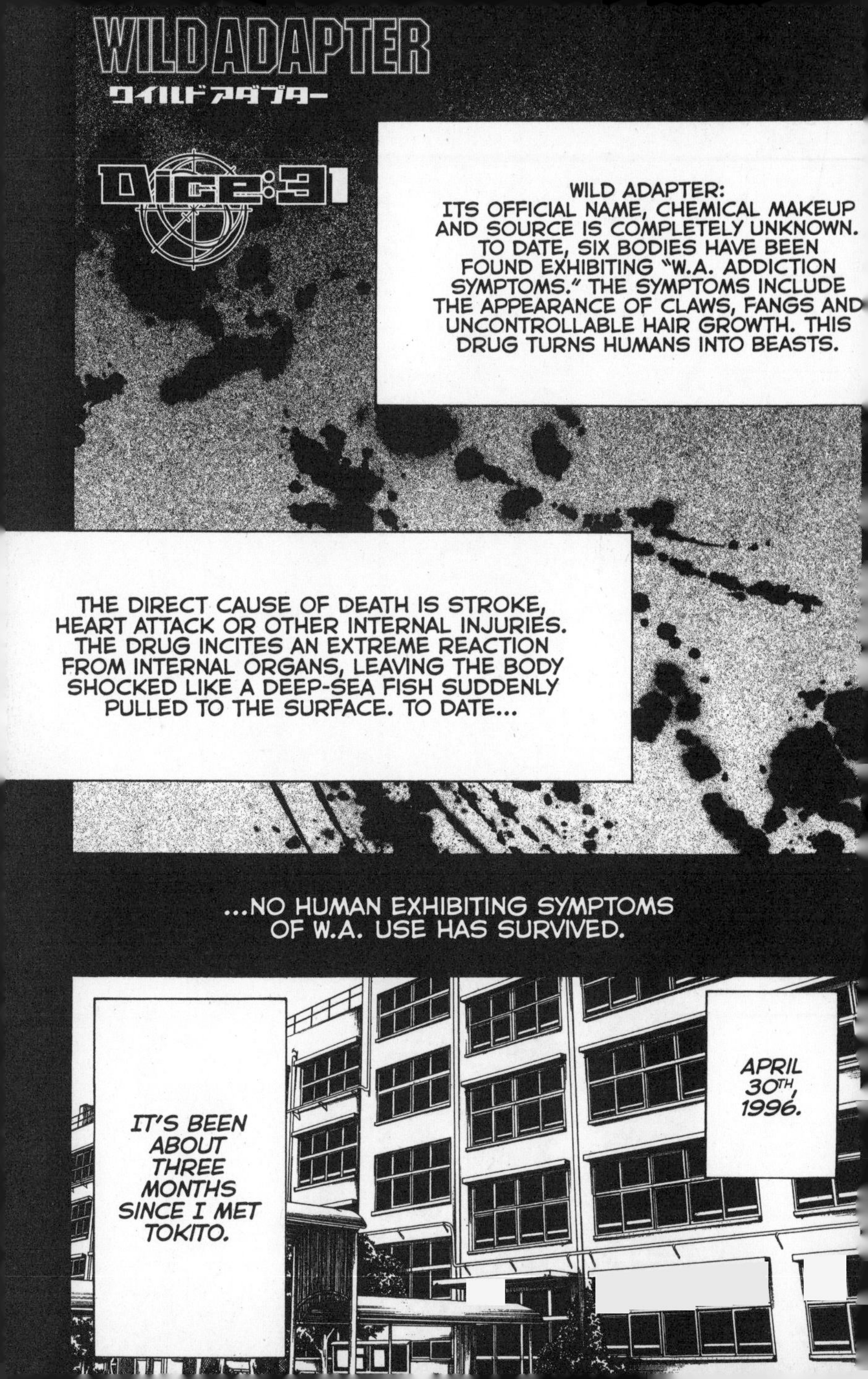
WILD ADAPTER
ワイルドアダプター
DICE:31
WILD ADAPTER: ITS OFFICIAL NAME, CHEMICAL MAKEUP AND SOURCE IS COMPLETELY UNKNOWN. TO DATE, SIX BODIES HAVE BEEN FOUND EXHIBITING "W.A. ADDICTION SYMPTOMS." THE SYMPTOMS INCLUDE THE APPEARANCE OF CLAWS, FANGS AND UNCONTROLLABLE HAIR GROWTH. THIS DRUG TURNS HUMANS INTO BEASTS.
THE DIRECT CAUSE OF DEATH IS STROKE, HEART ATTACK OR OTHER INTERNAL INJURIES. THE DRUG INCITES AN EXTREME REACTION FROM INTERNAL ORGANS, LEAVING THE BODY SHOCKED LIKE A DEEP-SEA FISH SUDDENLY PULLED TO THE SURFACE. TO DATE...
...NO HUMAN EXHIBITING SYMPTOMS OF W.A. USE HAS SURVIVED.
APRIL 30TH, 1996.
IT'S BEEN ABOUT THREE MONTHS SINCE I MET TOKITO.

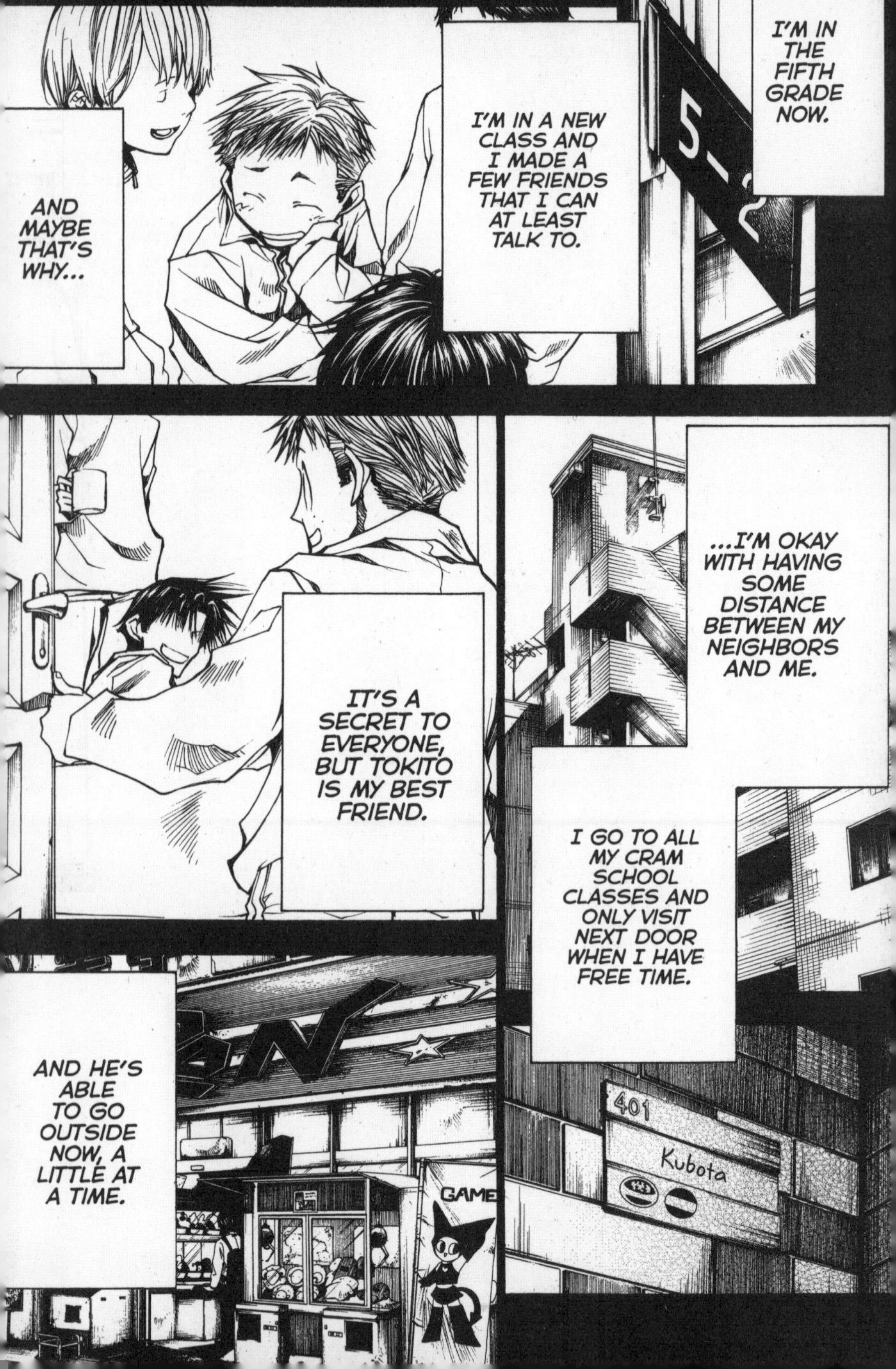
I'M IN THE FIFTH GRADE NOW.
I'M IN A NEW CLASS AND I MADE A FEW FRIENDS THAT I CAN AT LEAST TALK TO.
AND MAYBE THAT'S WHY...
...I'M OKAY WITH HAVING SOME DISTANCE BETWEEN MY NEIGHBORS AND ME.
I GO TO ALL MY CRAM SCHOOL CLASSES AND ONLY VISIT NEXT DOOR WHEN I HAVE FREE TIME.
401
Kubota
IT'S A SECRET TO EVERYONE, BUT TOKITO IS MY BEST FRIEND.
AND HE'S ABLE TO GO OUTSIDE NOW, A LITTLE AT A TIME.
GAME

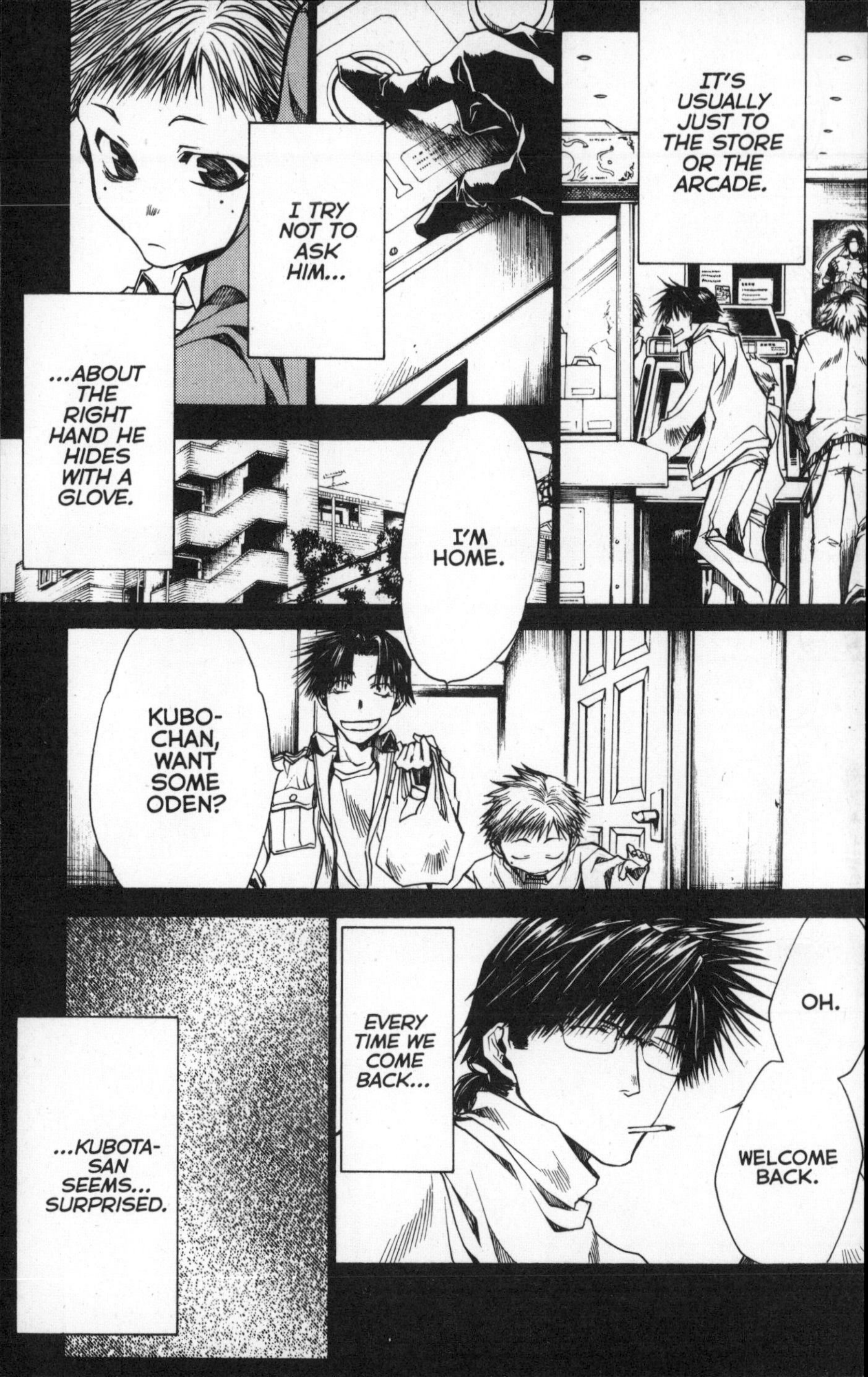
IT'S USUALLY JUST TO THE STORE OR THE ARCADE.
I TRY NOT TO ASK HIM...
...ABOUT THE RIGHT HAND HE HIDES WITH A GLOVE.
I'M HOME.
KUBO-CHAN, WANT SOME ODEN?
OH.
WELCOME BACK.
EVERY TIME WE COME BACK...
...KUBOTA-SAN SEEMS... SURPRISED.

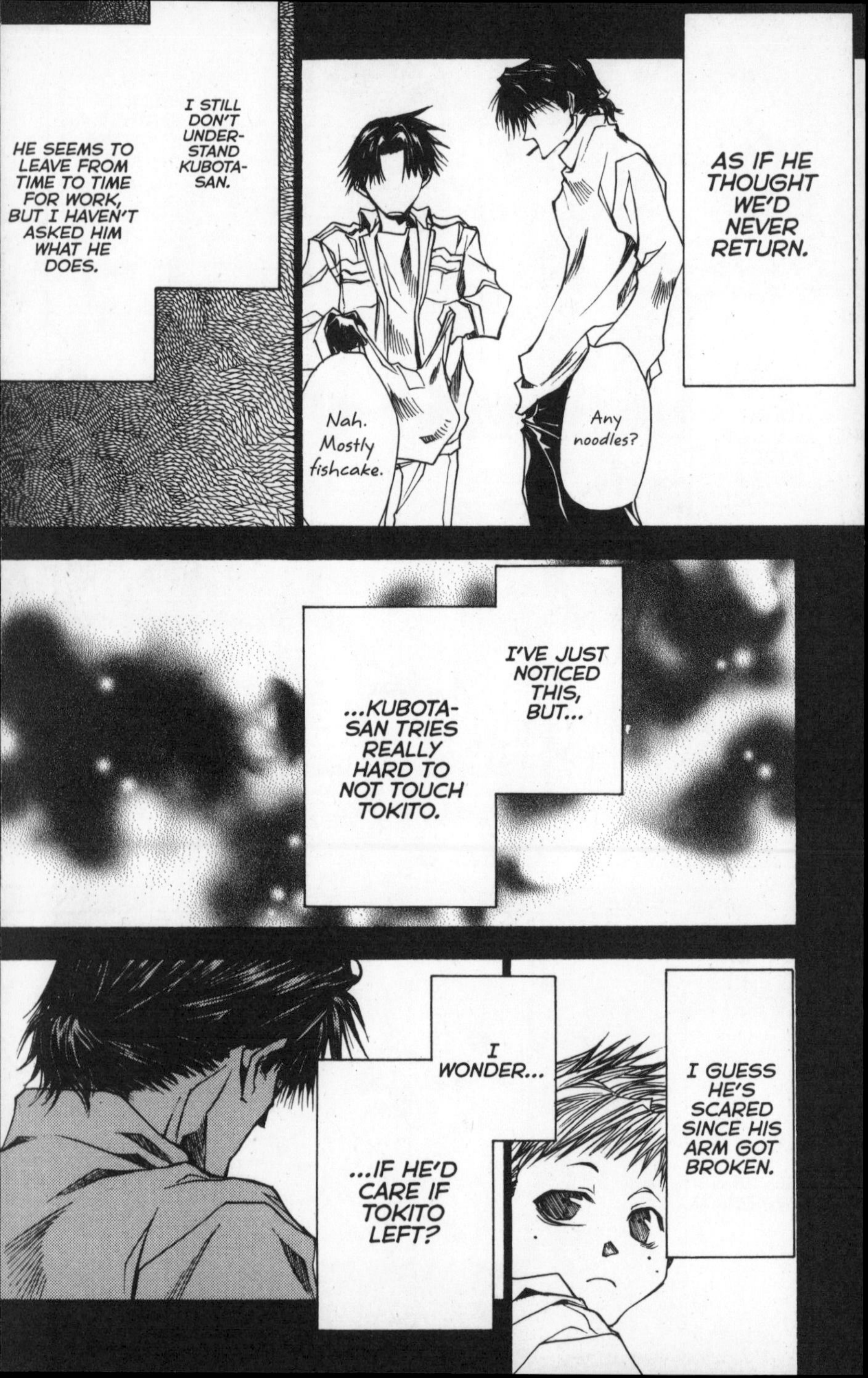
AS IF HE THOUGHT WE'D NEVER RETURN.
Any noodles?
Nah. Mostly fishcake.
I STILL DON'T UNDERSTAND KUBOTA-SAN.
HE SEEMS TO LEAVE FROM TIME TO TIME FOR WORK, BUT I HAVEN'T ASKED HIM WHAT HE DOES.
I'VE JUST NOTICED THIS, BUT...
...KUBOTA-SAN TRIES REALLY HARD TO NOT TOUCH TOKITO.
I GUESS HE'S SCARED SINCE HIS ARM GOT BROKEN.
I WONDER...
...IF HE'D CARE IF TOKITO LEFT?

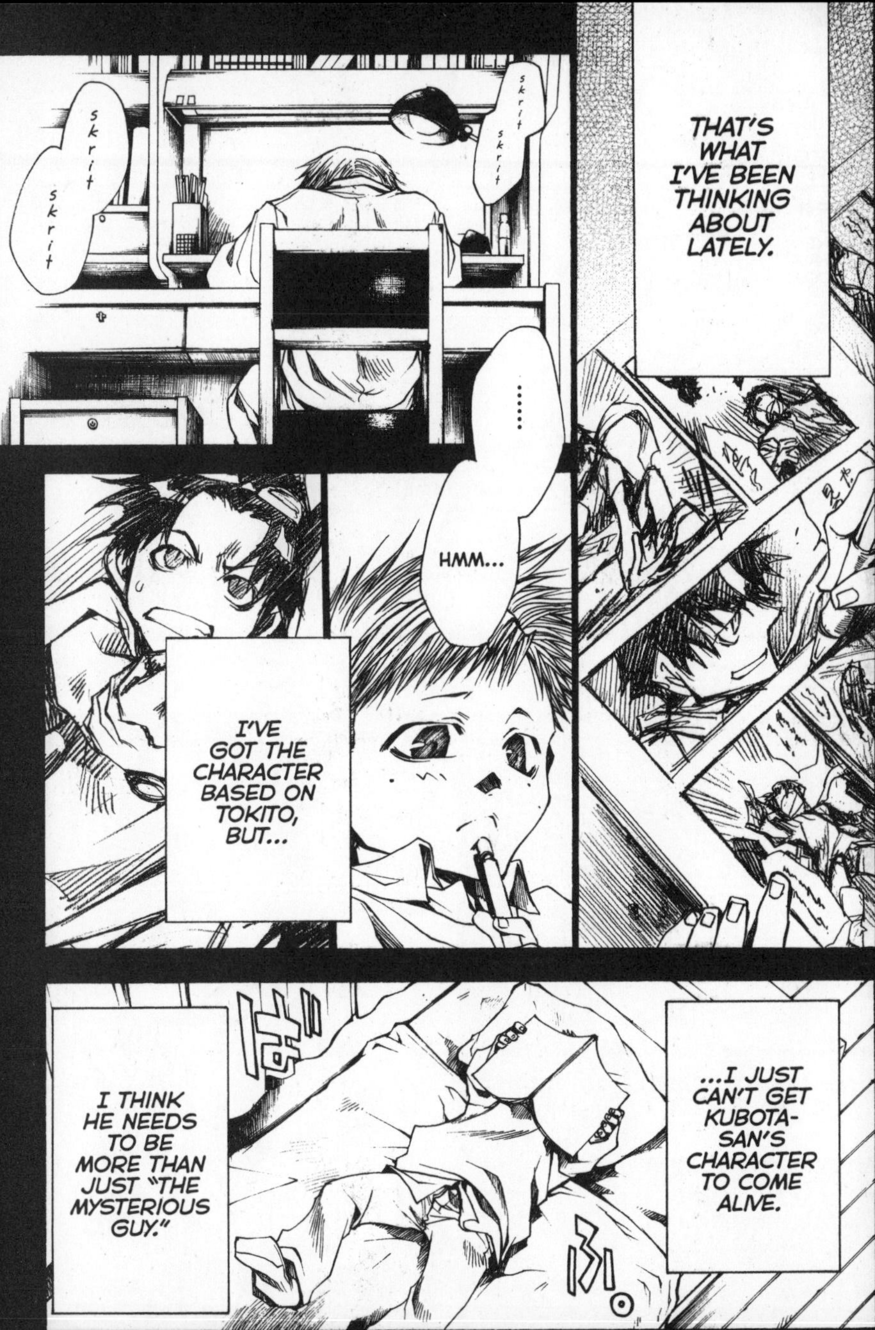
THAT'S WHAT I'VE BEEN THINKING ABOUT LATELY.
skrit skrit
skrit skrit
......
HMM...
I'VE GOT THE CHARACTER BASED ON TOKITO, BUT...
...I JUST CAN'T GET KUBOTA-SAN'S CHARACTER TO COME ALIVE.
ふ。
I THINK HE NEEDS TO BE MORE THAN JUST "THE MYSTERIOUS GUY."

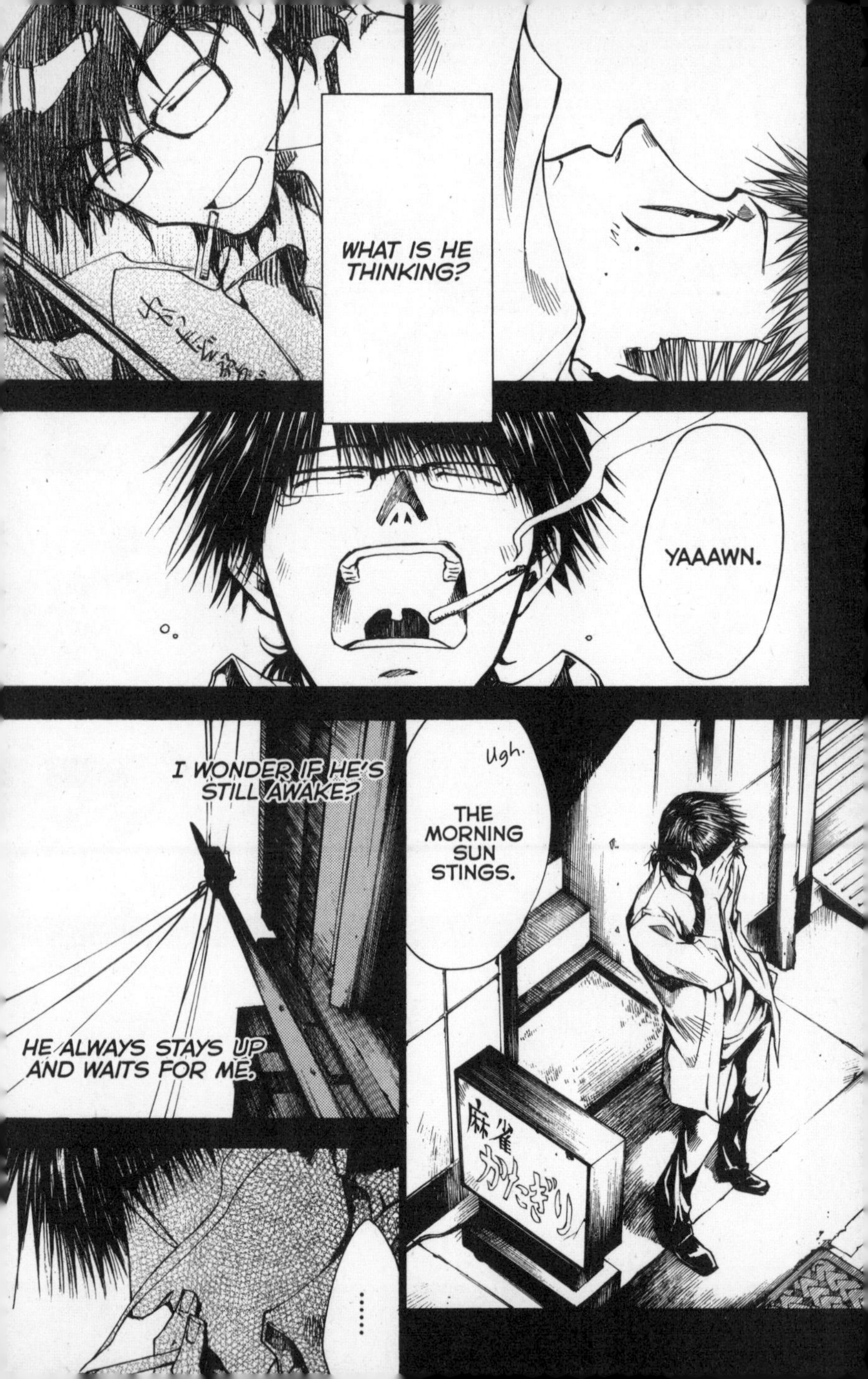
WHAT IS HE THINKING?
YAAAWN.
Ugh.
THE MORNING SUN STINGS.
麻雀 かたぎり
I WONDER IF HE'S STILL AWAKE?
HE ALWAYS STAYS UP AND WAITS FOR ME.
......

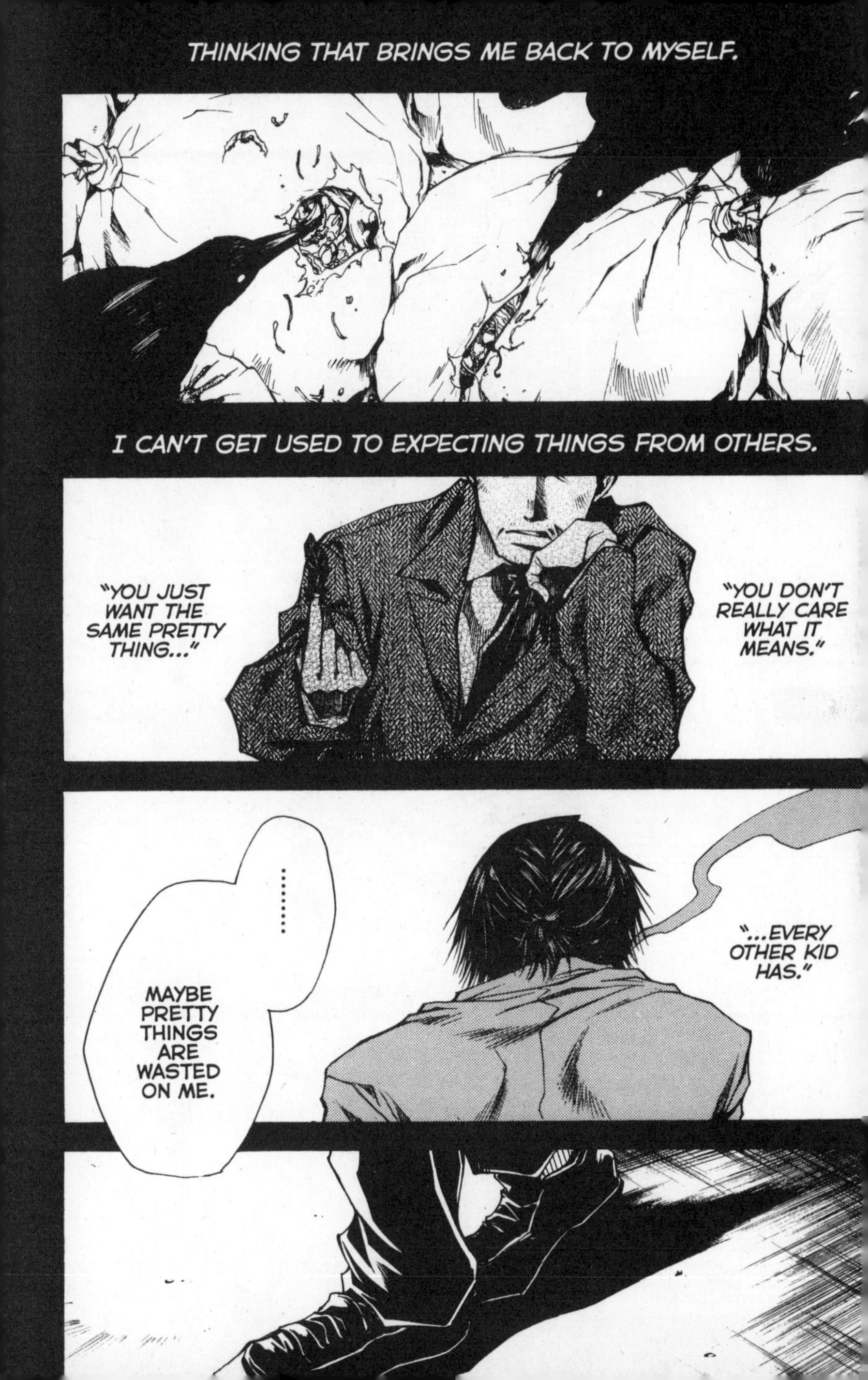
THINKING THAT BRINGS ME BACK TO MYSELF.
I CAN'T GET USED TO EXPECTING THINGS FROM OTHERS.
"YOU DON'T REALLY CARE WHAT IT MEANS."
"YOU JUST WANT THE SAME PRETTY THING..."
"...EVERY OTHER KID HAS."
......
MAYBE PRETTY THINGS ARE WASTED ON ME.

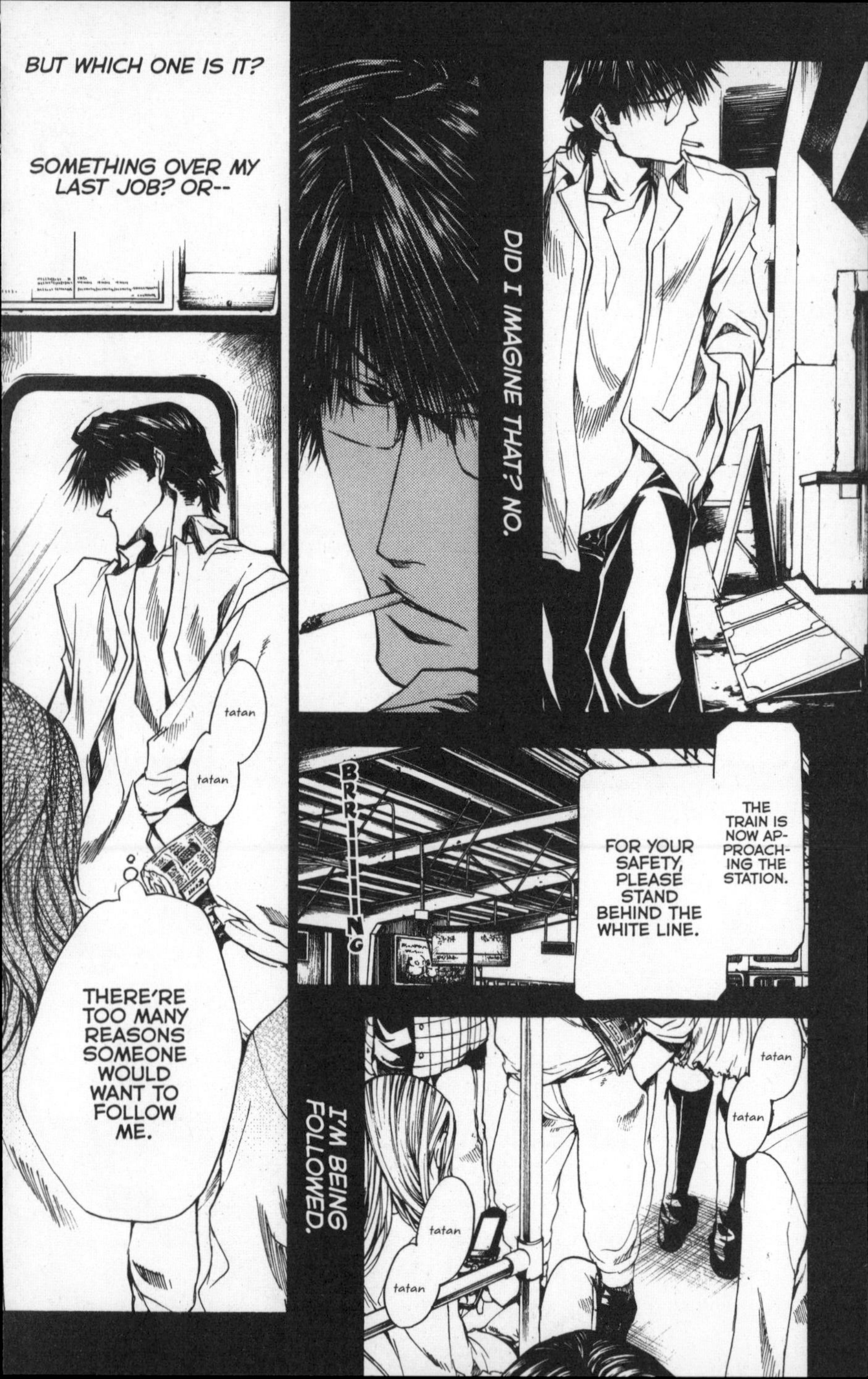

DID I IMAGINE THAT? NO.
THE TRAIN IS NOW APPROACHING THE STATION.
FOR YOUR SAFETY, PLEASE STAND BEHIND THE WHITE LINE.
BRRIIIING
I'M BEING FOLLOWED.
tatan
tatan
tatan
tatan
BUT WHICH ONE IS IT?
SOMETHING OVER MY LAST JOB? OR--
tatan
tatan
THERE'RE TOO MANY REASONS SOMEONE WOULD WANT TO FOLLOW ME.

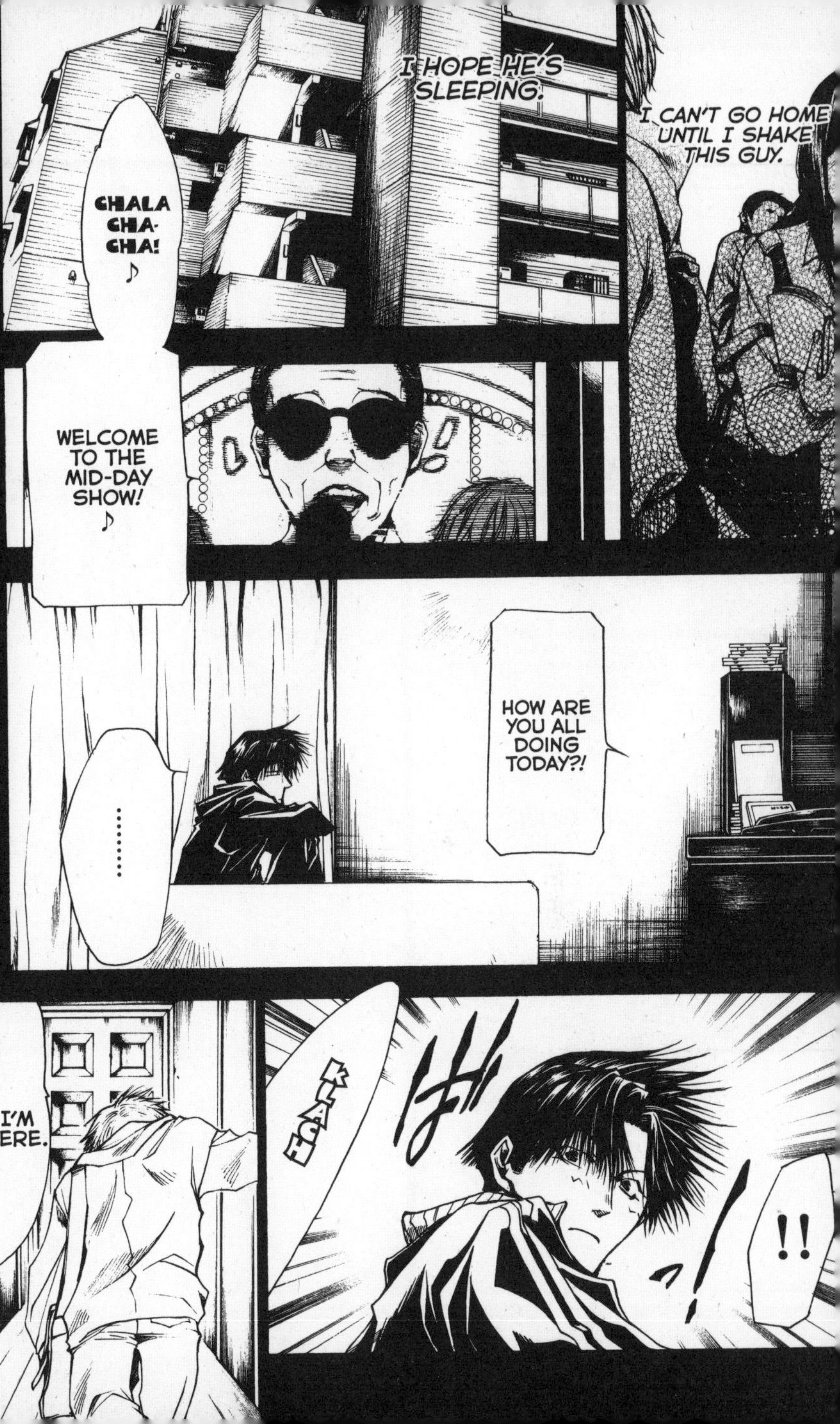
I CAN'T GO HOME UNTIL I SHAKE THIS GUY.
I HOPE HE'S SLEEPING.
CHALA CHA-CHA! ♪
WELCOME TO THE MID-DAY SHOW! ♪
HOW ARE YOU ALL DOING TODAY?!
……
!!
KLACH
I'M HERE.

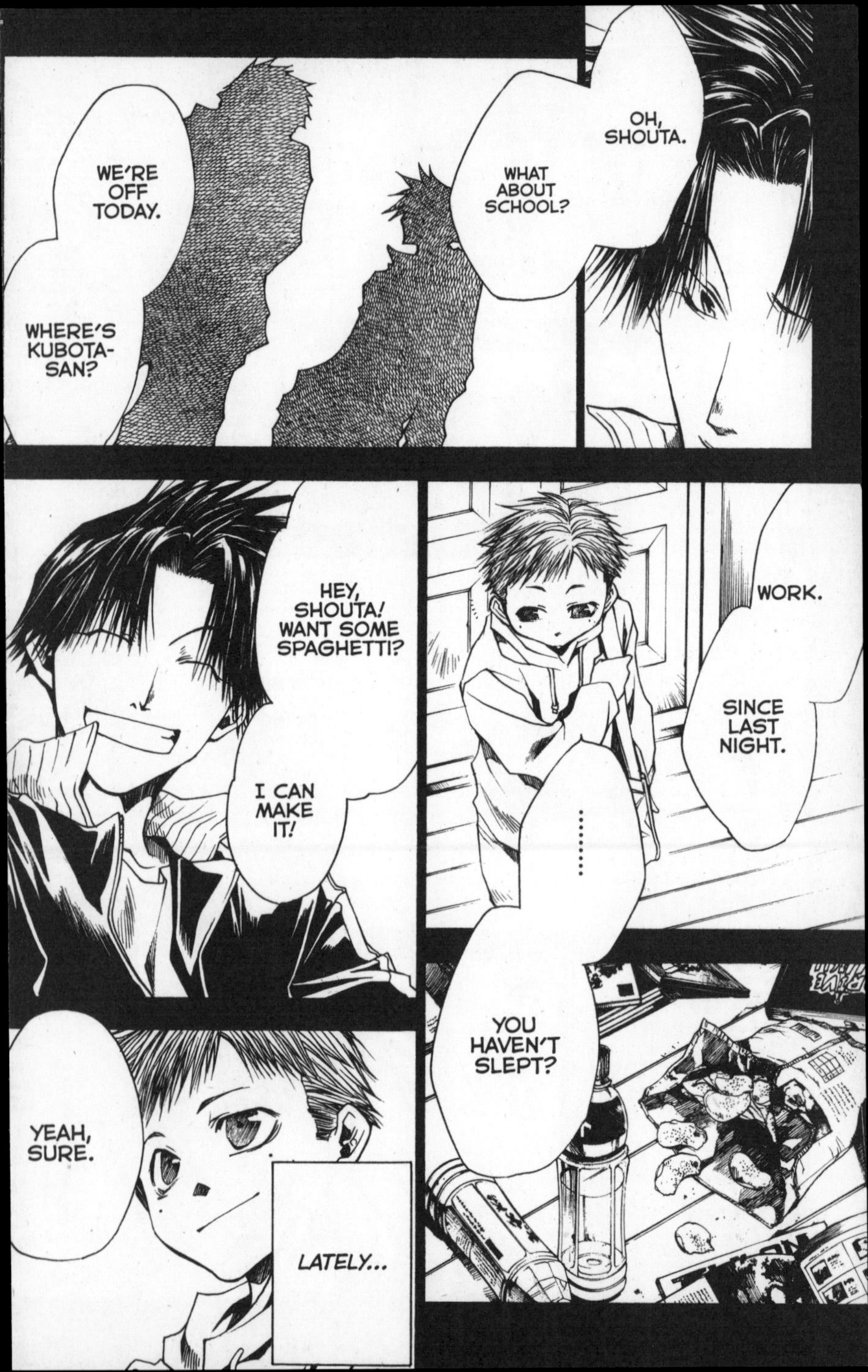
OH, SHOUTA.
WHAT ABOUT SCHOOL?
WE'RE OFF TODAY.
WHERE'S KUBOTA-SAN?
WORK.
SINCE LAST NIGHT.
......
YOU HAVEN'T SLEPT?
HEY, SHOUTA! WANT SOME SPAGHETTI?
I CAN MAKE IT!
YEAH, SURE.
LATELY...

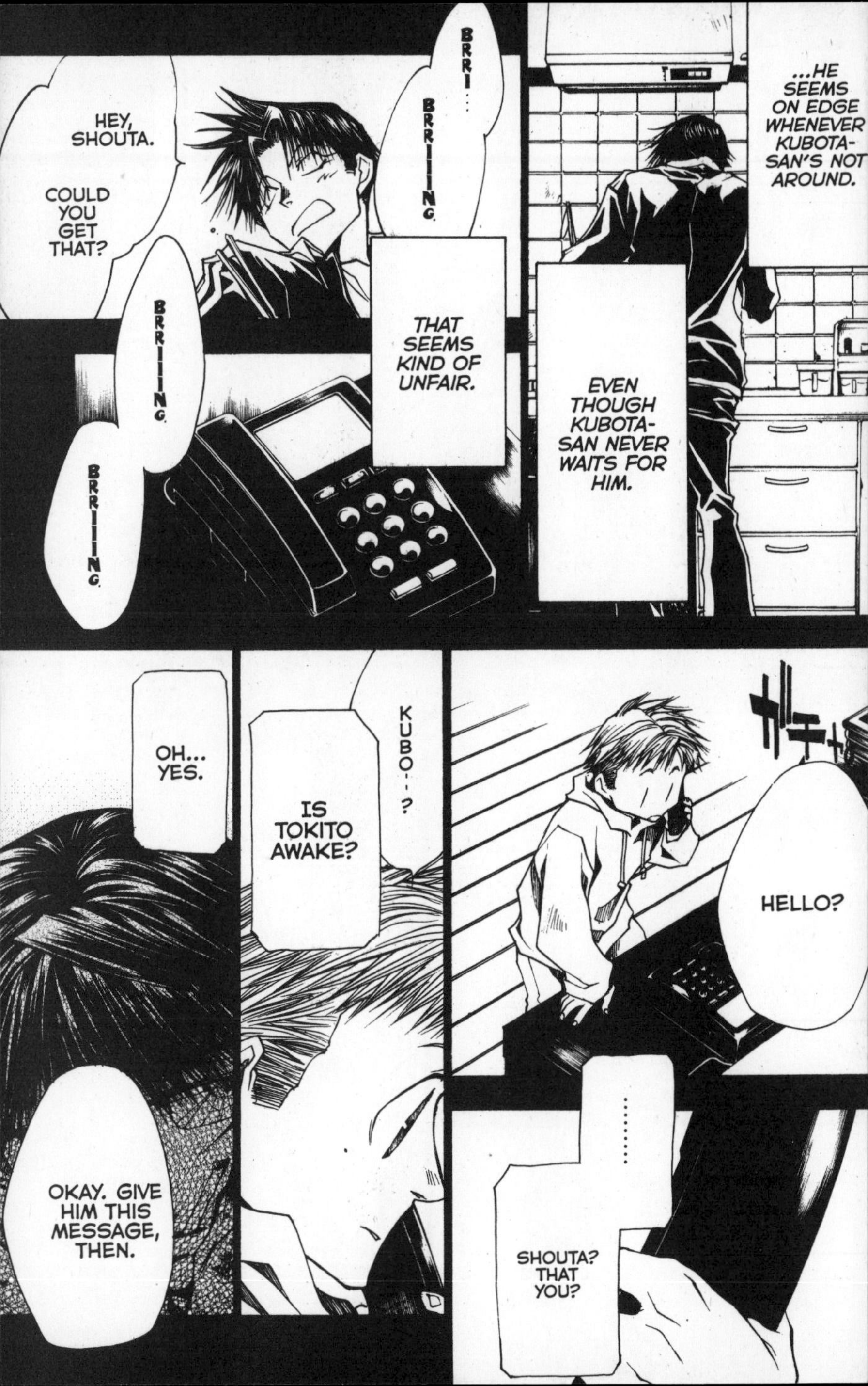
...HE SEEMS ON EDGE WHENEVER KUBOTA-SAN'S NOT AROUND.
EVEN THOUGH KUBOTA-SAN NEVER WAITS FOR HIM.
BRRI...
BRRIIING.
HEY, SHOUTA.
COULD YOU GET THAT?
THAT SEEMS KIND OF UNFAIR.
BRRIIING.
BRRIIING.
ガチャ
HELLO?
......
SHOUTA? THAT YOU?
KUBO...?
IS TOKITO AWAKE?
OH... YES.
OKAY. GIVE HIM THIS MESSAGE, THEN.

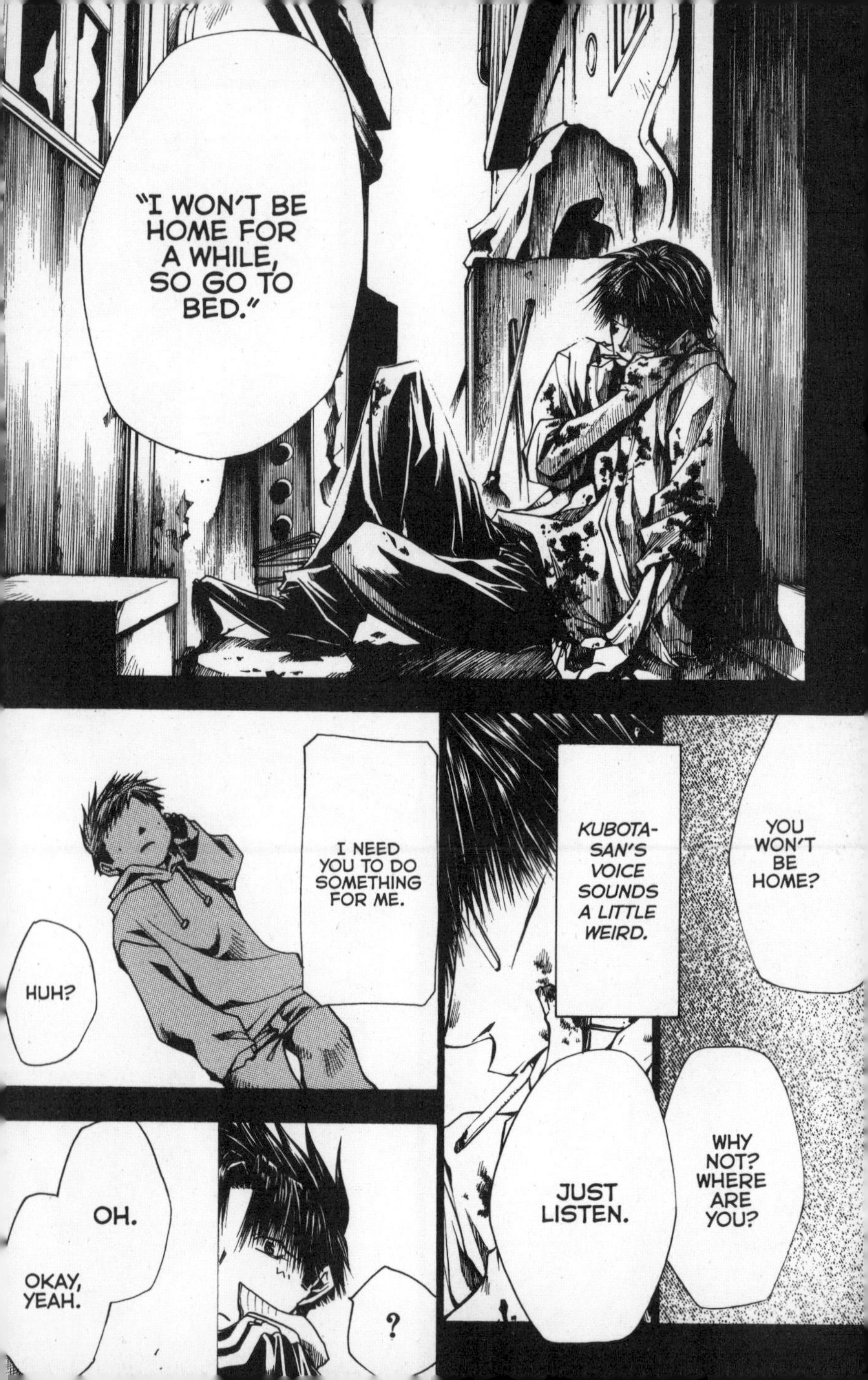
"I WON'T BE HOME FOR A WHILE, SO GO TO BED."
YOU WON'T BE HOME?
KUBOTA-SAN'S VOICE SOUNDS A LITTLE WEIRD.
WHY NOT? WHERE ARE YOU?
JUST LISTEN.
I NEED YOU TO DO SOMETHING FOR ME.
HUH?
?
OH.
OKAY, YEAH.

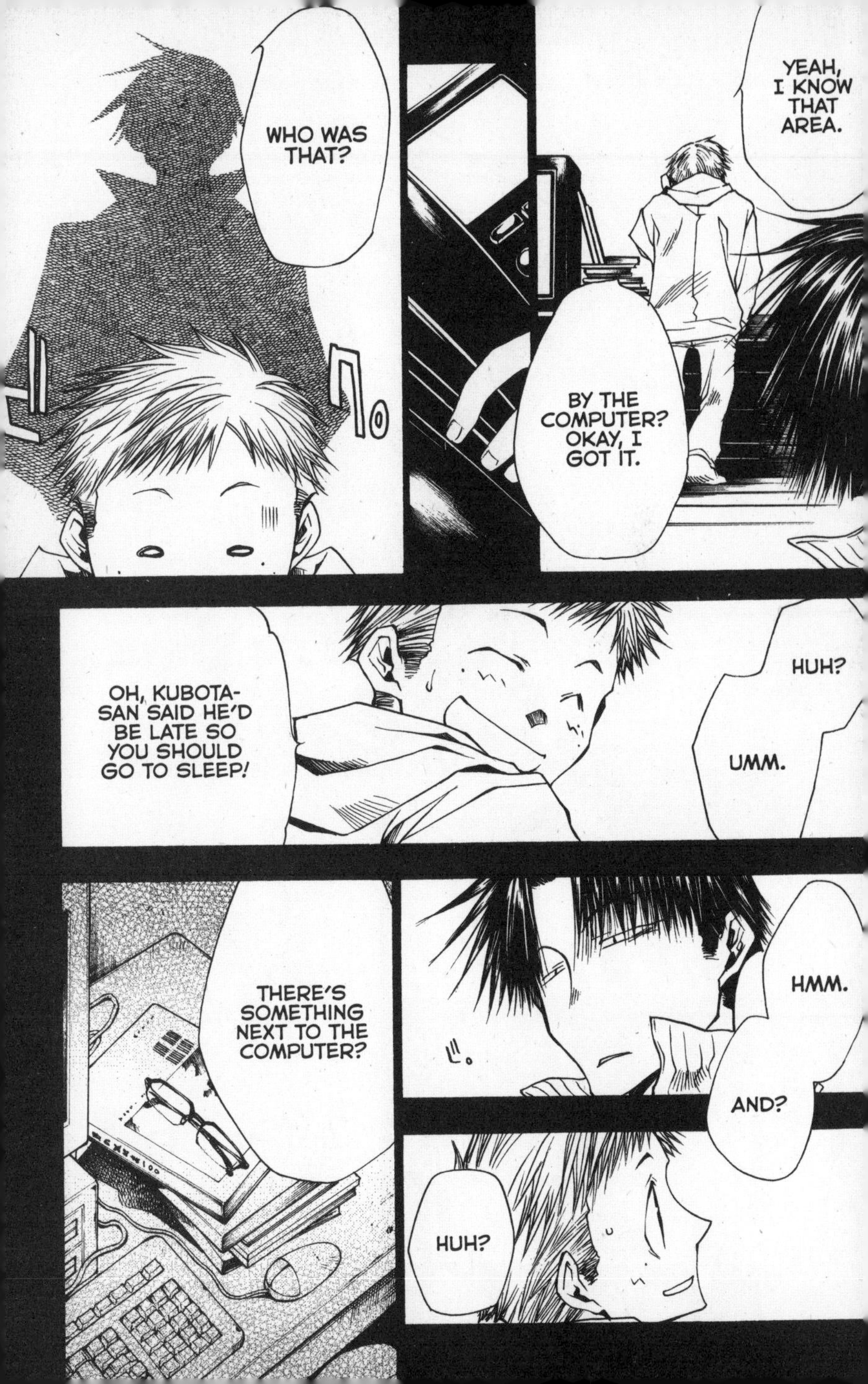
YEAH, I KNOW THAT AREA.
BY THE COMPUTER? OKAY, I GOT IT.
WHO WAS THAT?
HUH?
UMM.
OH, KUBOTA-SAN SAID HE'D BE LATE SO YOU SHOULD GO TO SLEEP!
HMM.
AND?
HUH?
THERE'S SOMETHING NEXT TO THE COMPUTER?

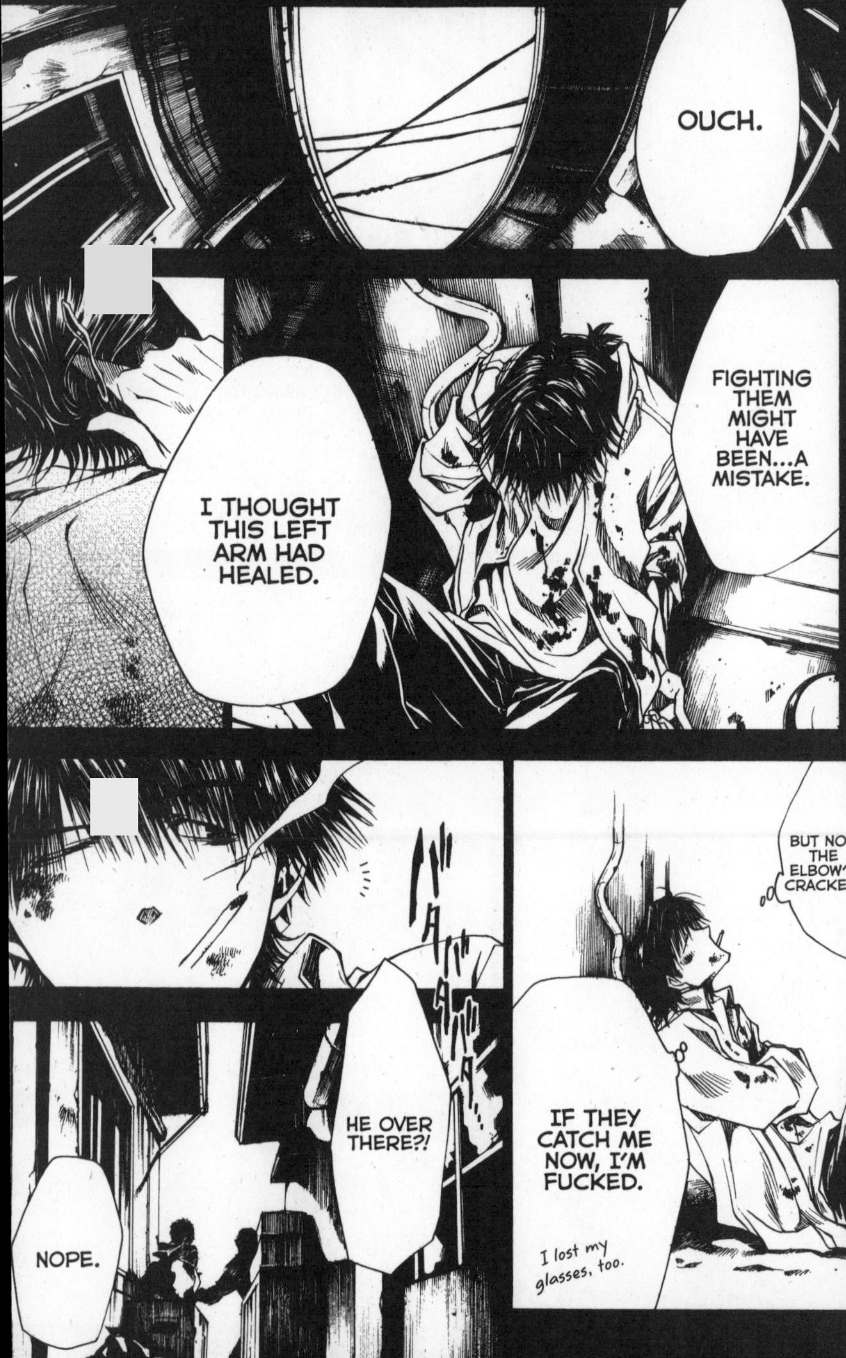
OUCH.
FIGHTING THEM MIGHT HAVE BEEN...A MISTAKE.
I THOUGHT THIS LEFT ARM HAD HEALED.
BUT NOW THE ELBOW'S CRACKED.
IF THEY CATCH ME NOW, I'M FUCKED.
I lost my glasses, too.
HE OVER THERE?!
NOPE.

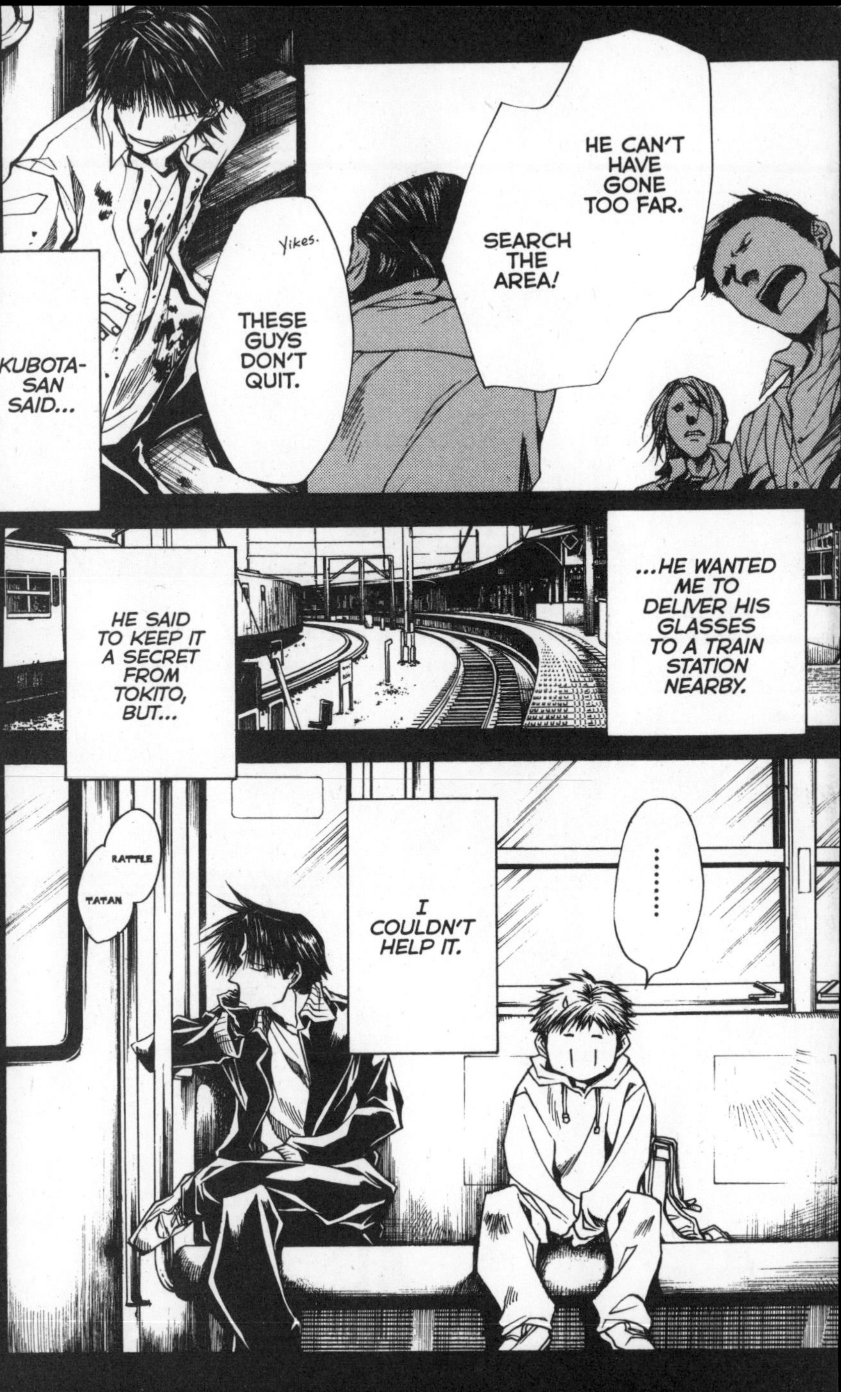
HE CAN'T HAVE GONE TOO FAR.
SEARCH THE AREA!
Yikes.
THESE GUYS DON'T QUIT.
KUBOTA-SAN SAID...
...HE WANTED ME TO DELIVER HIS GLASSES TO A TRAIN STATION NEARBY.
HE SAID TO KEEP IT A SECRET FROM TOKITO, BUT...
......
I COULDN'T HELP IT.
RATTLE
TATAN

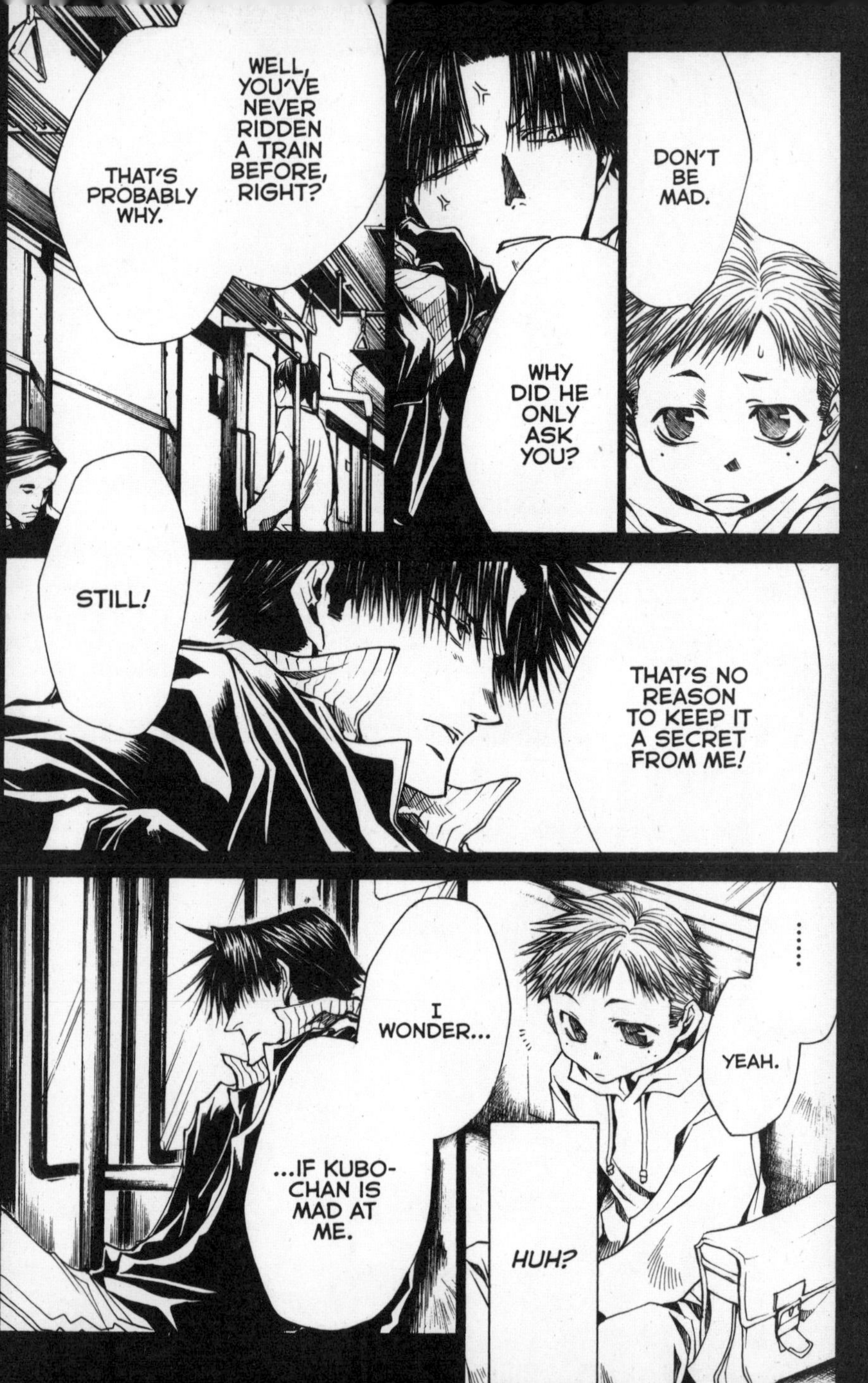
DON'T BE MAD.
WHY DID HE ONLY ASK YOU?
WELL, YOU'VE NEVER RIDDEN A TRAIN BEFORE, RIGHT?
THAT'S PROBABLY WHY.
STILL!
THAT'S NO REASON TO KEEP IT A SECRET FROM ME!
......
I WONDER...
...IF KUBO-CHAN IS MAD AT ME.
YEAH.
HUH?

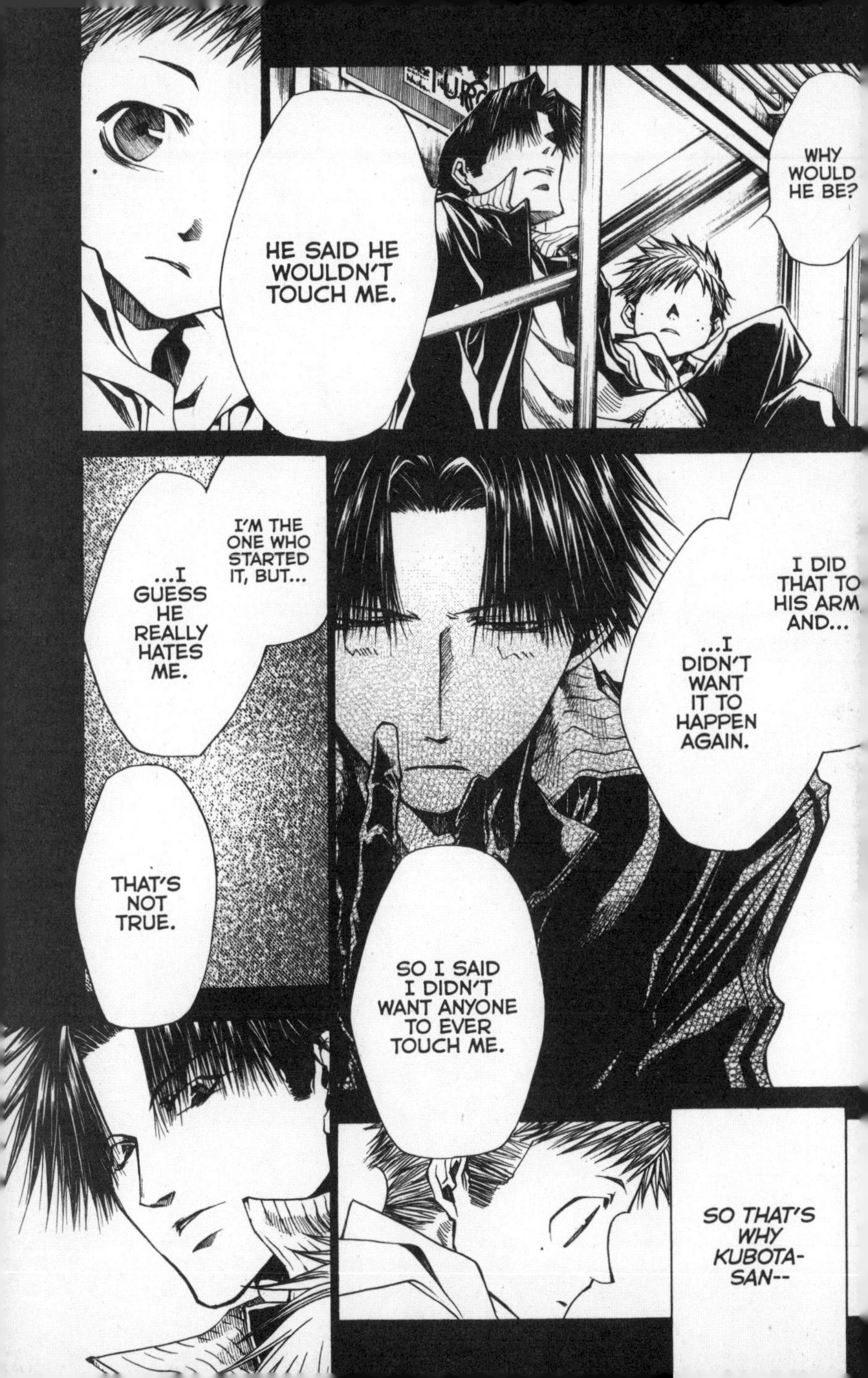
WHY WOULD HE BE?
HE SAID HE WOULDN'T TOUCH ME.
I DID THAT TO HIS ARM AND...
...I DIDN'T WANT IT TO HAPPEN AGAIN.
SO I SAID I DIDN'T WANT ANYONE TO EVER TOUCH ME.
I'M THE ONE WHO STARTED IT, BUT...
...I GUESS HE REALLY HATES ME.
THAT'S NOT TRUE.
SO THAT'S WHY KUBOTA-SAN--

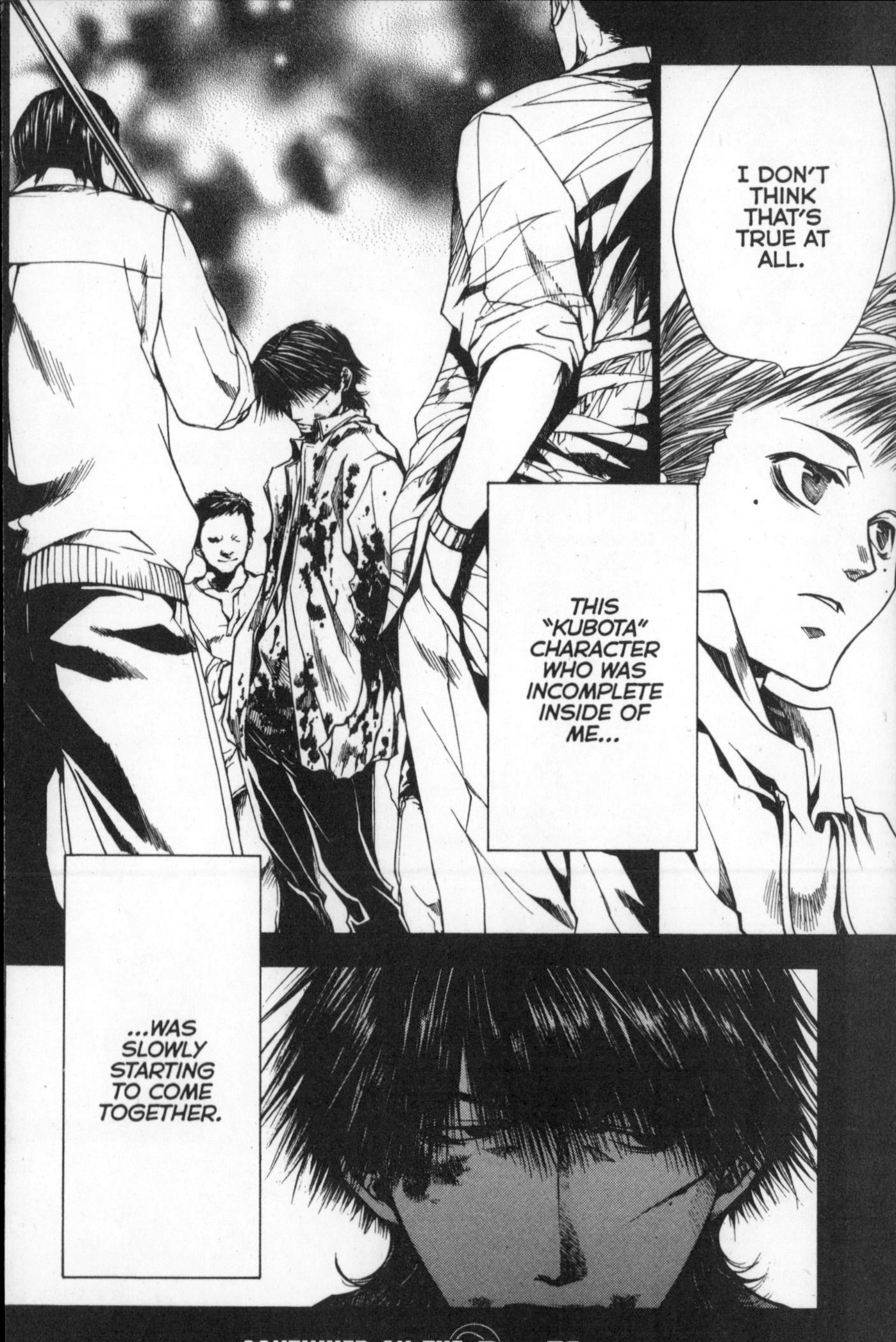
I DON'T THINK THAT'S TRUE AT ALL.
THIS "KUBOTA" CHARACTER WHO WAS INCOMPLETE INSIDE OF ME...
...WAS SLOWLY STARTING TO COME TOGETHER.

CONTINUED ON THE Dice:32

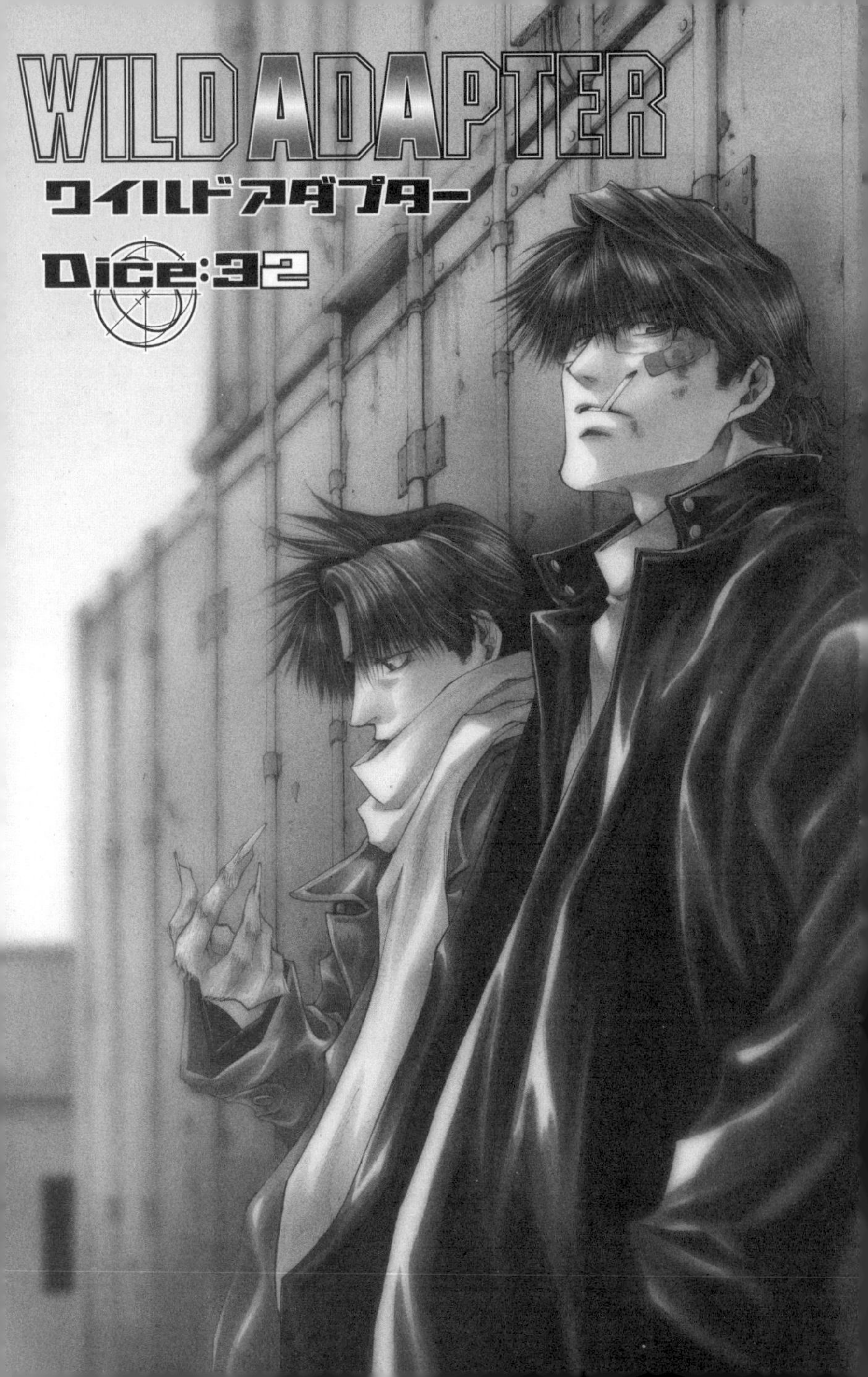
WILD ADAPTER
ワイルドアダプター
Dice:32

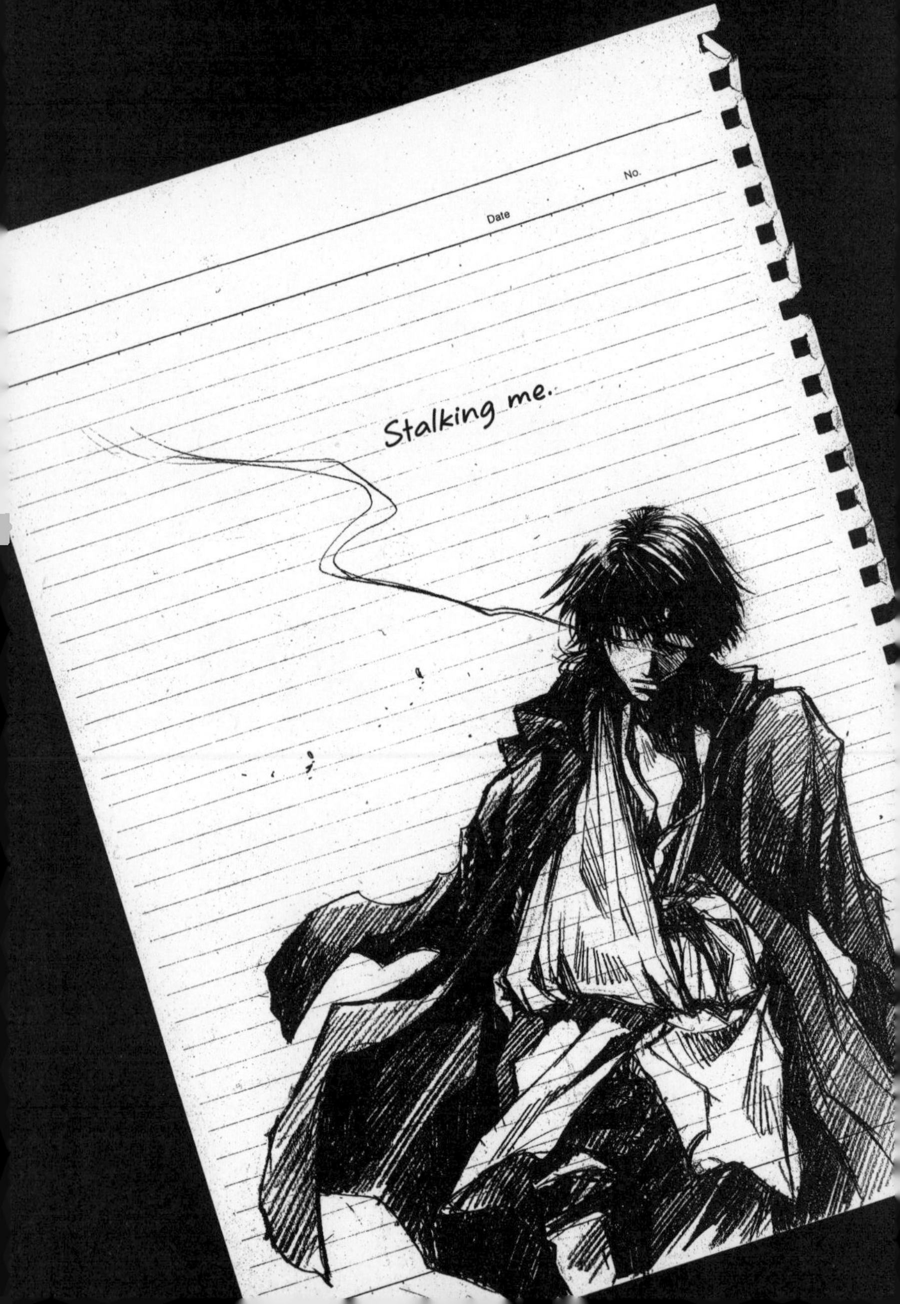
Date
No.
Stalking me.

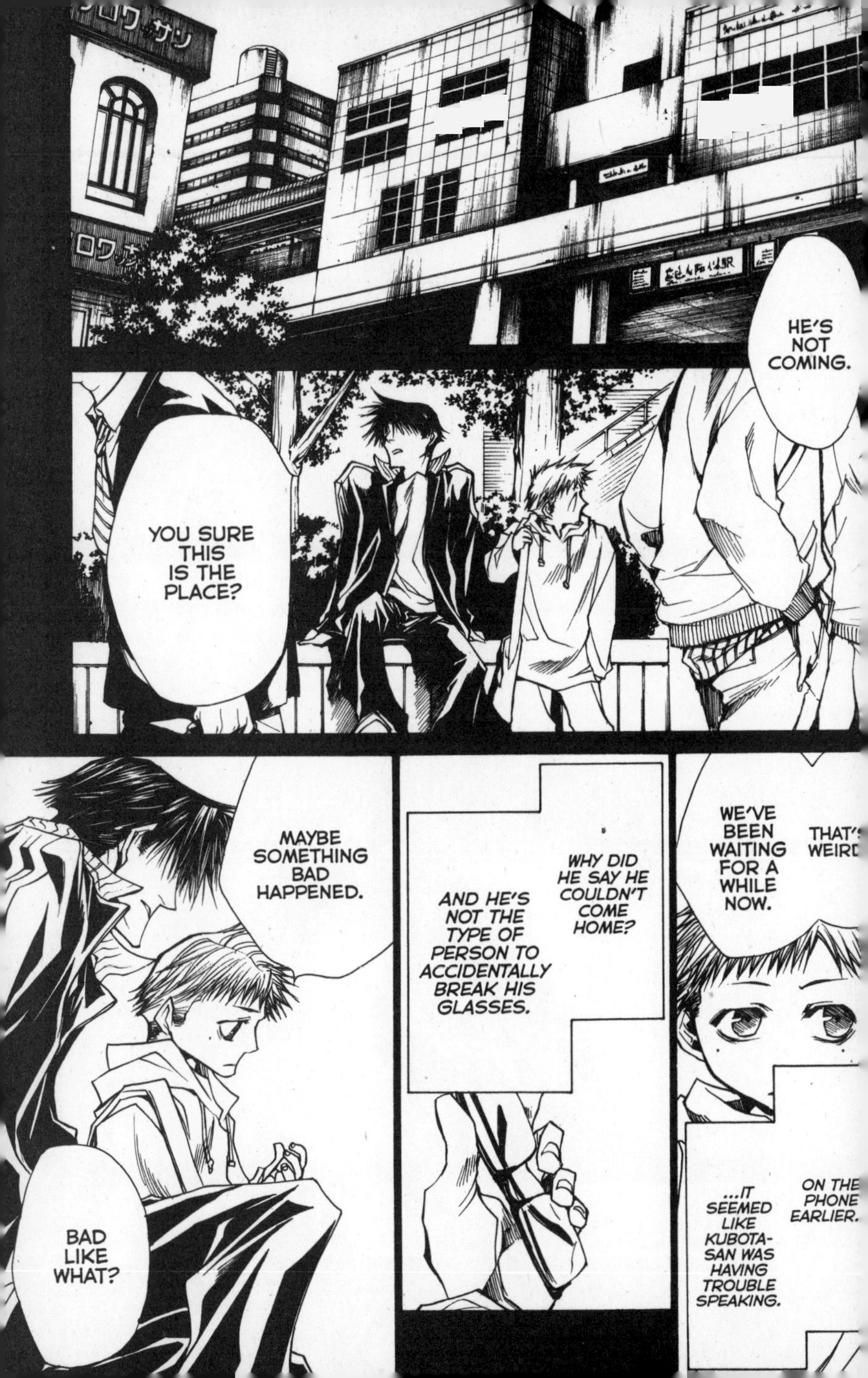
HE'S NOT COMING.
YOU SURE THIS IS THE PLACE?
THAT'S WEIRD
WE'VE BEEN WAITING FOR A WHILE NOW.
ON THE PHONE EARLIER.
...IT SEEMED LIKE KUBOTA-SAN WAS HAVING TROUBLE SPEAKING.
WHY DID HE SAY HE COULDN'T COME HOME?
AND HE'S NOT THE TYPE OF PERSON TO ACCIDENTALLY BREAK HIS GLASSES.
MAYBE SOMETHING BAD HAPPENED.
BAD LIKE WHAT?

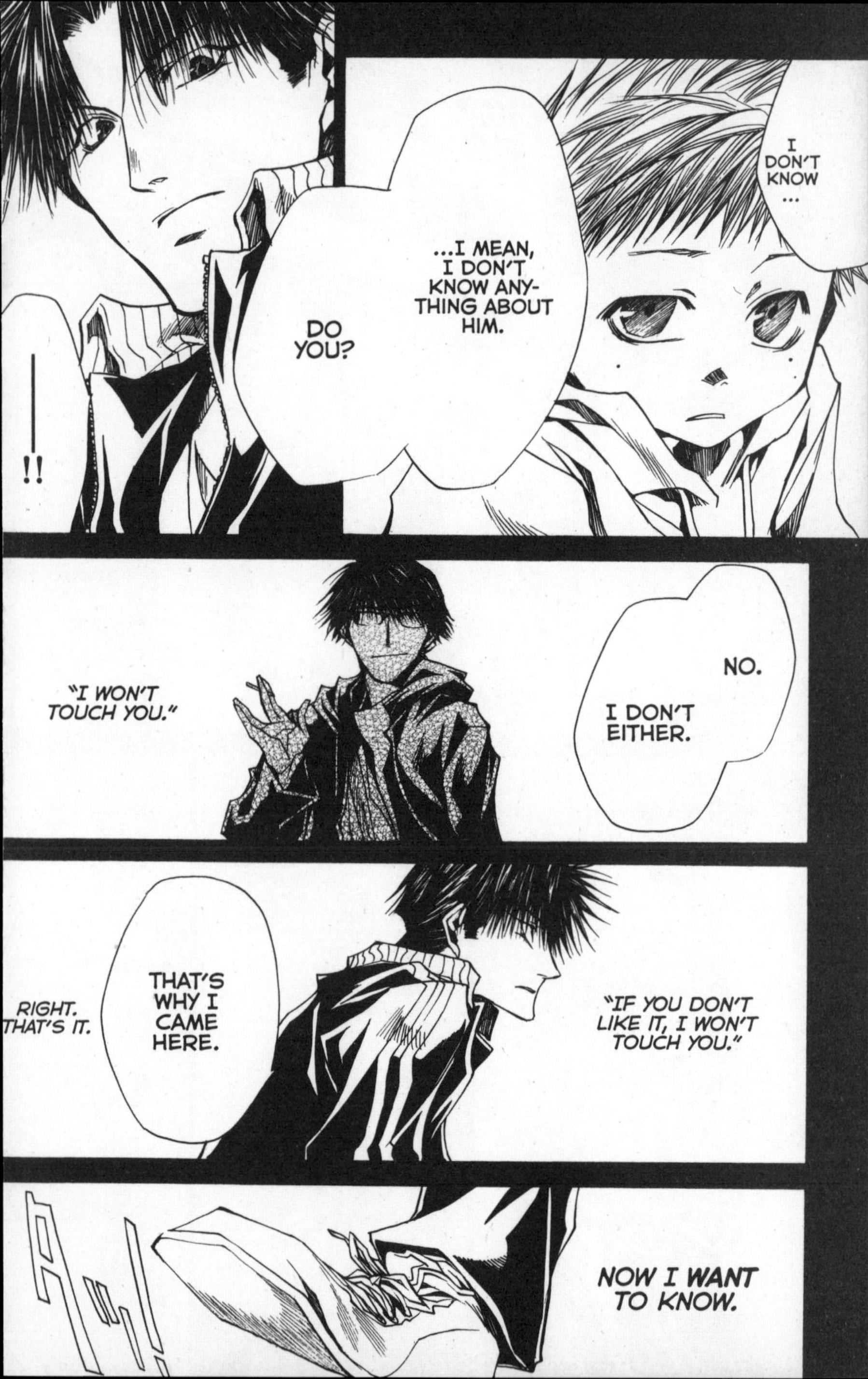
I DON'T KNOW ...
...I MEAN, I DON'T KNOW ANY-THING ABOUT HIM.
DO YOU?
—!!
NO.
I DON'T EITHER.
"I WON'T TOUCH YOU."
"IF YOU DON'T LIKE IT, I WON'T TOUCH YOU."
THAT'S WHY I CAME HERE.
RIGHT. THAT'S IT.
NOW I WANT TO KNOW.

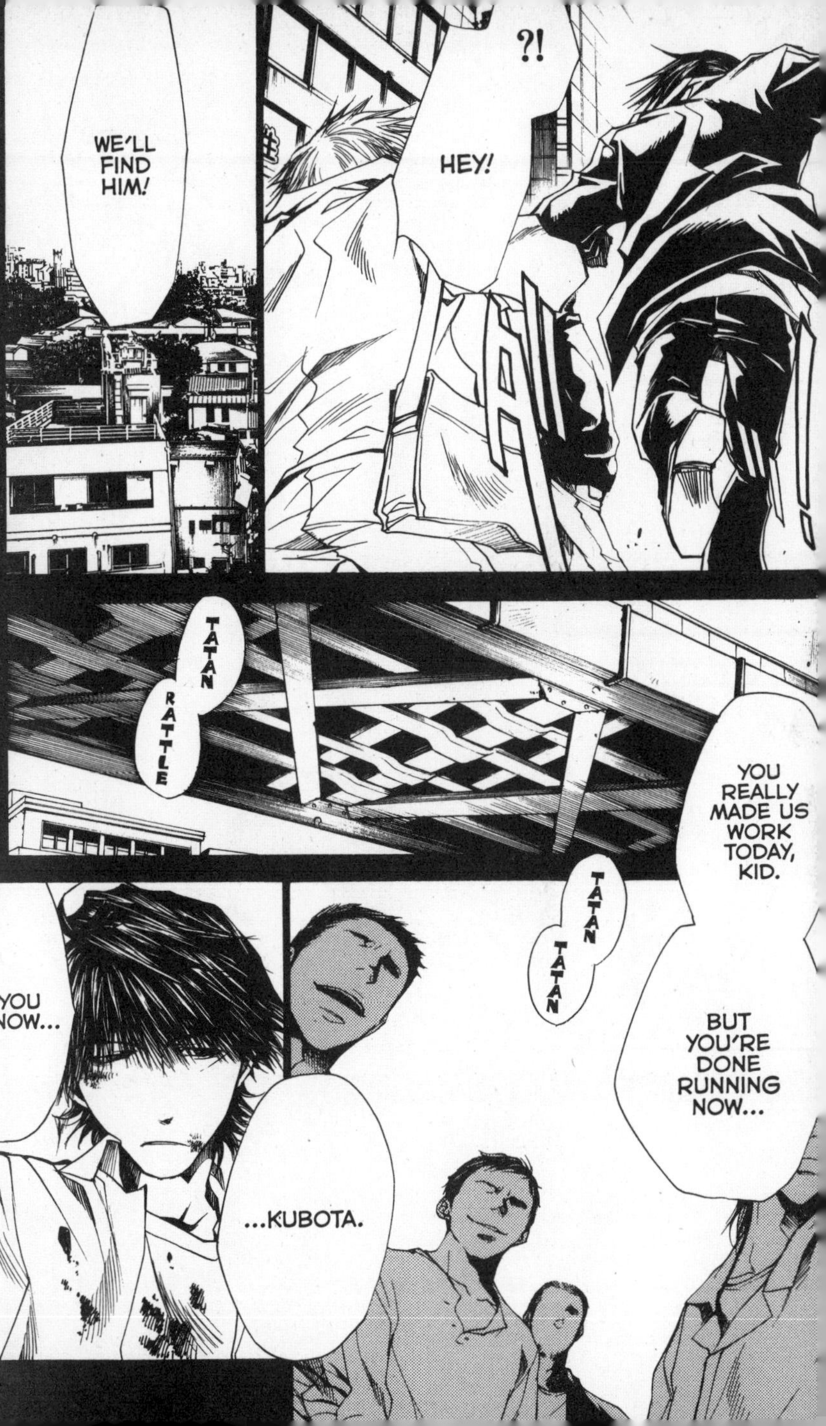
?!
HEY!
WE'LL FIND HIM!
TATAN
RATTLE
YOU REALLY MADE US WORK TODAY, KID.
TATAN
TATAN
BUT YOU'RE DONE RUNNING NOW...
YOU KNOW...
...KUBOTA.

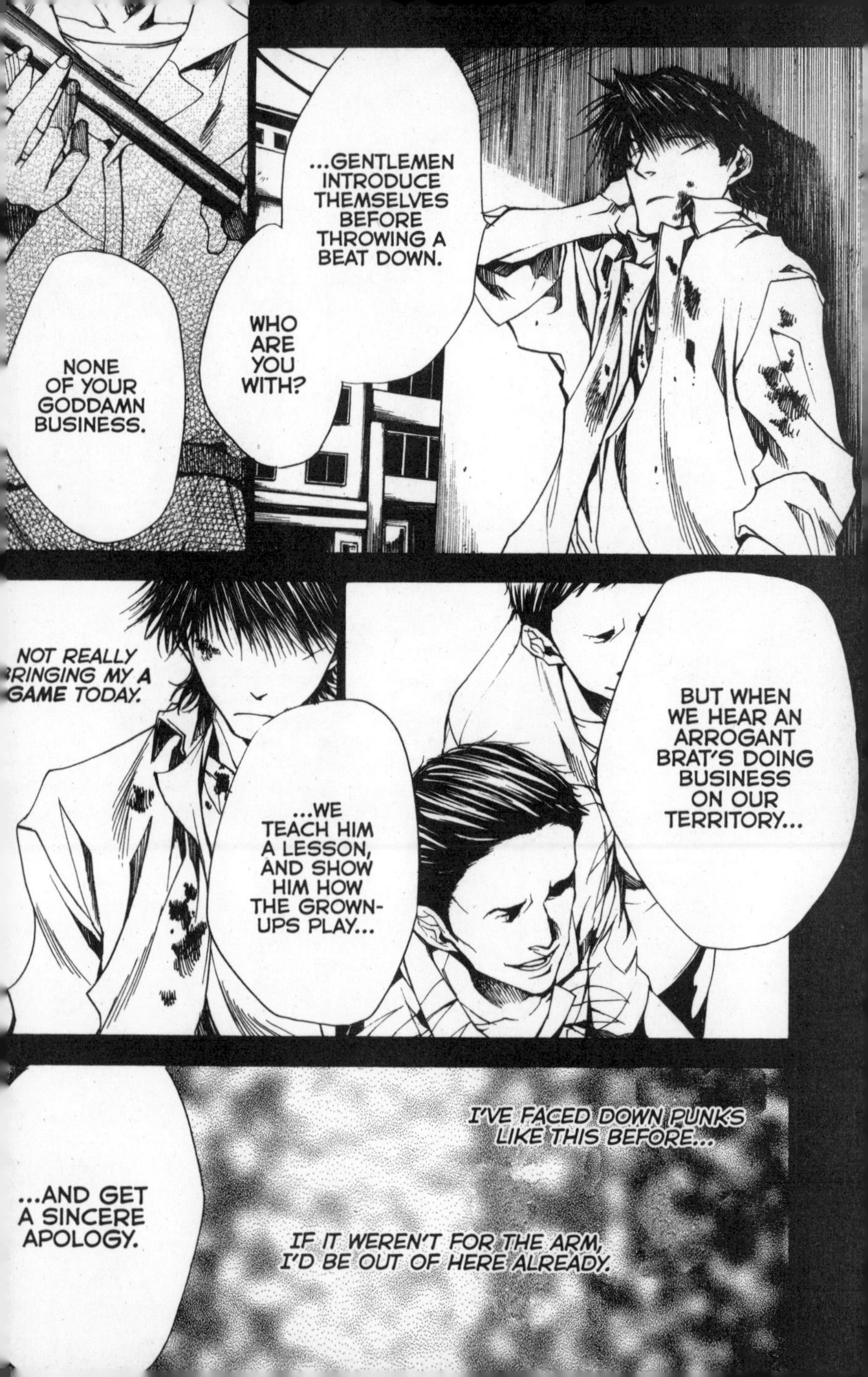
...GENTLEMEN INTRODUCE THEMSELVES BEFORE THROWING A BEAT DOWN.
WHO ARE YOU WITH?
NONE OF YOUR GODDAMN BUSINESS.
BUT WHEN WE HEAR AN ARROGANT BRAT'S DOING BUSINESS ON OUR TERRITORY...
...WE TEACH HIM A LESSON, AND SHOW HIM HOW THE GROWN-UPS PLAY...
NOT REALLY BRINGING MY A GAME TODAY.
I'VE FACED DOWN PUNKS LIKE THIS BEFORE...
IF IT WEREN'T FOR THE ARM, I'D BE OUT OF HERE ALREADY.
...AND GET A SINCERE APOLOGY.

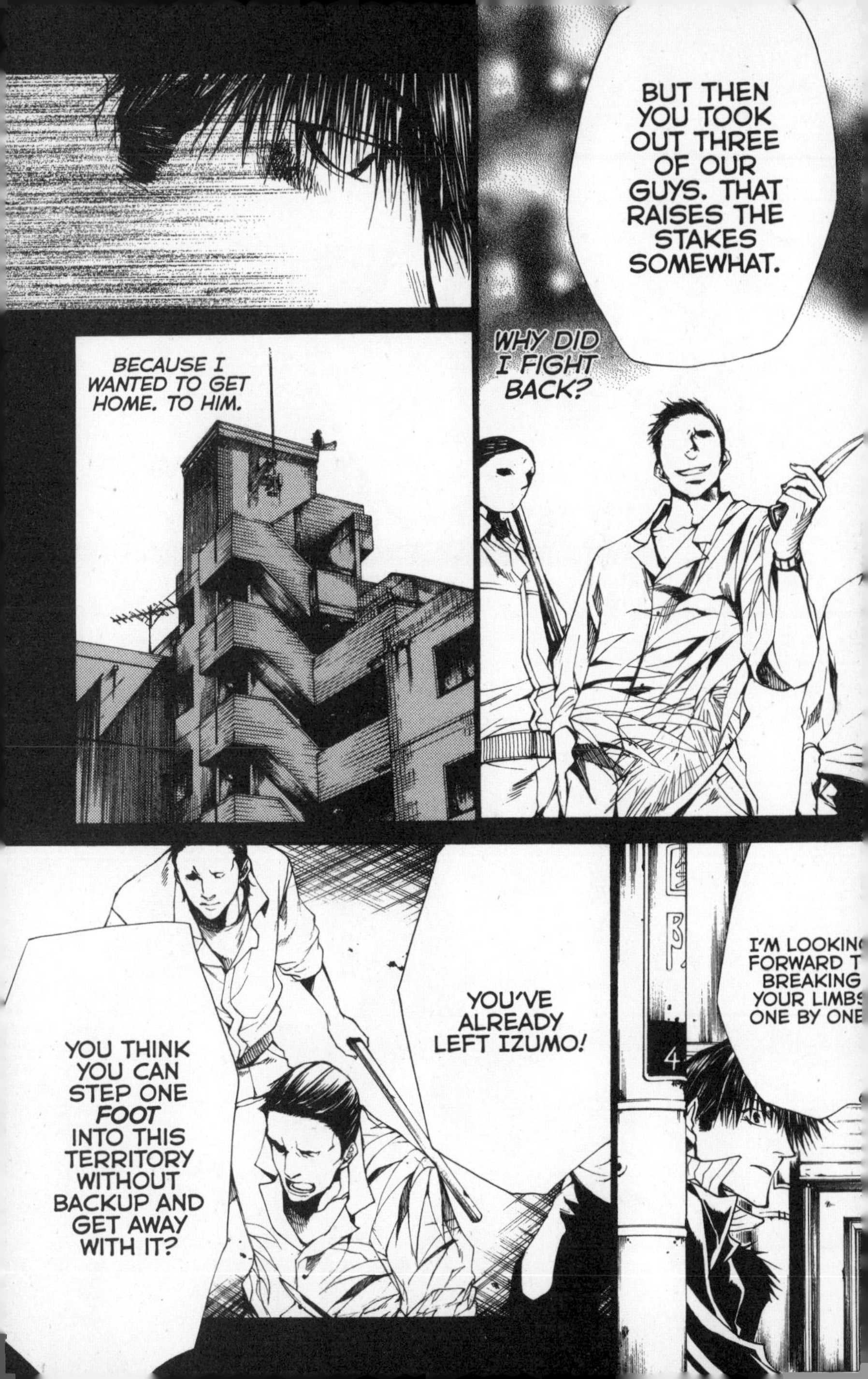
BUT THEN YOU TOOK OUT THREE OF OUR GUYS. THAT RAISES THE STAKES SOMEWHAT.
WHY DID I FIGHT BACK?
BECAUSE I WANTED TO GET HOME. TO HIM.
I'M LOOKING FORWARD T BREAKING YOUR LIMBS ONE BY ONE
YOU'VE ALREADY LEFT IZUMO!
YOU THINK YOU CAN STEP ONE *FOOT* INTO THIS TERRITORY WITHOUT BACKUP AND GET AWAY WITH IT?

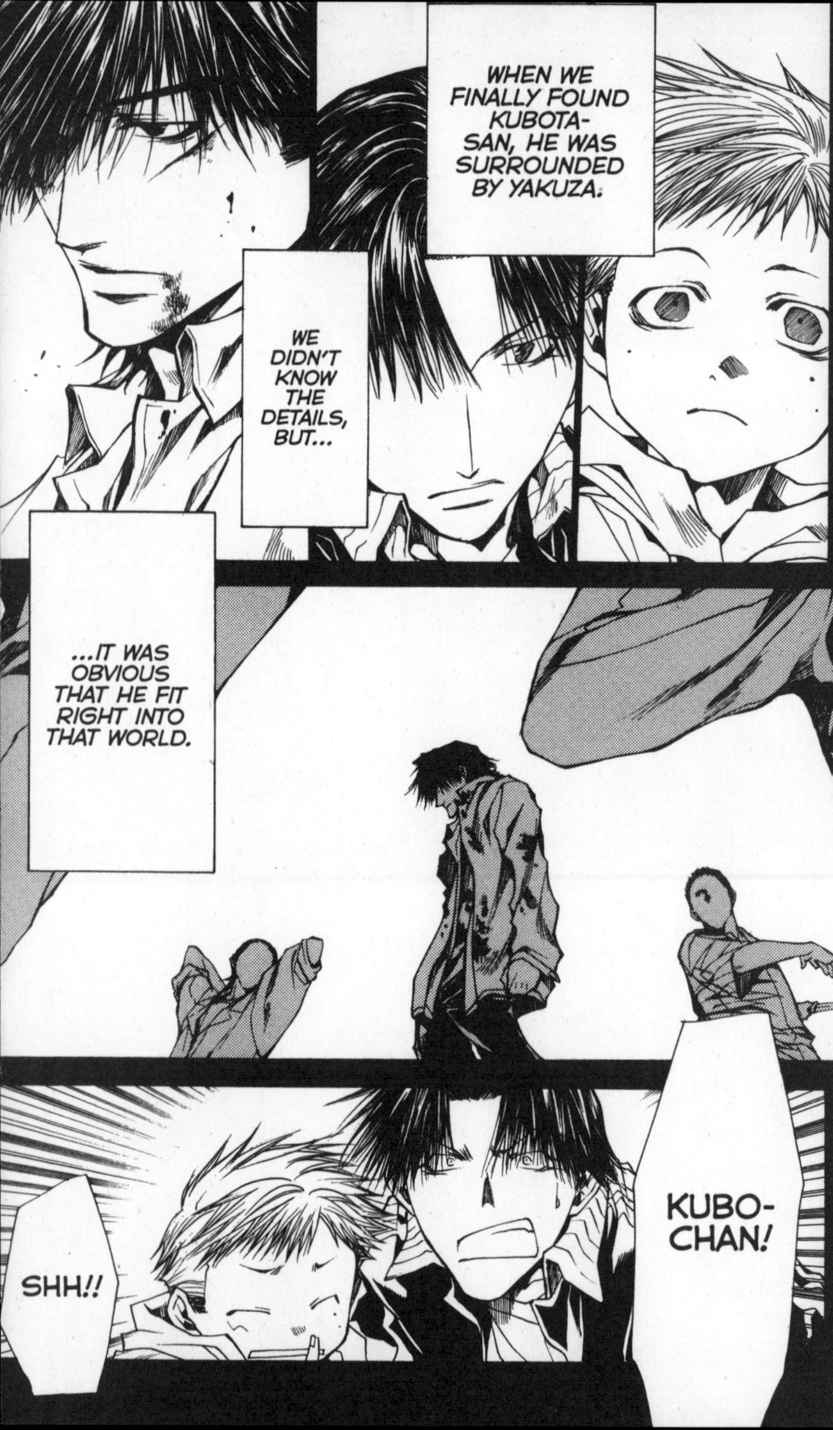
WHEN WE FINALLY FOUND KUBOTA-SAN, HE WAS SURROUNDED BY YAKUZA.
WE DIDN'T KNOW THE DETAILS, BUT...
...IT WAS OBVIOUS THAT HE FIT RIGHT INTO THAT WORLD.
KUBO-CHAN!
SHH!!

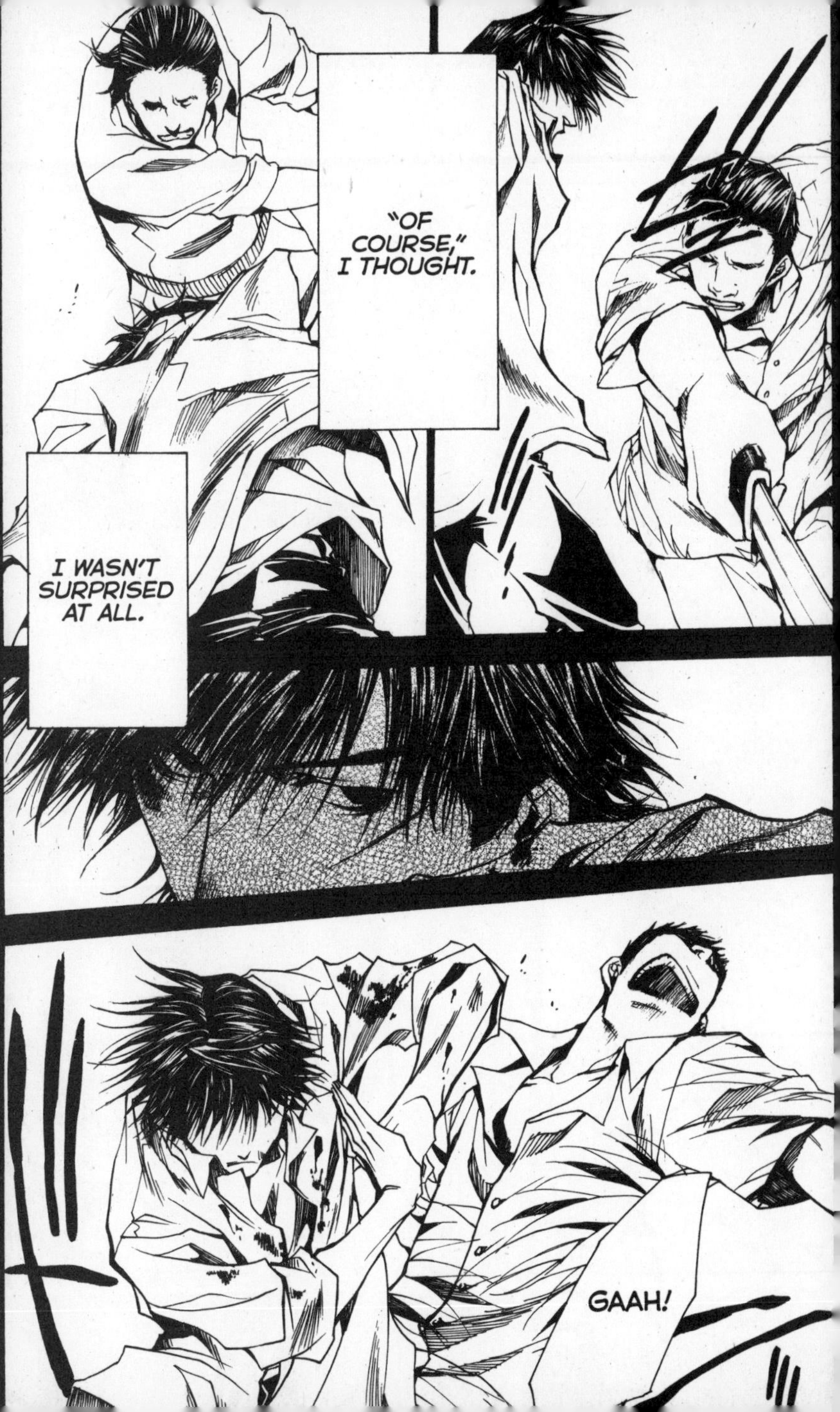
"OF COURSE," I THOUGHT.
I WASN'T SURPRISED AT ALL.
GAAH!

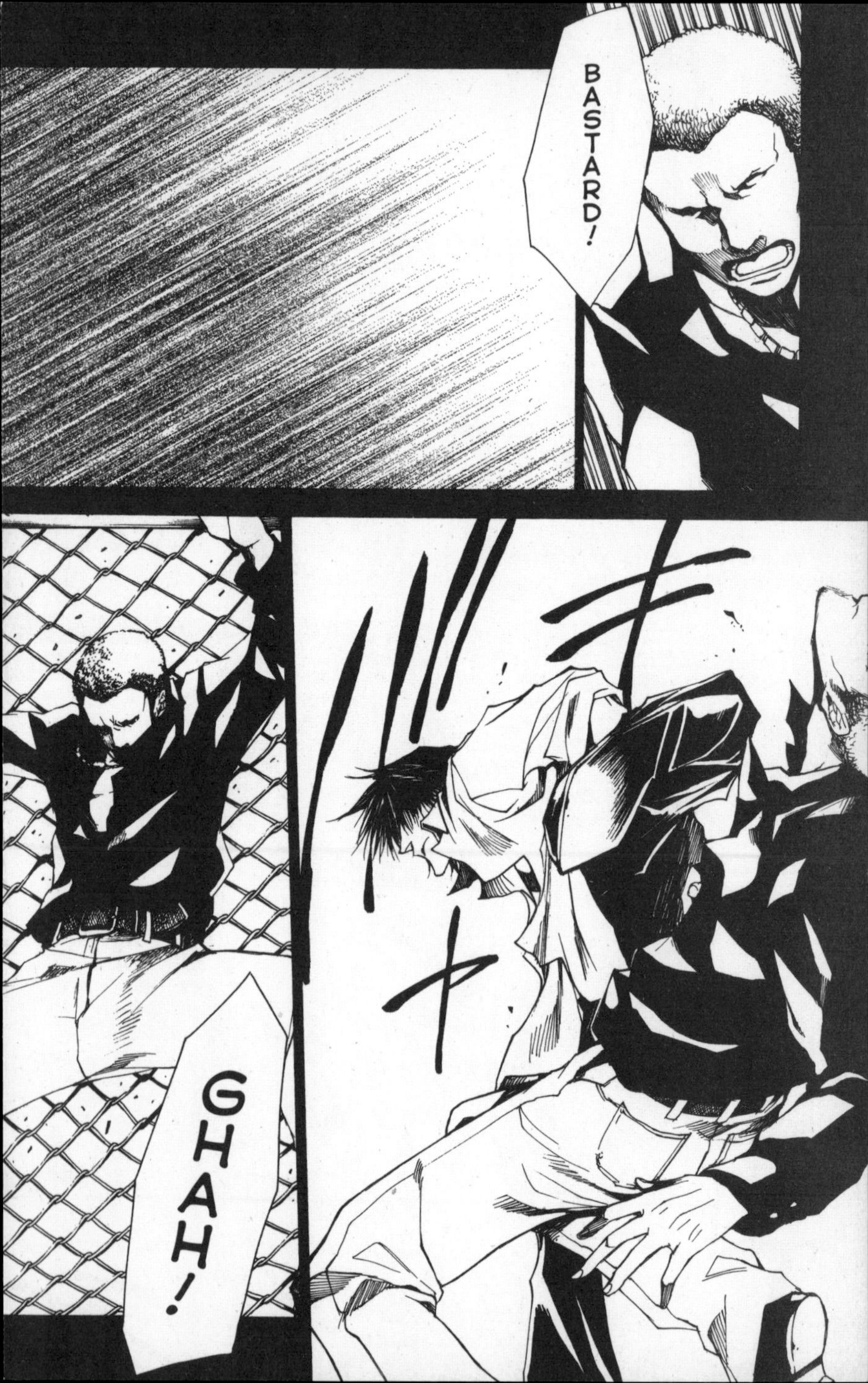
BASTARD!
GHAH!

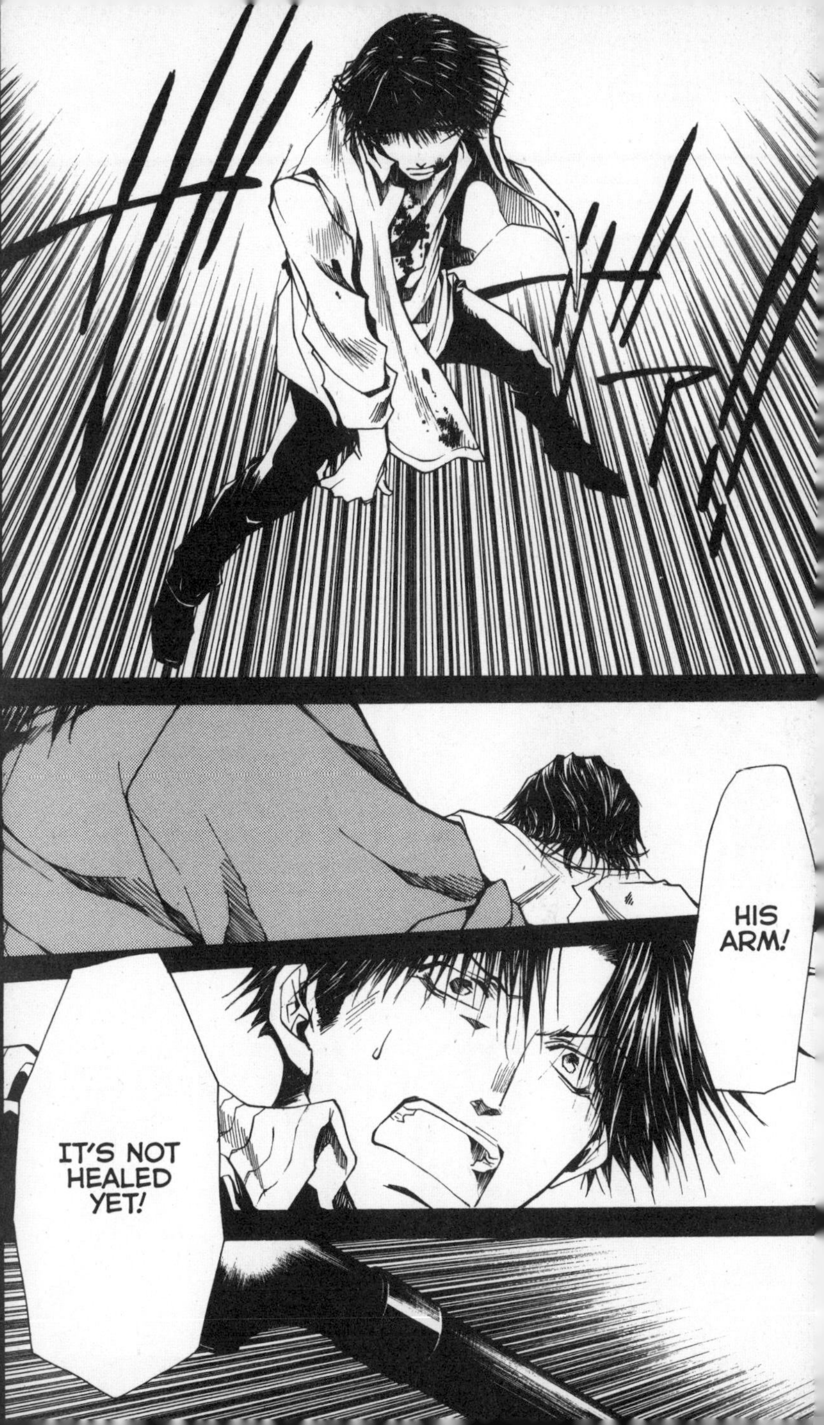
HIS ARM!
IT'S NOT HEALED YET!

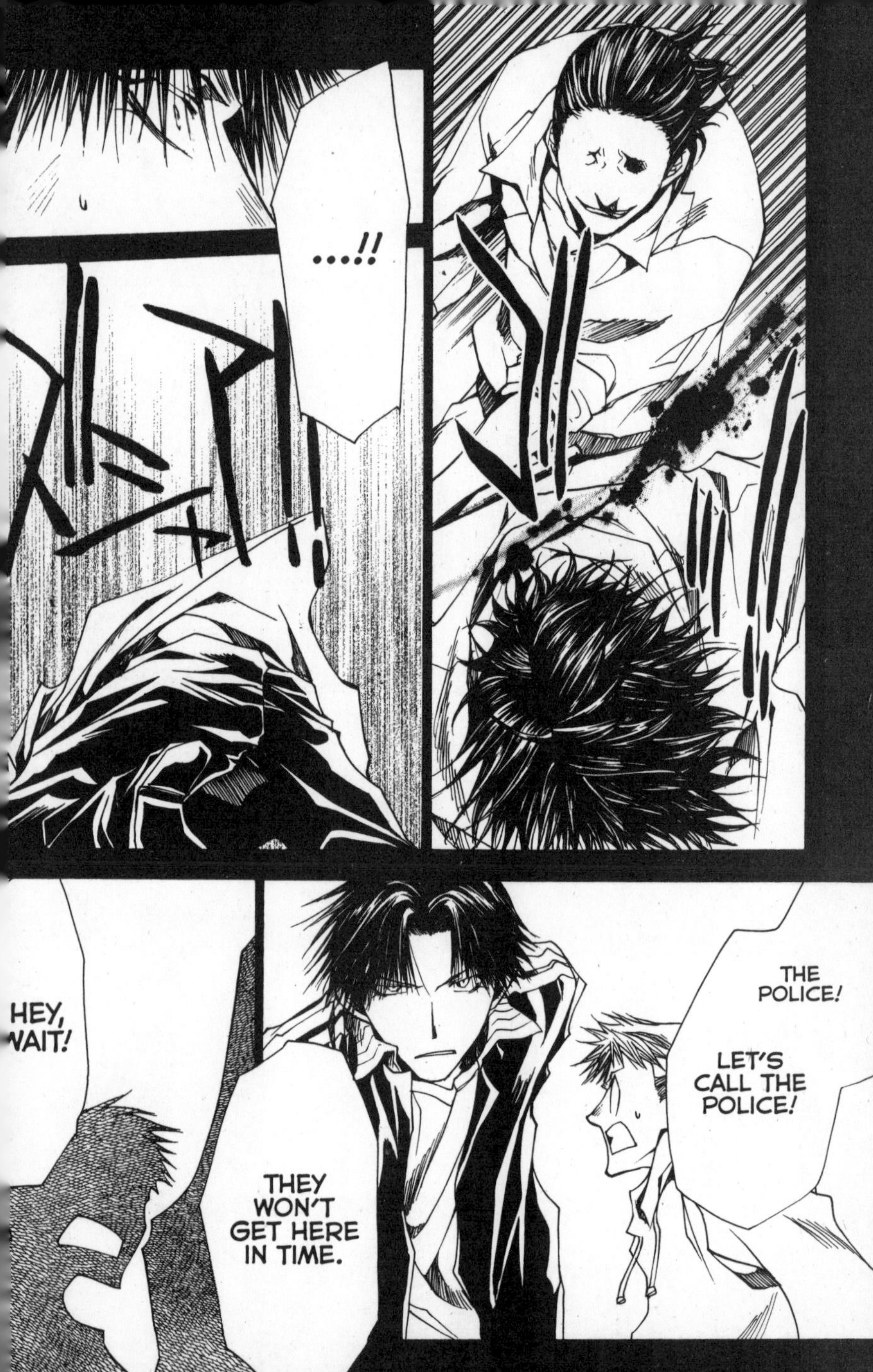

...!!
THE POLICE!
LET'S CALL THE POLICE!
THEY WON'T GET HERE IN TIME.
HEY, WAIT!

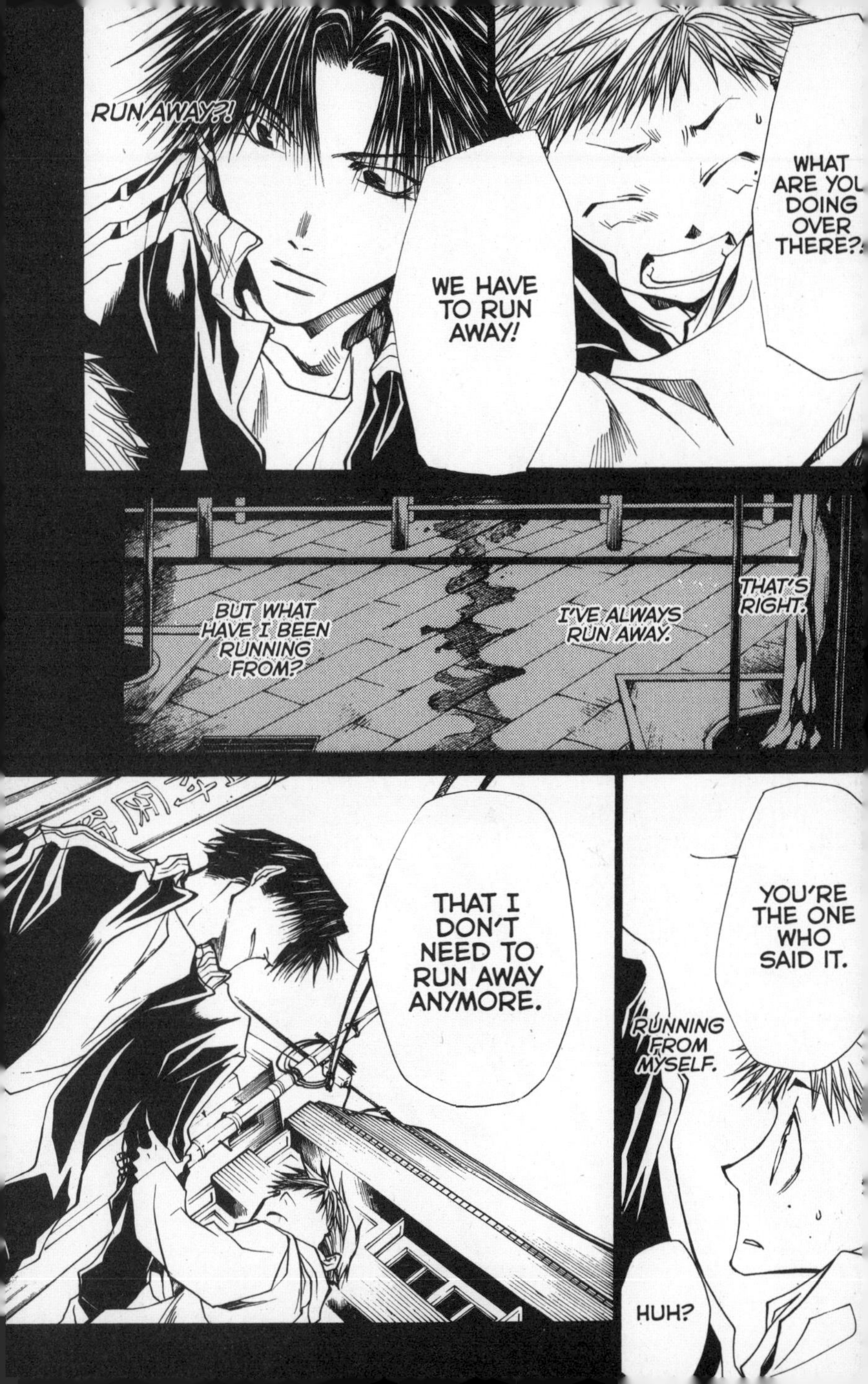
WHAT ARE YOU DOING OVER THERE?!
WE HAVE TO RUN AWAY!
RUN AWAY?!
THAT'S RIGHT.
I'VE ALWAYS RUN AWAY.
BUT WHAT HAVE I BEEN RUNNING FROM?
YOU'RE THE ONE WHO SAID IT.
RUNNING FROM MYSELF.
HUH?
THAT I DON'T NEED TO RUN AWAY ANYMORE.

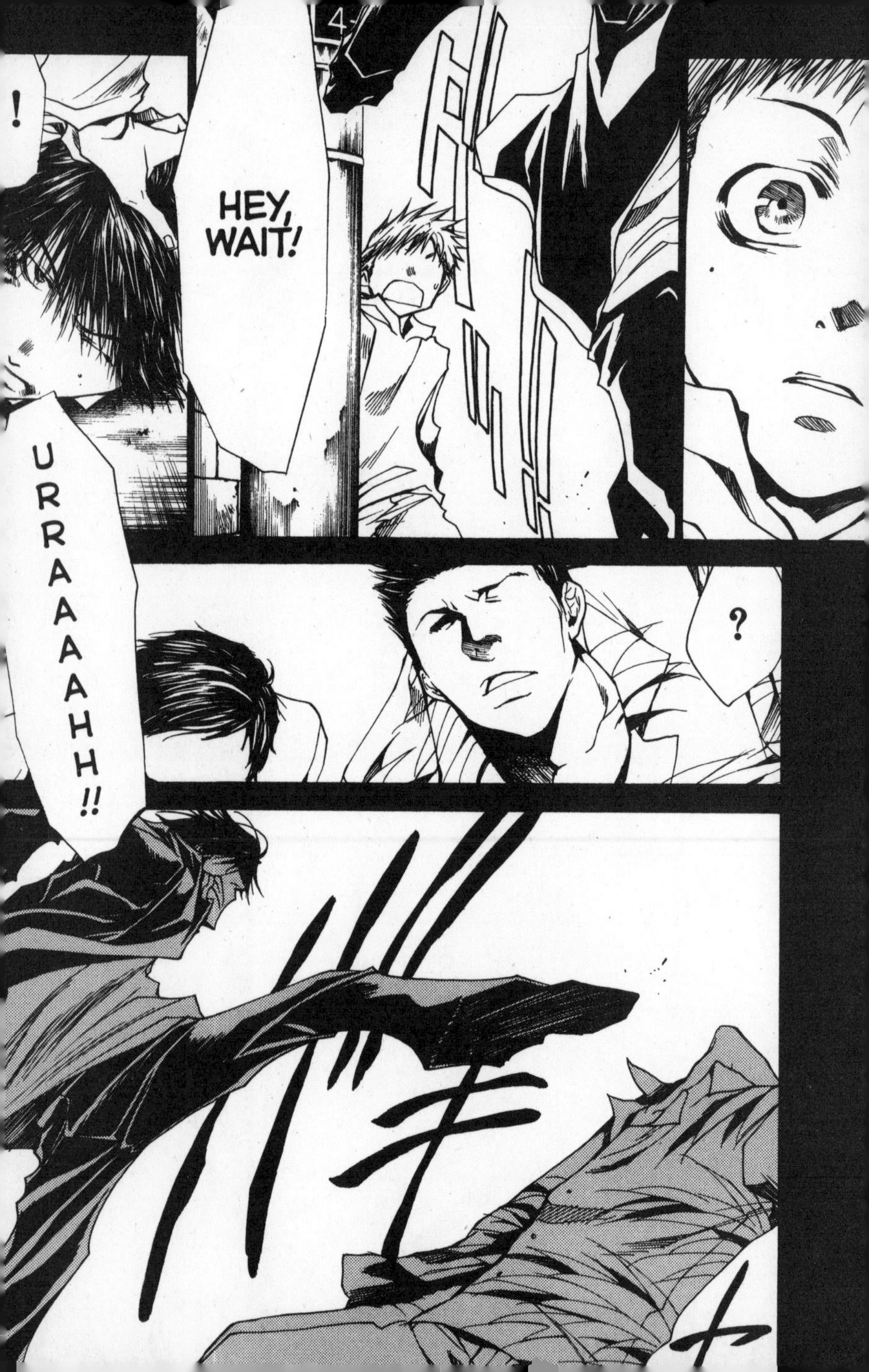
HEY, WAIT!
!
?
URRAAAAAHH!!

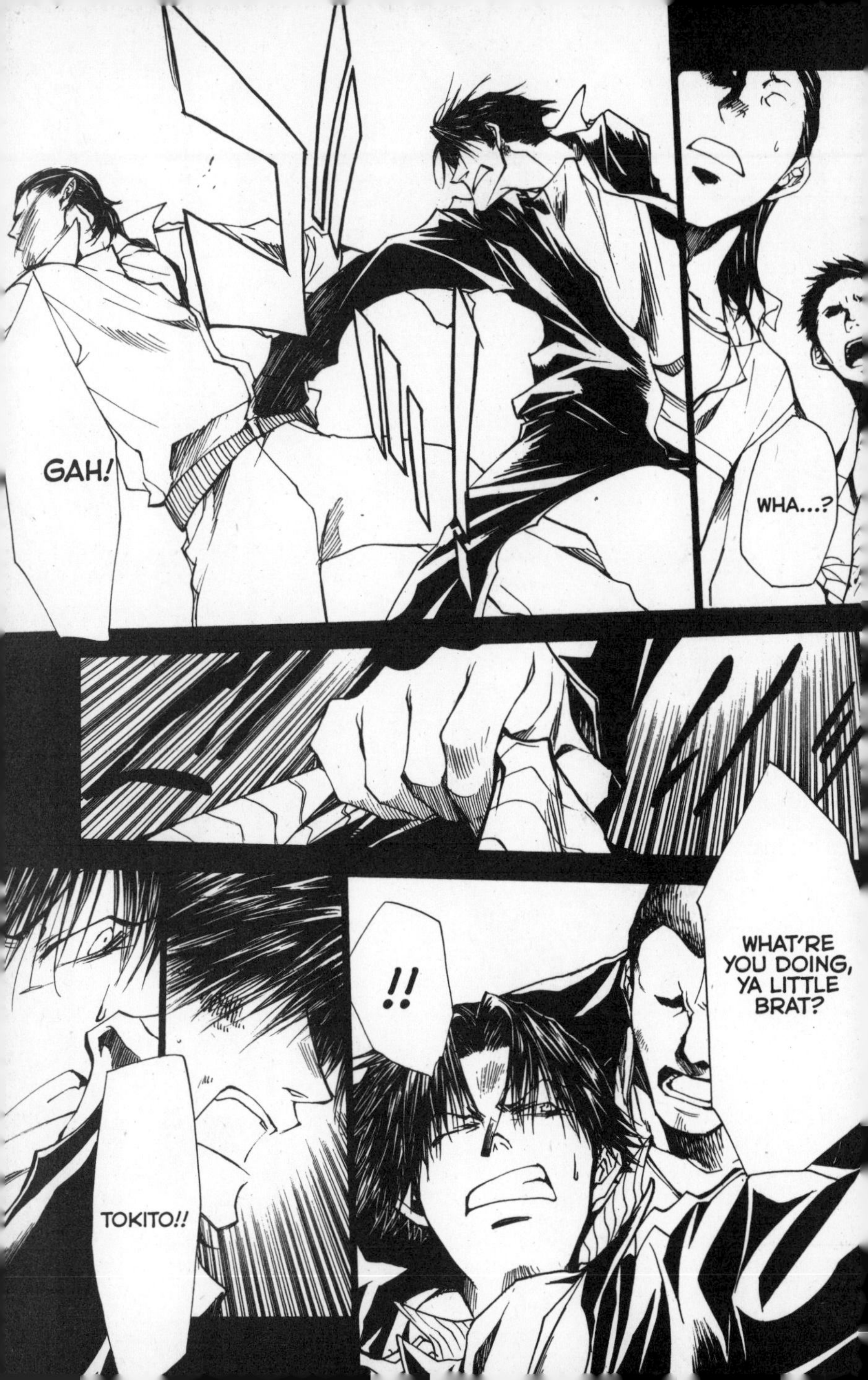
WHA...?
GAH!
WHAT'RE YOU DOING, YA LITTLE BRAT?
!!
TOKITO!!

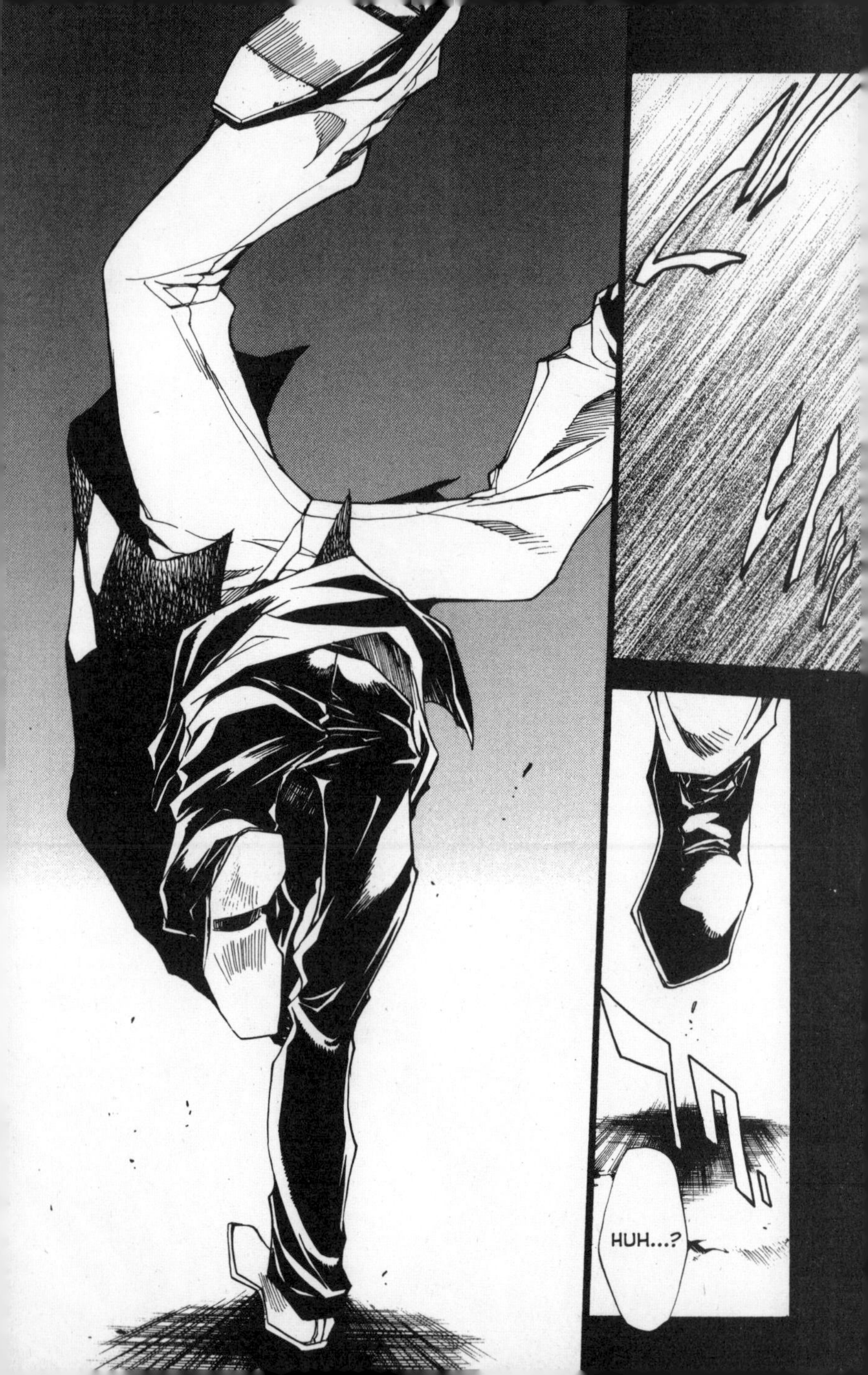
HUH...?

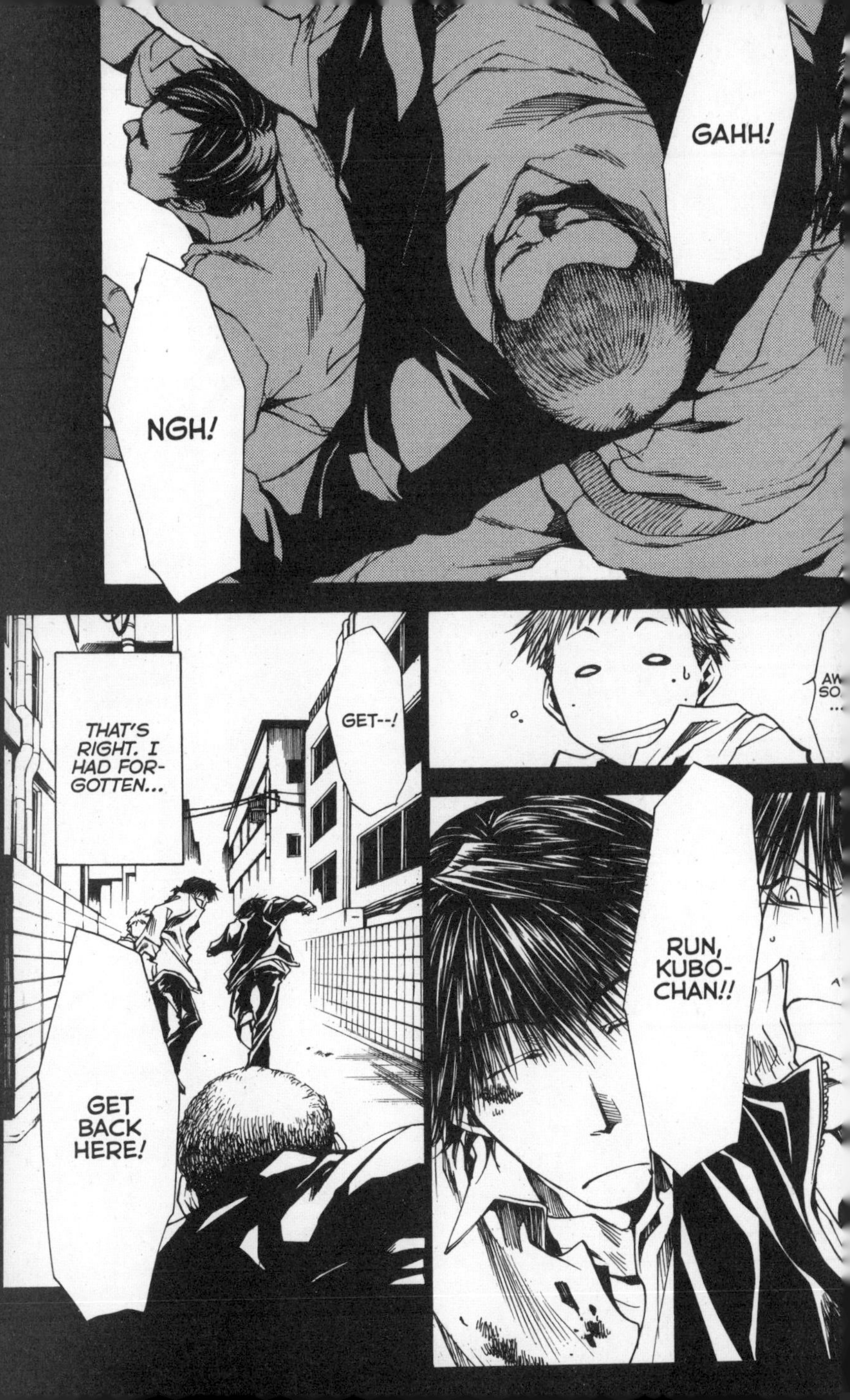
GAHH!
NGH!
RUN, KUBO-CHAN!!
GET--!
THAT'S RIGHT. I HAD FORGOTTEN...
GET BACK HERE!

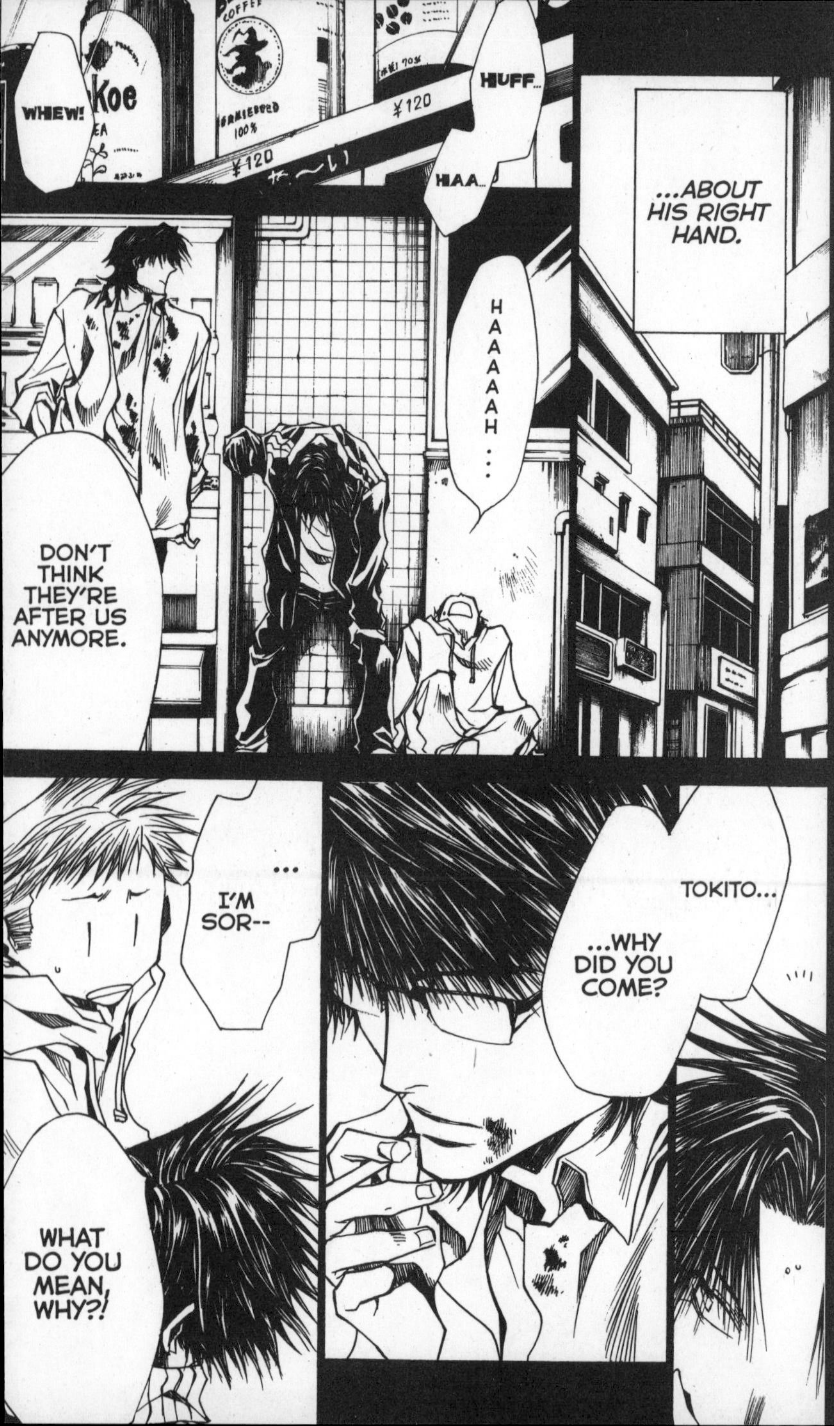
...ABOUT HIS RIGHT HAND.
HUFF...
HAA...
WHEW!
HAAAAAH...
DON'T THINK THEY'RE AFTER US ANYMORE.
TOKITO...
...WHY DID YOU COME?
...
I'M SOR--
WHAT DO YOU MEAN, WHY?!

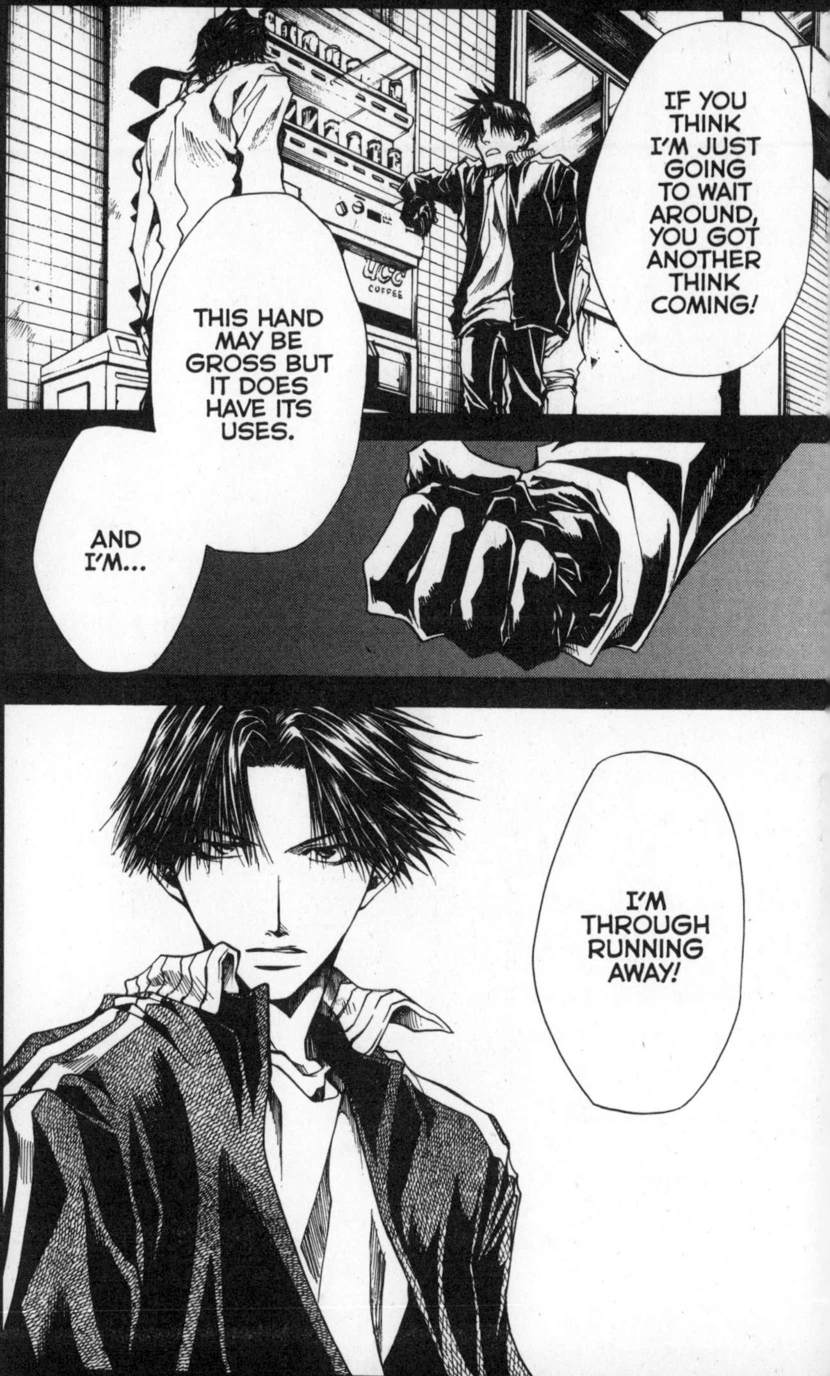
IF YOU THINK I'M JUST GOING TO WAIT AROUND, YOU GOT ANOTHER THINK COMING!
UCC COFFEE
THIS HAND MAY BE GROSS BUT IT DOES HAVE ITS USES.
AND I'M...
I'M THROUGH RUNNING AWAY!

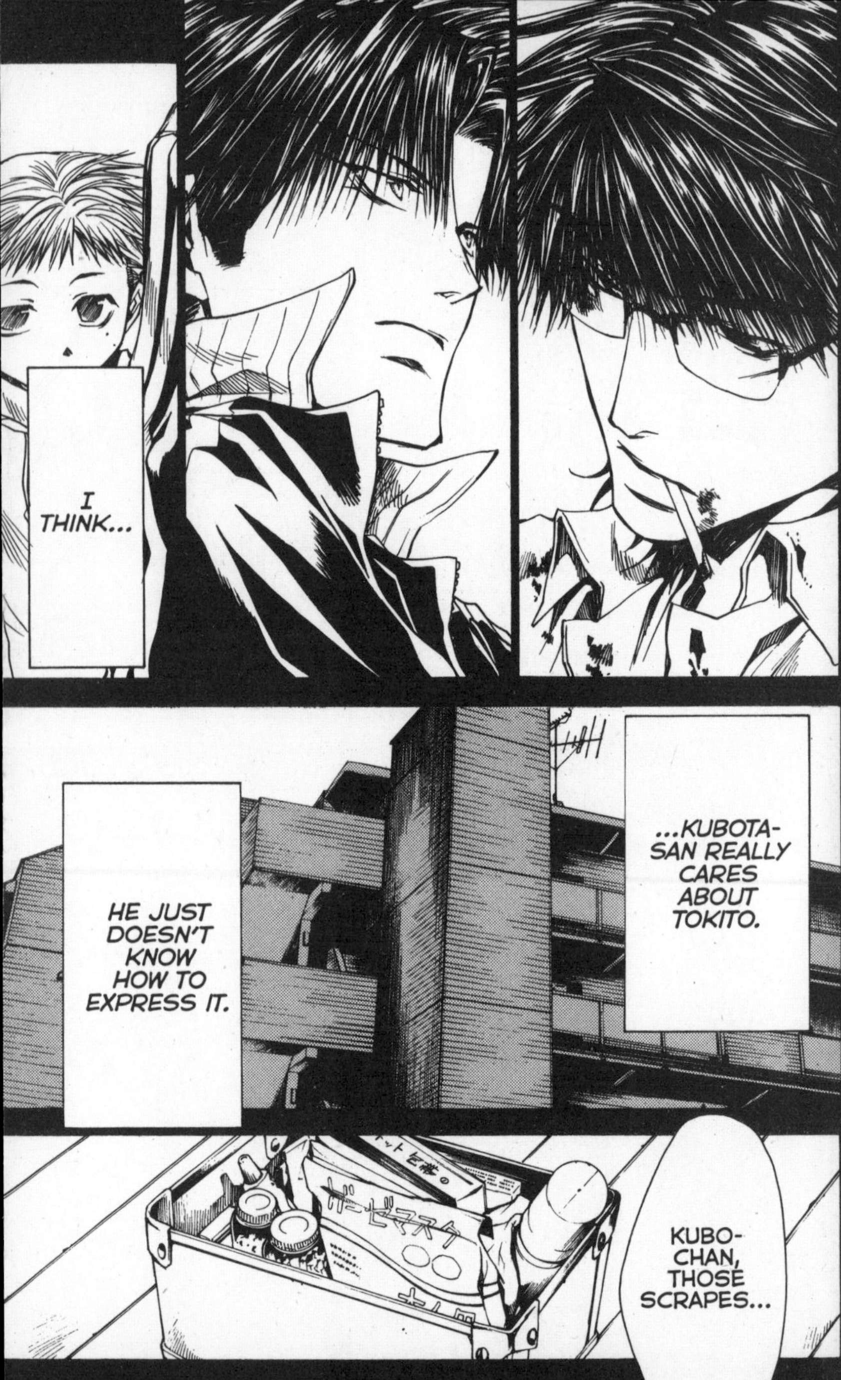
I THINK...
...KUBOTA-SAN REALLY CARES ABOUT TOKITO.
HE JUST DOESN'T KNOW HOW TO EXPRESS IT.
KUBO-CHAN, THOSE SCRAPES...

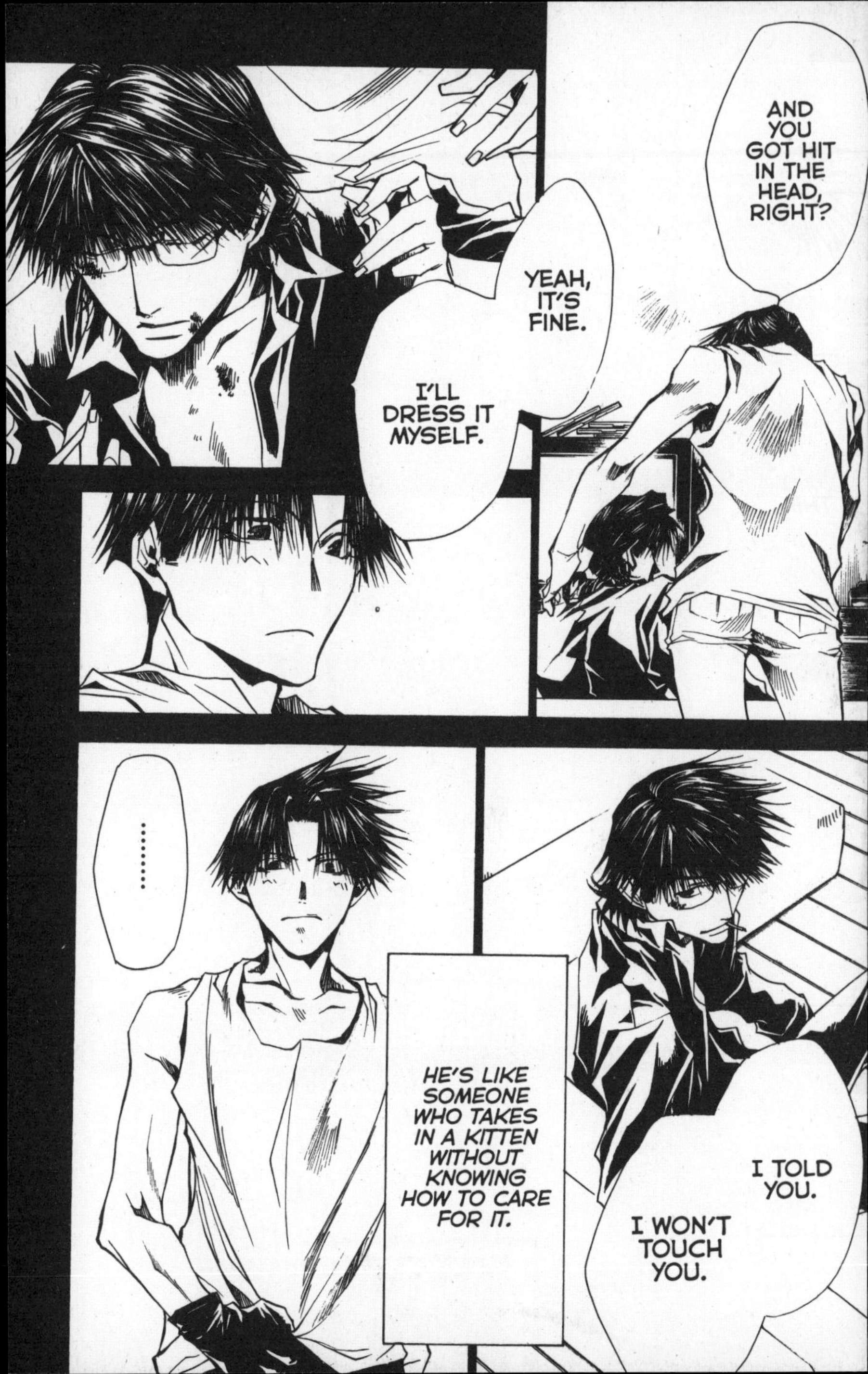
AND YOU GOT HIT IN THE HEAD, RIGHT?
YEAH, IT'S FINE.
I'LL DRESS IT MYSELF.
I TOLD YOU.
I WON'T TOUCH YOU.
......
HE'S LIKE SOMEONE WHO TAKES IN A KITTEN WITHOUT KNOWING HOW TO CARE FOR IT.

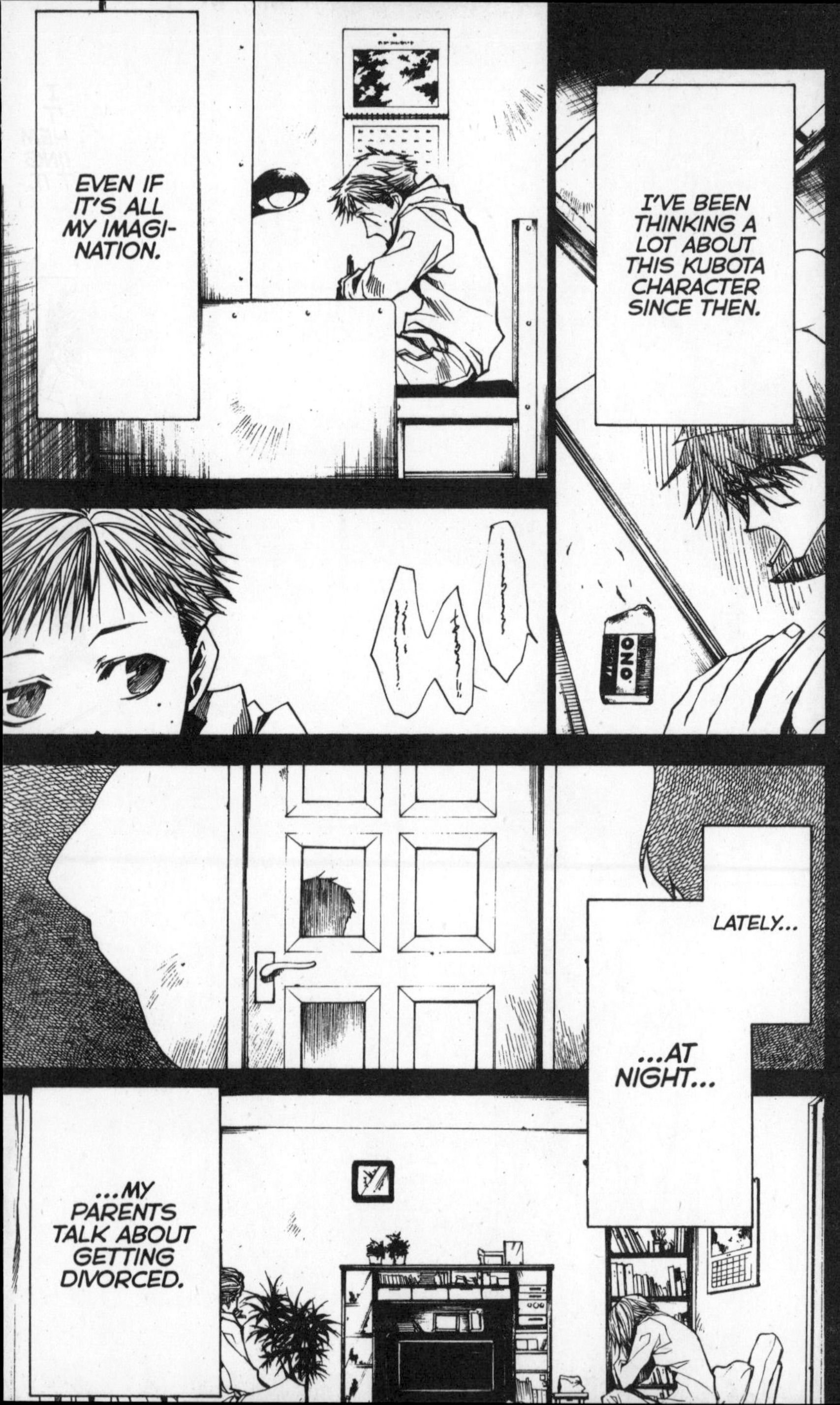
I'VE BEEN THINKING A LOT ABOUT THIS KUBOTA CHARACTER SINCE THEN.
EVEN IF IT'S ALL MY IMAGI-NATION.
LATELY...
...AT NIGHT...
...MY PARENTS TALK ABOUT GETTING DIVORCED.

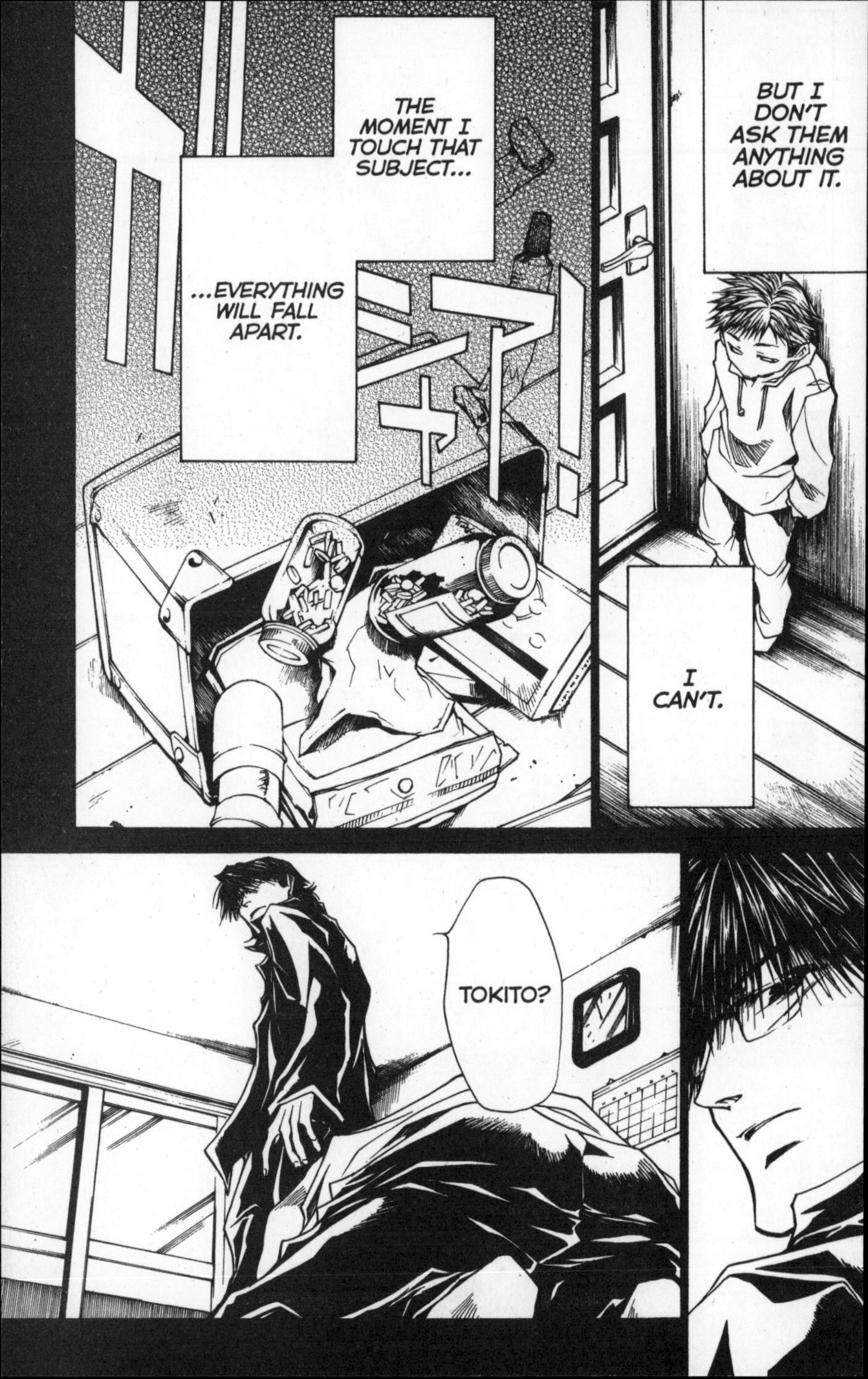
BUT I DON'T ASK THEM ANYTHING ABOUT IT.
I CAN'T.
THE MOMENT I TOUCH THAT SUBJECT...
...EVERYTHING WILL FALL APART.
TOKITO?

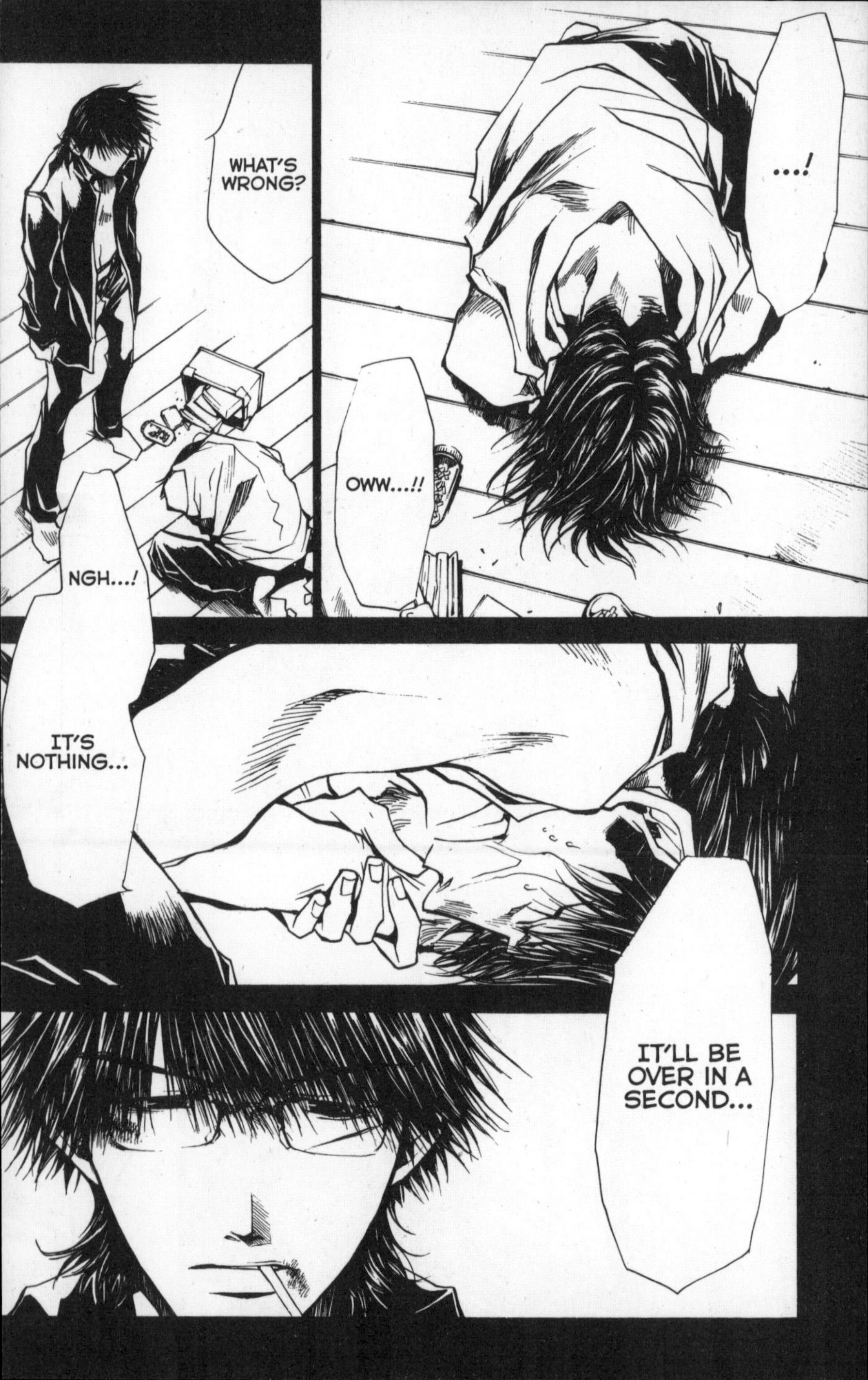
...!
OWW...!!
WHAT'S WRONG?
NGH...!
IT'S NOTHING...
IT'LL BE OVER IN A SECOND...

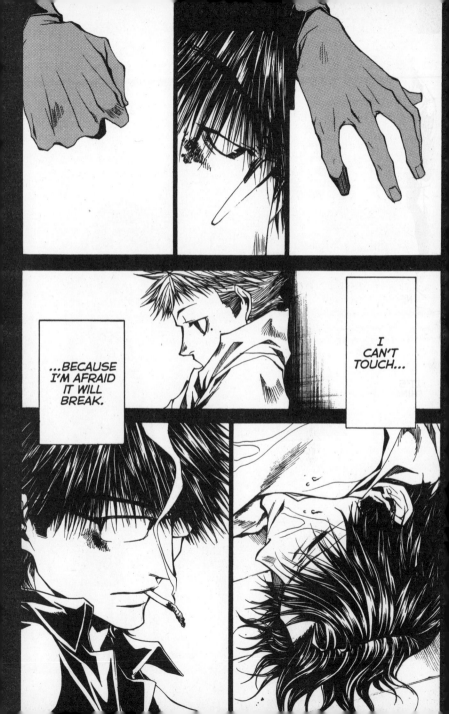

...BECAUSE I'M AFRAID IT WILL BREAK.

I CAN'T TOUCH...

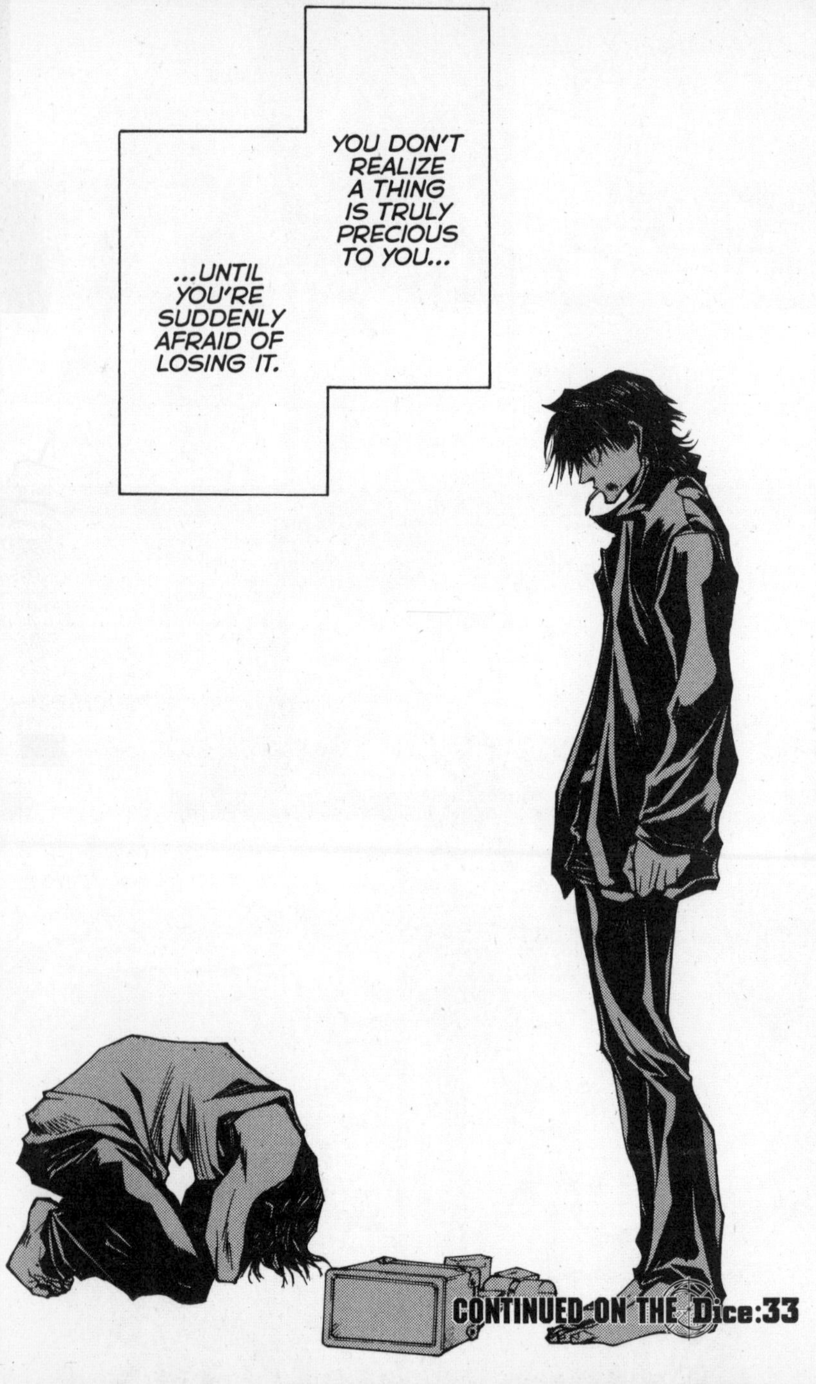

YOU DON'T REALIZE A THING IS TRULY PRECIOUS TO YOU...
...UNTIL YOU'RE SUDDENLY AFRAID OF LOSING IT.

CONTINUED ON THE Dice:33

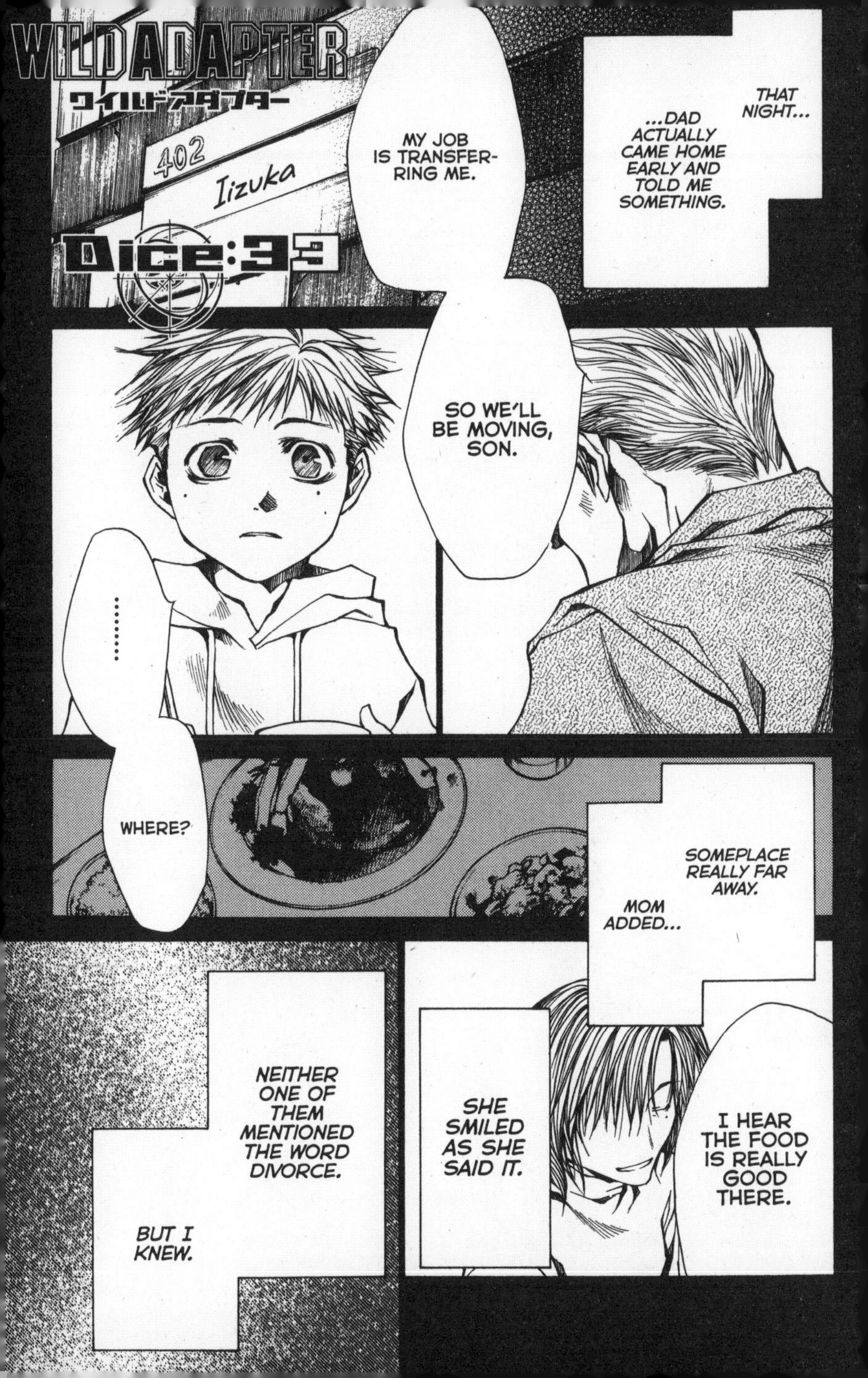
WILD ADAPTER
ワイルドアダプター
402
Iizuka
Dice:33
THAT NIGHT...
...DAD ACTUALLY CAME HOME EARLY AND TOLD ME SOMETHING.
MY JOB IS TRANSFERRING ME.
SO WE'LL BE MOVING, SON.
......
WHERE?
SOMEPLACE REALLY FAR AWAY.
MOM ADDED...
I HEAR THE FOOD IS REALLY GOOD THERE.
SHE SMILED AS SHE SAID IT.
NEITHER ONE OF THEM MENTIONED THE WORD DIVORCE.
BUT I KNEW.

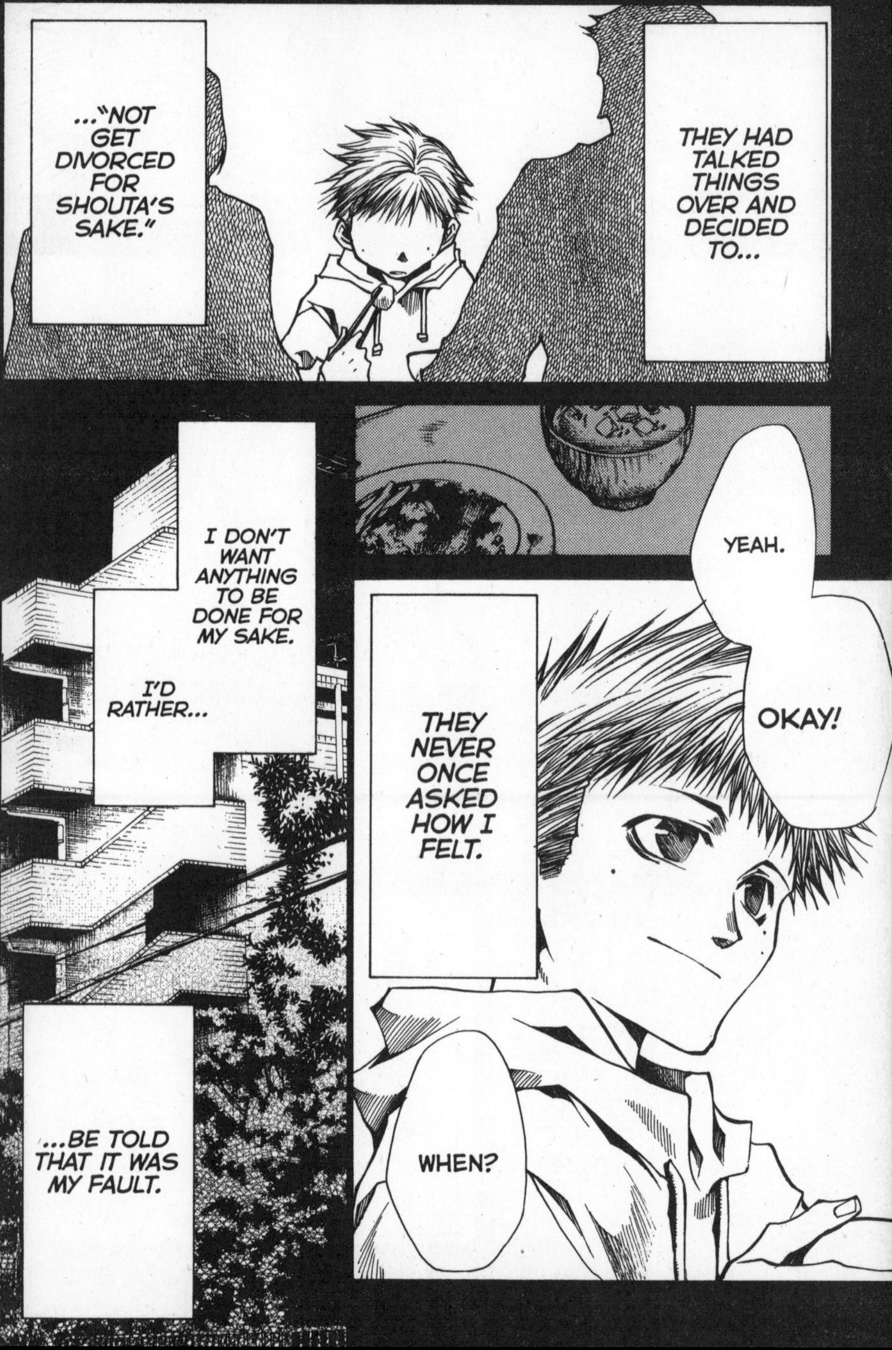
THEY HAD TALKED THINGS OVER AND DECIDED TO...
..."NOT GET DIVORCED FOR SHOUTA'S SAKE."
YEAH.
OKAY!
THEY NEVER ONCE ASKED HOW I FELT.
WHEN?
I DON'T WANT ANYTHING TO BE DONE FOR MY SAKE.
I'D RATHER...
...BE TOLD THAT IT WAS MY FAULT.

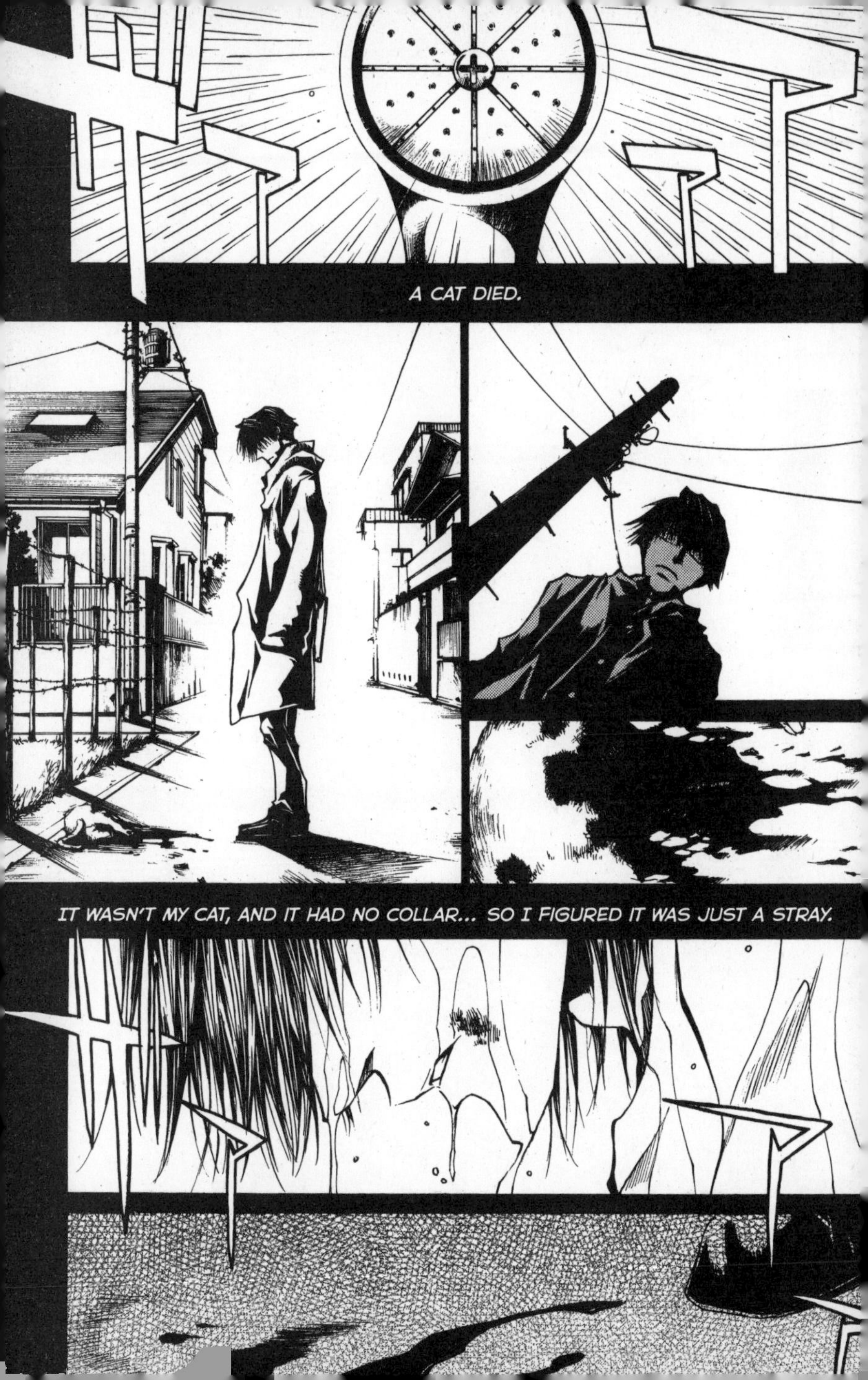
A CAT DIED.
IT WASN'T MY CAT, AND IT HAD NO COLLAR... SO I FIGURED IT WAS JUST A STRAY.

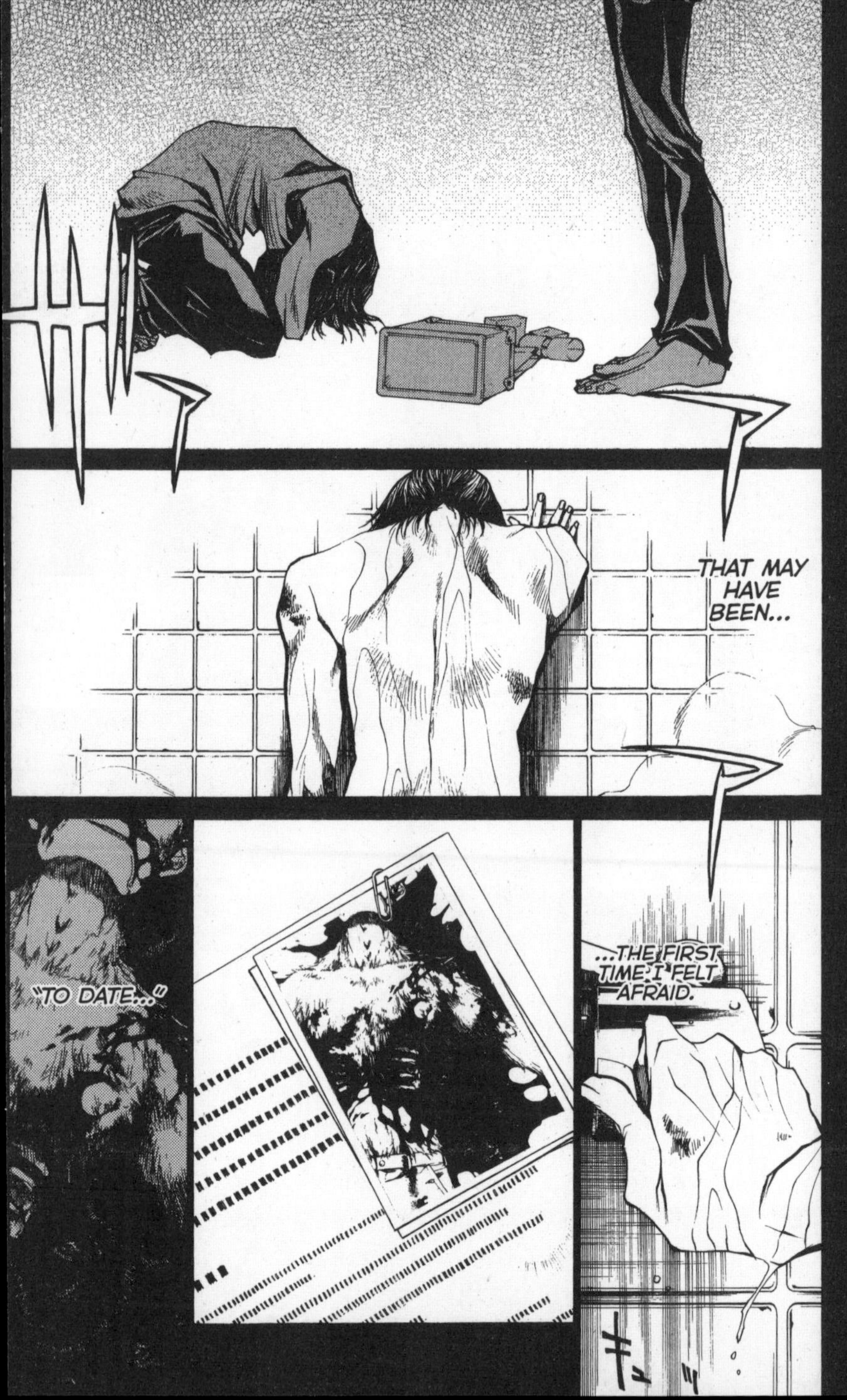
THAT MAY HAVE BEEN...
...THE FIRST TIME I FELT AFRAID.
"TO DATE..."

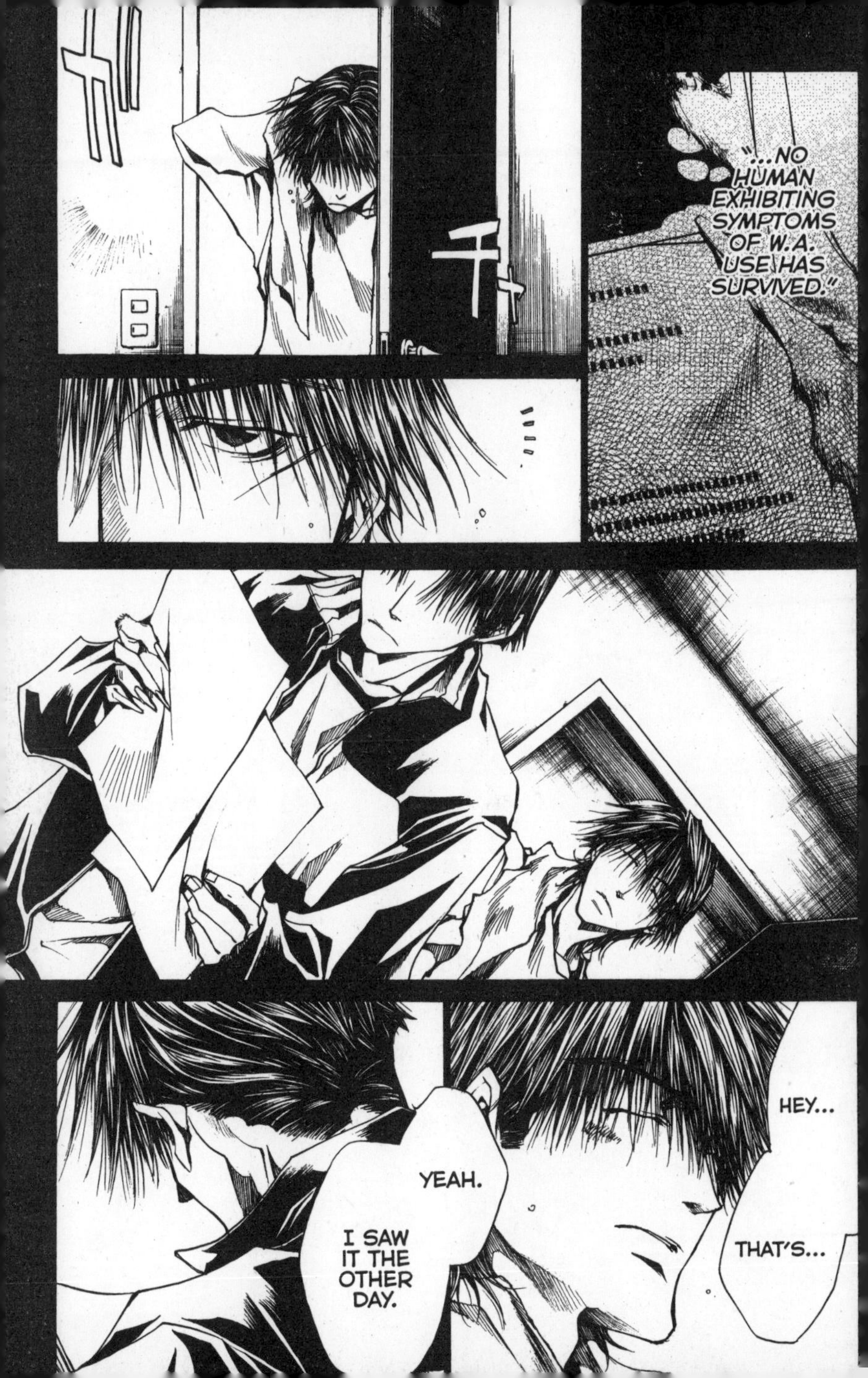
"...NO HUMAN EXHIBITING SYMPTOMS OF W.A. USE HAS SURVIVED."
ガチャ
HEY...
THAT'S...
YEAH.
I SAW IT THE OTHER DAY.

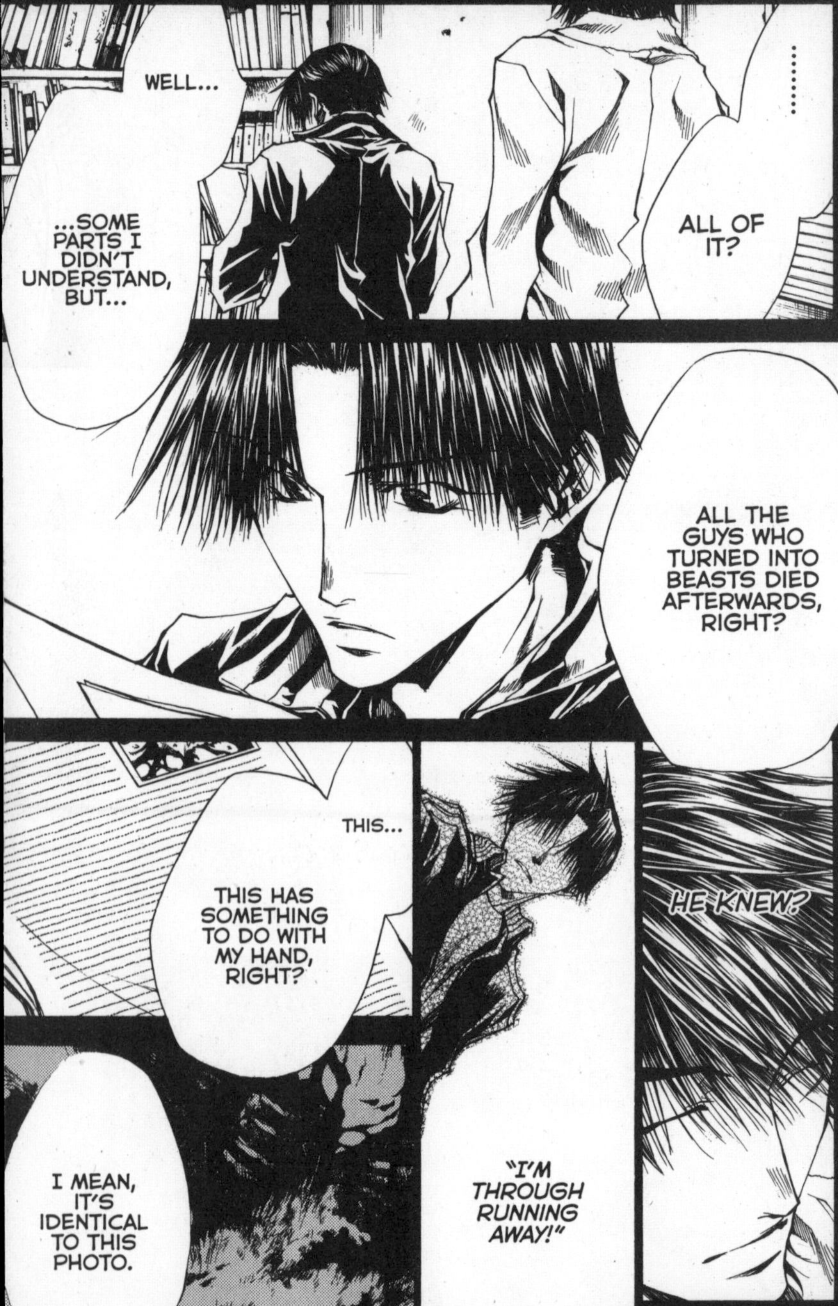
.....
ALL OF IT?
WELL...
...SOME PARTS I DIDN'T UNDERSTAND, BUT...
ALL THE GUYS WHO TURNED INTO BEASTS DIED AFTERWARDS, RIGHT?
HE KNEW?
"I'M THROUGH RUNNING AWAY!"
THIS...
THIS HAS SOMETHING TO DO WITH MY HAND, RIGHT?
I MEAN, IT'S IDENTICAL TO THIS PHOTO.

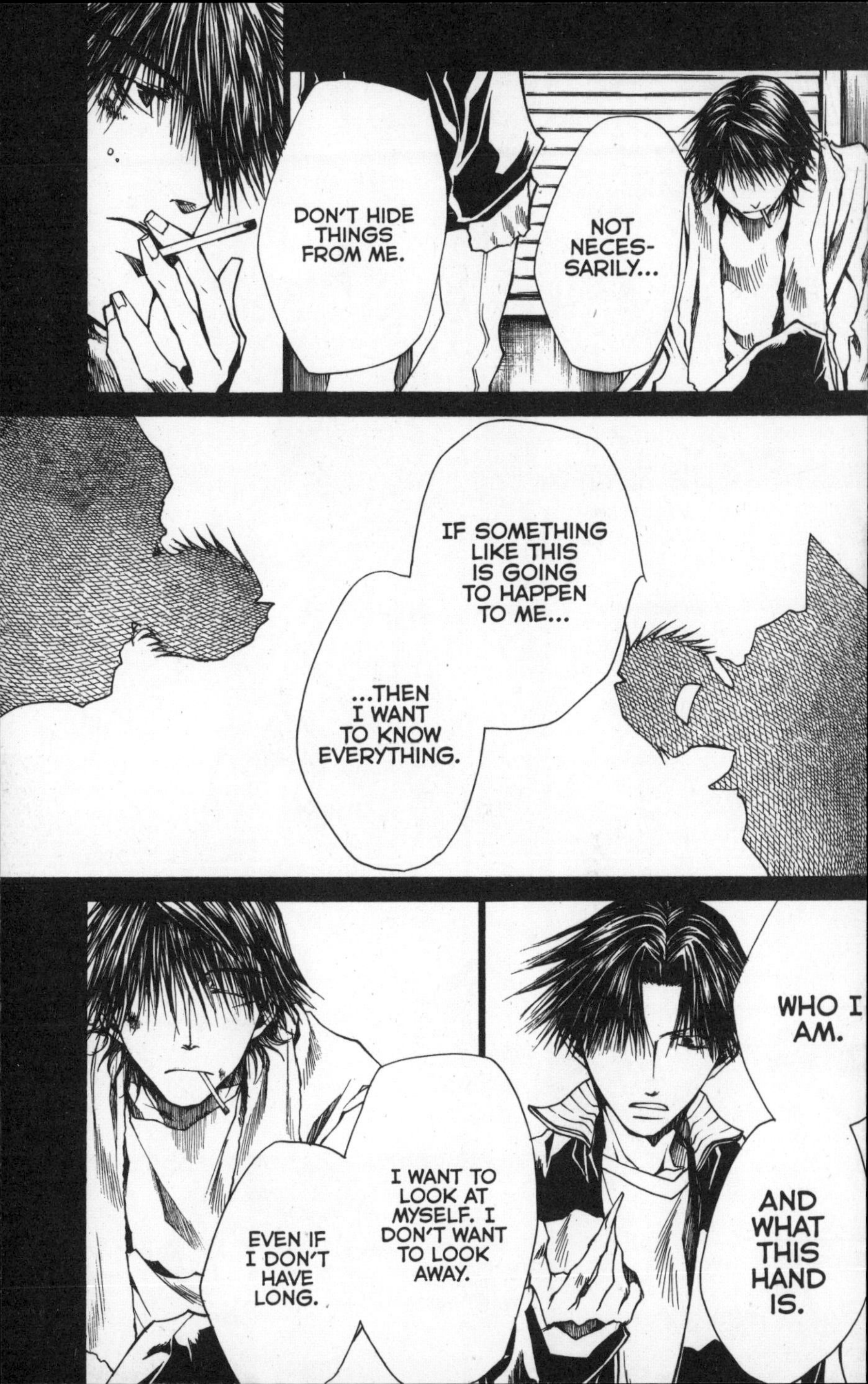
NOT NECES-SARILY...
DON'T HIDE THINGS FROM ME.
IF SOMETHING LIKE THIS IS GOING TO HAPPEN TO ME...
...THEN I WANT TO KNOW EVERYTHING.
WHO I AM.
AND WHAT THIS HAND IS.
I WANT TO LOOK AT MYSELF. I DON'T WANT TO LOOK AWAY.
EVEN IF I DON'T HAVE LONG.

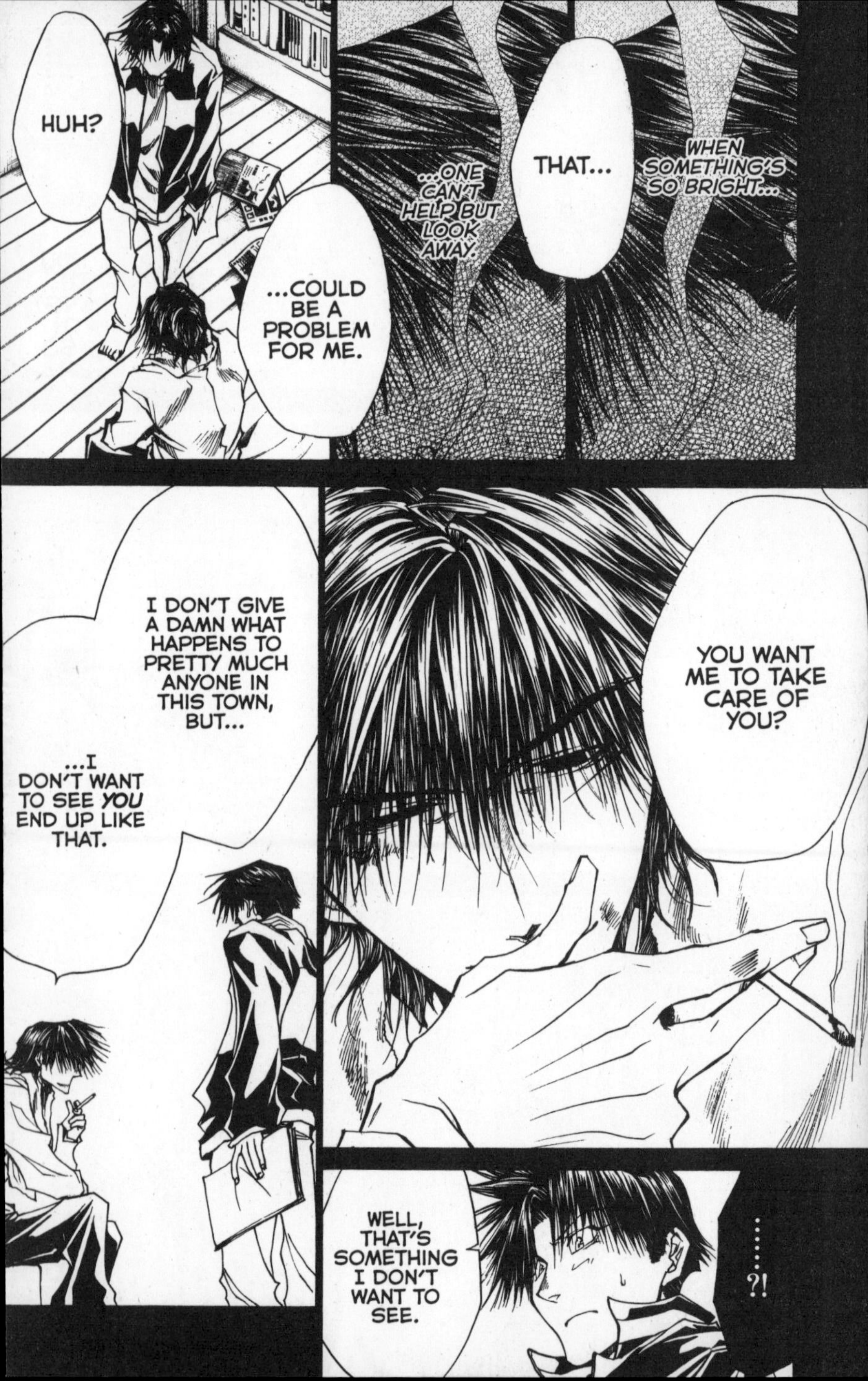
WHEN SOMETHING'S SO BRIGHT...
...ONE CAN'T HELP BUT LOOK AWAY.
THAT...
...COULD BE A PROBLEM FOR ME.
HUH?
YOU WANT ME TO TAKE CARE OF YOU?
I DON'T GIVE A DAMN WHAT HAPPENS TO PRETTY MUCH ANYONE IN THIS TOWN, BUT...
...I DON'T WANT TO SEE *YOU* END UP LIKE THAT.
......
?!
WELL, THAT'S SOMETHING I DON'T WANT TO SEE.

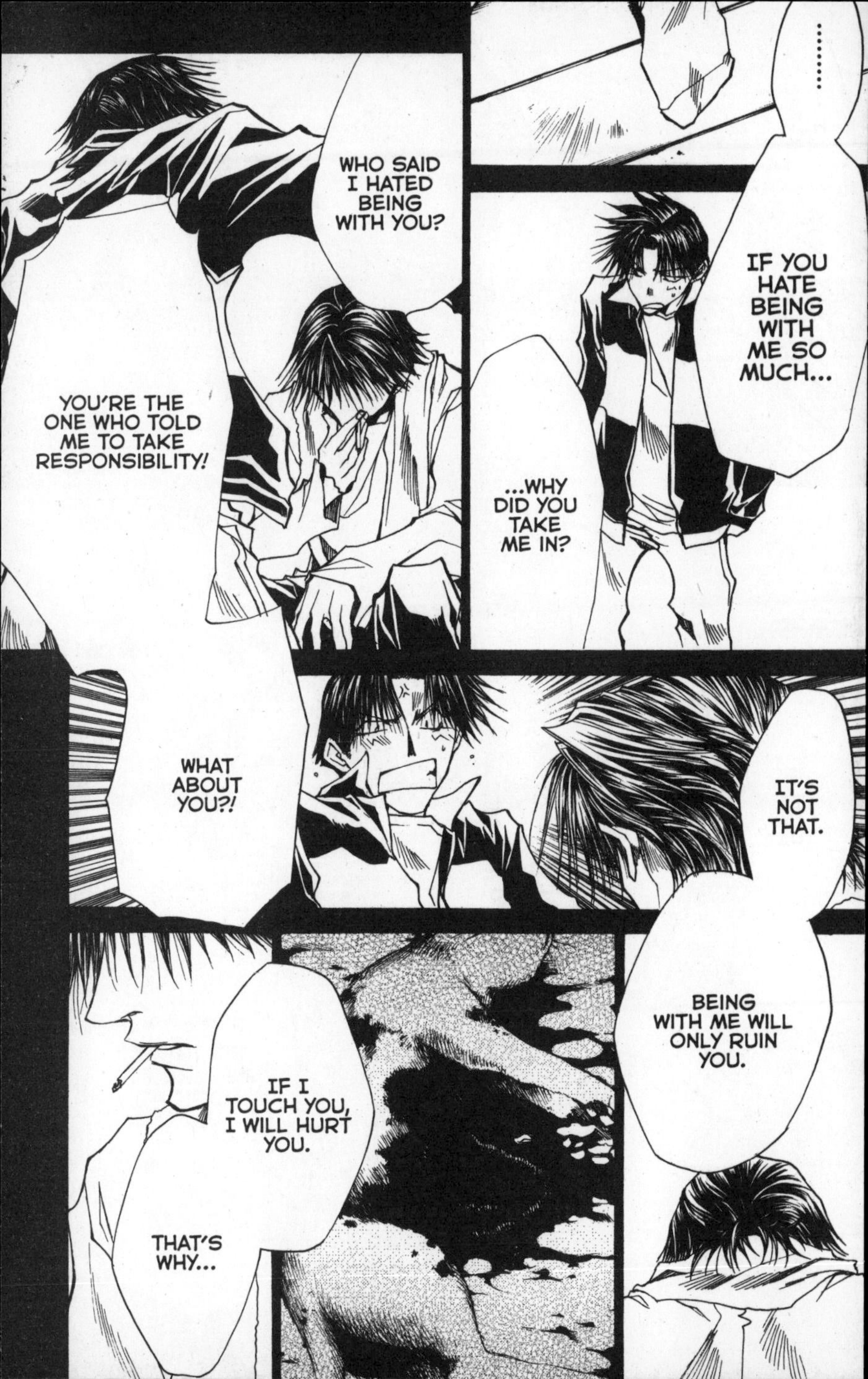
......
IF YOU HATE BEING WITH ME SO MUCH...
...WHY DID YOU TAKE ME IN?
WHO SAID I HATED BEING WITH YOU?
YOU'RE THE ONE WHO TOLD ME TO TAKE RESPONSIBILITY!
IT'S NOT THAT.
WHAT ABOUT YOU?!
BEING WITH ME WILL ONLY RUIN YOU.
IF I TOUCH YOU, I WILL HURT YOU.
THAT'S WHY...

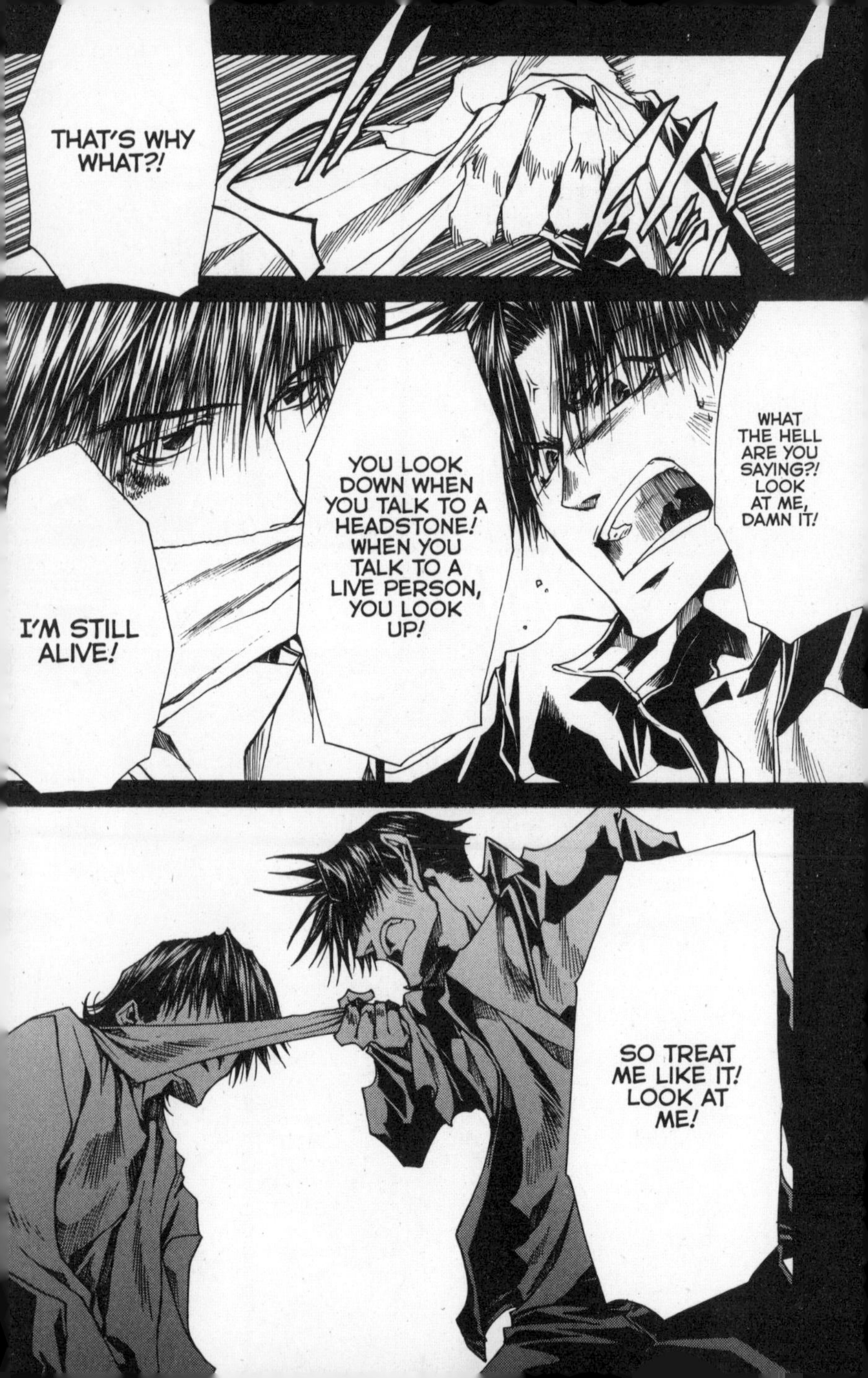
THAT'S WHY WHAT?!
WHAT THE HELL ARE YOU SAYING?! LOOK AT ME, DAMN IT!
YOU LOOK DOWN WHEN YOU TALK TO A HEADSTONE! WHEN YOU TALK TO A LIVE PERSON, YOU LOOK UP!
I'M STILL ALIVE!
SO TREAT ME LIKE IT! LOOK AT ME!

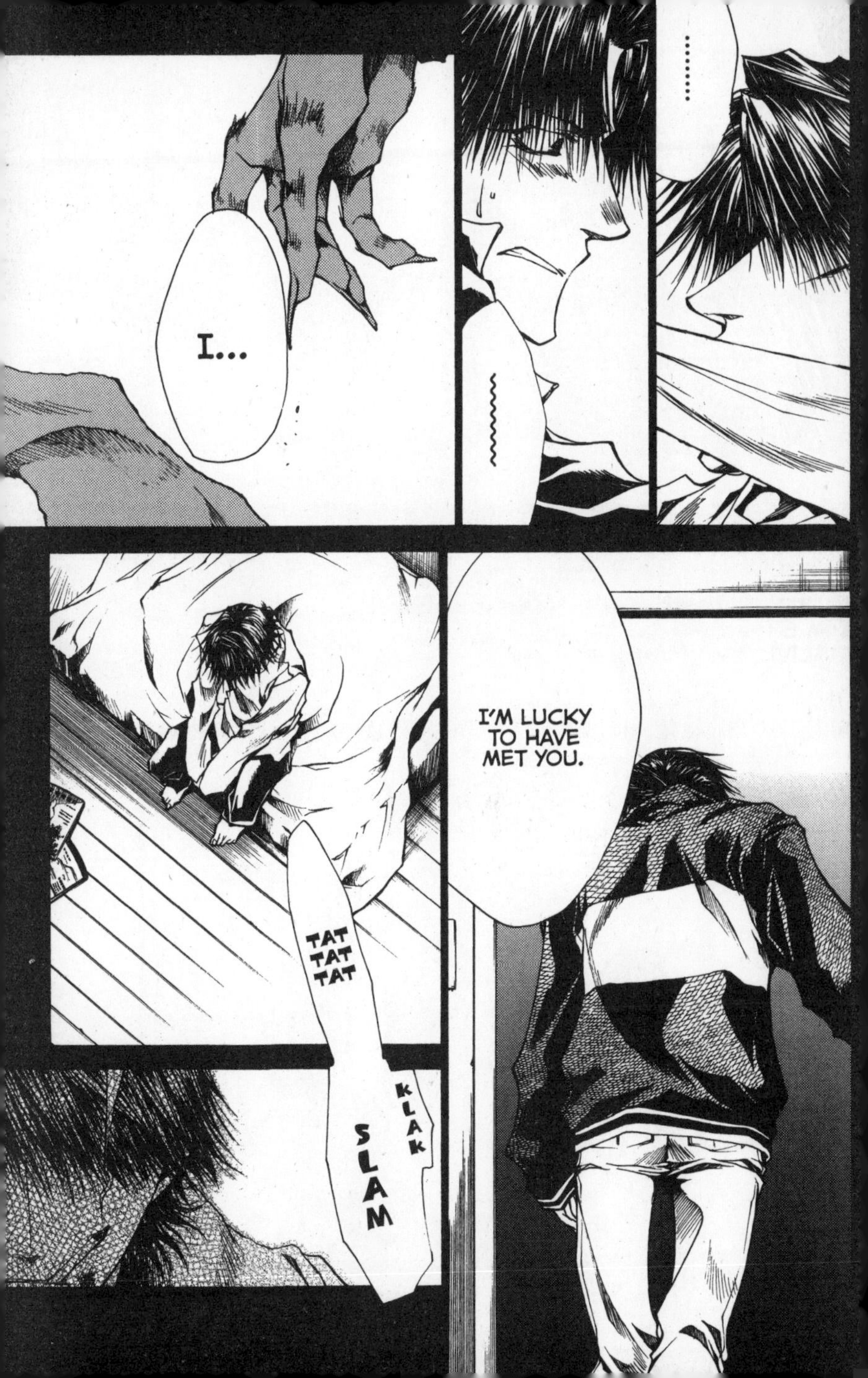
......
I...
I'M LUCKY TO HAVE MET YOU.
TAT TAT TAT
KLAK
SLAM

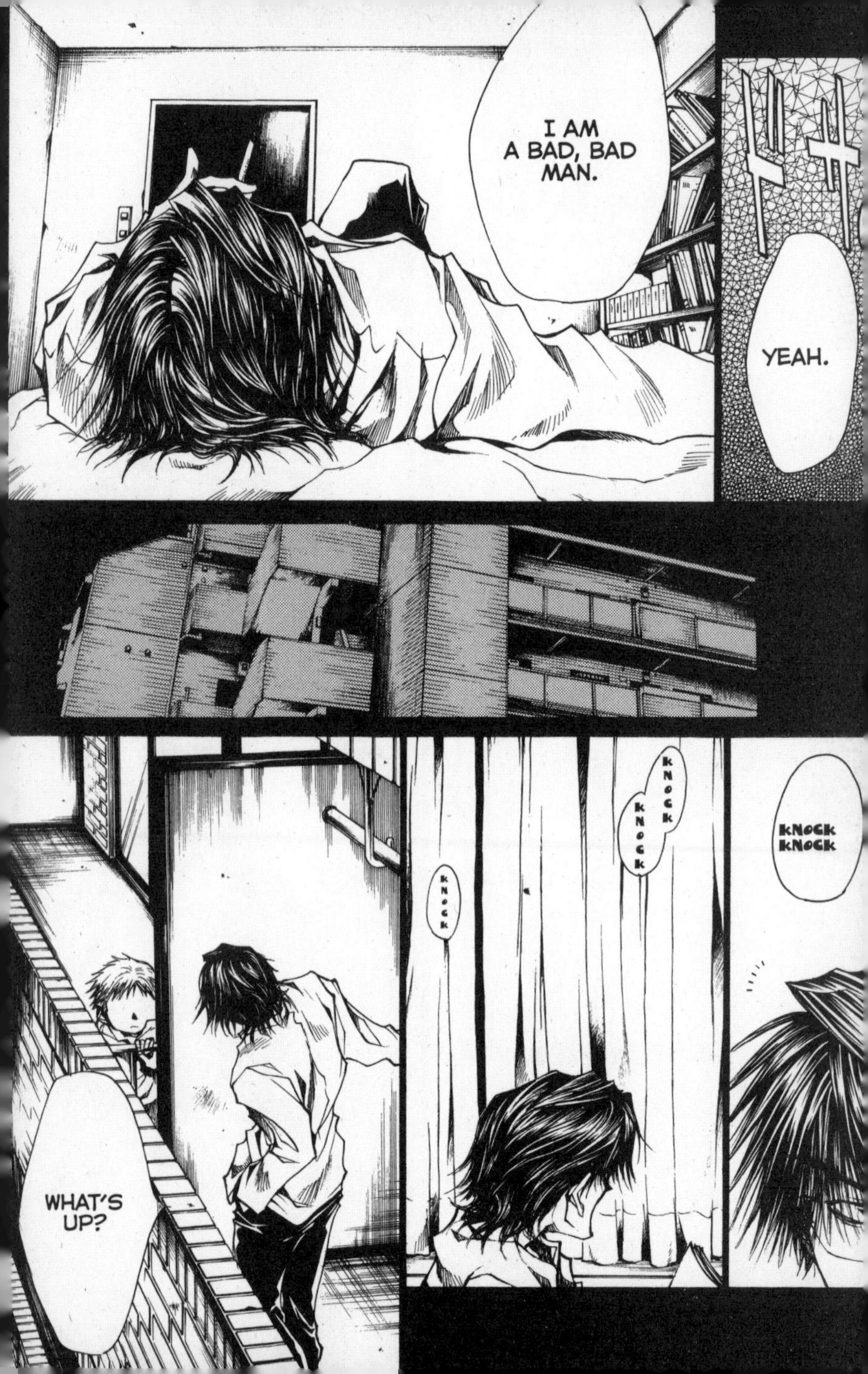
YEAH.
I AM A BAD, BAD MAN.
KNOCK KNOCK
KNOCK
KNOCK
KNOCK
WHAT'S UP?

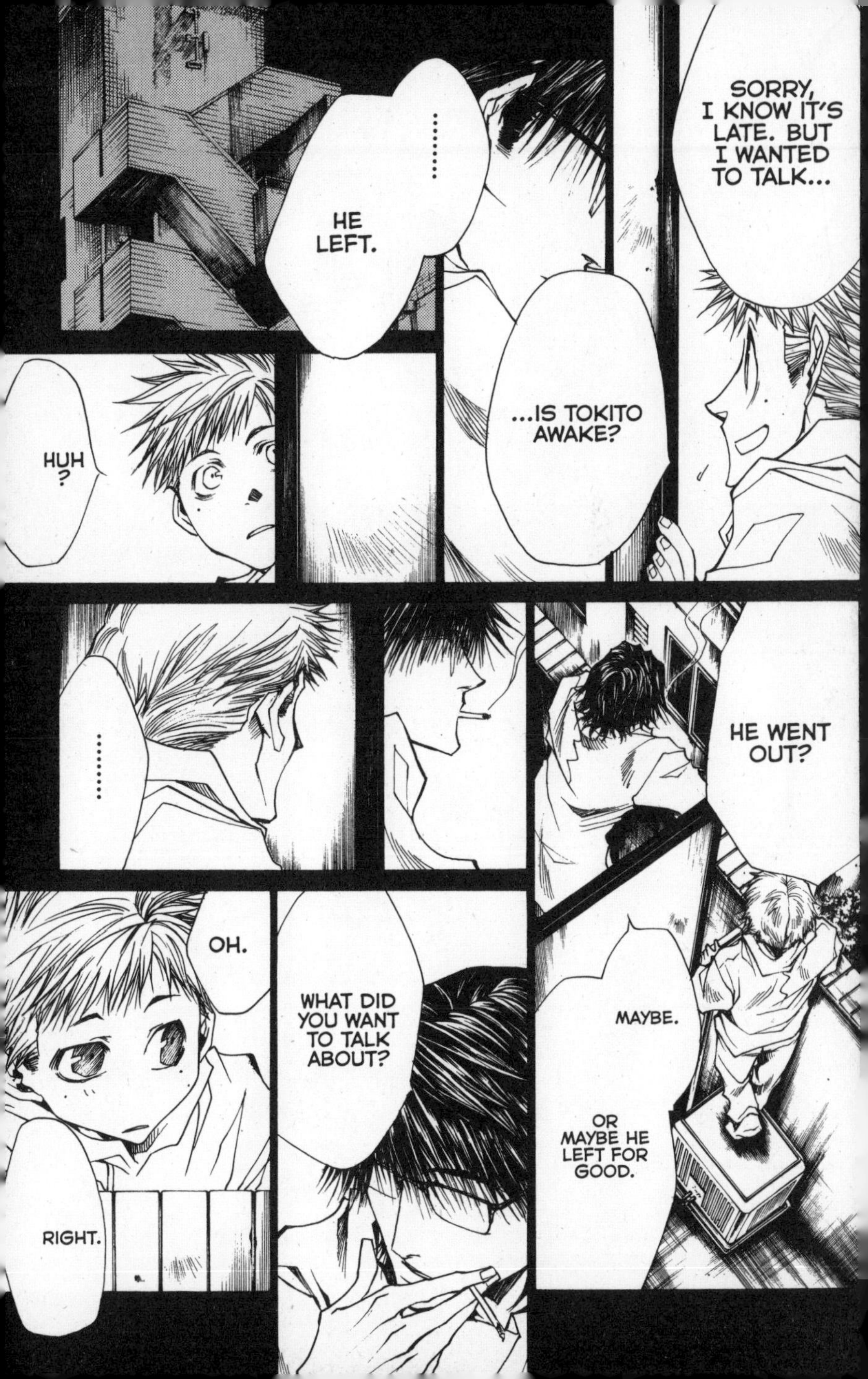
SORRY, I KNOW IT'S LATE. BUT I WANTED TO TALK...
...IS TOKITO AWAKE?
......
HE LEFT.
HUH?
HE WENT OUT?
MAYBE.
OR MAYBE HE LEFT FOR GOOD.
....
WHAT DID YOU WANT TO TALK ABOUT?
OH.
RIGHT.

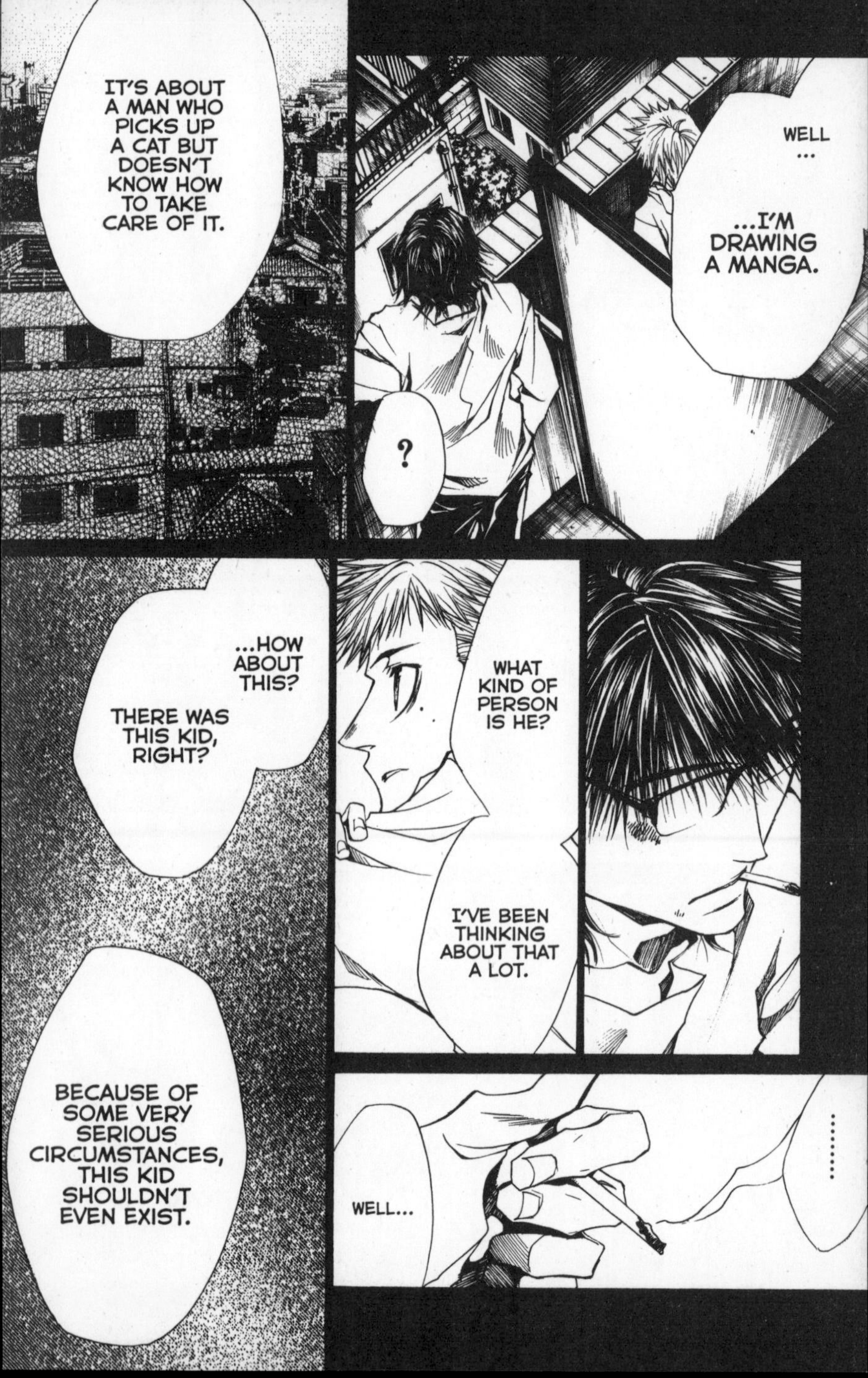
WELL ...
...I'M DRAWING A MANGA.
?
IT'S ABOUT A MAN WHO PICKS UP A CAT BUT DOESN'T KNOW HOW TO TAKE CARE OF IT.
WHAT KIND OF PERSON IS HE?
I'VE BEEN THINKING ABOUT THAT A LOT.
......
WELL...
...HOW ABOUT THIS?
THERE WAS THIS KID, RIGHT?
BECAUSE OF SOME VERY SERIOUS CIRCUMSTANCES, THIS KID SHOULDN'T EVEN EXIST.

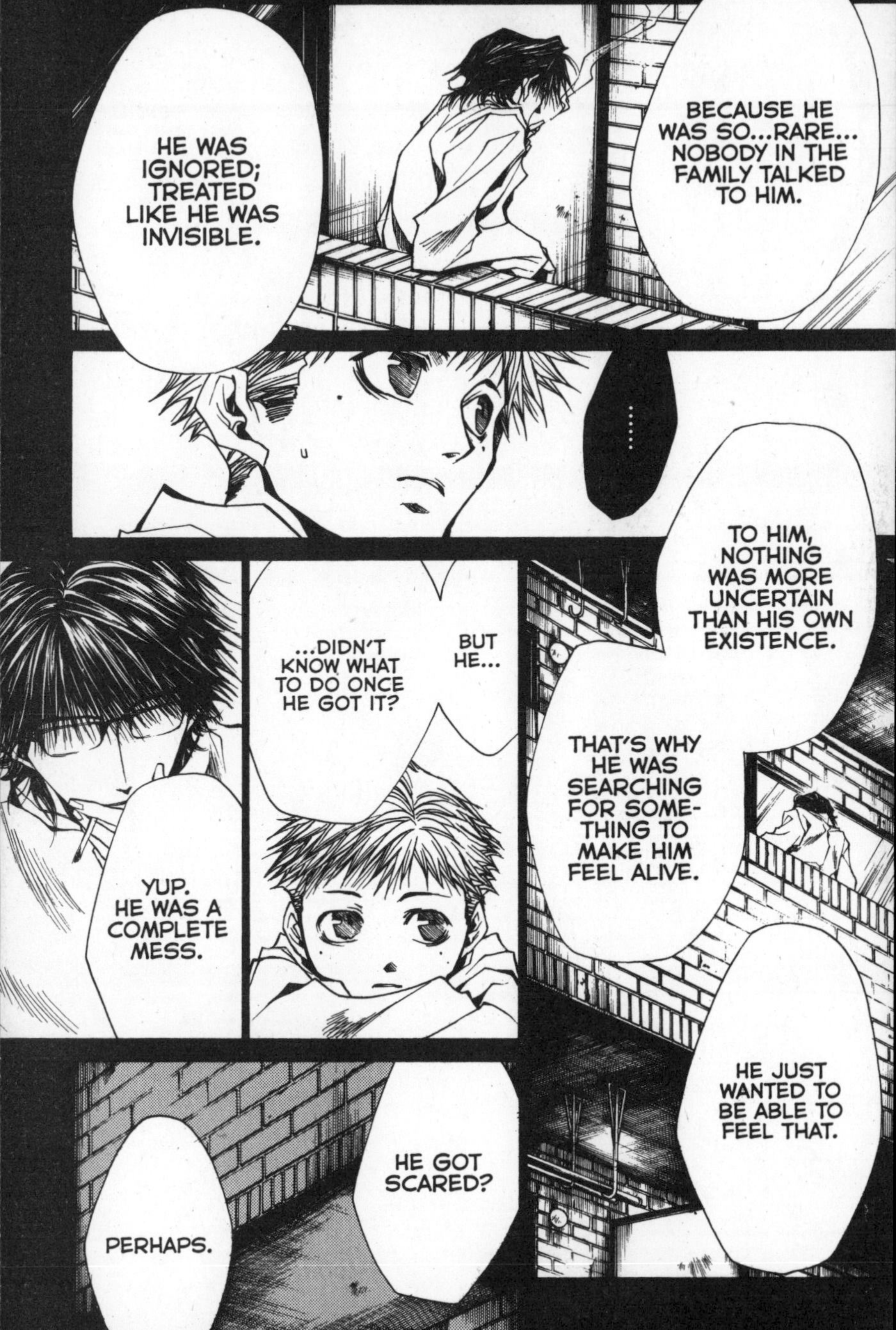
BECAUSE HE WAS SO...RARE... NOBODY IN THE FAMILY TALKED TO HIM.
HE WAS IGNORED; TREATED LIKE HE WAS INVISIBLE.
......
TO HIM, NOTHING WAS MORE UNCERTAIN THAN HIS OWN EXISTENCE.
THAT'S WHY HE WAS SEARCHING FOR SOME-THING TO MAKE HIM FEEL ALIVE.
HE JUST WANTED TO BE ABLE TO FEEL THAT.
BUT HE...
...DIDN'T KNOW WHAT TO DO ONCE HE GOT IT?
YUP. HE WAS A COMPLETE MESS.
HE GOT SCARED?
PERHAPS.

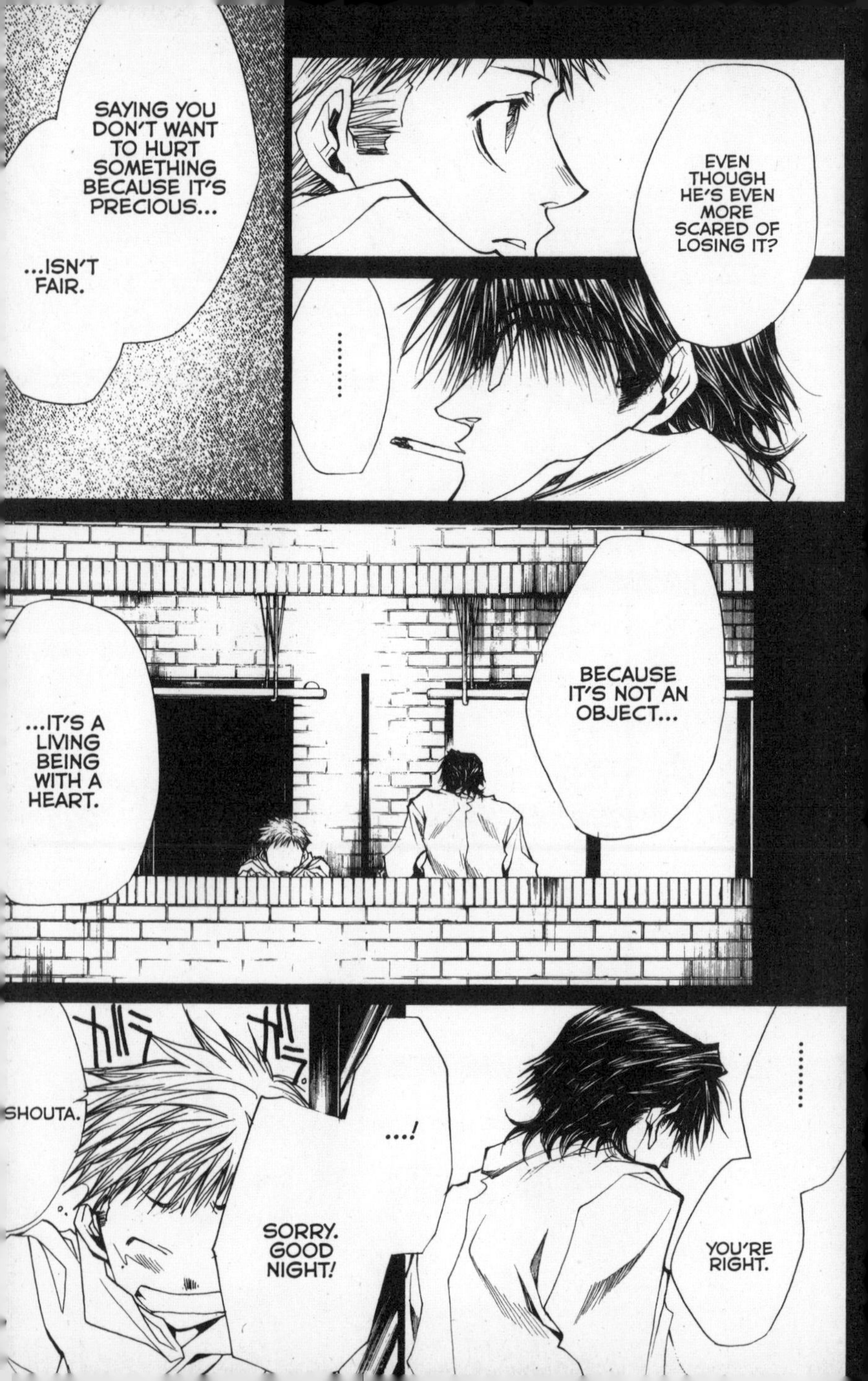
EVEN THOUGH HE'S EVEN MORE SCARED OF LOSING IT?
....
SAYING YOU DON'T WANT TO HURT SOMETHING BECAUSE IT'S PRECIOUS...
...ISN'T FAIR.
BECAUSE IT'S NOT AN OBJECT...
...IT'S A LIVING BEING WITH A HEART.
......
YOU'RE RIGHT.
...!
SHOUTA.
SORRY. GOOD NIGHT!

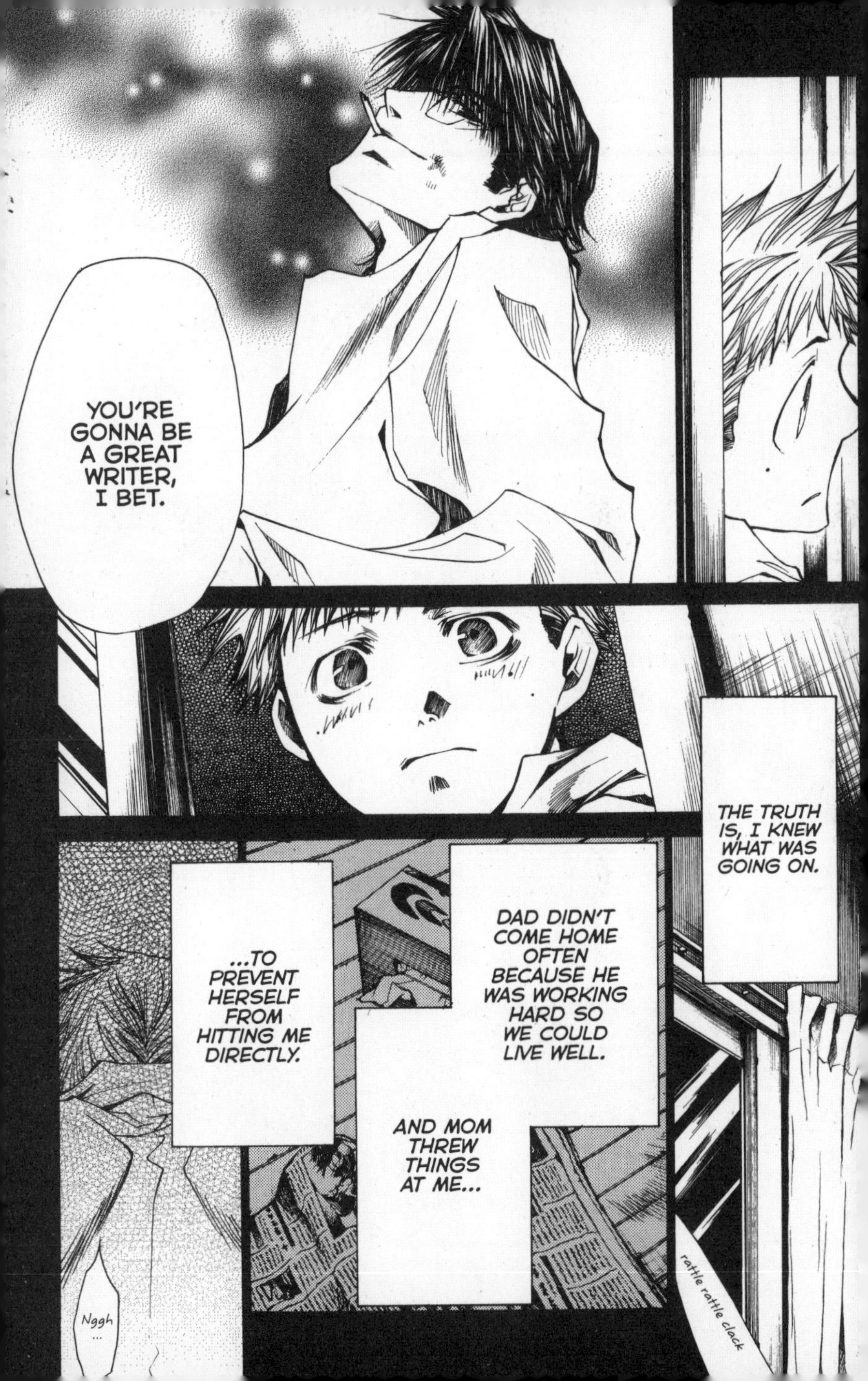
YOU'RE GONNA BE A GREAT WRITER, I BET.
THE TRUTH IS, I KNEW WHAT WAS GOING ON.
rattle rattle clack
DAD DIDN'T COME HOME OFTEN BECAUSE HE WAS WORKING HARD SO WE COULD LIVE WELL.
AND MOM THREW THINGS AT ME...
...TO PREVENT HERSELF FROM HITTING ME DIRECTLY.
Nggh...

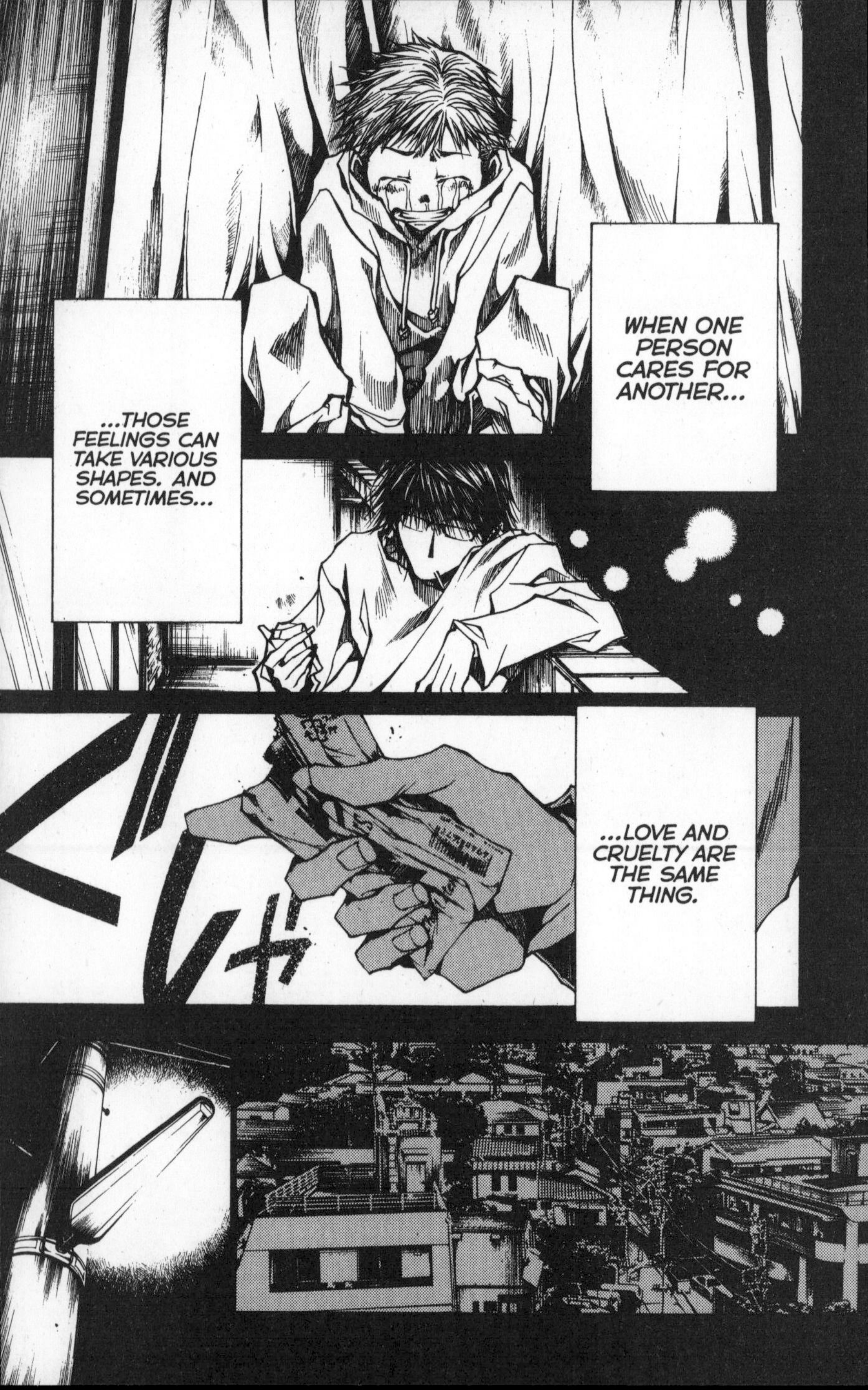
WHEN ONE PERSON CARES FOR ANOTHER...
...THOSE FEELINGS CAN TAKE VARIOUS SHAPES. AND SOMETIMES...
...LOVE AND CRUELTY ARE THE SAME THING.

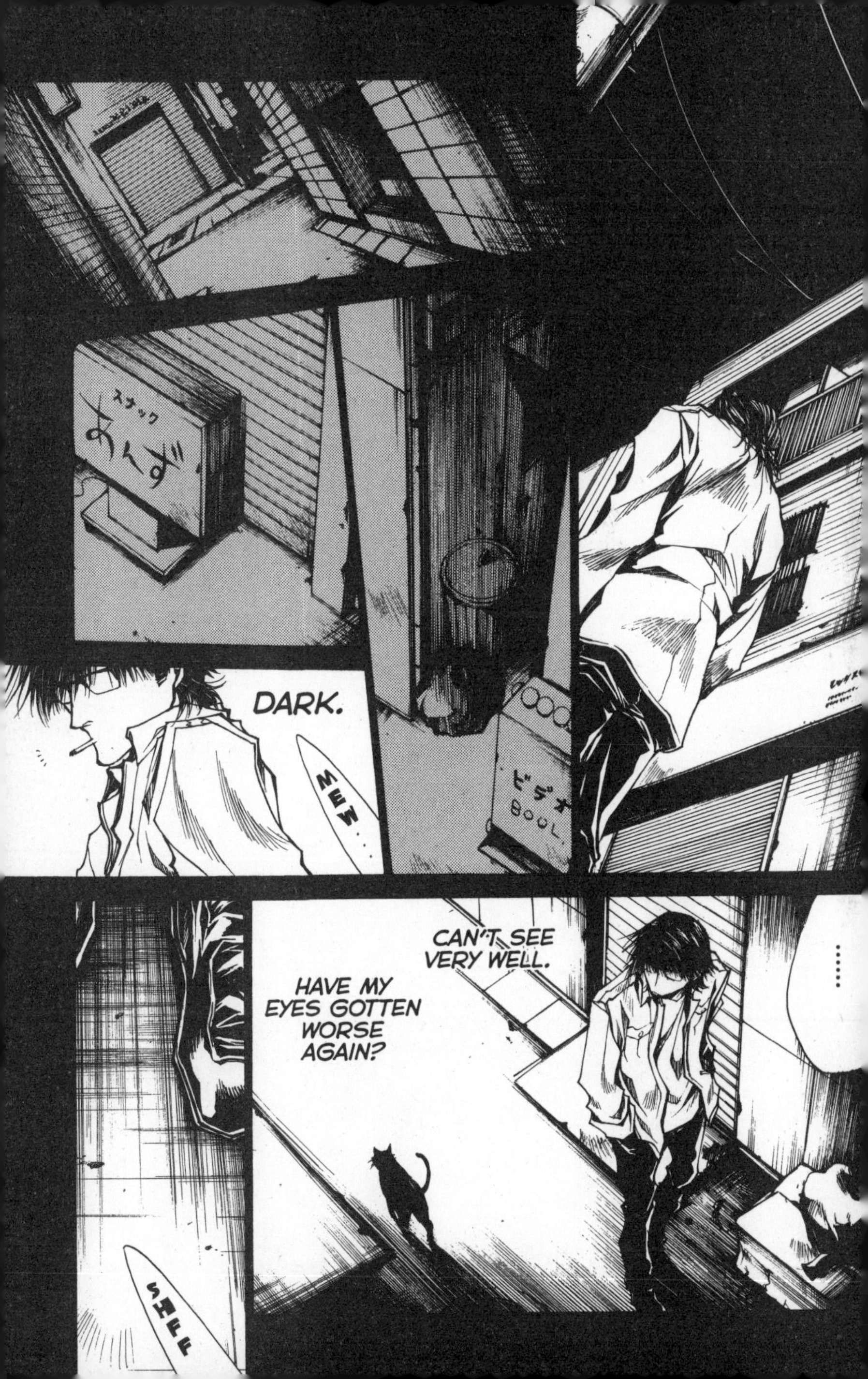

スナック
あんず
ビデオ
DARK.
MEW...
......
CAN'T SEE VERY WELL.
HAVE MY EYES GOTTEN WORSE AGAIN?
SHFF

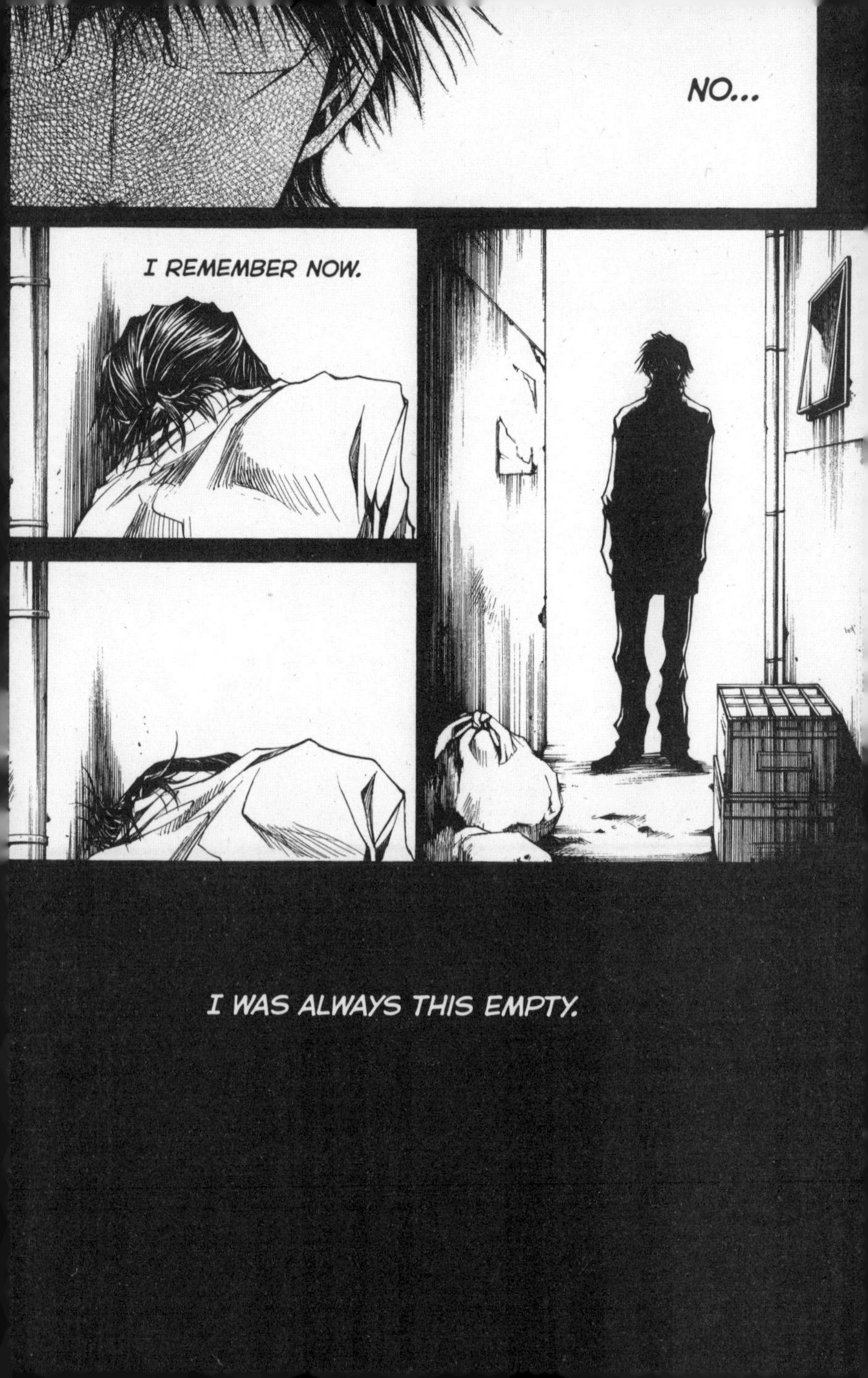
NO...
I REMEMBER NOW.
I WAS ALWAYS THIS EMPTY.

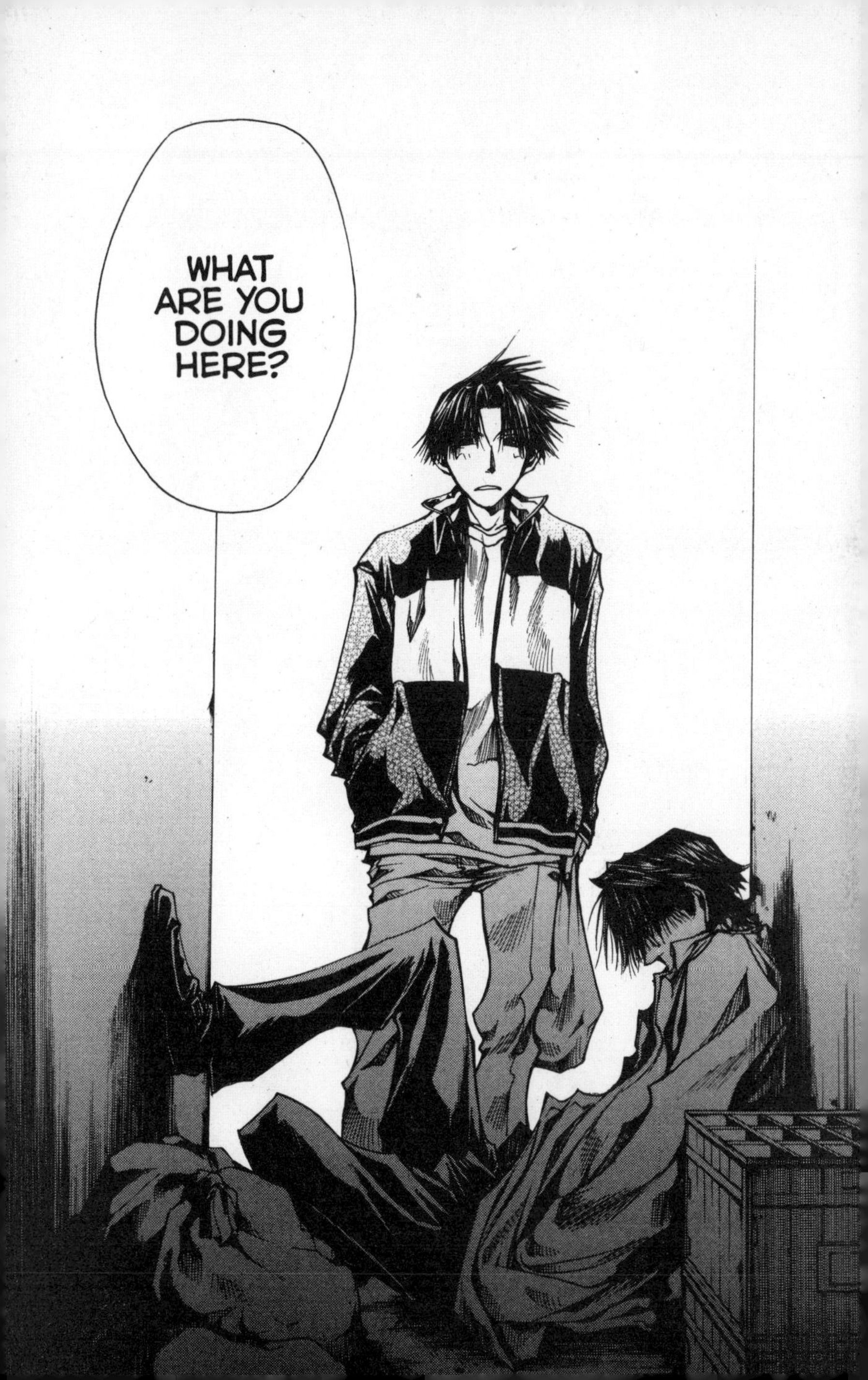
WHAT ARE YOU DOING HERE?

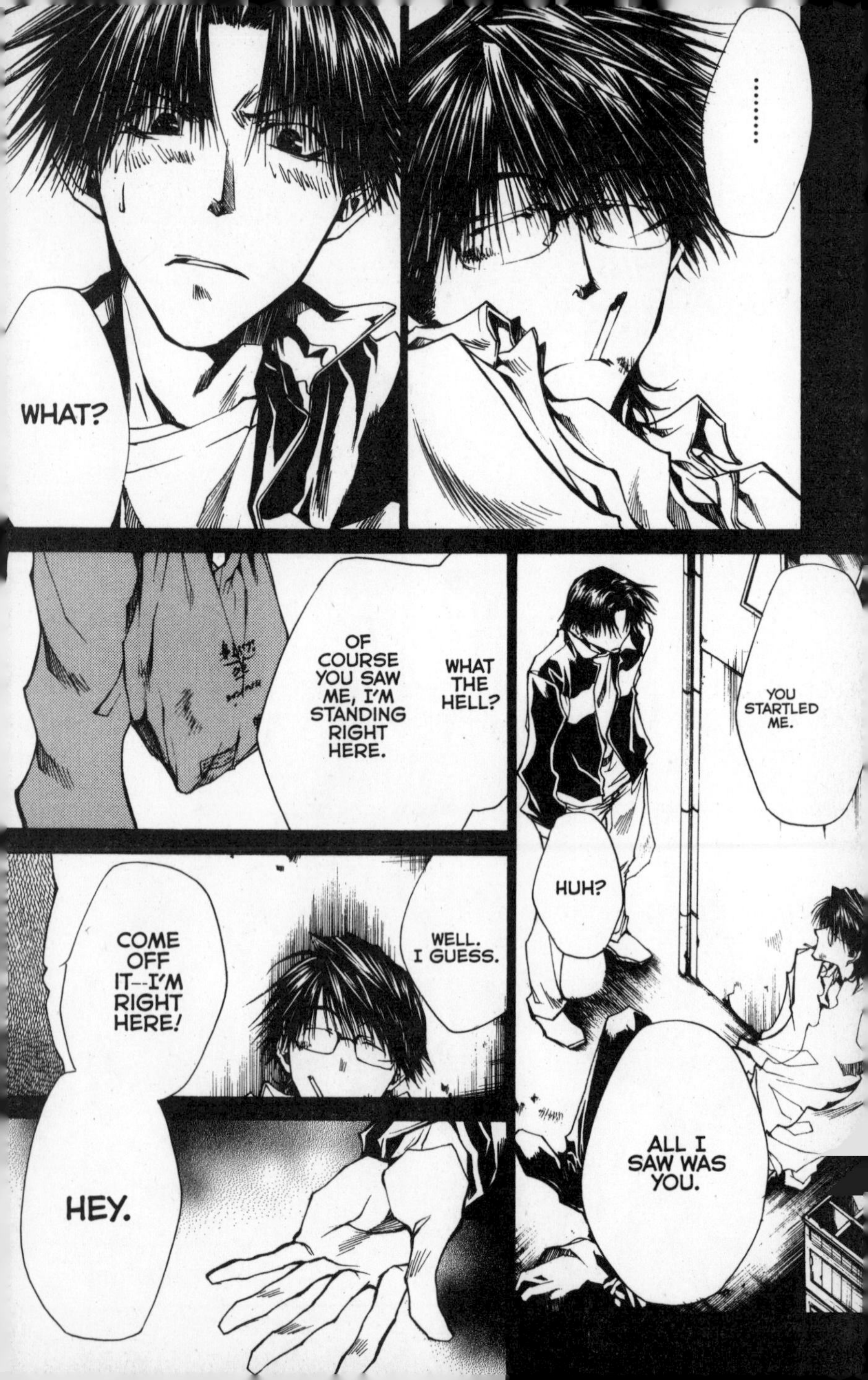
......
WHAT?
YOU STARTLED ME.
HUH?
WHAT THE HELL?
OF COURSE YOU SAW ME, I'M STANDING RIGHT HERE.
WELL. I GUESS.
COME OFF IT--I'M RIGHT HERE!
ALL I SAW WAS YOU.
HEY.

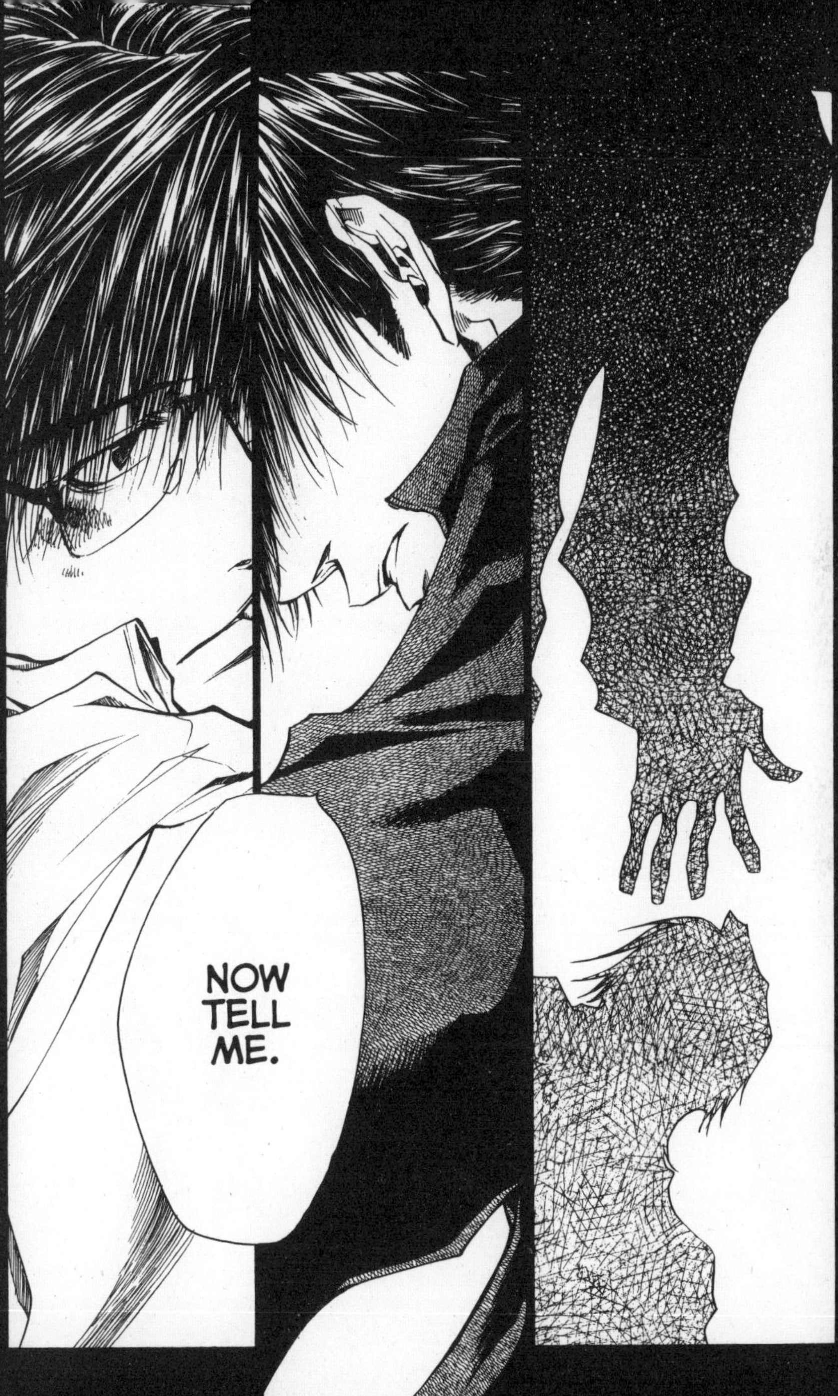
NOW TELL ME.

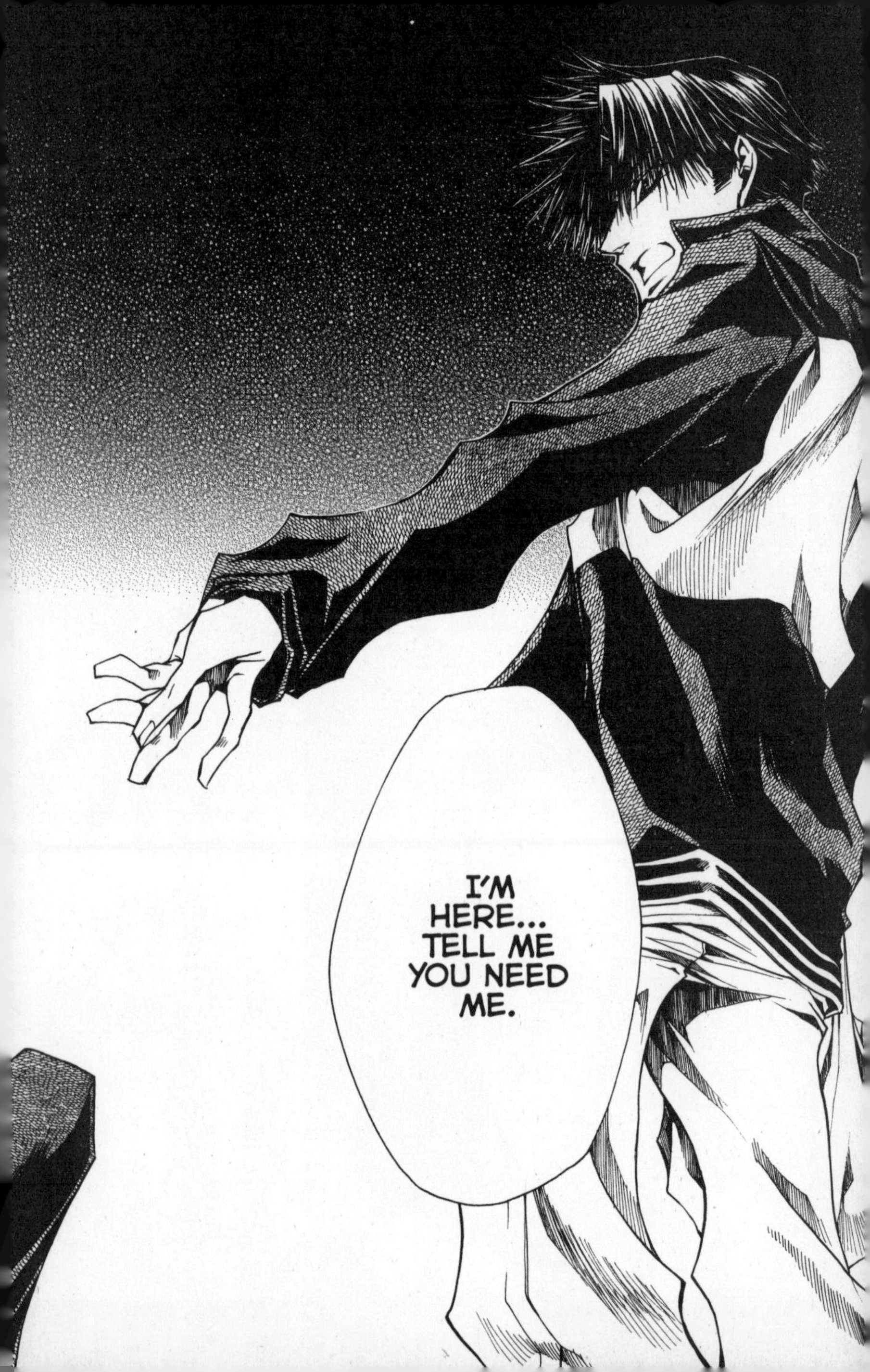
I'M HERE... TELL ME YOU NEED ME.

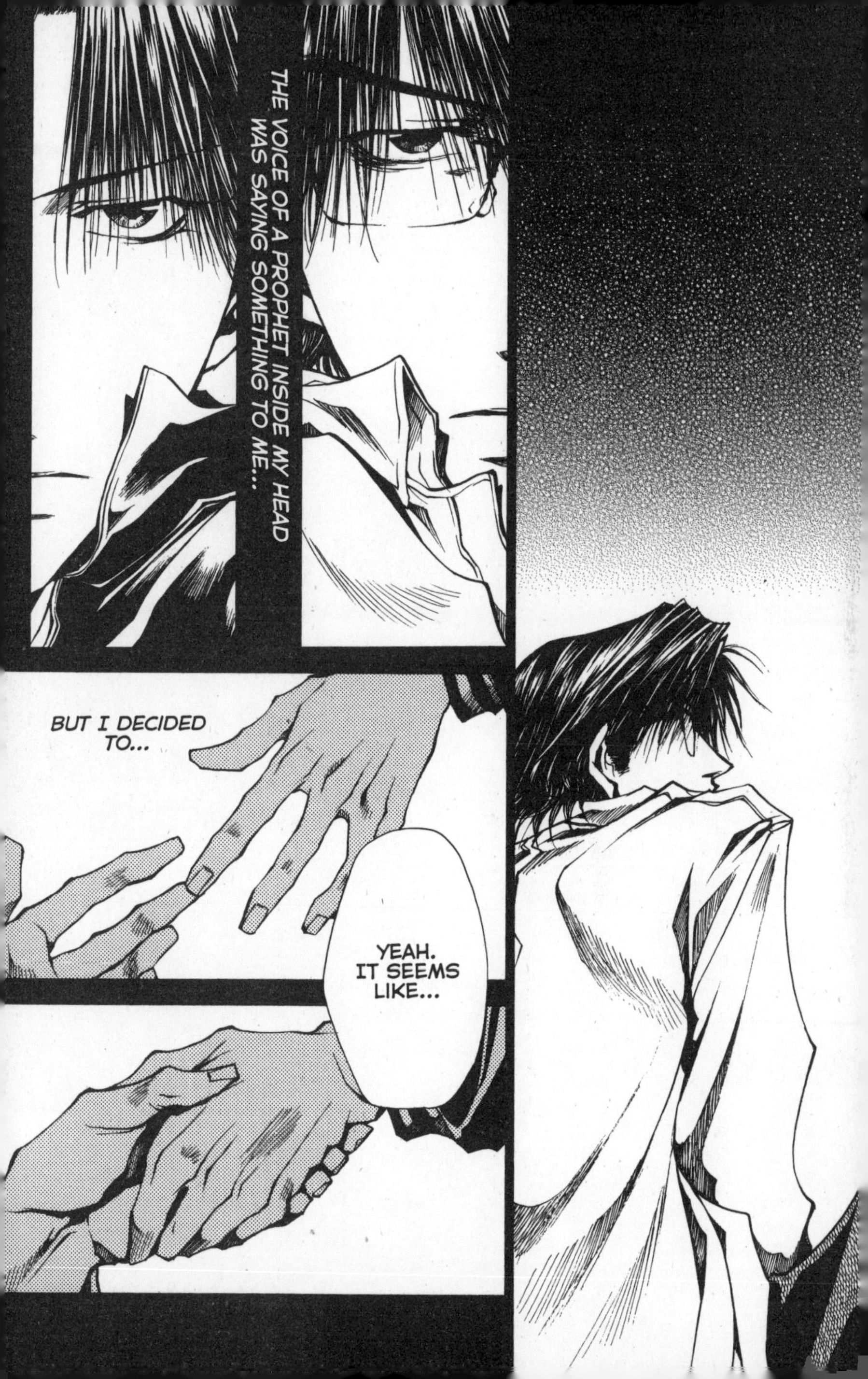
THE VOICE OF A PROPHET INSIDE MY HEAD WAS SAYING SOMETHING TO ME...
BUT I DECIDED TO...
YEAH. IT SEEMS LIKE...

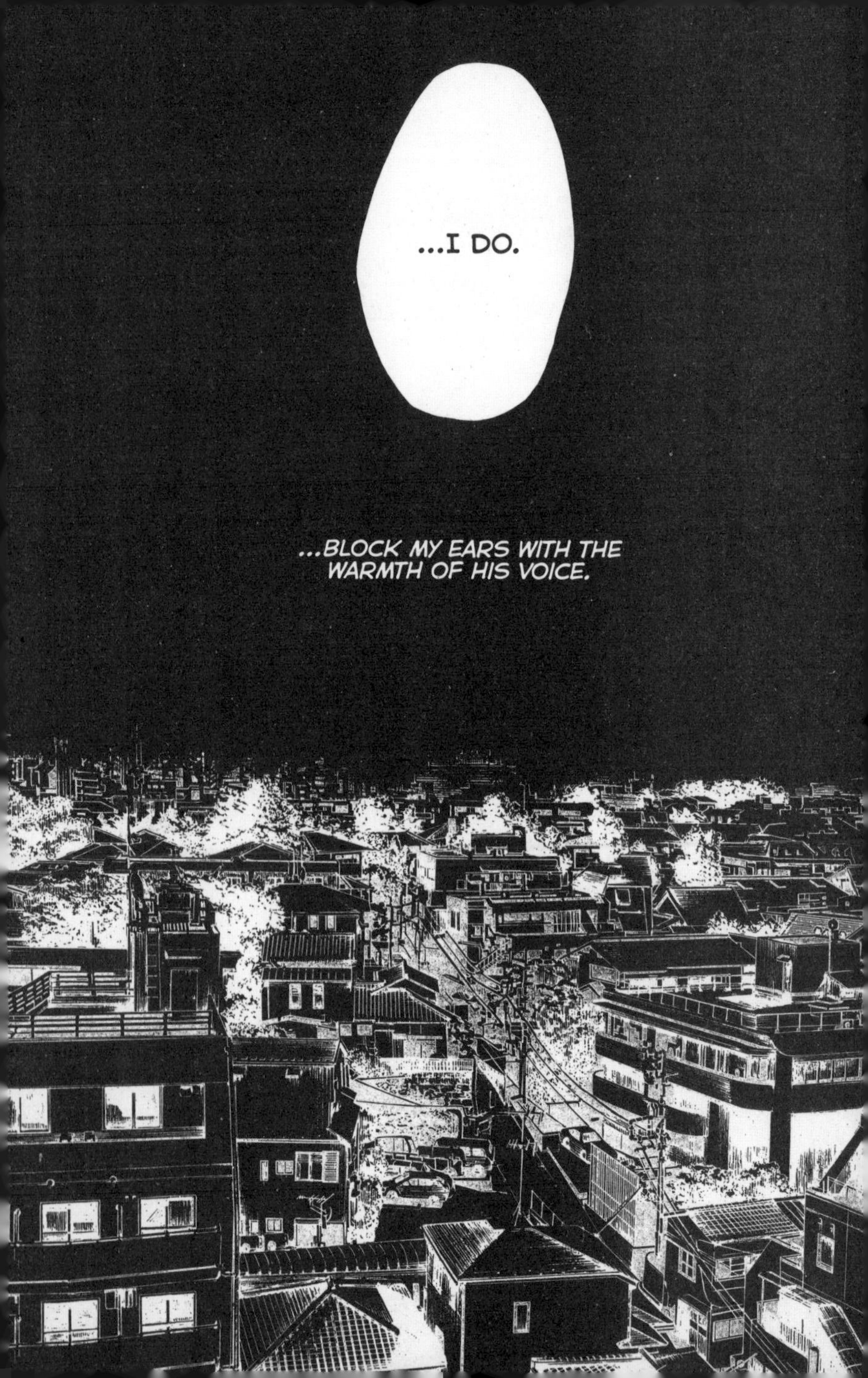
...I DO.
...BLOCK MY EARS WITH THE WARMTH OF HIS VOICE.

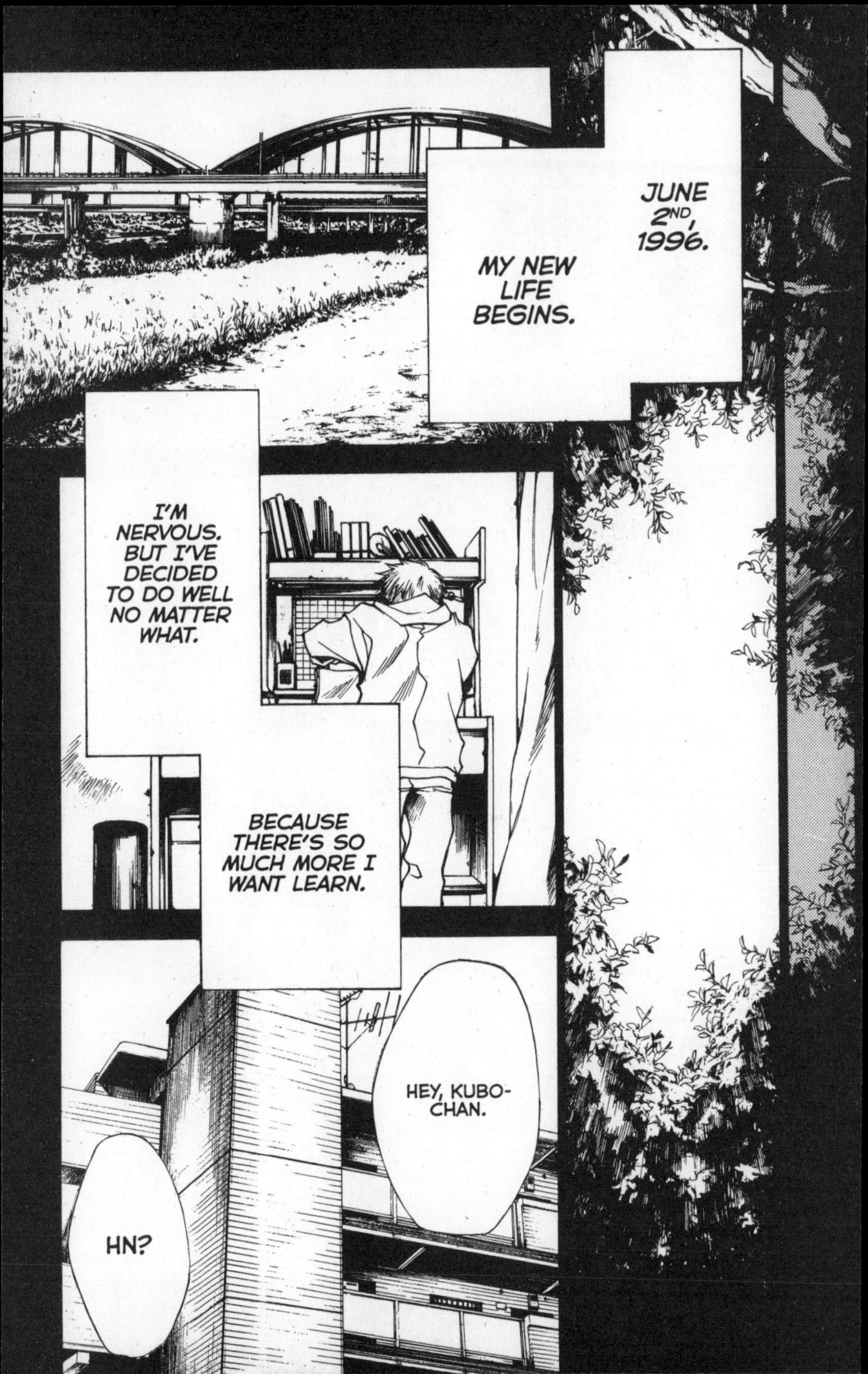
JUNE 2ND, 1996.
MY NEW LIFE BEGINS.
I'M NERVOUS. BUT I'VE DECIDED TO DO WELL NO MATTER WHAT.
BECAUSE THERE'S SO MUCH MORE I WANT LEARN.
HEY, KUBO-CHAN.
HN?

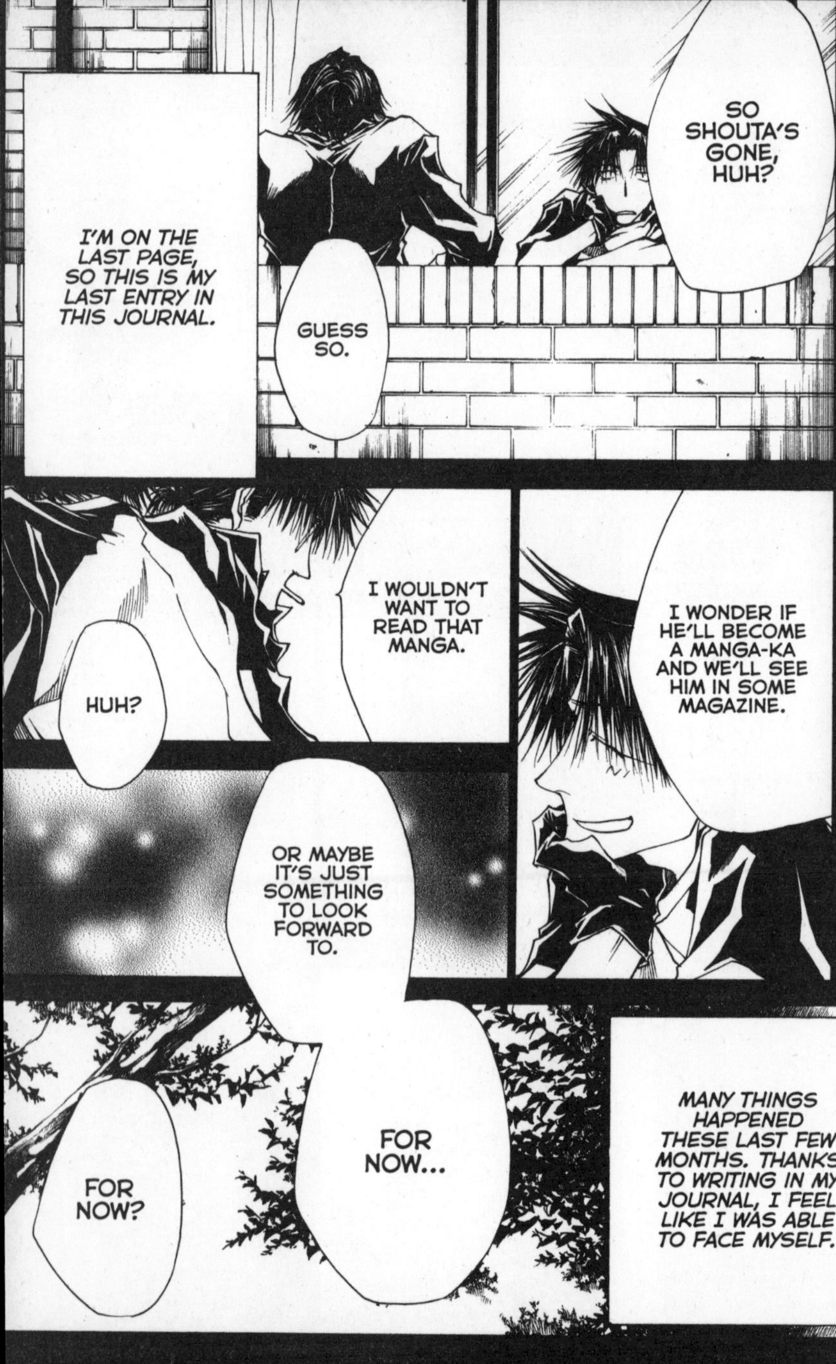
SO SHOUTA'S GONE, HUH?
GUESS SO.
I'M ON THE LAST PAGE, SO THIS IS MY LAST ENTRY IN THIS JOURNAL.
I WONDER IF HE'LL BECOME A MANGA-KA AND WE'LL SEE HIM IN SOME MAGAZINE.
I WOULDN'T WANT TO READ THAT MANGA.
HUH?
OR MAYBE IT'S JUST SOMETHING TO LOOK FORWARD TO.
MANY THINGS HAPPENED THESE LAST FEW MONTHS. THANKS TO WRITING IN MY JOURNAL, I FEEL LIKE I WAS ABLE TO FACE MYSELF.
FOR NOW...
FOR NOW?

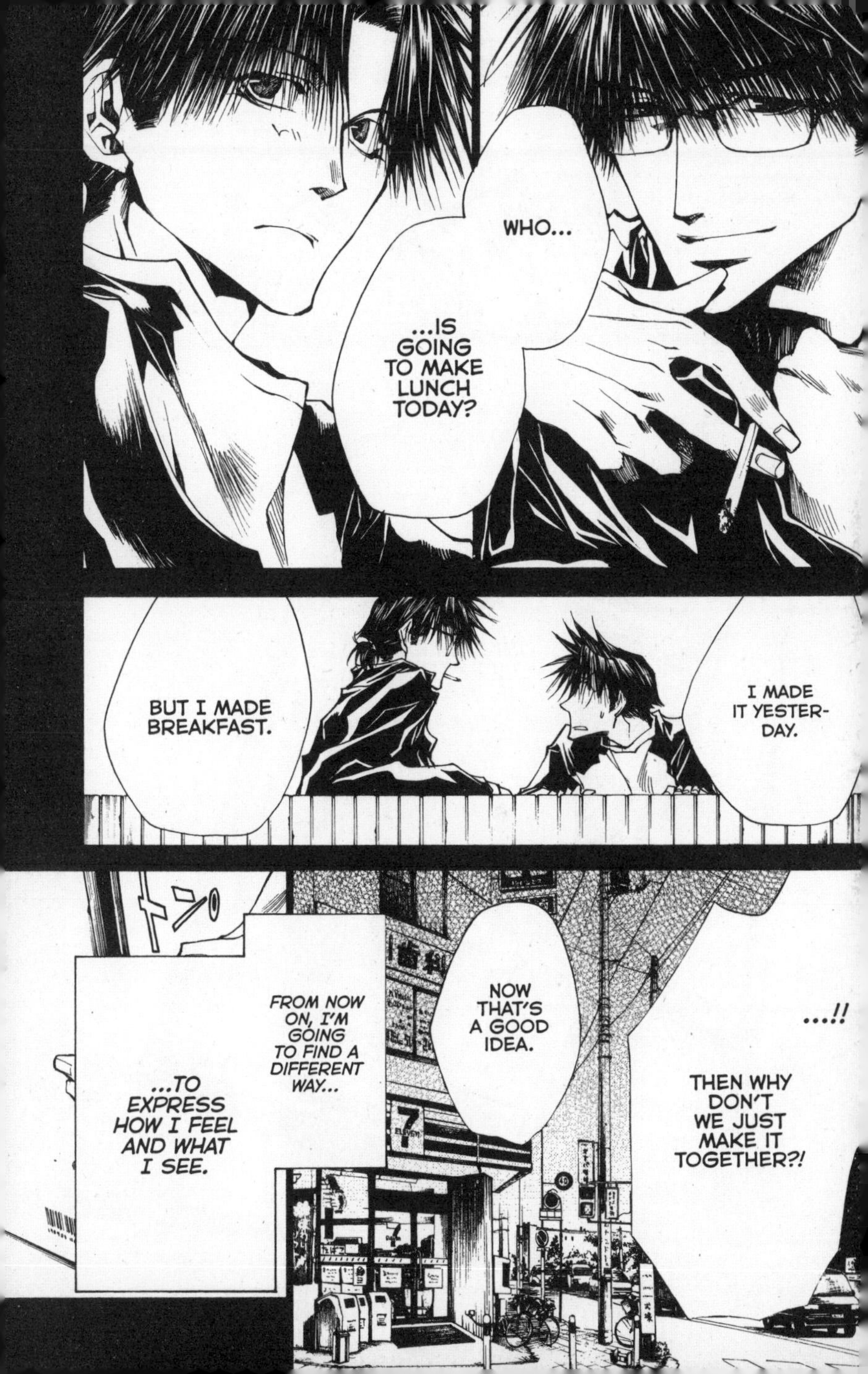
WHO... ...IS GOING TO MAKE LUNCH TODAY?
I MADE IT YESTER-DAY.
BUT I MADE BREAKFAST.
...!!
THEN WHY DON'T WE JUST MAKE IT TOGETHER?!
NOW THAT'S A GOOD IDEA.
FROM NOW ON, I'M GOING TO FIND A DIFFERENT WAY...
...TO EXPRESS HOW I FEEL AND WHAT I SEE.

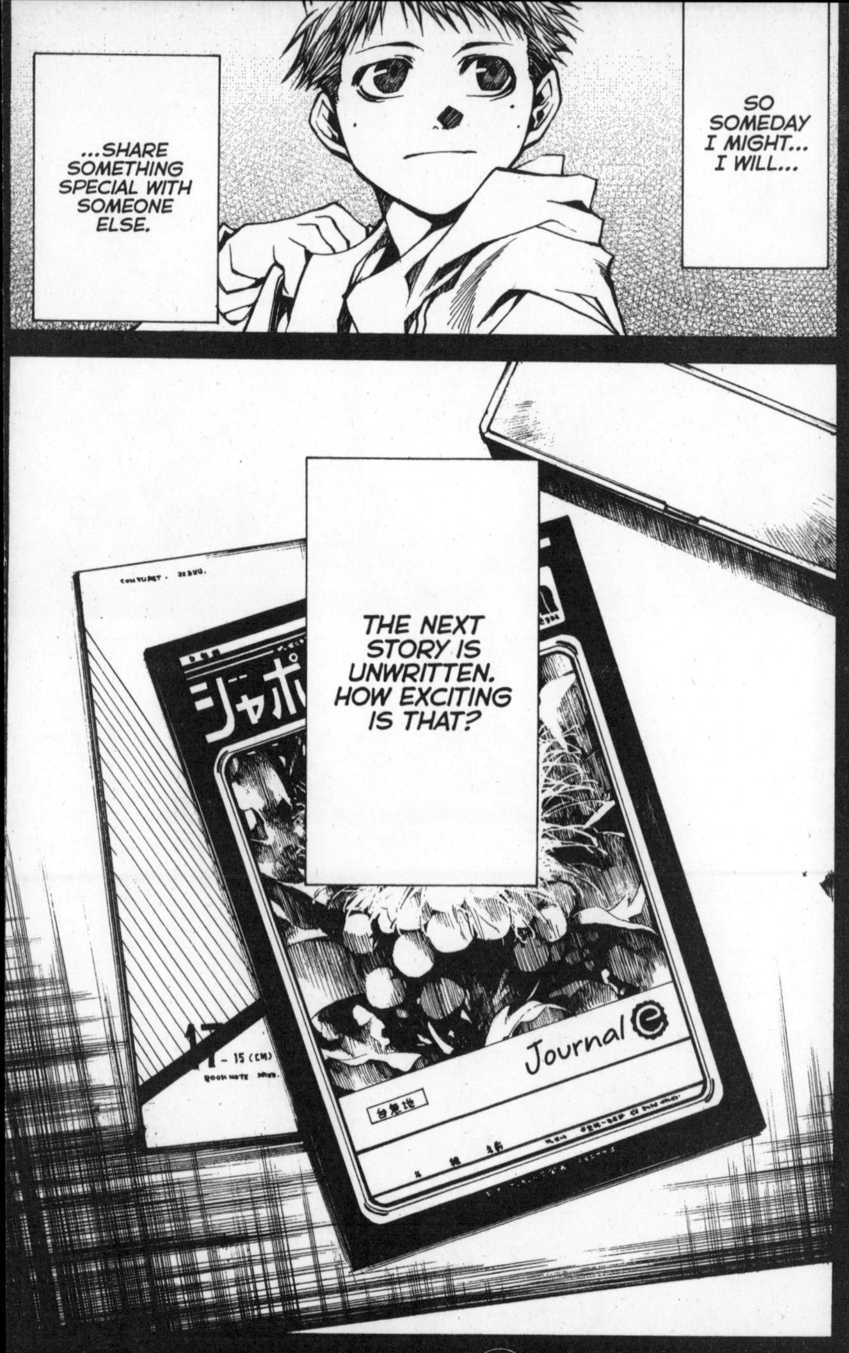
SO SOMEDAY I MIGHT... I WILL...
...SHARE SOMETHING SPECIAL WITH SOMEONE ELSE.
THE NEXT STORY IS UNWRITTEN. HOW EXCITING IS THAT?
Journal

WILD ADAPTER SCENE:05 **END** to be Next

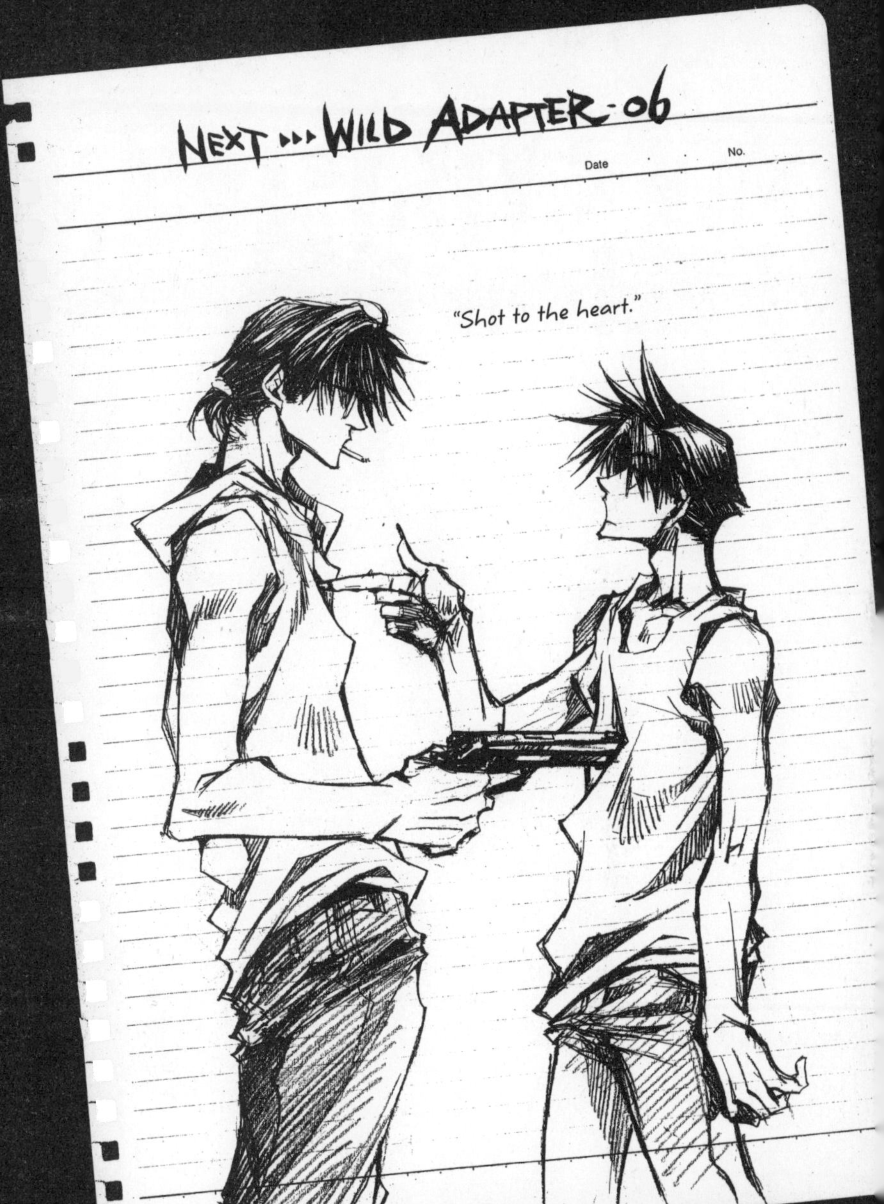
NEXT ▸▸▸ WILD ADAPTER-06
Date
No.
"Shot to the heart."

In the next volume of

WILDADAPTER

Sanada and the new youth leader
of the Izumo group finally make
their move—by kidnapping Tokito!
But after what happened to the
Tojou group when Kubota was
involved, they should have known
better. Kubota is on a mission,
and nothing will stand between
him and getting Tokito back.

TOKYOPOP®.com

WHERE MANGA LIVES!

JOIN the TOKYOPOP community: www.TOKYOPOP.com

COME AND PREVIEW THE HOTTEST MANGA AROUND!

CREATE...
UPLOAD...
DOWNLOAD...
BLOG...
CHAT...
VOTE...
LIVE!!!!

WWW.TOKYOPOP.COM HAS:

- Exclusives
- News
- Contests
- Games
- Rising Stars of Manga
- iManga
- and more...

TOKYOPOP.COM 2.0
NOW LIVE!

© Sang-Sun Park and TOKYOPOP

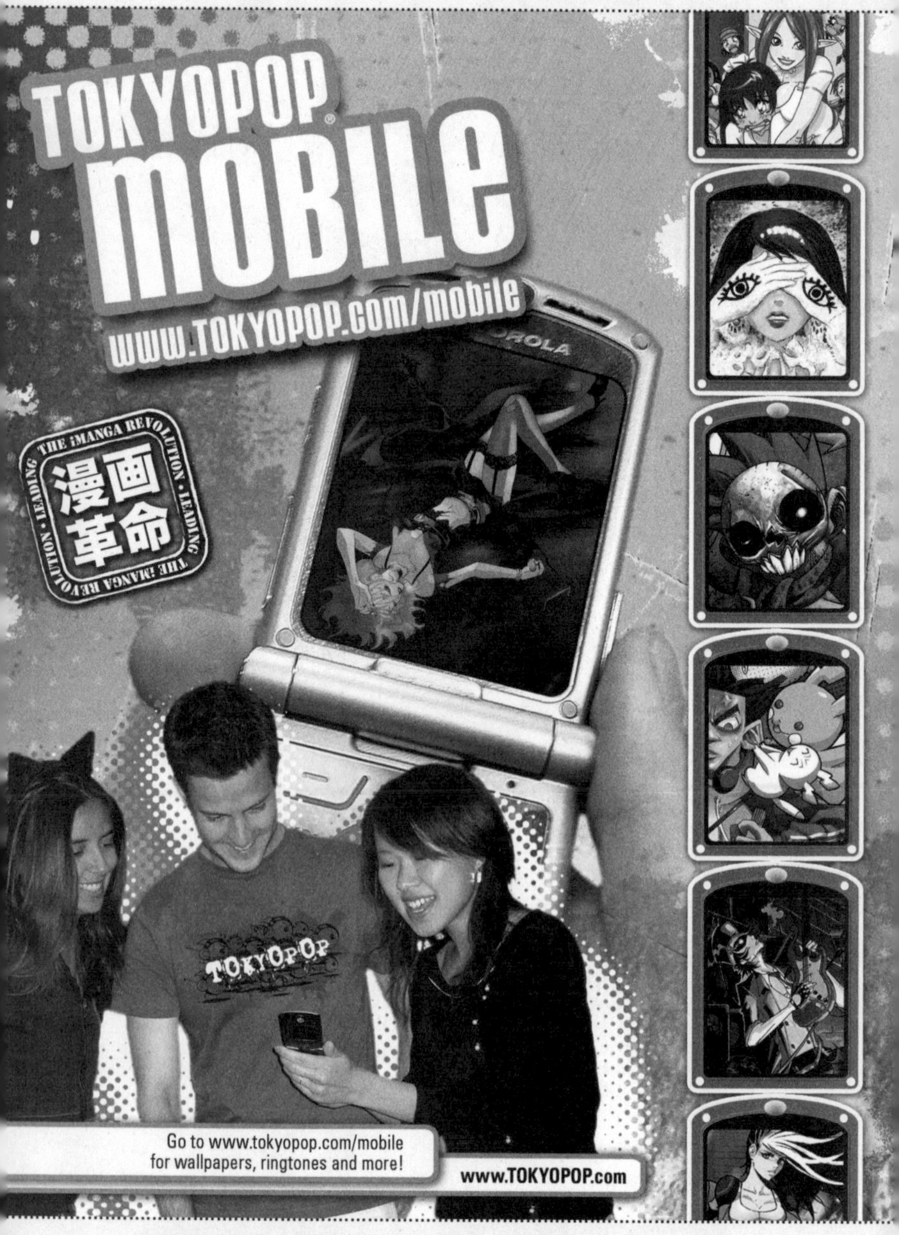
TOKYOPOP® MOBILE
www.TOKYOPOP.com/mobile
THE iMANGA REVOLUTION • LEADING THE iMANGA REVOLUTION • LEADING
漫画革命
TOKYOPOP
Go to www.tokyopop.com/mobile
for wallpapers, ringtones and more!
www.TOKYOPOP.com

TOKYOPOP MANGA SUPPLEMENT

SUPER HYPER AUDIOTISTIC SONIC REVOLUTION!!!

www.myspace.com/tokyopop

www.TOKYOPOP.com

TOKYOPOP RECORDS

Available at the iTunes Music Store
and everywhere music downloads
are available. Keyword: TOKYOPOP

New releases every month!
Check out these great albums
AVAILABLE NOW!!!

©2007 TOKYOPOP Inc.

FOR MORE INFORMATION VISIT: WWW.TOKYOPOP.COM

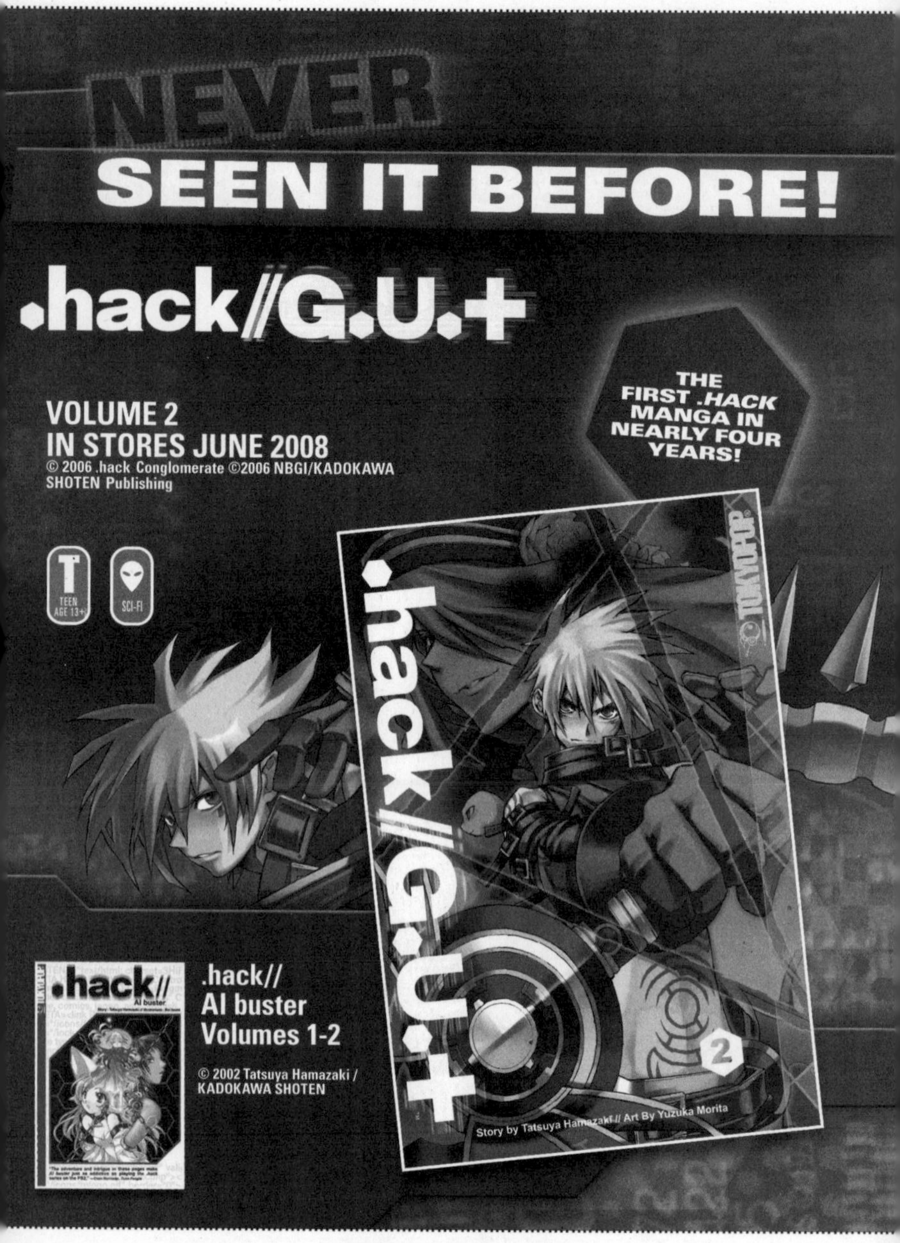
NEVER
SEEN IT BEFORE!
.hack//G.U.+
THE FIRST .HACK MANGA IN NEARLY FOUR YEARS!
VOLUME 2
IN STORES JUNE 2008
© 2006 .hack Conglomerate ©2006 NBGI/KADOKAWA SHOTEN Publishing
T
TEEN AGE 13+
SCI-FI
TOKYOPOP
.hack//G.U.+
2
Story by Tatsuya Hamazaki // Art By Yuzuka Morita
.hack//
AI buster
.hack//
AI buster
Volumes 1-2
© 2002 Tatsuya Hamazaki / KADOKAWA SHOTEN

.HACK UNIVERSE

"THE WORLD"
AS YOU'V

VOLUME 1
IN STORES JUNE 2008
© Project .hack 2002 - 2006/KADOKAWA SHOTEN

T
TEEN
AGE 13+

SCI-FI

BASED
ON THE
HIT VIDEO
GAMES!

ALSO AVAILABLE:

.hack//Legend
of the Twilight
Volumes 1-3

© 2002 Project .hack /
KADOKAWA SHOTEN

HALF A MILLION
COPIES SOLD!

.hack//
Another Birth
Volumes 1-4

© 2004 MIU KAWASAKI /
KADOKAWA SHOTEN

FOR MORE INFORMATION VISIT:

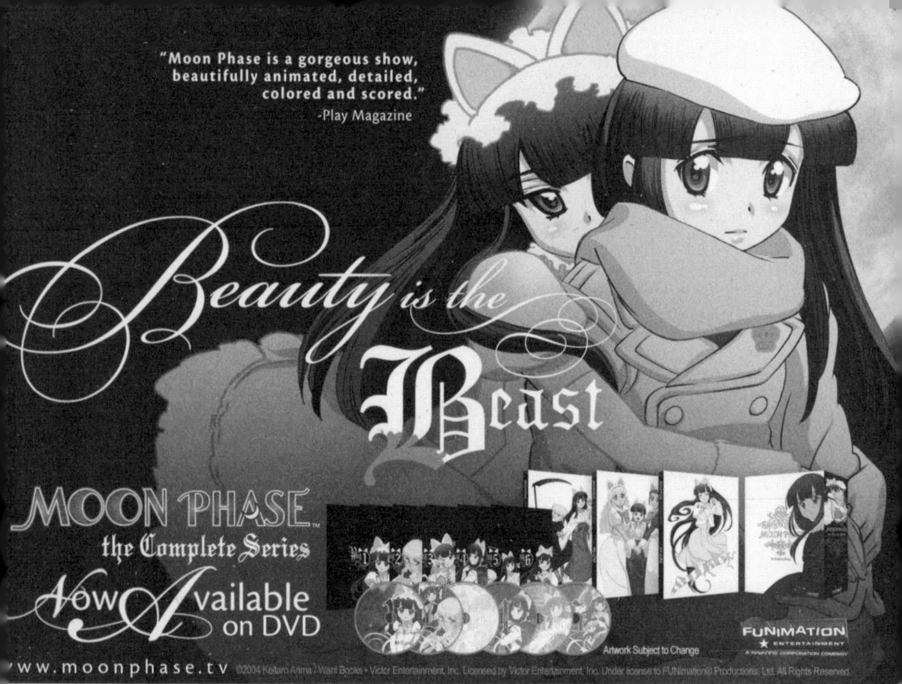
"Moon Phase is a gorgeous show, beautifully animated, detailed, colored and scored."
-Play Magazine
Beauty is the Beast
MOON PHASE
the Complete Series
Now Available on DVD
Artwork Subject to Change
FUNIMATION ENTERTAINMENT
www.moonphase.tv ©2004 Keitaro Arima / Wani Books • Victor Entertainment, Inc. Licensed by Victor Entertainment, Inc. Under license to FUNimation® Productions, Ltd. All Rights Reserved.

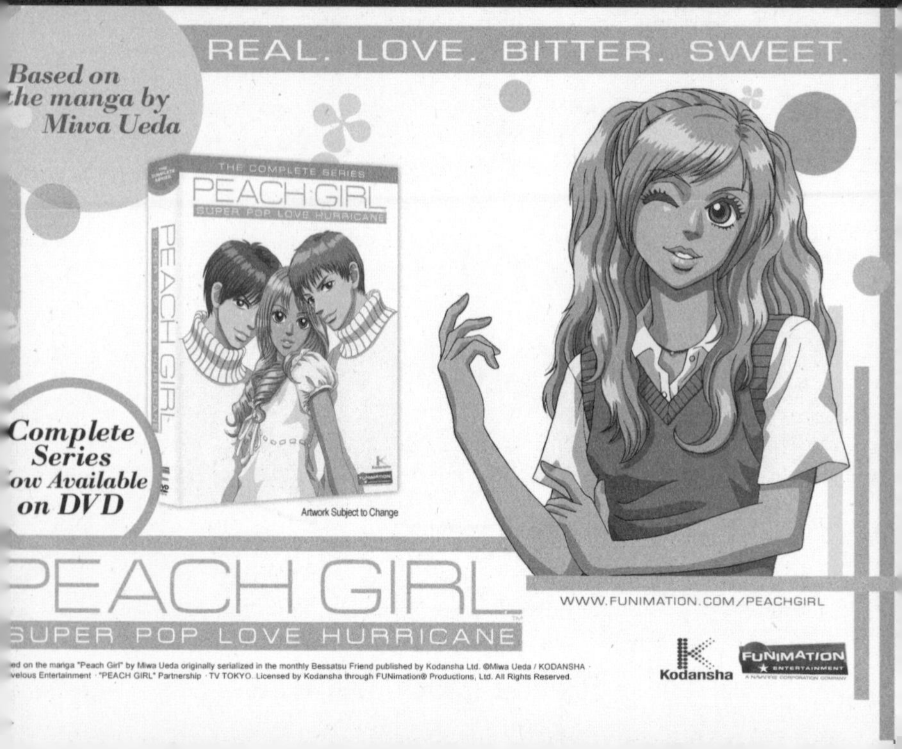
REAL. LOVE. BITTER. SWEET.
Based on the manga by Miwa Ueda
THE COMPLETE SERIES
PEACH GIRL
SUPER POP LOVE HURRICANE
Complete Series Now Available on DVD
Artwork Subject to Change
PEACH GIRL
SUPER POP LOVE HURRICANE
WWW.FUNIMATION.COM/PEACHGIRL
ed on the manga "Peach Girl" by Miwa Ueda originally serialized in the monthly Bessatsu Friend published by Kodansha Ltd. ©Miwa Ueda / KODANSHA ·
velous Entertainment · "PEACH GIRL" Partnership · TV TOKYO. Licensed by Kodansha through FUNimation® Productions, Ltd. All Rights Reserved.
Kodansha
FUNIMATION ENTERTAINMENT

FINALLY, A "HOW TO DRAW" MANGA FOR SHOJO ARTISTS!

Mangaka Selena Lin guides you in the basics of manga creation, from what tools to use and working with anatomy to panel composition and inking! More experienced artists will appreciate her up-to-date tutorial on Photoshop. Tutorials on coloring and a gallery of Selena's own adorable works are also included!

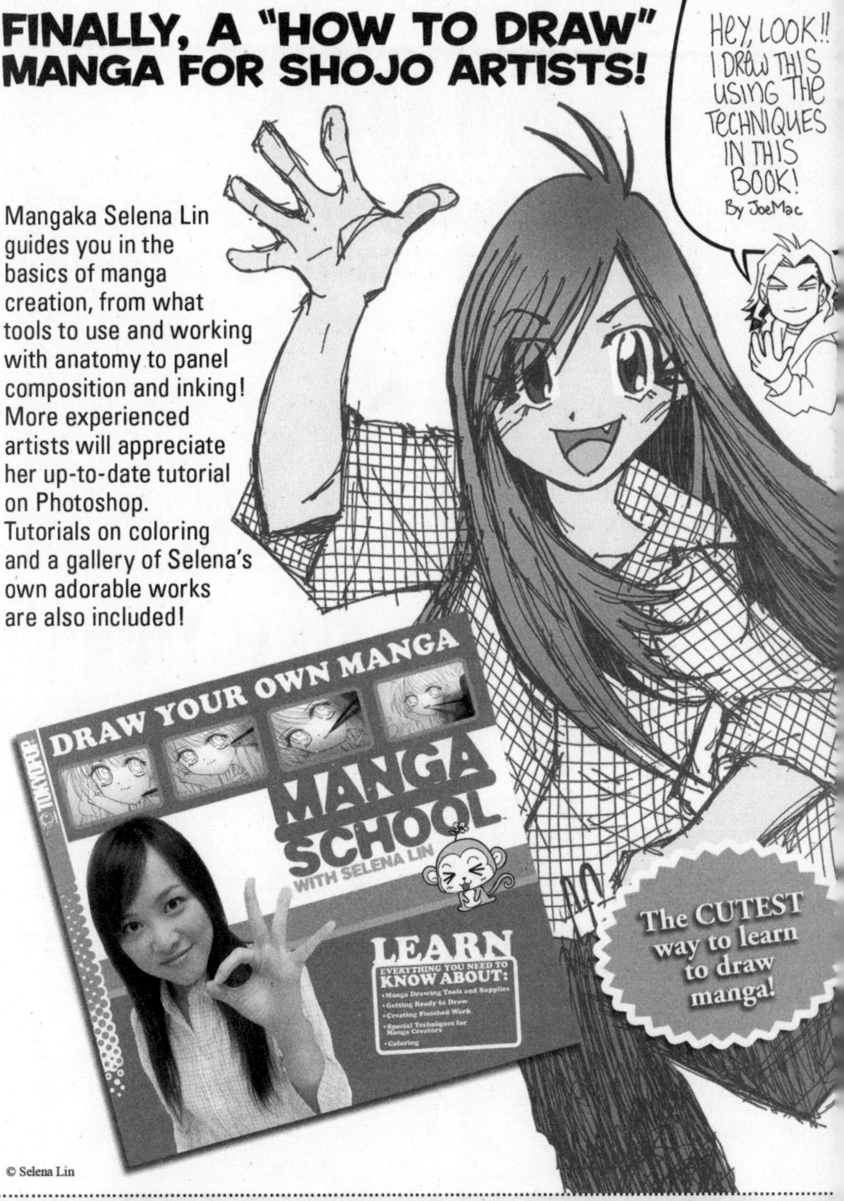
HEY, LOOK!! I DREW THIS USING THE TECHNIQUES IN THIS BOOK!
By JoeMac
The CUTEST way to learn to draw manga!
DRAW YOUR OWN MANGA
TOKYOPOP
MANGA SCHOOL
WITH SELENA LIN
LEARN
EVERYTHING YOU NEED TO KNOW ABOUT:
• Manga Drawing Tools and Supplies
• Getting Ready to Draw
• Creating Finished Work
• Special Techniques for Manga Creators
• Coloring

FOR MORE INFORMATION VISIT: WWW.TOKYOPOP.COM

STOP!

This is the back of the book.
You wouldn't want to spoil a great ending!

This book is printed "manga-style," in the authentic Japanese right-to-left format. Since none of the artwork has been flipped or altered, readers get to experience the story just as the creator intended. You've been asking for it, so TOKYOPOP® delivered: authentic, hot-off-the-press, and far more fun!

DIRECTIONS

If this is your first time reading manga-style, here's a quick guide to help you understand how it works.

It's easy... just start in the top right panel and follow the numbers. Have fun, and look for more 100% authentic manga from TOKYOPOP®!

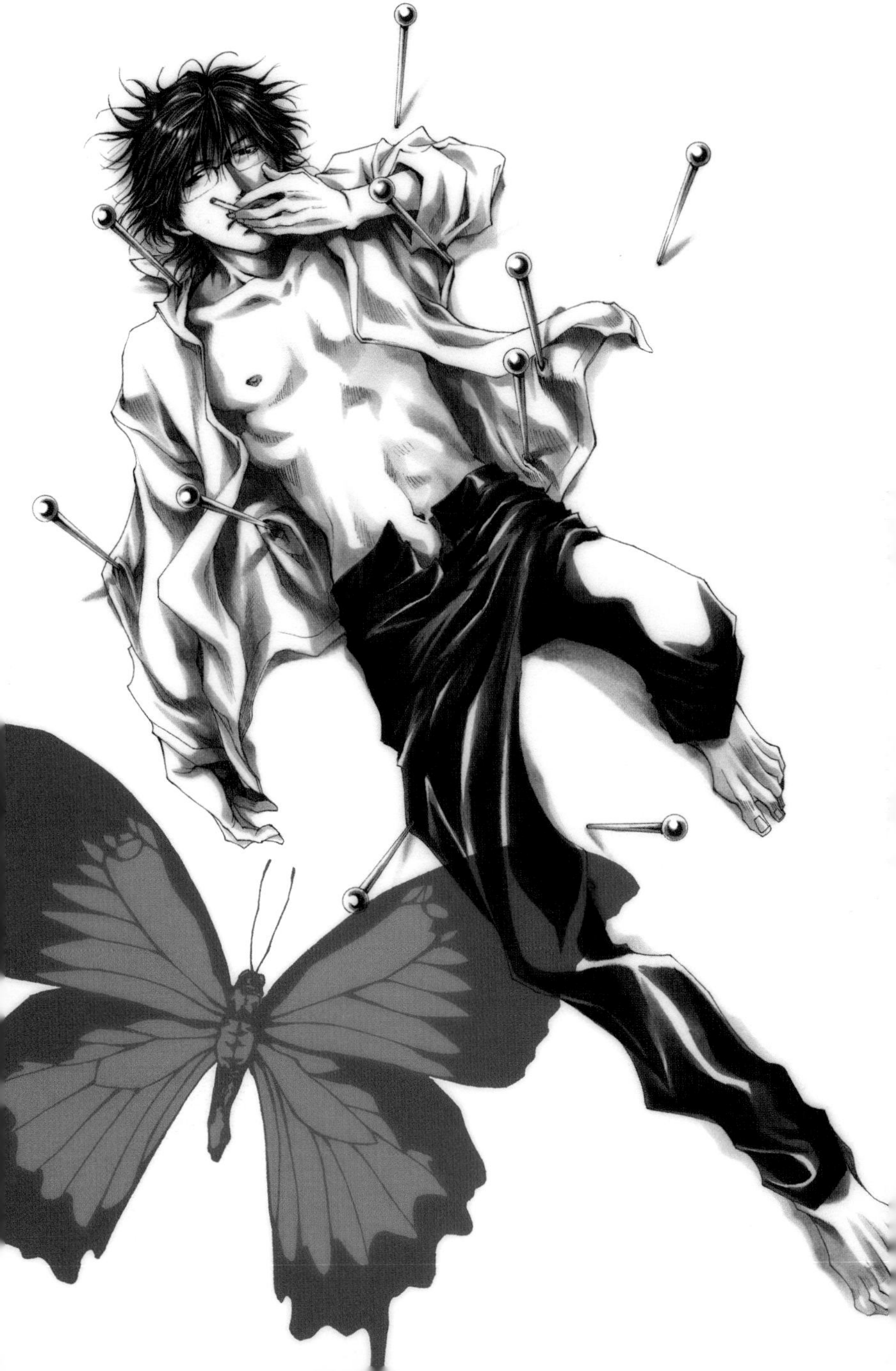

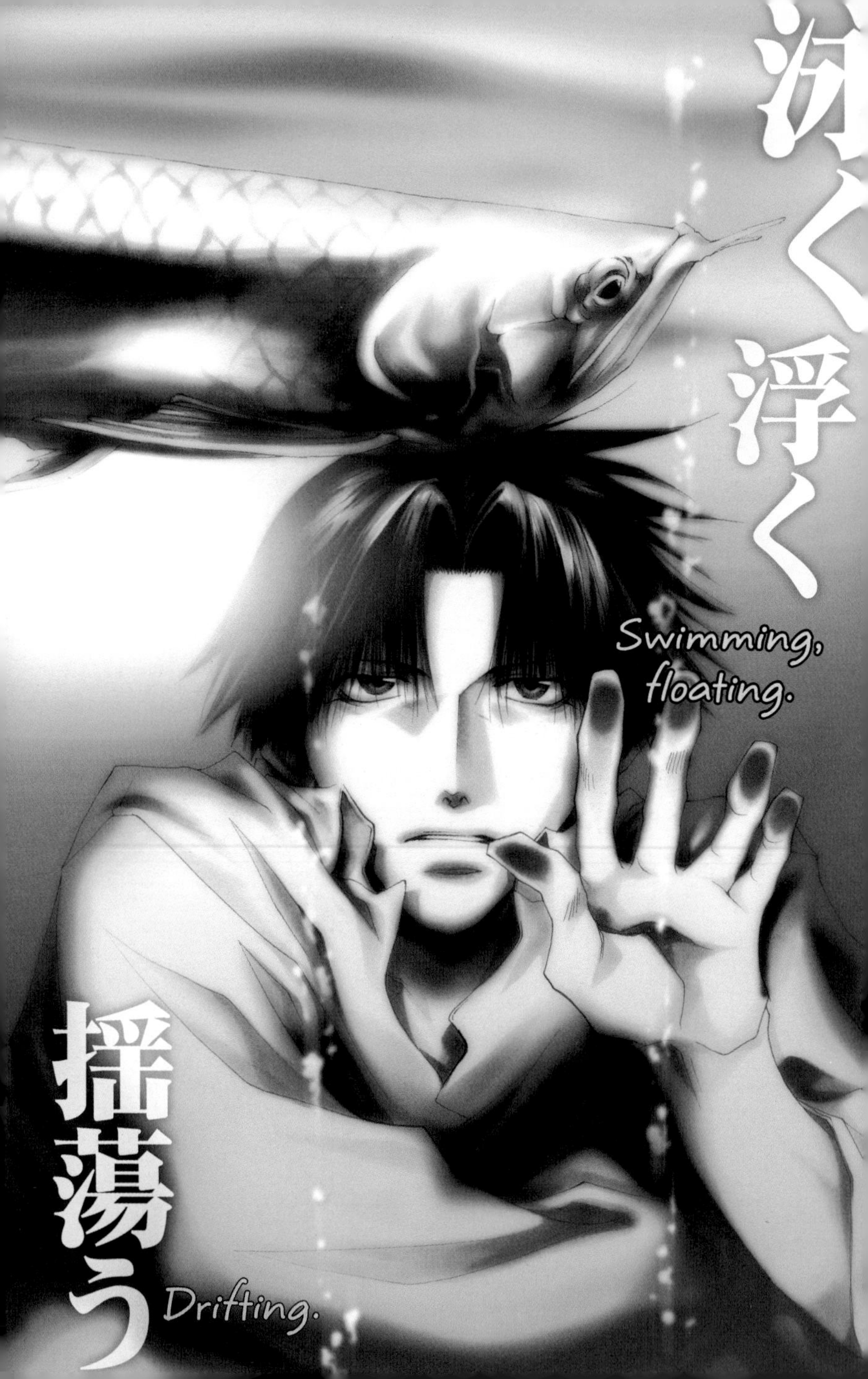
泳く浮く
Swimming, floating.
揺蕩う
Drifting.

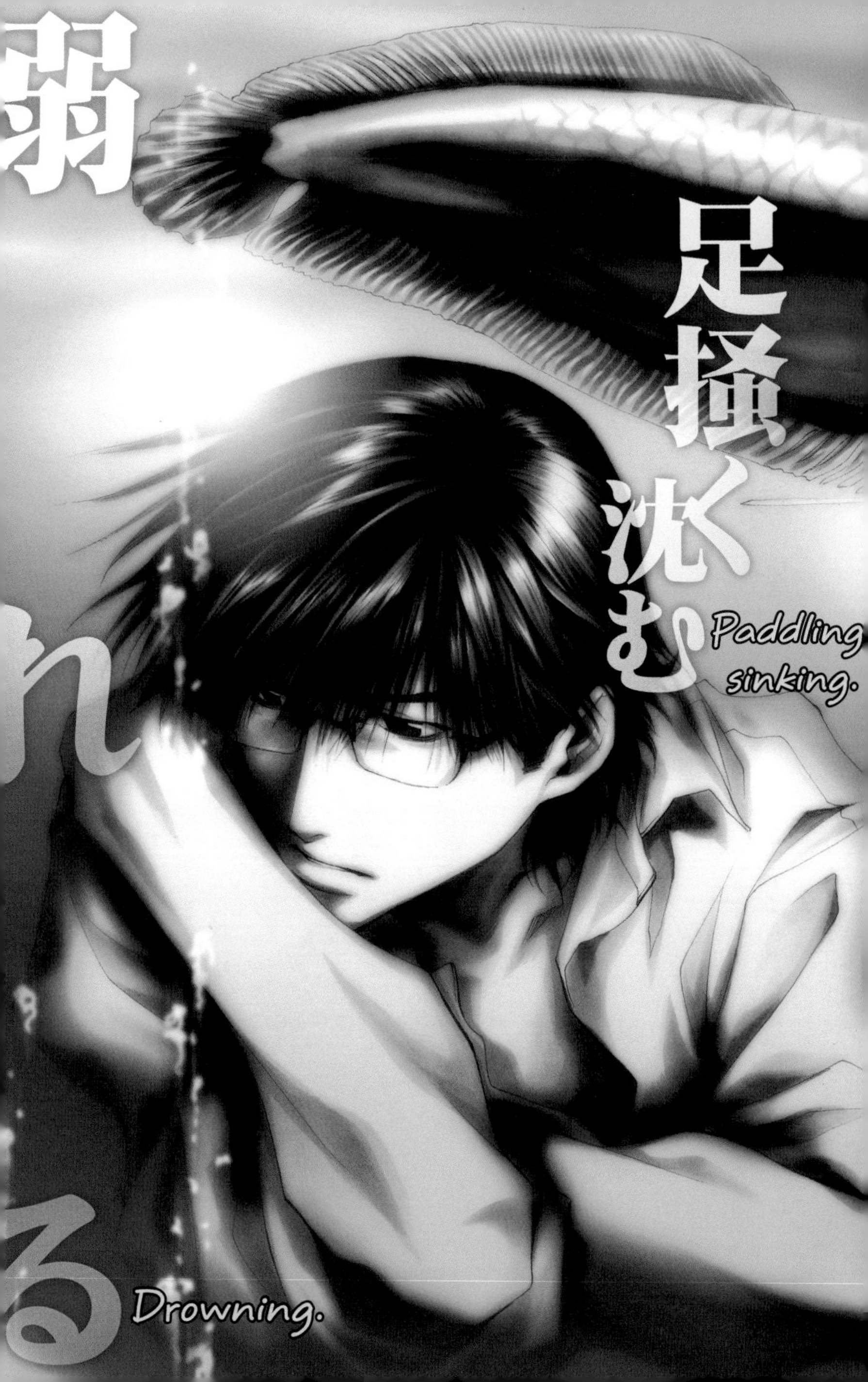

足掻く沈む
Paddling sinking.
溺れる
Drowning.

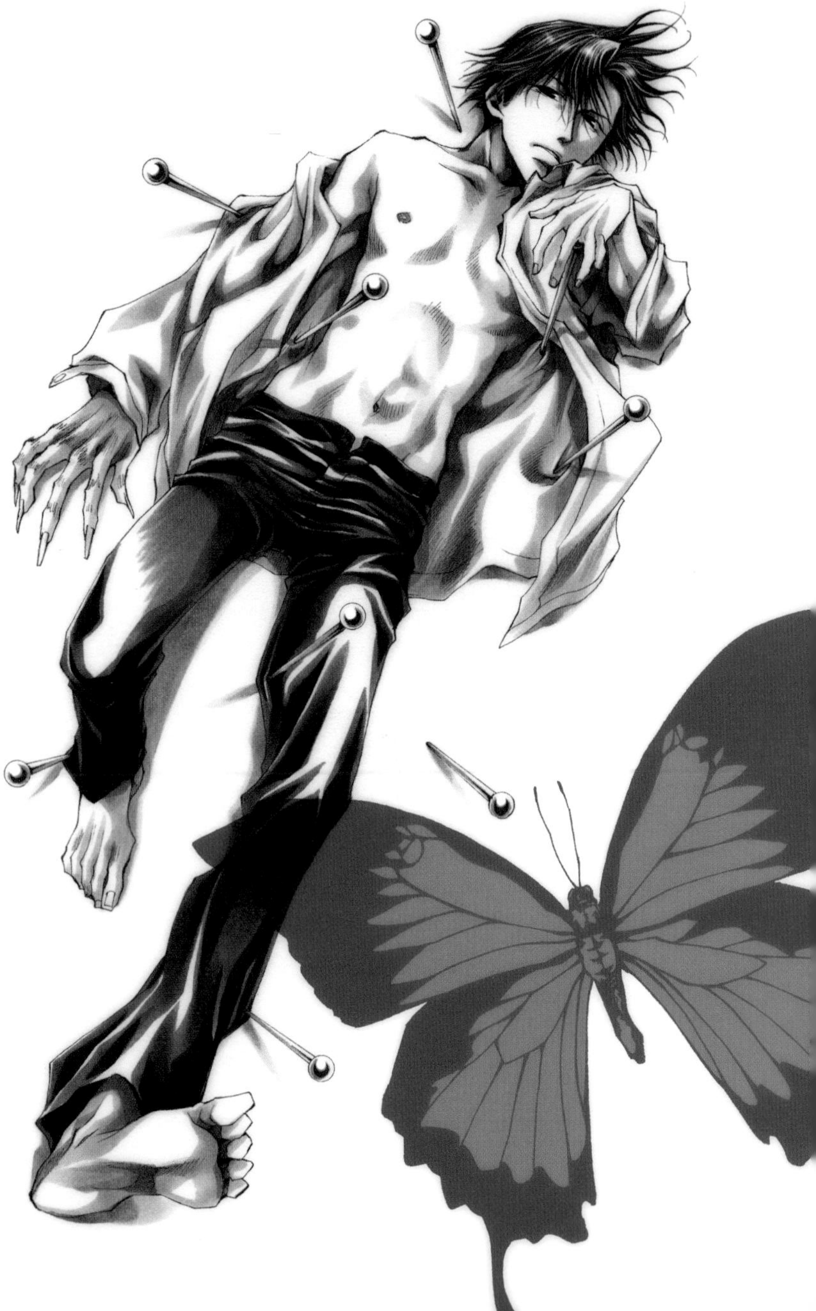